CROSSING BORDERS

Crossing Borders

Regional and urban perspectives on international migration

Edited by

CEES GORTER
Department of Regional Economics
Free University Amsterdam
The Netherlands

PETER NIJKAMP
Department of Regional Economics
Free University Amsterdam
The Netherlands

JACQUES POOT
Department of Econometrics and Economics
Victoria University of Wellington
New Zealand

Ashgate

Aldershot • Brookfield USA • Singapore • Sydney

© Cees Gorter, Peter Nijkamp and Jacques Poot 1998

Published by
Ashgate Publishing Ltd
Gower House
Croft Road
Aldershot
Hants GU11 3HR
England

Ashgate Publishing Company
Old Post Road
Brookfield
Vermont 05036
USA

British Library Cataloguing in Publication Data
Crossing borders: regional and urban perspectives on
    international migration
    1. Emigration and immigration
    I. Gorter, Cees II. Nijkamp, Peter, 1946- III. Poot, Jacques
    325

Library of Congress Catalog Card Number: 98-73397

ISBN 1 84014 882 9

Printed and bound by Athenaeum Press, Ltd.,
Gateshead, Tyne & Wear.

Contents

Figures and tables

ix

Contributors

Thomas Bauer
Selapo-Center for Human Resources
University of Munich
Ludwigstrasse 28RG
D-80539 Munich
Germany

Pieter Bevelander
Department of Economic History
Lund University
Box 7083
S-220 07 Lund
Sweden

Matthijs Breebaart
Faculteit der Ruimtelijke Wetenschappen
Universiteit van Amsterdam
Nieuwe Prinsengracht 130
1018 VZ Amsterdam
The Netherlands

Jouke van Dijk
Faculteit der Ruimtelijke Wetenschappen
Rijksuniversiteit Groningen
P.O. Box 800
9700 AV Groningen
The Netherlands

Peter Fischer
Faculty of Economics
Institute for Economic Policy Research
University of the Bundeswehr Hamburg
Holstenhofweg 85
D-22039 Hamburg
Germany

Hendrik Folmer
Department of General Economics
Agriucultural University Wageningen
Center Tilburg University
P.O. Box 8130
6700 EW Wageningen
The Netherlands

Manie Geyer
Department of Urban and Regional Planning
Potchefstroom University for Christian Higher Education
Private bag X6001
Potchefstroon 2520
South Africa

Cees Gorter
Department of Economics
Free University
De Boelelaan 1105
1081 HV Amsterdam
The Netherlands

Anne Green
Institute for Employment Research
University of Warwick
Coventry CV4 7AL
England

Henry W. Herzog Jr.
Department of Economics
College of Business Administration
University of Tennessee
Knoxville TN 37996-0550
USA

Bert van der Knaap
Department of Geography
Erasmus University
P.O. Box 1738
3000 DR Rotterdam
The Netherlands

Nadine Leiner
Faculty of Economics and Statistics
University of Konstanz
Postfach 5560 D140
D-78434 Konstanz
Germany

Gabriel Lipshitz
Bar-Ilan University
Department of Geography
52900 Ramat-Gan
Israel

Sako Musterd
Faculteit der Ruimtelijke Wetenschappen
Universiteit van Amsterdam
Nieuwe Prinsengracht 130
1018 VZ Amsterdam
The Netherlands

Peter Nijkamp
Department of Economics
Free University
De Boelelaan 1105
1081 HV Amsterdam
The Netherlands

Arend Odé
ISEO
Erasmus Universiteit Rotterdam
P.O. Box 1738
3000 DR Rotterdam
The Netherlands

Wim Ostendorf
Faculteit der Ruimtelijke Wetenschappen
Universiteit van Amsterdam
Nieuwe Prinsengracht 130
1018 VZ Amsterdam
The Netherlands

Jacques Poot
Department of Econometrics and Economics
Victoria University of Wellington
P.O. Box 600
Wellington
New Zealand

Alan M. Schlottmann
Department of Economics
College of Business Administration
University of Tennessee
Knoxville TN 37996-0550
USA

xiii

Harrie Visser
CBS
P.O. Box 959
2770 AZ Voorburg
The Netherlands

Brigitte Waldorf
Department of Geography and Regional Development
Harvill Building, Box #2
University of Arizona
Tuscon, Arizona 85721
USA

Leo van Wissen
Nidi
P.O. Box 11650
2502 AR The Hague
The Netherlands

Klaus Zimmermann
Selapo-Center for Human Resources
University of Munich
Ludwigstrasse 28RG
D-80539 Munich
Germany

Preface

Modern societies seem to be in a state of flux. The pace of change is more rapid than ever before. Crossing Borders – a rather adventurous undertaking in the past – has become a more pervasive response to change. Despite government efforts to control such flows, primarily on the receiving end, the permeability of borders is reinforced by globalization and a growing international mobility, which are the socioeconomic and spatial manifestations of the widening horizons of the modern world population. Against this background, international migration is a clear reflection of a more fluid type of locational behaviour of mankind at the turn of the century. Despite the large number of past studies on international migration, there are still many insufficiently explored aspects of long distance residential and job mobility.

Especially the regional and urban dimensions of cross-border migration need to be investigated more thoroughly. For example, what are the causes of the pronounced spatial selectivity in international migration patterns? Are cities offering the seedbed conditions for settlement in terms of job seeking, residential choices or access to new horizons and, in turn, what are the impacts of migrants on these cities? If prosperous regions or urban areas are attracting a disproportionately large share of foreign migrants, which categories of migrants settle there and why? How do migrants affect the public sector nationally and regionally? Can meaningful regional and urban policies be developed which try to exploit the potential benefit of international migration?

Seen from this perspective, the present volume brings together a collection of contributions in order to gain a better understanding of the complex phenomenon of international migration in the context of urban and regional development. The studies in this book cover a variety of theoretical and applied work. Most of the chapters emerged from an international workshop on 'International migration: regional and urban economic impacts and policies' in which the authors of contributions in this volume participated. The workshop was held in December 1995 at the Tinbergen Institute in Amsterdam. The papers were selected and revised following a review process.

For the publication of this volume we wish to thank firstly the authors for their cooperation in meeting deadlines and their efforts in putting together a high-quality volume. We also acknowledge the warm hospitality of the Tinbergen Institute (notably provided by Elfie Bonke). Finally, we thank Contact Europe (notably Dianne Biederberg) for their support in putting the various contributions in place.

Cees Gorter, Peter Nijkamp and Jacques Poot

1 Regional and Urban Perspectives on International Migration: An Overview

CEES GORTER, PETER NIJKAMP AND JACQUES POOT

1.1 Introduction

Throughout history, waves of migration have contributed to the shaping of societies across the world. Sometimes these flows were forced by nature, sometimes they were instigated by economic motives. During the first six decades or so of the present century, international migration was typically thought of as a movement of people from the Old World seeking better socioeconomic prospects in the New World. Since then, migration patterns have become more complex, affecting more countries, more people and for a greater variety of reasons.

Consequently, international migration is receiving increasing attention throughout the world. For Europe, three main geographical patterns of international migration can be identified: the migration between hinterlands and home countries, the migration streams from south to north, and recently, the east-west migration flows. It can also be observed that Western European countries have become reluctant to allow for inward (labour) migration. Nevertheless, the flows due to family reunification and asylum seeking have risen considerably in the recent past. Besides European countries, also Israel, the traditional English-speaking immigrant receiving countries (USA, Canada, Australia and New-Zealand), the Gulf states and some Asian countries (Japan, Singapore, Hong Kong and Malaysia) have experienced huge large inward migration streams during the last decade or so. However, the patterns are complex and sometimes rapidly changing. Some countries are both significant senders as well as recipients of migrants. It has been estimated that – in total – in the mid 1990s around 100 million people lived outside their country of birth, of whom one fifth were refugees.[1] In addition, the children of immigrants born in the host countries and subsequent generations contribute to a growing ethnic diversity of which the impact can be far greater than the immigration itself.

Migration is an inherently spatial phenomenon. By definition, an international migrant leaves one community and becomes part of another community in a foreign nation, at least for some minimum period of time.[2] Thus, for each migration we can identify regions, and urban or rural locations within regions, of origin and destination. In

1

addition, migration may not be a one-off event. Migrants may move again: within the host country, to a third country, or return home. The spatial patterns themselves have been described in surveys of global contemporary international migration such as Castles and Miller (1993) and Stalker (1994), whereas the economics of international labour migration have recently been studied by, for example, Van den Broeck (1996) from an institutionalist (or evolutionary) perspective in which the focus is on dynamic processes and human institutions. However, the *socioeconomic causes and consequences of the spatial patterns* have received surprisingly little systematic attention. Often migration is seen just from a host country perspective, or from a sending country perspective, without explicit consideration of the subnational origin and destinations of the flows or the linkages between countries.

It is well known that migration flows follow certain gravity-like properties, that there is chain migration, that certain regions attract more migrants than others, that migrants are highly urbanized, and that within urban areas there are also concentrations of migrants leading to a reshaping of the urban landscape. However, such observations are often the result of purely descriptive research or case study research. Consequently, there is still a need for an integrated multidisciplinary study of the spatial impact and the resulting socioeconomic and political issues concerning migration.

This book aims to fill this gap by bringing together a collection of chapters which are primarily concerned with the spatial impact of contemporary international migration patterns, and with related issues such as the impact on the (local) labour markets. The topics of the papers are wide ranging and the focus varies from broad international perspectives to specific urban areas. Two general themes run through the papers. The first of these is that migration is an inherently dynamic process which may have either equilibrating or self-reinforcing (cumulative) effects. The importance of considering international migration in a dynamic context has come to the fore in several theoretical frameworks which are available in the literature to study this phenomenon. In the next section we present an overview of a number of theoretical frameworks.

The second major theme of the book is the importance of personal networks in shaping international migration patterns, leading to pronounced clusters of (urban) areas from which migrants are drawn and of migrant settlement. Section 1.3 of this chapter reviews issues of spatial selectivity. Section 1.4 discusses briefly the related issue of absorption of immigrants in the urban labour market, with specific reference to the European situation where migration has suddenly become an important issue.

One or both of the main themes can be found in all the papers brought together in this book. Section 1.5 of this chapter outlines, and draws together, the findings of the remaining fourteen chapters of the book. These chapters have been grouped under four headings. Part A

2

(Chapters 2 to 5) addresses specific economic issues which have played an important role in the policy debate. Some theoretical results are derived, but the empirical evidence from the international literature to date is also reviewed. Part B (Chapters 6 to 8) focuses on linkages between sending and receiving countries and the spatial clustering that has emerged. Clustering at the subnational level and the related issue of assimilation of immigrants in local communities are addressed in the third part of the book (Chapters 9 to 12). Finally, Part D (Chapters 13 to 15) provides examples of new approaches to statistical modelling of migration, either in terms of a description or prediction of the actual flows, or in terms of the impact on local labour markets. The final section of this introductory chapter sets out some priorities for further research on international migration.

1.2   Theoretical Frameworks for International Migration Analysis

A variety of scientific explanations for international migration have been proposed in the literature. These differ in terms of the disciplinary perspective and the level of analysis (e.g. micro versus macro). Despite the myriad of publications on migration between countries, it is possible to group most of the explanatory theories into some main classes. Following Nijkamp and Spiess (1994), we will limit ourselves here to a concise description and evaluation of the following (non-exhaustive) classes: the equilibrium approach (Subsection 2.1); the utility maximizing approach (Subsection 2.2); the historical-structural approach (Subsection 2.3); the welfare state approach (Subsection 2.4); the regulatory approach (Subsection 2.5); the tension approach (Subsection 2.6); and the system approach (Subsection 2.7).

These approaches differ not only in terms of their main message, but also in terms of their disciplinary foundation. Considering only a single scientific discipline would lead, especially in the field of international migration research, to the loss of some very important aspects. In what follows we will provide for each approach one or more key references, which have been drawn from a range of disciplines (e.g. economics, sociology, political science). In addition to the survey in this section, Bauer and Zimmermann provide a more detailed overview of economic theories of labour migration in Chapter 4.

1.2.1 The Equilibrium Approach

The equilibrium approach to international migration represents a main direction in the explanation of causes and consequences of the international movements of people. A brief description of the consequences of international migration within the equilibrium approach can be found in, e.g. Greenwood (1994).

The equilibrium model of migration focuses primarily on the rational calculus of individual actors. Migration is in general regarded as the

3

outcome of a choice process for individuals or households. The choices can be explained by means of neoclassical economics. In general, the equilibrium approach conceptualizes migration as the geographical mobility of workers who are responding to imbalances in the spatial distribution of land, labour, capital and natural resources. Observed migration flows are seen as the cumulative result of individual decisions based on a rational evaluation of the benefits to be gained and the costs entailed in moving. On average, migrants are expected to move from low to high wage countries. When there is unemployment, migrants are also expected to be sensitive to observed differences in unemployment rates since these determine expected earnings when spells of unemployment are likely (see e.g. Harris and Todaro 1970).

By being seen as primarily a form of arbitrage in the labour market, migration is considered to raise wages in the sending country (because emigrants withdraw their labour) and lower wages in the receiving country (because immigrants will be seeking employment). Since we noted above that we expect migrants to move on average from low to high wage regions, the process therefore reduces such wage differentials. This, in turn, reduces the incentive for movement.

A crucial limitation of this approach is that restrictions on migration, usually by potential host countries, can distort the way in which observed flows are responding to international wage differentials. Thus, we expect the equilibrium approach to be more useful for understanding (free) internal migration patterns (for a survey of the evidence, see e.g. Greenwood 1975) or for understanding international migration between culturally and economically similar countries, as e.g. Poot (1995) demonstrated in the case of migration between Australia and New Zealand. However, Van Wissen and Visser show in Chapter 14 that international migration within the more diverse European Economic Area is only weakly responsive to income per head differentials.

Taking a longer term perspective, the equilibrium approach suggests that migration will lead to a gradual convergence in the rate of economic growth and social well being. This is, for example, shown by Fischer in the next chapter.

It is clear that this equilibrium approach may be criticized from various view points. Wood (1982) has pointed out three main critical points. The first relates to the fact that – especially in the context of developing countries – it is evident that geographic mobility of labour does not necessarily lead to an equilibrium situation, because migration is often an indicator of regional disparities which, e.g. due to the movement of skilled people, are reinforced by migration rather than reduced. Thus, inequalities may increase and the existence and nature of a long run equilibrium may depend on additional considerations, such as the emergence of eventual congestion effects in the receiving areas. This alternative perspective on the long run impact is highlighted by Fischer in the next chapter. He suggests that immigration may widen income differences due to, for example, positive agglomeration effects or human

4

capital externalities. The importance of such positive feedback loop effects of migration is reinforced by e.g. Geyer in Chapter 6 and Lipshitz in Chapter 7.

A second critical point mentioned by Wood (1982) concerns the non-historical character of the equilibrium approach. Some empirical facts run counter to this approach, notably that many 'backward' economies throughout history have not spontaneously exported labour and – when labour was needed – it had to be coerced out of them. As a third point, Wood criticizes the reductionism of the equilibrium approach, especially the failure to account for migration resulting from non-economic reasons, such as political developments, persecution, religious beliefs, etc.

1.2.2 The Utility Maximizing Approach

Borjas (1989) describes a more modern version and extension of the economic equilibrium approach to migration. This more recent approach is based on two key assumptions of neoclassical theory. The first assumption, that the individual is a utility maximizer, was already referred to above in the context of the equilibrium approach. Migrant behaviour is, however, constrained by the household's financial situation and by the migration policies of the sending and receiving countries. It is based on the second assumption, that exchanges among various players lead to an equilibrium in the market place, Borjas discusses extensively the existence of an immigration market, which is acting as a sieve for migrants across potential host countries. The different host countries function as the suppliers in this immigration market, making migration 'offers' with respect to a certain set of immigration regulations from which individuals on the demand side compare and choose. Hence, they allocate themselves in the end non randomly among countries.

Using these main assumptions, Borjas addresses three questions: the determinants of the size and skill composition of immigrant flows to any particular host country, the process of assimilation of migrants in the host country, and the adjustment process in the host countries' labour market after an immigration 'shock'. To answer these questions he develops a simple model of migration between two countries, a source and a host country. A special function relates in this model earnings to individual observable and unobservable skills. The assumption that observable skills (for example education) influence the rate of return to migration, enables Borjas to show how workers flow to the country that is willing to pay most for their human capital. An example of this type of model, but in the context of internal rather than international migration, is given by Van Dijk, Folmer, Herzog and Schlottmann in Chapter 15.

Borjas also shows that the self-selection of migrants on the basis of the unobserved abilities depends entirely on the extent of income inequality in the host and source country. He argues that there is no theoretical reason for presuming that immigration flows are always composed of the 'best and brightest'. His model predicts that the size, direction and composition of immigrant flows will change when economic and political conditions change: 'there is no universal law that must characterize all immigration flow' (Borjas 1989, pp. 471–72).

Borjas' model provides an innovative and flexible way to analyse migration decision making and migration flows. However, it remains a partial approach which does not concern itself with learning, social networks and adaptive behaviour at the micro level or regulatory regimes, historical and political influences and overall impacts at the macro level.

1.2.3 The Historical-Structural Approach

The third main direction of migration theories, the historical-structural approach, focuses on the origin of the costs and benefits faced by the potential migrants. Migration is seen as a macro-social process. This approach is – because of the variety of considerations included – more of a qualitative nature and not as easily characterized as the two previously mentioned approaches. Here, migration is seen with reference to a broader context of socioeconomic and political changes. For example, Goss and Lindquist (1995) provide a review of this approach and a comparison with the microeconomic approach. They refer to the latter as the functional perspective. However, Goss and Lindquist point to weaknesses in both approaches and suggest an alternative conceptualization which focuses particularly on migrant institutions. This so called structuration perspective was applied to labour migration from the Philippines.

Nonetheless, the historical-structural approach can aid the understanding of the processes of segmentation and polarization associated with the emergence of migrants clusters in urban housing market areas. These processes are exemplified by the analyses of Musterd, Ostendorf and Breebaart in Chapter 9 and Green in Chapter 10.

The principal insights of the historical-structural perspective are mainly to be found in historical materialism, according to which migration is deeply rooted in the pressures and counter pressures in national economies, which lead to changes in the organization of production. Structural factors, such as socioeconomic and political developments, influence labour mobility through their impact on the level and the spatial distribution of the demand for labour. Patterns of migration are thus explained in terms of changes in the organization of production which unequally affects the fortune of different social classes. Thus, migration is conceptualized as a class phenomenon where the unit of analysis is the migration stream.

A major advantage of the historical-structural approach is its attention to structural factors in migration patterns, but it has also various weaknesses. Wood (1982) notes that no attention is paid to the specific factors which motivate individual actors. The decision to migrate is implicitly assumed to be a rational one, but no attempt is made to conceptualize the nature of the decision making process. Moreover, Wood argues that migration is not necessarily class specific. Wood suggests a synthesis between the equilibrium and structuralist approaches in which the household becomes the central unit of analysis. Households would then be seen as decision units which seek 'sustenance strategies' which balance the available labour power and the consumption necessities, given the limitations imposed by the socioeconomic and physical environment. It appears however that, while the terminology is different, Wood's proposed approach is in content very similar to the utility maximizing approach, which nowadays also takes the household often as the micro level decision unit (see e.g. Borjas and Bronars 1991).

In contrast, Bach and Schraml (1982) provide a different perspective on the role of the household in the historical-structural approach. They argue that households are the central units in family and kinship relationships, which are the organizing force in the development of migration networks. They criticize the structuralist view that migrants are mere 'agents' of social change carrying the necessary labour attributes to satisfy accumulation in capitalist society. Instead, migration is seen as a 'collective action' by such families and local communities. They also note that a continuous influx of immigrant labour may not be a structural necessity for late capitalist societies.

1.2.4 The Welfare State Approach

An interesting class of migration analyses refers to the importance of the welfare state in connection with international migration. This approach, developed by Freeman (1986), emphasizes the tension which is created, on the one hand, by the need for the welfare state to restrain entry (to preserve the benefits to its members) and, on the other, by the need for the welfare state to be open to the global political and economic order. In line with the equilibrium migration approach, Freeman seeks the explanation for migration in wage differentials. But in contrast to this approach, he underlines the importance of welfare benefits: 'Along with the high real direct wages, the social wage is part of the package of compensation that exerts an attractive pull on workers in less prosperous societies drawing them to the rich countries in anticipation of better lives' (Freeman 1986, p. 55).

It is not just a simple attraction of migrants to the welfare state, but rather the availability of the welfare state benefits to indigenous workers which helps the sequence of events which create the demand for foreign labour. In this context, foreign labour is seen as the only real alternative to the elimination of the privileges of the indigenous work force, but only if new workers are excluded from the rights of the welfare state. Yet, in practice, immigrants do have access to welfare state privileges and this explains why even unemployed migrants stay in their host country.

7

The benefits of the welfare state may overcompensate for factors like language difference or unfamiliar culture, which otherwise would be strong reasons for return migration (or for not even leaving the home country). Given this pull force of a welfare state and the moral and legal difficulty of excluding migrants from it, Freeman concludes that migration is a threat to the welfare state.

Similarly, it is not surprising that policies which encourage higher levels of immigration would need to coincide with social policies which reduce the generosity of the welfare state.[3] Leiner's analysis, in Chapter 3, of the possible immigration induced congestion in publicly provided goods is a clear theoretical example of the welfare state approach. She argues for an entrance fee levied on migrants to compensate natives for the congestion externality conferred on them.

1.2.5 The Regulatory Approach

International migration is rarely a free movement of people across borders, but usually strongly influenced by various physical and non-physical barriers. Zolberg et al. (1986) and Zolberg (1989) have drawn attention to the importance of borders and regulations (both incentives or disincentives) for migration. Zolberg argues that the political perspective may help to overcome the limitations of the historical-structural and the equilibrium approaches.

The regulatory approach is macro analytical and historical in nature. As in the utility maximizing approach, individuals aim to maximize their welfare by exercising a variety of choices from which migration is only one. In addition, there are organized states which maximize collective goals by controlling the exit or entry of individuals. Thus, there is a fundamental tension between the interests of individuals and between the sending and receiving countries. Taking into account that several states tend to interact as parts of a larger whole – a situation which Zolberg calls 'an international social system' – the overall structural configuration of the international social system provides an analytical matrix for analysing migration policies. An example of the regulatory approach can be found by Lipshitz's study in Chapter 11 of the impact of immigration and housing policies on the settlement of Jewish people from the former Soviet Union in Israel. The importance of politics and policies is also highlighted by Lipshitz in Chapter 7 and by Odé in Chapter 8.

Zolberg (1989) notes in the context of restricted entries that it is important to realize that – in the current post communist era – most countries from which people would like to emigrate do not restrict their movements, but countries to which people would like to go do so. It is the policy of potential recipient countries which determines whether a movement can take place and of what kind. Therefore, Zolberg adds to Bhagwati's (1984) opinion that migration can be better influenced by disincentives rather than incentives. In this respect, entry restrictions are a central issue in understanding international migration patterns and they deserve closer analytical attention.

1.2.6 The Tension Approach

There are only a few approaches to international migration which try to explain migration in the context of one general, global theory. The sociological approach of Hoffmann-Nowotny (1981) is one. Penninx (1986) notes that this approach, in contrast with other migration theories, is rather more deductive than inductive. Hoffmann-Nowotny aims to explain international migration as a specific field of social reality within a general Theory of Societal Systems. This allows for a discussion of migration on the level of three different system units: the individual, the class and the collective system unit. Characteristic for Hoffmann-Nowotny's analysis on all levels is that migration is seen as the result of structural and anomic tensions. Structural tensions are due to a divergence of power and prestige. Anomic tensions are an empirical consequence occurring at the moment when structural tensions exceed a certain threshold level, which is not further specified.

At the individual system unit, Hoffmann-Nowotny distinguishes two cases in which migration occurs. The first case is that an individual may have a more or less balanced status configuration within a societal system, but may experience anomic tension because he or she is a member of a power deficit system. The individual is reducing the power deficit by migrating. In the second case, an individual experiences an anomic tension which cannot be traced back to the external position of the system, but to the internal status quo. The individual is migrating for an improvement of his or her status.

Hoffmann–Nowotny considers these two cases at the level of the individual rather than as an exception and migration is more frequently expected to be 'a means of a tension management policy' at the societal level (Hoffmann–Nowotny 1981, p. 71). A policy of migration is seen as one possibility for realizing a balance between power and prestige, which is less difficult than other possibilities which require financial expenses and also affect the status quo. Migration is also related to a conservation of the structures of the social system of origin. Moreover, the social systems should be seen in the context of the global system.

Within the Hoffmann–Nowotny framework, emigration can be interpreted as a reduction of tension at the level of a societal system in the same way as it does at the level of the individual system unit. However, it is important to note that this reduction can only be realized if the individuals succeed in balancing their status configuration in the immigration system. Analogously, immigration can be interpreted as the building of tension, because of internal rank distances which may be increased by immigrants. Thus, on the one hand, systems with lower tension absorb immigrants who try to reduce tension by migrating, but on the other hand, immigration creates new tensions which can be turned partly into a new, possibly negative, development. Some of the features of this sociological approach are implicit in the studies of urban clustering of migrants by Musterd et al. in Chapter 9 and Green in Chapter 10. Moreover, this approach can perhaps aid the understanding of the (largely economic) analysis of migrant assimilation in Sweden by Bevelander in Chapter 12.

We conclude that Hoffmann-Nowotny's framework is quite remarkable because of his attempt to explain migration in the context of a global theory. On the other hand – as the above description shows – his approach is rather abstract.[4] In addition, Hoffmann-Nowotny himself pointed out that an application of his 'theory is restricted mainly to modern mass migration from less to more developed contexts' (Hoffmann-Nowotny 1981, p. 83) and therefore does not encompass all types of contemporary international migration.

1.2.7 The System Approach

One approach which has gained in popularity in recent years is the system approach. This approach recognizes that the study of changing trends and patterns of contemporary international migration requires a dynamic rather than a static perspective. A further main characteristic of the system approach is that a so called migration system, i.e. two or more places or more specific countries connected to each other by flows and counterflows of people, is used as the basic unit of analysis (Kulu-Glasgow 1992).

Figure 1.1, reproduced from Kritz and Zlotnik (1992), illustrates how in the system approach other flows and linkages between countries matter too. Migration flows occur within national contexts whose political, demographic, economic and social dimensions are changing partly in response to the feedbacks and adjustments that stem from migration itself.

When international migration is analysed as embedded in a system like the one described in Figure 1.1 it is evident that micro as well as macro elements are part of the analysis. The individual has in this system the role of an active decision maker, who develops strategies to migrate which are embedded in the different influences of the system.

Kritz and Zlotnik (1992) point out that – in addition to the spatial dimension that demarcates all countries in a system – a time dimension should also be included. The time dimension allows a historical perspective on migration, an analysis of structural conditions, and economic and political linkages.

Networks play also a key role in the system approach. Combined with the emphasis on time, Kritz and Zlotnik stress that 'networks must be looked at as dynamic relationships and variable social arrangements that vary across ethnic groups and time and shape migration and its sequel' (p.6). They point out that networks of institutions and individuals link the various countries together into a coherent migration system. They also note that networks at the origin restrain or encourage an individual to migrate depending on the extent to which such networks provide economic and social support. Networks at the destination may give migrants access to various resources. Finally, networks between origin and destination countries can play a role in channelling information, migrants, remittances and cultural norms.

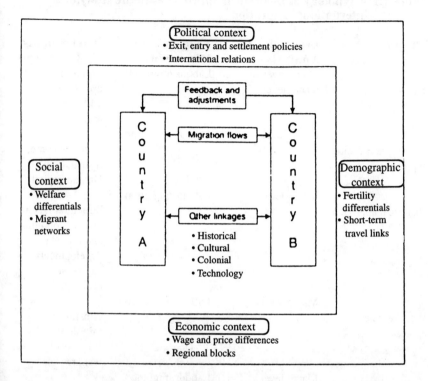

Figure 1.1   A system framework for international migration

Source: Kritz and Zlotnik 1992, p. 3.

Different types of migrants make use of different types of networks: migration of elites, for example, is facilitated by elite institutional networks (such as multinational corporations). Networks of legal institutions can be conceptualized as being top-down, while migrants networks operate in the reverse direction. Moreover, networks may sustain the momentum of migration flows, even when economic incentives to migrate are reduced in different parts and migration controls are tightened by the country of destination. Many of the authors in the present volume emphasize the importance of networks. These are important for understanding specific flows such as the

11

migration of Polish workers to The Netherlands discussed by Odé in Chapter 8 and the broader systemic frameworks developed by Geyer in Chapter 6 and Waldorf in Chapter 13.

Table 1.1 A typology of theoretical approaches to the study of international migration

Theory	Level of Analysis	Type of Migration	Determinants
Equilibrium approach	Micro level and macro level	Labour migration	Employment opportunities with higher returns
Utility maximizing approach	Micro level	Labour migration	Higher income distribution Human capital
Historical approach	Macro level	Labour migration	Structural factors (socio economic and political developments of capitalist economies
Welfare state approach	Macro level	Labour migration	Kinship migration Benefits of welfare state
Regulatory approach	Macro level	Labour migration and refugees	Immigration regulations
Tension approach	Micro level and macro level	Ethnically diverse labour migration	Tension
System approach	Micro level and macro level	All types of approach	Many factors, including social networks

We conclude that a system framework has – compared to the other approaches – the big advantage that it tries to take into account a large variety of factors which play a role in the migration process. This approach is not restricted to a special type of migration and it does not

12

only explain the existence of migration but also how the size, especially of social networks, is nowadays important because a large proportion of the migration flows may be characterized as family migration. But on the other hand, the system approach has the character of a conceptual framework rather than a specific theory. However, in the end, it may not provide much guidance in specifying functional relationships or testable hypotheses in empirical research.

As a conclusion to this section, we show in Table 1.1 for all the above described approaches their level of analysis, the type of migration analysed and their main determinants.

1.3 Spatial Selectivity

In the previous section, we have presented the dominant factors of international migration which lead to the decision of individuals or groups to migrate. Of course, these main determinants are also of great importance in getting settled in a foreign country (i.e., in the absorption process).

The choice of destination depends largely on the motives for migration and the expectations and perceptions which immigrants have about a possible country of destination. A rational individual will in principle choose an area – within his or her opportunity set – that will lead to the expected maximization of socioeconomic and cultural opportunities. These opportunities have a clear geographical component, as the decision where to go is essentially a choice – and ultimately a competition – for alternative (activity and contact) spaces.

For instance, a 'wealth' based motive will lead to a selection among countries of destination where skills are best useable and where higher wages, employment possibilities or social security benefits are available. This also explains why it is very difficult to make a distinction between economic migrants and forced migrants, once they have left their country of origin: despite the differences in 'push' factors, they will maximize their utility via the choice of an appropriate country of destination.

Fawcett and Arnold (1987) distinguished three contextual factors (state to state relations and comparisons, mass culture connections, family and social networks) which form linkages between places. These factors partly explain the choice of destination of immigrants. Fawcett and Arnold developed in this context a framework for the socio-psychological processes within an immigration system, beginning with the decision stage and proceeding through the transition stage to the adaptation stage.

The first stage, the decision stage, contains two main components: the potential mover's motivation for change and the emigration decision process. The interaction of motivation, opportunity for improvement, and a family incentive determines the articulation of the decision stage. With the inclusion of the family in the decision stage, Fawcett and

Arnold consider also the family as a major influencer in the decision making process.

The transition stage refers to the overcoming of all barriers such as bureaucratic steps, travel and financial arrangements, etc. which determine whether a move really occurs. The regulations of official gatekeepers in the countries of origin and destination play in this stage an important role in the choice of destination and the actual move.

Finally, the adaptation stage relates to the adjustment and settlement process in the place of destination. Labour market opportunities, psychological support and the help of family and friends are important for a successful move at this stage.

Mirroring Fawcett and Arnold's (1987) three stages, Nijkamp and Voskuilen (1996a) put together a simple conceptual framework for immigration flows. This has been reproduced in Figure 1.2. The process of migration is modelled in a single structure that consists of three steps which are influenced by the macroeconomic conditions of origin and of destination.

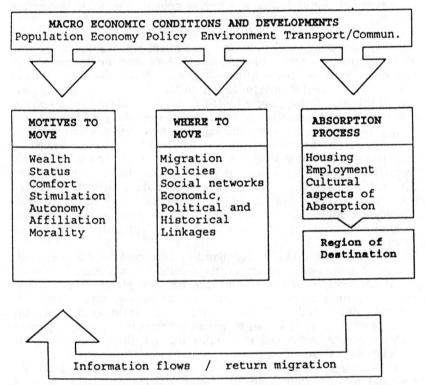

Figure 1.2   A conceptualization for analysing international migration decisions

14

An important feature of Figure 1.2 is that the choice of destination ('where to move') must be seen within the context of controls and regulations set by the countries of origin and destination. The increasing international migration flows have led to a growing pressure on host countries, mainly in the developed regions. As we already stressed in the previous section, we cannot exclusively look at motives and expectations at a micro level to explain international migration patterns, but we have to consider also these decisions in the context of migration policies set by governments and by the international community.

Rogers (1992) has recently distinguished fourteen steps to manage international migration from the perspective of a country of destination. It is useful to summarize these steps here in order to highlight the diversity within the range of possible immigration policies:

1 Controls. This means a more strict policing of borders, use of carrier sanctions, etc. The trend in host countries has been towards increased controls; however, controls do not alter the basic mechanism that causes migration pressures.

2 Opening up new migration opportunities and/or restructuring old ones. To ease migration pressures, a policy admitting temporary workers from sending regions is a possibility. For instance, migration pressure from eastern European countries may be reduced if temporary contracts − with a commitment by sending countries of taking back workers after expiration of the contracts − are possible.

3 Permanent immigration. This means enlarging immigration opportunities by increasing occupational quotas and accepting a greater diversity of immigrants. The key idea here is that a proactive management of immigrant flows may be more effective than a reluctance by governments to accept that 'temporary migration policies' of the past have been instrumental in the supply of new permanent immigrants.

4 New accessions to the UN Convention Relating to the Status of Refugees. Several Eastern European countries, which formally contributed to the refugee problem, have become members of the international refugee regime.

5 Voluntary repatriation. With the end of the superpowers' involvement in several refugee generating countries (e.g. El Salvador, Afghanistan), peace has become possible in some cases. Voluntary repatriation, assisted by the international community, may be an option when a lasting peace is established.

6   Restructuring refugee resettlement opportunities. Recent changes in the international system offer an opportunity to strengthen the focus on protection while moving away from using resettlement as a surrogate immigration channel.

7   Bilateral quid pro quo's. To reduce demand for access to its territory, a host country may enlist the cooperation of the country of origin, or of transit, in return for certain monetary concessions or specific, limited migration opportunities.

8   Multilateral efforts to resolve complex refugee situations. The Schengen agreement in Europe is a recent procedural European agreement for dealing with asylum claims and migration control.

9   Keeping migrants at home by providing information. Information programmes may give would be migrants a better idea of the problems they may face in the host country.

10   Keeping migrants at home by means of intervention. Countries that are potential or actual creators of refugees can be confronted with various types of intervention by international organizations, ranging from economic embargoes to military intervention (e.g., the UN intervention in Bosnia).

11   Keeping migrants at home by means of trade instead of migration. Protectionist policies against sending countries contribute to migratory pressures. However, trade must be seen as a long term solution.

12   Keeping migrants at home by means of taking jobs to the home country. Host country firms can locate factories in migrant sending countries to save labour cost, thereby creating additional employment in those countries. However, it may not be practical or economically desirable for governments to guide firms' Overseas Direct Investment (ODI) decisions.

13   Keeping migrants at home by means of long term development aid. The results of development aid have been mixed, but when successful, such aid should also have the long run effect of diminishing migration pressures.

14   Providing incentives for migrants to return and to invest in their home countries. Experience with this policy has shown that the monetary incentive given by the host country to return migrants was used by return migrants who most likely would have returned in any case.

Although effective immigration policies ultimately determine whether a migration can take place, the actual situation has been rather confused and fluid in many developed countries since migration pressures increased. These countries, such as those of Western Europe, are nowadays taking steps in the direction of more restrictive regulations and controls in an attempt to control the growing number of immigrants to their country (see, for example Briggs Jr. 1996).

In this context, social networks play an important role in finding legal possibilities within new regulations. Fawcett and Arnold (1987) noted that once the pioneering wave of immigrants has settled, linkages are established that motivate and facilitate further migration. Immigrants often develop complex family strategies to maximize the opportunities available under prevailing immigration laws. Family formation, a type of family reunification, is one of these strategies. For example, Muus (1990) found that the number of marriages between migrants already living in the Netherlands and partners from Turkey or Morocco doubled in the period 1987–1989. Furthermore, social networks offer opportunities for illegal immigrants because in the first period of their settlement these networks make it possible to adapt in the host country.[5]

It is also noteworthy that migration preferences change over time. For example, labour migration during the sixties was mainly determined by the industrialization of Northern European countries in certain manufacturing regions. This can be illustrated by the case of Germany where Munich, Stuttgart and the Ruhr area were among the first areas where the demand for guest workers developed (King 1993). Recent migrants have also chosen the same regions as their destination, a phenomenon which can be explained by chain migration and (expected) labour market opportunities (Van Imhoff et al. 1994).

Another example is the situation in the Netherlands. Immigrants there, like elsewhere, are highly urbanized but the labour market opportunities only partly explain this disproportional distribution. Immigration can be mainly explained in recent years by family reunion, family formation and asylum seeking. This increases the spatial concentration further (De Mas and Haffmans 1984). As a consequence, social factors and networks explain nowadays the continuing growth of the immigrant population in these areas. In addition, as will also be elaborated in several other chapters of this book, the housing market also contributes to the spatial concentration of immigrants (King 1993). The stock of relatively cheap (often inferior) houses in certain parts of major cities are often the only option for new immigrants.

1.4 Labour Market Absorption Policies

It has already been highlighted in the introduction that international migration patterns are changing considerably. Moreover, we also observe a major change in the composition of the immigrants flows in the recent past. These changes call for a profound analysis of policies

17

for the absorption of immigrants on the (urban) labour market. This is a particularly important issue in Europe, due to the persistently high unemployment levels in most of the countries (especially in the cities). An overview of the various policy responses which can be found in European countries is given by Cross (1989) and Schierop (1989). The policy approaches regarding the absorption of new immigrants in the labour market and their success rate vary considerably among the different countries.

There is some evidence that the effects of immigration on the labour market in the traditional immigrant receiving countries in North America and Australasia are on a structural basis often positive, or at least rather neutral (see for instance Chiswick 1978; Poot 1986; Greenwood and McDowell 1986; Withers 1987; Wright and Maxim 1993; Simon 1994). In contrast, migration is considered to have fuelled unemployment in the European labour markets, although the econometric evidence for this is rather inconclusive (see e.g. Zimmermann 1995). Any difference between these two situations may be due to structural differences in the labour markets of the former and the latter countries, the skill composition of the immigrant flows, and differences in policies oriented towards the absorption of immigrants in the region of destination. The policy approach in the USA and in other traditional immigration countries such as Canada and Australia has permanent settlement as the core objective. The integration in these host countries is aided by the usual availability of a range of coordinated services assist in labour market absorption. Furthermore, such countries make a clear distinction between family, refugee and independent categories. In contrast, few labour market initiatives are exclusively targeted to new immigrants in European OECD countries. The training programmes and policies in these countries were targeted to problem groups in general and were not designed for new immigrants. In this respect it is important to develop training programmes aimed at social and economic integration of immigrants at a city level, because immigrant absorption is a problem which mainly concerns city areas.

In general, the policy responses towards the absorption of new immigrants in European countries appear to show some similarity. Policies have been developed which range from language training programmes to programmes specifically aimed at the assimilation of immigrants in the labour market. The objectives of these policies are to accelerate the economic integration of immigrants. At an urban level, a series of different complementary projects has been developed to meet this objective. They aim on the supply side at the enhancement of skills of immigrants and on the demand side at stimulating companies to employ new immigrants. These projects are diverse in nature and can be clustered in the following way (see Nijkamp and Voskuilen 1996b):

a   Projects aimed at the training of basic skills. These projects help the new immigrants in the first period after arrival in the host country.

Examples of immigrant integration programmes are: language training programmes, cultural adaptation programmes, etc.

b   Vocational training programmes. These programmes are developed to improve the educational level and the professional skills of immigrants in order to provide a better match with the current demand in labour market demand. Examples of these programmes are: vocational guidance, self-employment programmes, etc.

c   Labour market absorption programmes. These programmes are developed to improve the labour market outcomes for immigrants. Examples of supply side oriented absorption programmes are: application training, labour market intermediaries, temporary in-company training programmes, etc. An example from The Netherlands is the Project Integration New immigrants (PIN), which was developed to teach new immigrants the basic skills they need to fit into Dutch society. Similar projects can be found in Germany to integrate 'Aussiedler' from central and eastern Europe.

Another way to improve the labour market absorption process of foreign immigrants in local labour markets could be a demand side oriented policy directed towards reducing the existing barriers to obtain available jobs. This strategy might be accomplished by subsidizing the employment of disadvantaged workers, for example to encourage firms in the primary sector to employ such workers. Another approach may be the introduction of antidiscrimination legislation in the form of quotas, registration, affirmative action, etc. In addition, governments could remove institutional barriers in order to stimulate self-employment activities of the new immigrants.

1.5 An Outline of the Book

Following this introductory chapter, Part A of this book is concerned with the economic dimension of the impact of international migration. In Chapter 2, Fischer presents a macroeconomic perspective on the impact of migration in a set of (international) regions which are economically integrating, such as we have witnessed in the European Union recently.

Fischer makes the important distinction between short, medium and long run effects. Migration is a welfare enhancing form of arbitrage in the short run standard neoclassical model. It may speed up regional integration in the short run, and lead to general equilibrium effects on the demand for labour in the medium term, but in the long run it does not matter for the rate of growth from this perspective.

Fischer also predicts that capitalists in the host country, remaining workers in the sending country and migrants themselves are those who gain from migration in the short run, while capitalists in the sending

19

country and native workers who would act as substitutes for immigrants in the host country would be worse off. These distributional effects influence the politics of immigration, but – since migration is welfare enhancing – public transfers to redistribute the gains could make everyone better off.

Fischer shows that in the competing perspective of the 'new economic geography', in which regional growth may be subject to economies of scale and human capital externalities, migration may encourage divergence both in the short run and the long run and policy action may be needed. Thus, the conclusions of the theoretical analysis depend strongly on the assumptions made. The impact of immigration on economic growth consequently deserves close empirical scrutiny.

Fischer's chapter does not address any possible negative externalities due to immigration. An example of this type of externality is the increasing consumption of publicly provided goods which are subject to some congestion. The impact of immigration in the presence of such 'club goods' is an issue addressed by Leiner in Chapter 3 by means of a theoretical two-country trade model. The congestion effects are likely to accrue to the residents of the host country in densely populated areas and may also lead to a decline in the terms of trade. Consequently, they are one reason why countries which pursue free trade policies strongly restrict immigration. Leiner shows that what matters is not the fact that migrants gain a share of the existing public capital stock (for which the costs are sunk), but the possibility that there are congestion effects, that residents believe that their rights are 'diluted' or that the public capital stock must be expanded. In such situations a case can be made for compensating entrance fees to be levied on migrants.

Bauer and Zimmermann provide in Chapter 4 a more detailed review of the economic and econometric approaches to international migration than was addressed in (compound overview of) Section 1.2. They distinguish between the standard neoclassical approach, the human capital approach, the role of asymmetric information, family migration and network migration. Bauer and Zimmermann note that these theories still warrant extensive testing, but that the usually available data, namely macro level time series, are unsuitable for this purpose. Such data tend to have too few observations to apply modern time series econometric methods and, moreover, are in any case unsuitable to test hypotheses about the complicated micro level decision making that is characteristic of the migration phenomenon. They recommend that micro level survey (panel) data should be generated and that these would be particularly useful to obtain a better understanding of the current immigration problems in Europe.

The final contribution of Part A, by Poot, provides a survey of some recent findings regarding the impact of immigration on labour markets and urban infrastructure in Australia and New Zealand, two countries which still encourage some further immigration. Differences and similarities between the findings for the two countries, also in relation to the experience of other high income countries, are mentioned. Poot

20

reinforces Fischer's paper by noting that the distinction between micro and macro level approaches, and between short run and long run impacts, is important. There appears to be little evidence of immigration affecting wage levels and unemployment rates at the macro level in Australasia. While analyses of migrant earnings show a process of generally successful adaptation, although not necessarily catch up, there are clear differences between migrants groups – related to characteristics such as birthplace, ethnicity and occupation. With respect to the spatial impact, immigrants are disproportionally attracted by certain regions and by the largest cities. Their presence may lead to short run upward pressure on house prices and rents. Finally, Poot emphasizes that urban population growth due to immigration generates both positive and negative externalities. However, these are difficult to identify empirically.

Part B of the book is concerned with the international patterns and linkages in international migration systems. The spatial selectivity of the migration flows and clustering of the migrant stocks come to the fore. In Chapter 6, Geyer applies the idea of differential urbanization, which he developed for studying internal migration patterns, to the case of international migration. Differential urbanization refers to a sequential urban development pattern, in which the core of an urban area initially grows rapidly, subsequently grows slower than the suburbs, at some stage even experiences population loss, but eventually may gain population again in a phase of reurbanization. These phases are driven by both intraurban relocation and internal migration. Another important aspect of this theory is that there may be mainstream and substream migration flows in different directions and of a different composition. Geyer also focuses on the motives of migrants and distinguishes between productionism and environmentalism. In early stages of development, households are driven by the quest for income gains (productionism). However, because space and amenities have a positive income elasticity, eventually a demand for quality of life takes over (environmentalism).

Geyer shows that these concepts are also fruitful for studying international migration. He emphasizes the impact of globalization on the patterns of urban growth and the distinction between core and peripheral regions. This has direct implications for mainstream and substream migration flows. Yet the present global urban hierarchy may expect a further shakeup and this will again lead to further changes in international migration flows.

Lipshitz describes in Chapter 7 the spatial dimension of internal migration as the result of relative demands for labour driven by the patterns of development on the one hand and the political processes and resulting immigration regulations on the other. Like Geyer, he emphasizes the role of globalization (the new world economic order), but also stresses the impact of the new political world order. He refers to migration at the international level, but briefly discusses subnational

21

spatial patterns also. Lipshitz notes that migrants are drawn to the main cities but few countries have a spatial immigration policy.

The reason for restricting immigration is mainly political: it alleviates the fear of an eroding position of unskilled native workers. Globalization will lead to further growth in the migration of professionals, but this is unlikely to create political tensions. However, policies can have a strong impact on the intraurban locational decisions of migrants through the availability and location of public housing.

Odé describes in Chapter 8 the contemporary patterns of labour migration to The Netherlands by means a study of the size and composition of employment permits issued to migrant workers. Prior to discussing the Dutch case, he also provides a brief discussion of general economic and political aspects of contemporary labour migration, with specific reference to Europe.

Odé's chapter highlights the presence of some very specific and strong spatial linkages. Namely, after discussion the occupational composition and origins of Dutch migrant workers, Odé zooms in on the presence of Polish migrant workers in Dutch horticulture. These workers are not only spatially concentrated in the Netherlands, but they also come from just a few areas in Poland. Personal networks play an important role. Also important is the seasonality of the work. The question would arise to what extent the seasonal work will lead to permanent immigration.

The situation in The Netherlands is one which can still be found in many developed countries: despite a public fear of immigration, employers in certain specific industries - particularly in the primary sector – push for the recruitment of unskilled migrant workers for positions which are not being filled by the native unemployed workers.[6]

Chapters 9 to 12 focus on regional and urban clustering of migrants. Attention is also given to the assimilation of immigrants in local urban areas and labour markets. Musterd, Ostendorf and Breebaart study in Chapter 9 segregation, polarization and policies concerning ethnic minorities in Amsterdam by means of a comparison with London, Brussels and Frankfurt. They find that there is significant spatial segregation in European cities, although not to the same extent as in the USA. London and Brussels are more ethnically segregated and polarized than Amsterdam and Frankfurt. Tensions also flare up more often in the former two cities. Yet the latter two cities have been more active in formulating policies to address these problems and segregation does not seem to have led to growing polarization in Amsterdam. One cause of the difference in segregation across the four cities is the international variation in housing market conditions and housing policies. A spatial dispersion policy may not be constitutional in some countries.

The observed spatial patterns are due to many factors. Musterd et al. emphasize the negative externalities of segregation, but we should note that clustering can also create positive externalities in terms of the knowhow, financial and other support which it can provide to newcomers.

Musterd et al. review the specific policies available to ethnic minorities in terms of the availability of education and assistance in the labour market. The policies may have been effective in The Netherlands, but Musterd et al. feel that it is too early to consider this proven. Finally, they note that the processes of growing liberalization and market reforms worldwide may have a negative impact on the relative position of migrants and ethnic minorities in the big cities.

Green describes in Chapter 10 the spatial distribution of ethnic minorities in the United Kingdom and the socioeconomic well being and labour market experience of these people. As we noted earlier in this chapter, we should also consider the second and subsequent generations when we analyse the long run impact of the immigration of people on the social structure of the host society. Green therefore rightly focuses on the composition of the population of Great Britain in terms of country of birth as well as ethnicity. The geographical scale of analysis ranges from the national level through regions to the level of London boroughs. The observed patterns are rather complex and vary between ethnic groups. However, a general feature is that immigrants and ethnic minorities are concentrated in Greater London and the South East of Britain. The strong ethnic clustering within Greater London mentioned by Musterd et al. in the previous chapter is reinforced by Green.

Green's research provides evidence for the disadvantaged position of certain ethnic minorities in the local labour markets. The observed outcomes would be consistent with the notion of a dual labour market in which the ethnic minorities are overrepresented in the secondary market with low pay, low job security and unfavourable working conditions (Doeringer and Piore 1971). However, in addition to occupational and industrial segmentation, we may also observe a spatial segregation of ethnic minorities which in itself may be a source of discrimination.

Lipshitz describes in Chapter 11 the integration of immigrants from the former Soviet Union in the Israeli housing and labour markets. An interesting feature of this migration is that, despite having been a very large flow concentrated over only a few years (with a peak in 1989–90), absorption in Israel seems to have been largely successful. One reason may be the high level of human capital of many of the ex-Soviet Union immigrants. The professional immigrants tend to be the most mobile and they preceded a flow of industry workers from the ex Soviet Union.

Lipshitz finds that the presence of skilled immigrants in a periphery is in itself not sufficient to attract high tech and other rapid growth activities to these areas. Consequently, the core-periphery dichotomy is modified but not broken by immigration.

The current Israeli policy for absorption is market driven with migrants being provided with a lump sum settlement grant. Private housing investment follows the migrants rather than vice versa. Lipshitz finds that subsidized housing in the periphery attracted the weaker (unskilled, retired) migrants, but many of these considered those locations as temporary only. Generally speaking, migrants went where jobs were. Internal migration patterns after settlement reflect upward mobility and life cycle related changes.

The final chapter of Part C is concerned with economic integration of immigrants in Sweden, both at the national level and in the Malmö labour market. Bevelander uses in this chapter employment rates – i.e. the proportion of a certain population group registered as employed – as the statistical indicator to compare the labour market performance of different immigrant groups. Bevelander finds that the employment rate declined among immigrants over the period 1970–1990. Unlike much of the literature of labour market absorption, which gives supply side explanations only, Bevelander finds that labour market absorption is a function of both the demand side and the supply side of the labour market.

On the supply side, absorption is inter alia related to education, occupation and language skills, while on the demand side the business cycle, economic restructuring and discrimination against immigrants may also play a role. Thus, low growth and a transformation towards the service sector also contributed to the deteriorating labour market outcomes for immigrants. The results for Malmö strengthened the conclusions obtained for Sweden generally.

Part D, which contains the final three chapters of the book, provides some examples of theoretical and empirical modelling of aspects of migration. Waldorf describes in Chapter 13 a model of Markov transition probabilities of moves between an origin country and destination regions in a way which takes various important phenomena into account. The presence of clusters of immigrants is the first of these. They are according to Waldorf due to network dynamics which go beyond the narrow economic calculus. However, these clusters may have strong economic implications. Another aspect of the model is that interregional migration and return migration following an initial move are also both taken into account.

The transition probabilities in Waldorf's model are a function of relative population sizes of origins and destinations, which is consistent with a broad push/pull interpretation of migration and this idea can be found in the empirical work by Van Wissen and Visser in Chapter 14 also. Finally, duration of stay effects are also considered.

Van Wissen and Visser provide in Chapter 14 an exploratory analysis of international migration flows within the European Economic Area (EEA). They note that there are big problems with obtaining good quality data of gross EEA migration data. Van Wissen and Visser use a statistical model based on the Poisson distribution. However, the basic model performs rather unsatisfactorily and two less constrained models provide betters results. The results confirm the importance of the gravity property of migration flows. There are several ways of explaining this property in terms of migrant behaviour, e.g. by means of search behaviour in the labour market (e.g. Poot 1995). The importance of networks of migrants and return migration is again highlighted in this chapter. The migration flow from A to B is related to the number of residents of A born in B and the number of residents of B born in A.

It is surprising that the economic variables turn out to be unimportant in the Van Wissen/Visser model. The authors point to small differences in economic indicators within the EEA at the national level, but the aforementioned data problems may have affected the results also.

The final chapter of the book is concerned with the efficiency of migration in terms of the extent to which migration brings actual and potential earnings closer. Chapter 15 focuses on internal migration and potential earnings in the USA and The Netherlands but the results have some significance for international migration studies also. Van Dijk et al. point to institutional causes for the inter-country differences in the attainment of potential earnings, such as labour market policies, unionization and the wage setting environment.

Earnings attainment among internal migrants in The Netherlands was much higher relative to earnings attainment among US internal migrants. Van Dijk et al. explain the difference in terms of institutional differences between the two countries. Van Dijk et al. also find that employed migrants within the US obtain higher wages than non-migrants. In the Netherlands there appears to be no noticeable difference between migrants and non-migrants in this respect. We suggest that one reason may be the difference in geographic scale of the two labour markets. If this indeed matters, we can conclude that migration will pay off more on average when countries are economically integrating following an opening of borders to migration.

1.6 Research Agenda

Despite the progress which has already been made in our understanding of the causes and consequences of immigration in a spatial context, an issue to which the papers in this volume aim to make a contribution, there is still a significant set of issues which ought to be addressed in future research. In this section we will briefly outline several such issues. A further discussion of a research agenda with an economic focus is given by Bauer and Zimmermann in Chapter 4 and by Poot in Chapter 5.

Our first point is that the global pattern of migration systems and migration networks deserves full scale attention. Too often, international migration flows are analysed as a two dimensional flow without reference to the possibility that such flows are not independent of other flows. Systemic modelling, which has been fruitful to study internal migration (see e.g. Nijkamp and Poot 1987), could be extended to the case of cross border migration. Layton (1983) found, for example, that migration from the United Kingdom to New Zealand was influenced by competing opportunities in Australia.

Second, the development of migration streams over time – in relation to gender, education, age and country of origin – needs to be mapped out in greater detail. Several authors in this volume stress the importance of a dynamic perspective. It will also be fruitful to pay greater attention to the interaction between international migration and other forms of international linkages, such as trade, ODI and information exchange through media networks (see Poot 1996).

Next, the spatial concentration effects of immigration – in relation to local housing markets and local labour markets – should be investigated more thoroughly, witness also terms like the 'new ethnic division of labour'.

There is also still a need to evaluate systematically the various labour market absorption programmes in order to judge potential projects on their effectiveness and critical success factors. This will be particularly of importance in the European context. At the same time, a comparison should be made of the impact of cultural, economic-social and institutional differences across countries on the labour market absorption process of immigrants.

Finally, the structure of receiving regional or urban labour markets and the general welfare impacts on new foreign entrants are a subject to be studied in greater detail, as otherwise effective policies are hard to develop and implement. The effect of immigrants on public expenditure and income, an issue partly addressed by the theoretical analysis of Leiner in Chapter 3, is still highly debated in terms of the available empirical evidence (e.g. Simon 1996, Borjas 1996).

In general, much more empirical work needs to be done with micro level data, as there are limitations in this context to the statistical inferences that can be made with macro level data. This point is also stressed by Bauer and Zimmermann (Chapter 4) and by Poot (Chapter 5). Even at the micro level, the available data are often not specifically generated for studying migration problems. Hence, new micro level data – particularly of a panel nature – will need to be generated and the sampling problem inherent in the study of minorities must be addressed.

To end, we consider two specific questions of predominant importance in future international migration research. The first research question is related to the functioning of urban labour markets: 'Is the unfavourable labour market position of immigrants a result of ethnic-specific job search behaviour?'. In the literature, it is found that new immigrants make use of existing social networks (usually present in urban areas) to get acquainted in a country of destination and also to acquire a job in the urban labour market (see. e.g. Zimmermann 1994). To test this network hypothesis – which seems to be valid in third world countries – in the labour market setting of the developed countries, one could use the so called 'flow or matching' approach to the labour market which emphasizes the dynamic nature of the job finding and job losing process on the one hand, and the job creation and job destruction on the other hand (see e.g., Blanchard and Diamond 1992).

In this respect, it can also be taken into account that the matching of jobs and immigrants is not only influenced by the job search strategies chosen by the job seekers, but also by employers recruitment strategies via which they can implicitly reveal their preferences towards certain groups in the labour market (see e.g., Gorter et al. 1993). Modelling the labour market by means of this flow approach will also allow the application of simulation scenarios to access the effectiveness of various labour market policies which aim to improve the position of new immigrants.

The second research question addresses the issue of economic development impacts of new immigrants in host countries: 'Do the international migration flows have a positive economic development effect on the country of destination, specifically in the urban areas?' The socioeconomic impact of foreign immigrants on the economic development of the host country or region has been extensively studied outside Europe, especially in the United States. Research on the effects of immigration shows evidence of such a positive relationship in the US (see for a survey, Greenwood 1994). However, the long run impact on economic growth and technical change has as yet not been firmly established due to the difficulty of testing such effects with macro level data. Moreover, results for countries such as the United States or Australia cannot directly be translated to other countries, such as in Europe – due e.g. to strong institutional differences. Therefore, empirical evidence is needed to test under which conditions the labour market and macroeconomic results also hold for regions in Europe.

The basic hypothesis to be investigated, which we will refer to as the 'Greenwood hypothesis', is the existence of positive, endogenously generated, growth in certain (usually urban) areas as a result of economic activities of immigrants (such as, for example, new entrepreneurship). Clearly, this endogenous growth effect will only show up in the long run (given that it exists) and therefore, a longitudinal meso analysis of regional/urban development is asked for in which the focus should be on the economic impact of immigration flows. One of the main questions to be answered is whether the economic position of the regions of origin and of destination diverge of converge (see also Goria and Ichino 1994). A relevant aspect of this kind of research is, of course, the choice of indicators of regional/local development. At the end, one would like to appraise the policy implications of the validity of the 'Greenwood hypothesis' in settings where this has not been done yet, such as in Europe.

References

Bach, R.L. and Schraml, L.A. (1982), 'Migration, Crisis and Theoretical Conflict', *International Migration Review*, vol. 16, pp. 320–41.

Bhagwati, J.N. (1984), 'Incentives and Disincentives: International Migration', *Weltwirtschaftliches Archiv*, vol. 120, pp. 320–41.

Blanchard, O.J. and Diamond, P. (1992), 'The Flow Approach to Labor Markets, American Economic Review', *Papers and Proceedings*, pp. 354–59.

Böhning, W.R. (1991), 'Integration and Immigration Pressures in Western Europe', *International Labour Review*, vol. 13a, no. 4, pp. 445–58.

Borjas, G.J. (1989), 'Economic Theory and International Migration', *International Migration Review*, vol. 23, pp. 457–78.

Borjas, G.J. (1996), 'Reply to Julian Simon's Rejoinder', *Journal of Economic Literature*, vol. 34, no. 3, pp. 1332–333.

Borjas, G.J. and Bronars, S.G. (1991), 'Immigration and the Family', *Journal of Labor Economics*, vol. 9, no. 2, pp. 123–48.

Briggs, Jr. V.M. (1996),' International Migration and Labour Mobility: The Receiving Countries', in Van den Broeck, J. (ed.), *The Economics of Labour Migration*, Edward Elgar, Cheltenham, UK

Castles, S. and Miller, M.J. (1993), *The Age of Migration*, Macmillan: London.

Chiswick, B.R. (1978), 'The Effect of Americanization on the Earnings of Foreign-born Men', *Journal of Political Economy*, vol. 86, pp. 897–921.

Cross, M, (1989), 'Migrants and New Minorities in Europe', in Entzinger, H. and J Carter (eds) *International Review of Comparative Public Policy, Vol. 1*, JAI Press Inc., Greenwich, Connecticut.

De Mas, P. and Haffmans, M.A.F. (1993), *De Gezinshereniging van Marokkanen in Nederland,* Centrum Migratie Onderzoek, Instituut voor Sociale Geografie, Amsterdam

Doeringer, P.B. and Piore, M.J. (1971), *Internal Labor Markets and Manpower Analysis*, Heath, Lexington Mass.

Fawcett, J.T. and Arnold, F. (1987), 'Explaining Diversity: Asian and Pacific Immigration Systems', in Fawcett, J.T. and B.V. Carino (eds) *Pacific Bridges: The New Immigration from Asia and the Pacific Islands*, Center of Migration Studies:, New York.

Freeman G.P. (1986), 'Migration and the Political Economy of the Welfare State', *Annals of the American Academy of Political and Social Science*, vol. 485, pp. 51–63.

Goria, A. and Ichino, A. (1994), 'Migration and Convergence among Italian Regions', Paper 51.94, Fondazione Eni Enrico Mattei, Milano.

Gorter, C., Nijkamp, P. and Rietveld, P. (1993), 'The Impact of Employers' Recruitment Behaviour on the Allocation of Vacant Jobs to Unemployed Job Seekers', *Empirical Economics*, vol. 18, no. 2, pp. 251–69.

Goss, J. and Lindquist, B. (1995), 'Conceptualizing International Labor Migration: A Structuration Perspective', *International Migration Review*, vol. 29, no. 2, pp. 317–51.

Greenwood, M.J. (1975), 'Research on Internal Migration in the United States', *Journal of Economic Literature,* vol. 13, pp. 397–433.

Greenwood, M.J. (1994), 'Potential Channels of Immigrant Influence on the Economy of the Receiving Countries', *Papers in Regional Science,* vol. 73, no. 3, pp. 211–40.

28

Greenwood, M.J. and McDowell, J.M. (1986), 'The Factor Market Consequences of US Migration', *Journal of Economic Literature*, vol. 24, pp. 1738–772.

Harris, J. and Todaro, M.P. (1970), 'Migration, Unemployment and Development: a Two Sector Analysis', *American Economic Review*, vol. 60, no. 1, pp. 126–42.

Hoffmann-Nowotny, H.J. (1981), 'A Sociological Approach Towards General Theory of Migration', in Kritz, M.M., Keely, Ch.B. and S.M. Tomasi (eds) *Global Trends in Migration: Theory and Research on International Population Movements*, The Center of Migration Studies, New York.

King, R. (1993), *Mass Migration in Europe: The Legacy and the Future*, Belhaven Press, London.

Kritz, M.M. and Zlotnik, H. (1992), 'Global Interactions: Migration Systems, Process, and Policies', in Kritz, M.M., Lim, L. and H. Zlotnik (eds) *International Migration Systems: A Global Approach*, Clarendon Press, Oxford.

Kulu-Glasgow, I. (1992), 'Motives and Social Networks of International Migration Within the Context of the Systems Approach: A Literature Review', Netherlands Interdisciplinary Demographic Institute (NIDI): The Hague, unpublished paper.

Layton, T.B. (1983), 'British Migration to New Zealand after World War II', *Australian Economic History Review*, vol. 23, pp. 219–37.

Muus, P.J. (1990), 'Migration, Minorities and Policy in the Netherlands: Report for the Continuous Reporting System on Migration', SOPEMI, Department of Human Geography, University of Amsterdam.

Nijkamp, P. and Poot, J. (1987), 'Dynamics of Generalised Spatial Interaction Models', *Regional Science and Urban Economics*, vol. 17, no. 3, pp. 367–90.

Nijkamp, P. and Spiess, K. (1994), 'International Migration in Europe: Critical Success Absorption Factors', *Journal of Regional Studies*, vol. 12, no. 4, pp. 331–35.

Nijkamp, P. and Voskuilen, M. (1996a), 'International Migration: A Comprehensive Framework', *European Spatial Research and Policy*, vol. 3, no. 1, pp. 5–28

Nijkamp, P. and Voskuilen, M. (1996b), 'Urban Migrant Absorption', in M. Chatterji and R. Domanski (eds) *Urban and Regional Management in Countries in Transition,* Polish Academy of Sciences, Warsaw, pp. 93–114.

Penninx, R. (1986), 'Theories on International Labour Migration: between Micro and Macro Analysis', paper presented at the XIth World Congress of Sociology, New Delhi.

Poot, J. (1986), *Immigration and the Economy: A Review of Recent Australian Findings on the Economic Consequences of Immigration and the Relevance of These Findings for New Zealand*, Victoria University Press, Wellington

Poot, J. (1995), 'Do Borders Matter? A Model of International Migration in Australasia', *Australasian Journal of Regional Studies*, vol. 1, no. 2, pp. 159–82.

Poot, J. (1996), 'Information, Communication and Networks in International Migration Systems', *Annals of Regional Science,* vol. 30, no. 1, pp. 55–73.

Rogers, R. (1992), 'The Politics of Migration in the Contemporary World', *International Migration*, vol. 30.

Schierop, C. (1989), 'Immigrants and Immigrants Policy in Denmark and Sweden', in H. Entzinger and J. Carter (eds) *International Review of Comparative Public Policy, Vol 1*, JAI Press Inc., Greenwich, Connecticut.

Simon, J.L. (1994), 'On the Economic Consequences of Immigration', in Giersch, H. (ed.) *Economic Aspects of International Migration*, Springer-Verlag, Berlin.

Simon, J.L. (1996), 'Reply to a Review by George Borjas', *Journal of Economic Literature*, vol. 34, no. 3, pp. 1331–332.

Stalker, P. (1994), *The Work of Strangers: A Survey of International Labour Migration*, International Labour Office, Geneva.

Van den Broeck, J. (ed) (1996), *The Economics of Labour Migration*, Edward Elgar: Cheltenham, United Kingdom

Van Imhoff, E., Schoorl, J., Van De Erf, R. and Van Der Gaag, N. (1994), 'Regionale Prognose Bevolking van Turkse, Marokkaanse, Surinaamse of Antilliaanse Afkomst, 1992–2000', NIDI report no. 33, Den Haag.

Withers, G. (1987), 'Migration and the Labour Market: Australian Analysis', *The Future of Migration*, OECD, Paris.

Wood, C.H. (1982), 'Equilibrium and Historical-Structural Perspectives on Migration', *International Migration Review*, vol. 16, pp. 298–319.

Wright, R.E. and Maxim, P.S. (1993), 'Immigration Policy and Immigrant Quality: Empirical Evidence from Canada', *Journal of Population Economics*, vol. 6, no. 4, pp. 337–52.

Zimmermann, K.F. (1994), 'Some General Lessons for Europe's Migration Problem' in Giersch, H. (ed.), *Economic Aspects of International Migration*, Springer Verlag, Berlin.

Zimmermann, K.F. (1995), 'European Migration: Push and Pull', in *Proceedings of the World Bank Annual Conference on Development Economics 1994*, Supplement to the World Bank Economic Review and The World Bank Research Observer.

Zolberg, A.R. (1989), 'The Next Waves: Migration Theory for a Changing World', *International Migration Review*, vol. 23, pp. 403–29.

Zolberg, A.R., Suhrke, A. and Aguayo, S. (1986), 'International Factors in the Formation of Refugee Movements', *International Migration Review*, Vol. 20, pp. 151–69.

Notes

1. Castles and Miller (1993), p. 4.

2. In statistical collections, migration is usually defined as a geographical relocation for 12 months or more.

3. The policy changes in New Zealand in the early 1990s would be a good example. See chapter 5. Similarly, Freeman (1986) notes that international migration has led to an Americanization of European welfare policies in which immigration has reduced the power of organized labour by dividing it into national and immigrant camps.

4. His theory was nonetheless empirically verified by means of studies of migration problems in Switzerland.

5. For example, Böhning (1991) estimated that at least some 600,000 illegal people entered western Europe in the period 1983–1989.

6. This raises several issues for further research: the missing incentives for local unemployed, the difference in motivation between migrants and locals, and the impact of immigration on (sub-standard) working conditions.

Part A
Theory and Evidence: An Economic Perspective

2 Migration, Economic Integration and Regional Growth

PETER FISCHER

2.1 Introduction

After the traumatic experience of World War Two, nations concurred in their aim for peace and economic prosperity. They established an ever denser network of informal and formal cooperation and thereby allowed economic boundaries to be detached from political frontiers. Markets have been merging with increasing speed and international specialization and globalization have been taking place generating increasing economic welfare: present times have become the age of economic integration, of which the realization of the European Common Market programme represents just the most recent notable step.

Economic integration may take place through three different instruments: free trade the (legally) free flow of capital (international investment) and the free migration of people. While the well known obstacles to trade usually leave plenty of room for national borders to matter in economic terms, a liberalization of the remaining two instruments of international integration, capital flows and migration, reduces the economic importance of borders significantly and strengthens locational competition between integrating regions. With economic integration proceeding, the focus of institutional economic integration has shifted from pure liberalization of trade to the liberalization of trade *and* factor flows. This chapter presents an investigation of part of the latter, namely the (allocative and distributive) effects of free migration on regional growth and income convergence in the context of economic integration.

Traditionally, economists have dealt with the 'Nature and the Causes of the Wealth of Nations' (Adam Smith 1776). Political decisions divide the world into different single nations. Thereby the 'holistic axiom of a 'national' economic as a basically homogeneous system' (Giersch 1990:1) dominates the analysis of international relations. Nations were reduced to dimensionless points.

The distinction between the political and the economic area and thus the geographic aspects of economic transactions have been practically ignored in the neoclassical literature for a long time. Using the term 'regional' in our analyses we want to stress that in the context of economic integration it is not the politically determined entity 'country' or 'province' that matters but the economically defined 'region': places of economic activity and market spaces which are locationally concentrated, which differ from each other through their relative endowment with specific production factors and which constitute economic 'subareas' of an integrating area. They may sometimes correspond to agglomerations only but can also extend in size beyond national borders. In the latter case, institutional economic integration is particularly effectual in removing obstacles connected to political borders and thereby allow 'natural' economic regions to develop freely. In using the term 'regional' we would also like to emphasize that what we are focusing on here is economic integration and migration between geographically and culturally not too distant places like the regions of the European Common Market, rather than economic growth trends between the less and the more developed countries.

In what follows, we discuss (allocational and distributional) effects of migration on regional growth and income convergence in the context of economic integration from different points of view. Following a general overview of the effects of migration in Section 2.2, Section 2.3 provides the traditional neoclassical point of view. It is shown that from a neoclassical point of view, free migration is expected to increase overall wealth and to enhance economic convergence between integrating regions. Economic integration is not a necessary condition for convergence, but if regions integrate, convergence can be expected to gain in speed. Trade and capital flows may partly substitute for the lacking mobility of labour. While the overall allocational effects of migration tend to be positive, some groups in society will be affected adversely. Indeed, native workers who compete on a substitutive basis with immigrants may in the short run constitute the principal 'losers' of economic integration through migration and therefore object to immigration. But workers whose work is complementary to jobs done by immigrants will gain, and in the medium run allocation affects are likely to dominate. In the long run, however, limited migration will not influence stead-state equilibrium wealth in a neoclassical setting. Migration may speed up integration and ease adjustment processes in the short run, but in a neoclassical environment, migration does not matter in the long run.

Section 2.4 departs from the traditional neoclassical analysis of the effects of migration and introduces technological difference between emigration and immigration regions, the exploration of economies of scale, imperfect competition and human capital externalities. It is argued that in an environment where economies of scale and imperfect competition matter – an environment which we consider particularly relevant for highly developed and specialized regions undergoing a process of fostered economic integration – migration may encourage divergence in the short as well as in the long run. Migration can then become an important factor in locational competition. On the one hand,

36

the ability to attract mobile production factors may then decide whether a region becomes centre or periphery. On the other hand, the low mobility of labour in some highly developed societies may constitute the limitational factor to concentration processes as implied by models of 'economic geography' and locational competition. Both arguments have policy implications, which we will outline in the concluding section of this chapter. But in almost all models, migration generates only pecuniary externalities that are common features of the general price mechanism and do not hamper the allocative efficiency of market solutions. 'Winners' can compensate 'losers' ex post. Only in endogenous growth models that identify 'human capital' (or population density) as 'engines of growth' can migration exhibit social externalities that may call for ex ante policy action.

2.2   Effects of Migration – An Overview

There are many approaches to study the impact of migration on regional growth. In what follows, we will adopt a macroeconomic perspective that treats migration as merely mobility of labour. But even within this narrowed scope of analysis, there remain various ways of looking at certain effects of migration.[1]

In macroeconomic terms, migration represents in the short to medium run a change in a location's relative endowment of labour relative to other production factors. The magnitude of these relative endowment changes depends on the extent to which migrants carry capital with them, import it or remit it home. In the short to medium run, one may distinguish between labour market, remittance, public transfer and trade effects of migration on growth and development. Comparative-static analyses of labour market effects predominate (for a recent review see e.g. Borjas 1994, 1995; Friedberg and Hunt 1995). Migration increases the amount of labour supplied to the immigration region and is thus usually expected to reduce the average wage level there. In the emigration region, it decreases the labour supply and thus may increase the average wage level (*the immediate quantity effect*). To what extent this quantity effect of migration affects immobile labour depends on the substitutability of mobile and immobile labour. If migration follows economic incentives and people migrate from where labour productivity is low to where it is higher, then mobility improves the allocation of production factors. In the medium run, the improved allocation of production factors may further exert positive *dynamic allocation effects* on wages, employment and total value added produced. Finally, migration will also redistribute the relative compensation of the different kinds of production factors. These *distributive effects* of migration can explain group specific resistance to free migration even if net allocative welfare effects are unambiguously positive.

Obviously the effect of migration on the factor intensity of production crucially depends on whether migrants carry capital with them, which in

37

turn depends on the characteristics of migrants. In the medium run, remittances of migrants to their dependants may stimulate capital formation in their home economy and slow down investments in capital in the host region. The short to medium turn importance of the *remittances effect* largely depends on whether financial transfers of migrants will be used for investment or rather for consumption purposes.

Public transfer effects capture the net contribution of migrants to the financing of public services. These contributions increase or decrease the after tax output disposable for savings and investment which helps to determine the changes in capital stock in the immigration and emigration regions. Again, these allocational effects of public transfers are complemented by an intergroup redistribution over the tax system. Under a progressive tax system, the relatively poorest profit most from a positive net contribution of immigrants to the financing of public services.

In international economics literature, particular attention has been paid to *trade effects* of migration which may be conceived as the open economy part of allocation effects of migration.[2] On the one hand, resulting from the Rybcyzinski theorem, a migration induced change in the supply of the production factor labour will increase the output of the good that uses labour relatively intensively and may therefore lead to a change in relative prices, decreasing the price of labour intensive goods and thus altering a region's (country's) terms of trade. On the other hand, the Stolper-Samuelson theorem shows that a (small) change in relative prices and in factor rewards will increase the real reward of the factor intensive in the production of the good whose relative price has risen (i.e. here the capital intensive good) and reduce the real reward of the other factor.

Given that growth is almost entirely a matter of long run dynamic processes that necessarily take time, it is somewhat paradoxical that the described short to medium term effects and their comparative static analysis have up to now by and large dominated research on impacts of migration on economic growth. In the long(er) run the initial changes in relative factor endowment caused by migration as well as their influence on labour market imbalances are bound to be largely outweighed by migrants' own intertemporal behaviour and thus their long run impact on the accumulation of production input factors. Migration induced changes in investment behaviour, human skill formation and technology will determine the impact of migration on the long run 'steady-state' level and eventually on the path to convergence or divergence of economic development and growth (i.e. the growth effect of migration we are mainly interest in). Migration induced long run macroeconomic changes determine the impact of migration on the production structure and thus whether migration finally stimulates or hampers structural change (*structural change effect*).

Long term effects of migration on economic growth are probably much less explored because they are difficult to capture theoretically and even more difficult to quantify empirically. From a theoretical point of view they do not depend only on the characteristics and habits of migrants, but even more so on assumptions about the nature of the macroeconomic production function. In short, there are two contrasting traditions of thinking, the so called convergence and divergence school. In what follows we will provide a stylized introduction to the modelled functional relations, their short and long run implications and underlying assumptions about these two schools. First we begin with the more rigid neoclassical 'balanced growth' convergence school.

2.3 The 'Balanced Growth' and Convergence Point of View

2.3.1 The Basic Model

The convergence school of thinking about the impact of migration on growth is closely connected to traditional neoclassical economics. We commonly think of a world where the regions of emigration and immigration are both economies producing under conditions that may be represented as:

$$Y_t = eT \, K_t^\beta \, L_t^\gamma \tag{2.1}$$

where $\beta + \gamma = 1$ (constant return to scale). Y equals total output produced with given quantities of production factor inputs of labour L, capital K and non-accumulative (eventually exhaustible), location specific resources A (arable land, etc.). The technology T and the efficiency level e determine the relationship between factors used and output produced. Moreover, it is generally assumed that the following neoclassical assumptions hold:

a   migrants are a homogeneous group of working people (labour);
b   labour markets are in equilibrium, there is no unemployment;
c   production technologies are identical and exogenously given across regions;
d   production of goods and services takes place under constant returns to scale (i.e. $\beta + \gamma = 1$);
e   different kinds of production factors are (imperfect) substitutes;
f   transport and transaction costs are negligible;
g   markets are efficient and fully competitive;
h   individual and collective interests are identical; there are no externalities of individual action.

A key feature of neoclassical models of growth is that their emphasis is not on technology. Neoclassical theories assume that technology spreads relatively fast and that therefore the technological information and possibilities are similar across all regions. Differences in efficiency parameters are usually not within the scope of such theories. They are simply assumed to be determined exogenously and to capture system specific imperfections. In terms of the neoclassical school of thought, locations therefore do not differ by the technology they have access to nor by the way they make use of these, but by the different availability of production input factors. The different factor endowments explain why wages, interest rates, prices and growth may differ from one imperfectly integrated region to another.

A further important characteristic inherent to neoclassical economics is the assumption (d) that production takes place under constant returns to scale. Each single input, however, yields decreasing partial returns to scale. Different production factors may substitute for each other, though not perfectly. This (rather realistic) assumption is crucial for our allocation effect of migration.

The optimal working of the allocation effect of migration, trade and investment in a neoclassical world does not only depend on the constant returns, decreasing marginal products and factor substitution assumption. One usually also supposes that markets are perfect and production factors get paid their marginal return. Finally, externalities from individual actions are ruled out in neoclassical macro models of development and growth.

2.3.2 Convergence Effects of Migration on Development – the Short to Medium Run Perspective

The most immediate effects of migration on regional economic growth are via labour market effects. Within a neoclassical world they can be easily demonstrated from a comparative-static point of view by means of a simple diagram (see Figure 2.1).

Figure 2.1 draws a neoclassical aggregate labour market equilibrium for two regions R and Q, the regions of immigration R and the region of emigration Q – that we assume to be imperfectly integrated due to political obstacles at the outset. Trade or changes in investment have not yet assured factor price and growth equalization and migration between Q and R has been severely restricted. Suppose that the emigration region at time t1 is endowed with relatively abundant labour ($k_Q^{ti} < k^*$) and the immigration region has relatively abundant capital at its disposal ($k_Q^{t1} > k^*$). In brief, initial equilibrium wages $w_R^{t1}(k)$ in R surpass equilibrium wages $w_Q^{t1}(k)$ in Q.

Now consider institutional changes that remove the political obstacles and allow economic integration of the two regions. Macroeconomic models do not usually introduce any micro foundation of migration decisions. They simply assume that people move from where wages are low to where wages are high. For the sake of a simple demonstration of the key forces at work, let us therefore assume that people may freely and without cost migrate to the immigration region as long and as much as they want. In the (theoretical) corner solution where no (pecuniary and psychic) costs of migration exist and labour is perfectly mobile, the

40

two regions would integrate perfectly. In both regions, migration would ultimately bring about the long run steady state labour-capital endowment k*.[3] As allocation effects would generally take some time to materialize due to 'natural' rigidities, short and medium term labour market effects will differ, however, in the short run, migration in the presence of economic integration would lead to a new labour market equilibrium at time t2. Firstly, immigration from region Q has *increased* relative labour supply in region R. The aggregate labour supply curve shifted to the right and the wage level *decreased* until the new short run equilibrium wage in R – $w_{Q+R}^{t2}(K_O)^*$ – on the new labour supply curve L_R^{S2} equalled the (increased) wage level in Q.

Secondly, emigration *reduced* hours desired to work in W at a given wage level and thus shifted the aggregate labour supply curve to the left. The wage level *increased* until it reached a new equilibrium where on the supply curve L_Q^{S2} the short run equilibrium wage level in Q – $w_{Q+R}^{t2}(k)^*$ – equals the one in the region of immigration R. Moreover, total employment *increased* in R by $E_{RTot}^{t2} - E_R^{T1}$ and *decreased* in Q by $E_Q^{t1} - E_Q^{t2}$.

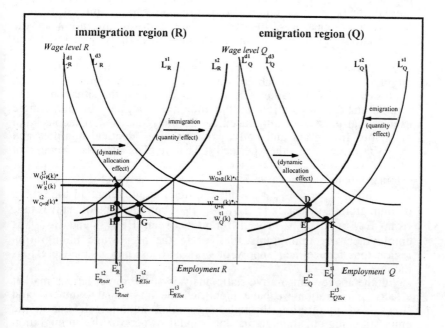

Figure 2.1   Direct labour market effects of migration

41

Due to the improved factor allocation total factor compensation in the integrated region R+Q has improved already in the short run. Given our neoclassical assumptions, the net welfare gain from migration for the receiving region may be roughly approximated by the areas within the triangle ABC. The foregone migrant income in the economy of emigration is more than compensated by the migrants' income in the immigrant region. Indeed, if the area BGH represents the additional immigrant income that outweighs the lost capital compensation DEF in the emigration region, net short run allocational gains for the integrated area as a whole can be approximated roughly by the area ABGC in Figure 2.1. By this resulting immediate net allocative 'migration gain' is likely to be relatively small in scale and dependent on the elasticities of the labour demand and supply curves (Borjas 1995).

More prominent in scale than the immediate allocative gains from migration are the short run redistributive effects of the altered relative factor endowments. Labour in the emigration region benefited from a relative income redistribution away from the owner of capital to workers because emigration made labour more scarce in relation to the, in the short run, inelastically supplied) capital and the compensation used for labour increased. In contrast, in the immigration region migration made labour relatively more abundant than capital and induced a reduction in labour compensations relative to returns on capital. Indeed, without redistributive measures, the net welfare gain of migration in the immigration region will – in the short run – be entirely used for capital compensation.

The above captures the short run direct labour market effects of migration on the *total* labour force. In practice, we may further be interested in labour market effects of migration on the situation of the original native population in the immigrant region. In our simple neoclassical model, we introduced, so far, only one homogeneous kind of labour. Immigrant and native workers have identical qualities and may substitute each other perfectly. That implies that also immigrant and native workers' wages have to be equal at $w_{Q+R}^{t2}(k)^*$. From our original labour supply curve L_R^{s1} we know that at $w_{Q+R}^{t2}(k)^*$ natives are only willing to work E_{Rnat}^{t2}. While thus total employment in the region of immigration increases by $E_{RTot}^{t2} - E_R^{t1}$, employment of natives falls from E_R^{t1} to R_{Rnat}^{t2}. The different between E_{RTot}^{t2} and E_{Rnat}^{t2} is employment by immigrants. Natives in the high wage immigration region thus reduce their supply of work and lose part of their previous income.

With the above comparative-static analysis of the direct labour market effects of migration we have identified the traditional 'winners' and 'losers' of integration through migration.[4] Immobile labour in the emigration region, immigrants and capital owners in the immigration region win, while native labour in the immigrant region and capital owners in the emigration region lose in their relative income position. From a neoclassical point of view, we may thus expect immobile labour

42

immigration regions (and capital owners in emigration regions) to oppose international labour mobility. In order to 'convince' them to support a liberal migration policy, one might consider redistributing part of the net allocational gains of free labour mobility away from the winners towards the losers.[5]

The evidence empirical studies produced on the *effects of migration on natives' wages* is surprisingly mixed. Direct effects depend heavily on the characteristics of immigrants and results are highly sensitive to the assumptions underlying the different studies. Different authors studying the same labour markets may come up with different directions of effects of migration on natives' wages (see for example Borjas 1994 for an overview). Most authors find negative direct labour market effects of immigration on native wages in the immigration regions, but they are typically very small (Gang and Rivera-Batiz 1994). It seems that wage effects are the more positive the more *skilled* immigrants are. A small negative impact of immigration on low skilled workers' real wages in the US was found by Grossman (1982); Borjas (1990); LaLonde and Topel 1991 and Borjas, Freeman and Katz (1992). Ekberg (1983) found the effect for low skilled wages in Sweden in the late seventies. McDowell and Singell (1993), however, analysed the composition of US immigration in more detail and found considerable variation in immigrants' characteristics. This, in turn, explained immigration induced effects on regional wage variations rather well. Borjas, Freeman and Katz (1992) arrive at similar results.

A first explanation why the available empirical evidence does not reveal the expected negative impact of immigration on native wages may be found in the shortcoming of the usual comparative-static analysis as described above: it accounts for the (probably relatively minor) immediate quantity effect of migration only and neglects more long term dynamic effects. We expect that in the medium term, the allocational gains from the increased economic integration between the integration and immigration regions, exert positive dynamic effects on total output and increase labour demand. This *dynamic allocational effect* of migration makes the economy more productive and increases incentives for capital accumulation and investment. In our figure, we have drawn the dynamic demand effects of labour mobility as a rightward shift of the labour demand curves from L^{d1} to L^{d3}. These dynamic allocational gains (of economic integration) materialize in both locations. Therefore, migration in the context of perfect regional economic integration establishes in the long run a (steady state) time t3 equilibrium where the labour demand curve in the region of immigration shifts from L_R^{d1} to L_R^{d3} as the labour demand curve in the region of emigration shifts from L_Q^{d1} to L_Q^{d3}. As a consequence, the wage level increases in the immigration and emigration regions rather simultaneously from $w_Q^{d1}(k)^*$ to $w_{Q+R}^{t3}(k)^*$. Correspondingly, employment in the emigration as well as in the immigration region increases also. In our graph, we have depicted the dynamic allocation effect such that also in the immigration region the new equilibrium wage $w_{Q+R}^{t3}(k)*$, total employment E_{RTot}^{t3} as well as the employment of natives E_{RNat}^{t3} exceed the levels before immigration. In other words, the effect of immigration on wages and employment of natives is in the medium term ambiguous. Whether natives in the immigrant region really face an absolute decrease in their wages and employment depends on the relative importance of the two labour market effects, the immediate quantity and the dynamic allocation effect.[6]

2.3.3 Departing from Classical Assumptions

Heterogeneous labour Apart from these medium term dynamic effects, complementarity between mobile and immobile labour may explain why empirical evidence usually does not reveal a considerable negative impact of immigration on native wages. The negative effect of immigration on wages and employment of natives is essentially due to the fact that in the traditional neoclassical model we distinguish only between two homogeneous production inputs, capital and labour. Immigrants are therefore perfect substitutes for natives. However, there is often sound reason to think of them as at least partial complements. Most simply, consider the production function:

$$Y_t = eT\, K_t^\alpha\, IL_t^\beta\, ML_t^\chi$$

(2.2)

where production results from inputs of capital, immobile labour (IL) and mobile labour (ML, the migrants) and where $\alpha+\beta+\chi=1$. Again, all different categories of input factors may substitute each other, but not perfectly. For illustration purposes, imagine that mobile labour consists dominantly of specialists while immobile labour represents unskilled workers. In such a neoclassical model, economically driven immigration of labour decreases its relative scarcity and thus allows distribution of factor income away from mobile to the benefit of immobile natives. As there will again be a technologically optimal combination of factor inputs, migration will improve allocational efficiency by evening out relative scarcities and will increase total factor compensation available.

If immobile and mobile labour are not perfect substitutes, their relationship can be perceived in terms similar to the relationship between capital and labour. If mobile labour migrates more or less freely from where it is relatively abundant to where it is relatively scarce (i.e. from low to high migrant wage locations), positive allocational and distributional effects of labour mobility are most likely to dominate the substitution effect and immobile labour profits from the migration of mobile ones: immobile natives should be interested in allowing mobile ones in on economic reasons. As the allocation effect takes some time, the negative substitution impact of immigration on native employment may dominate in the very short run and determine native labours' stance on immigration.

If we summarize the key message of the neoclassical model with respect to the short to medium term, we conclude that migration will tend to equalize factor compensation levels and their relative distribution after economic integration. Migration may even in the short run be a strong force of macroeconomic convergence, provided our basic neoclassical assumptions apply and provided the development gap between immigration and emigration regions is predominantly due to differences in factor endowments. Potential 'losers' in this convergence process may be wage earners in the immigration region, but allocational effects make it undetermined whether they will really face a decrease in the absolute level of their wages and employment. As far as economic integration is concerned, the neoclassical model would thus predict it to result in regional wage *convergence* and to induce dynamic growth effects in all regions involved. These effects also depend on the observed intensity of migration between different integrating regions.

There is some empirical evidence for the convergence function of migration. In a recent paper Boyer et al. (1993) argued for example that the massive emigration from Ireland prior to World War I contributed significantly to the convergence of real wages from Ireland, the UK and the US. The convergence effect of the free movement of labour is also emphasized by Taylor and Williamson (1994), who investigate population movements during the late 19th century.

The convergence effect of migration may not only help to balance international development gaps, but can also help to balance out the effects of macroeconomic shocks. This mechanism becomes even more important in situations where other possible channels of adjustment are not sufficiently available. Blanchard and Katz show that between the different states of the USA, migration has played an important rule in balancing out temporary regional labour market effects (Blanchard and Katz 1992), more important than that between different European regions and nations (Decressin and Fatas 1994). Indeed, the low interregional mobility in Europe has raised concerns about the future of European integration and the feasibility of a European Monetary Union (Neven and Gouyette 1994).

However, a concern has been raised about potentially deteriorating effects of migration of highly skilled on the development of emigration regions (the so called 'brain drain'). This discussion was triggered by the observation that migrants from 'southern' countries often belonged to the most highly skilled of their home societies.

Whereas there is no distinction between the skill levels in the traditional neoclassical model, some economists used a simple 'trick' to analyse the 'brain drain' within this framework. Bhagwati and Hanada (1994), for example, model the skills of migrants as capital which they carry with them. Emigration of such migrants has labour market effects which are very different from those discussed above. Their immigration does not make labour in the immigration region more abundant relative to capital, but more scarce. Henceforth, wages are lowered in the emigration and increased in the immigration region: 'brain drain' leads

45

to diverging short to medium term development effects in the immigration and emigration economies.[7]

Alternatively, the neoclassical model can be slightly altered by accounting for human skills as a particular production input which is linked to the migrants. Assume for example a neoclassical production function of the following form:

$$Y_t = eT \, K_t^{\alpha} \, L_t^{\beta} \, HC_t^{\gamma} \tag{2.3}$$

where $\alpha + \beta + \chi = 1$ (CRS).

The above representation should look rather familiar. The spirit of this specification is obviously just like our previous distinction between mobile and immobile labour as separate production factors. Output is again produced under the usual neoclassical assumptions, but using at least three different kinds of production factors which may imperfectly substitute each other: 'unskilled labour' L, 'capital' K and 'human capital' HC. Human capital and capital can be accumulated. All factors are compensated according to their marginal profitability. An individual migrant is thus compensated for her or his unskilled labour capacity as well as for her or his accumulated amount of human skills. In such a scenario we find then first, that differences between unskilled and highly skilled migration can again be analysed in terms of the usual partial comparative-static analysis of substitution, allocation and distribution effects on the labour market. Secondly, as long as standard neoclassical assumptions apply, the 'brain drain' reflects relative scarcities. Labour and skill both migrate from where they are more abundant to where they are more scarce, thereby balancing out relative endowment differences and speeding up growth and development convergence.

Note the different implications of the brain drain in the simple neoclassical model and the modified human capital model: in the simple two factors neoclassical model, the brain drain has a short term negative effect on wages in the emigration region and increases labour compensation in the immigration region. This provides a first argument for the view that migration *may cause divergence.* In a modified neoclassical model that distinguishes between skilled and unskilled labour, the brain drain will tend to *enforce convergence* between emigrant and immigrant regions, rather than hamper it.[8]

In a pioneering article, Mankew, Romer and Weil (1992) first employed a model that explicitly distinguishes between unskilled labour and 'human capital'. By including skills as a production input factor they managed to explain differences in growth and convergence patterns between different nations quite convincingly. According to their estimations, labour, capital and human capital all derive roughly similar (decreasing) marginal productivity patterns. Their results imply that in equilibrium the three production factors are most efficiently used in about equal proportions, yield equal returns and would thus each earn roughly one third of the total output produced.

2.3.4 Departing from Classical Assumptions

Unemployment Another not too realistic assumption of the standard neoclassical setting is full employment. As much as emigration has traditionally been referred to as a suitable tool to reduce unemployment in emigration regions, fears of spreading unemployment have been put forward as an argument to restrict immigration. But notwithstanding its intuitive plausibility, the conclusion that migration has adverse welfare effects in the presence of unemployment (Brecher and Choudri 1987; Razin and Sadka 1995a, 1995b) is not necessarily appropriate. As much as emigration has traditionally been regarded as a suitable tool for the reduction of unemployment in emigration regions, fears of unemployment have been put forward in immigration regions as arguments for the restriction of immigration. But whether immigration really increases unemployment depends firstly on the *relative importance* of the immediate quantity effect vis-à-vis the (dynamic) allocation effects and secondly on the *degree of substitutability* between immigrants and native labour.

If native and migrants are perfect substitutes and if the quantity effect dominates the allocation effects, immigrants who already work for lower wages will decrease the wage level in the immigration region and crowd natives out of the labour market. However, if immigration leads to strong demand effects or if immigrants complement native labour, they will create additional jobs and thus help to reduce native unemployment rather than augment it. The same holds if immigration helps to overcome the structural rigidities in the labour market that cause structural unemployment (Schmidt, Stilz and Zimmermann 1994).

Negative employment effects are not a particularly likely effect of migration according to the majority of empirical studies. Simon (1989), Pope and Withers (1993) and Mühleisen and Zimmermann (1994) all share the conclusion that natives do not have to fear unemployment due to competition from immigrants. Zimmermann (1993) also argues that negative effects of migration on wages and employment opportunities of natives are not normally identifiable. In a recent survey article this assumption is shared by Friedberg and Hunt (1995). They look specifically at immigration effects on the US labour market whereas Pischke and Velling (1994) and Smolny (1991) who investigate immigration effects on the German labour market also support that point. Despite some dissenting views, e.g. Winkelmann and Zimmermann (1993), DeNew and Zimmermann (1994) and Franz (1993), these articles also lend some support to the conclusion that immigrants are usually complements rather than substitutes. After all, even those scholars who arrive at somewhat more pessimistic conclusions do not find very strong negative effects for employment and remuneration of natives.[9]

47

If economic integration stimulates labour mobility between previously unconnected regions, migration is likely to increase overall employment in the area concerned. Empirical evidence supports the view that it is unlikely that in the medium term migration jeopardizes the employment situation of immobile labour in the immigration region even if both regions suffer from unemployment problems. On the contrary, it may remedy the underlying structural causes of unemployment.

To finish our discussion of short to medium run allocative and distributive effects of migration in the neoclassical model, let us look at *public transfers*. Migrants contribute to the public household of their host economy by paying taxes and they use social security and other public services. The difference between what they pay and what they get is called the absolute net public transfer. The difference between the net transfer of natives and of immigrants is usually called relative net transfer. Calls for less immigration are often based on the 'argument' that immigrants are a drain on public resources. This argument is not generally supported by empirical evidence. Migrants are often larger per capital net contributors to public finances than natives. The demographic composition, qualifications and labour market integration of migrants have an important impact on their effect on public expenditure (for a summary of empirical findings, see Simon 1989 and 1994). Generally speaking, the younger and the better educated migrants are, the less likely it is that they are net recipients of public expenditure in the immigration regions. An especially favourable situation for the immigration region (and an especially problematic one for the public sector of the emigration region) comes about if migrants are dominantly highly skilled (see for example Borjas 1995: 18–19).

2.3.5 Convergence Effects of Migration – In the Long Run Little Matters

In the short run, migration leads to a change in the availability of labour relative to other production factors. In the longer(er) run, this effect will not last in a purely neoclassical world. In the long run it is not the comparative-static analysis of the factor intensities before and after immigration, but the *intertemporal optimization behaviour of individuals* that determines growth and development in a neoclassical setting. If temporary immigration makes labour relatively more abundant and capital more scarce, this initial change increases the return on capital investments and creates strong incentives to save and invest. In a neoclassical economy these incentives will last until the actual capital intensity equals the technologically and demand determined optimal 'steady state' level which is independent of limited migration phenomena (in a 'homogeneous' world).

Long run development problems have been analysed in neoclassical growth theory which started with Solow (1956) and has been greatly extended since.[10] These models determine wealth and growth dependent on a regional economy's accumulation of production input factors.

48

K_{t+1}, the stock of accumulative factors at a given time t+1 depends on technologically determined factor depreciation and on people's investment behaviour:

$$K_{t+1} = K_t - \delta_t K_t + I_t , \qquad (2.4)$$

where $I_t = q(i, \varphi) Y_t$, i.e. the capital stock K at time t+1 equals capital at time t minus the amount that was used up through depreciation δ plus the amount newly invested I, given the restraining condition that overall investments have to equal the share of output that is used for investment qY. People optimize their investment behaviour so as to equalize marginal (discounted) returns. Return on investment is dependent on the interest rate i and people's preference for consumption now to consumption later, the rate φ they discount future returns with.

Given a certain technology, any discount rate of future returns unambiguously defines an optimal long run capital intensity k* where people just save enough to compensate for the reduction of the per capital stock through depreciation and population growth. Each such k* determines a long run 'steady state' level of per capital output and development where growth of per capital output just equals zero. People's intertemporal maximization of income according to their time preference makes sure that in the long(er) run – all other things being constant – the economy reaches the corresponding optimal capital intensity k* and its 'steady state' level of development. In equilibrium, the classical condition:

$$q^* (i,\varphi) . f(k)^* = (\delta + \eta) . (k)^* , \qquad (2.5)$$

has to be satisfied. The steady state level of the region's development is therefore determined by the preferences of people for present consumption (incorporated into their discount rate φ), the available technology (marginal profitability of investment incorporated into the interest rate), the depreciation rate of the capital stock δ and the population growth rate (defining the speed at which additional new borns endowed with no capital yet 'decrease' the average capital intensity). All these determinants are usually assumed as being exogenous which means that differences in income levels between macro level units reflect either permanent differences in people's preference for the present, in population growth or exogenously determined (temporary) departures from the long run stead state level of growth. Positive (or negative) growth rates of *per capita* wealth can only come about due to macroeconomic adjustment processes, altered partial returns to capital or investment (technology or international integration or demand determined) or changed preferences for present consumption.[11]

49

Figure 2.2 illustrates the working of long run growth and convergence in the neoclassical model development graphically. The two (neoclassical) model economies, the potential immigration region R and the potential emigration region Q are identical except for differences in their relative factor endowments k at time t. We assume the absence of trade due to prohibitive costs. Since people's preferences are by definition identical, the initial difference in factor endowment (capital) intensities are not stable. The marginal return on investment in $Q(k_{Qt})$ is higher than people's preference for the present and higher than in $R(k_{Qt})$.[12] Intertemporal optimization of saving and consumption behaviour induces people in the relatively labour abundant region to save and invest more than what depreciation (δ) and population growth (η) 'eat up'. This increases capital intensity in S and leads it to converge towards its steady state equilibrium level k*.

In the relatively capital abundant region R, the relatively low marginal return on investment is insufficient to cause people to save and invest enough to replace capital stock losses due to depreciation and population growth. As a consequence capital intensity in Q and R converge. In the long run, that will be true even in the absence of economic integration and migration.

At the steady state level, factor proportions and thus output per capita are identical in our two neoclassical model economies. As long as there are no new exogenous shocks, the equilibrium is steady, net investment is zero and gross investment keeps the (optimal) capital intensity constant. As a consequence, per capita regional growth remains zero in this long run equilibrium. Positive or negative growth rates reflect adjustment processes that occur after exogenous shocks and bring the involved economies converging to their (old or new) long run steady state level.

We conclude that within the neoclassical long run model the steady state level of per capita regional development is independent of temporary migration flows; temporary migration does not matter. In the long run it is not temporary migration, but rather the *intertemporal optimization behaviour of individuals* that determines growth and development.

In the medium term, temporary migration may matter as a possible instrument to *speed up* the convergence process. International investment and trade would be alternative instruments. *Speed, intensity* and *structure* of migration flows influence transition and may be potential tools to minimize the costs of adjustment to the long run steady state.

Unlike temporary flows, permanent migration can affect the steady state *level* of a region's development because it amounts to a change in the population growth rates in the migration regions. Assuming that migrants do not carry any physical capital with them, the net migration rate (μ) will affect the per capita capital stock in exactly the same way as the rate of domestic population growth (η). Total capital dilution per capital now changes to $(\delta+\eta+\mu)(k)$ which corresponds to the

50

immigration region to a left and upwards rotation of the capital dilution curve in Figure 2.2. It decreases the immigration region's steady state level of development and increases it in the emigration region, as long as population growth in both economies differs due to migration.

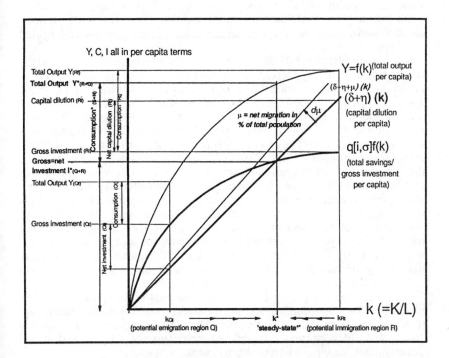

Figure 2.2   Long run growth, convergence and migration in the neoclassical model of development

Neoclassical growth models have frequently been tested empirically. These tests usually demonstrate that absolute convergence (i.e. not conditional on any further exogenous explanatory variables) takes place at least within 'convergence clubs' of not too different regions, but at a surprisingly slow rate of about 2 to 3 percent per annum (Dowrick and Nguyen 1989; Barro 1990; Barro and Sala-i-Martin 1991, 1992). Especially on a regional level convergence depends on the structural features of the investigated group of regions (Martin 1995). However, most of the development *growth* process cannot be explained by neoclassical convergence processes, but rather by (exogenously determined) changes in technology (total factor productivity) and the impact of other disequilibrating factors. Indeed, while one finds

51

convergence within the group of Northern countries and the group of Southern countries, surprisingly little convergence takes place between 'South' and 'North'. As mentioned previously, Mankiw, Romer and Weil (1992) obtain more explanatory power than traditional approaches by including 'human capital' in a neoclassical production function. But from our point of view, they also do not give any convincing explanation why there are no more equilibrating flows of 'human capital' and migration to speed up the convergence process and bridge the development gaps.

In a review of empirical data, Barro and Sala-i-Martin (1995) analyse the influence of migration on growth in US states since 1880, prefectures of Japan since 1930 and European countries since 1950. They find that migration has responded positively at initial levels of per capital income. Locations that enjoyed above average development levels at the outset of the study period tended to report higher than average immigration rates (and slowing down growth processes). These results were stronger for the US and Japan than for Europe. But as far as the influence of net migration flows on convergence is concerned, Barro and Sala-i-Martin's results are inconclusive. Migration seemed to have a rather minor influence on growth processes during this century. Since this contrasts sharply with the conclusions of a study by Taylor and Williamson (1994) who identified net migration as the major driving force of convergence between European countries and the development in America and overseas at the end of the 19th century, it seems likely that migration has only had minor importance of 20th century growth processes, *because* only little migration took place.

From a theoretical point of view, there are possibilities to explain why incentives for migration, capital accumulation and investment may lead to something else than convergence. These explanations lead us to the so called 'divergence school' of the impact of migration on development we would like to discuss next.

2.4   The Divergence Point of View

Since Marx, Myrdal (1956/1957), Hirschmann (1958) and Wallerstein (1974) there have always ben scholars arguing that migration increases rather than decreases development differences between macro level units. These divergence theorists usually combine different ideas deriving from the relaxation of at least one of the neoclassical assumptions of identical production technologies, constant returns to scale in production, perfectly competitive markets or the absence of positive or negative externalities of production. In what follows, we will demonstrate these mechanisms by discussing the implications of dropping these assumptions.[13]

2.4.1 Departing from Classical Assumptions

Differences in production technology A major characteristic of divergence theories is the argument that in contrast to what we assumed previously, technological progress does not necessarily spread from developed core locations to the periphery. In other words, different locations may rather persistently use different kinds of technologies. An alternative way to think of causes for such persistent technological differences is in terms of the efficiency of the location specific institutional framework, the *'Ordnungpolitik'* that may be more or less productivity prone.[14] This alteration can be incorporated into our simple specification introduced earlier, if we add to our familiar production function:

$$Y_t = eT\, K_t^a L_t^b$$

where $\alpha+\beta=1$ (constant returns to scale) the remaining condition:

$$eT_R \gg eT_Q. \tag{2.6}$$

It does not matter whether the efficiency advantage in production comes about due to superior technology or other factors. It is sufficient to assume that eT in the potential immigration region R is absolutely superior to eT in the potential emigration region Q. If a given combination of input factors produces a higher output in R than in Q, the input factors in R will be better paid than those in Q.[15] If both factors (capital and labour) are mobile, it will pay for both of them to migrate to R a long as factor proportions do not become too unfavourable and as long as technology differences persist. Therefore provided both production factors are mobile, economic integration allowing for migration does not induce convergence as long as absolute technological differences between locations persist.[16] Wages and/or returns on investment will therefore remain low in the disadvantaged region and will not fall in the immigration region as long as there are no constraints from immobile factors. Convergence or divergence patterns depend on technology diffusion and efficiency improvements rather than on migration. The disadvantaged emigration region can only catch up by improving its technology and efficiency which becomes more difficult once its factors of production begin to leave.

Second, if in the long run all capital and labour is mobile and there are no constraints from immobile factors, economic integration will in the long run confront the disadvantaged location with a total outflow of production factors until 'the last person turns off the light'.

As long as the emigration and immigration regions produce under constant returns to scale and as long as both factors flow so as not to alter factor proportions, the wealth of the immobile population does not

53

become affected. There are no 'losers' and no other 'winners' from economic integration through migration than the migrants. If factor mobility changes factors proportions, the above analysis of short and long run allocative and distributive aspects applies.

The radical corner solution to our simple model predicting a total evacuation of the disadvantaged region may be replaced by a more realistic one if we introduce location specific fixed factors:

$$Y_t = eT \, \bar{A}^{-\chi} \, K_t^{\alpha} \, L_t^{\beta} \tag{2.7}$$

where $\alpha+\beta+\chi=1$ (constant returns to scale) and $\bar{A}$ represents the amount of location specific immobile input factors (non-tradable resources, natural amenities, infrastructure, provision of public goods, etc.). Given the restricting condition that its technology is inferior, the emigration region has less output to pay its three factors. Given similar initial factor proportions in both locations, it will benefit mobile factors to move away. The resulting outflow from the emigration region makes mobile factors more scarce relative to immobile, location specific fixed factors. Distribution effects assure returns on mobile factors to rise until it no longer pays off for mobile factors to emigrate. Consequently, compensation of immobile, location specific factors decreases. If party of the so far immobile, location specific factors may also become mobile, potentially, the incentives to emigrate increase.[17]

Consequently, we conclude that firstly the existence of location specific immobile factors prevents a disadvantaged location from experiencing total outflow of its mobile production factors. Economic integration enforcing migration will induce returns on mobile factors to converge interregionally, but returns on immobile ones to diverge.

Secondly, if there are distinguished production factors of which some are mobile at the outset and others immobile but may potentially become mobile, like e.g. 'immobile' labour in agriculture, then increasing mobility of mobile production factors in technologically disadvantaged locations increases the incentives for so far immobile factors to emigrate as well (cumulative causation).

Finally, the more mobile factors of production in a technologically disadvantaged location are, the lower the monetary incentives to exploit the location specific factors and the more difficult catching up may become.

In brief, in our modified model with technological differences and location specific factors, economic integration through migration increases the incentives for further migration, increases overall allocational efficiency but decreases it in the disadvantaged emigration region and hence widens the original development gap. Provided that e.g. international companies increase the mobility of parts of the local workforce, this may indeed worsen the situation of the immobile workforce. For immobile factors, economic integration no longer leads to compensation convergence.

54

So far, we have assumed constant returns to scale. Is this realistic? Theoretically, output expansion may happen at constant returns to scale (CRS), decreasing returns to scale (DRS) or increasing returns to scale (IRS). As far as IRS are concerned, we can distinguish between:

a   increasing returns to scale internal to the firm;
b   increasing returns to scale internal to the industry;
c   economy wide increasing returns to scale.

On the aggregate level type a) IRS merely determine the size of a representative plant. If the size is large enough to allow for sufficient competition, they are not relevant in the context of our previous discussion. But the situation is different in cases b) and c). The larger the industry or total economic activity becomes, the more productive each firm will be.

The c) type IRS can easily be expressed in our production function. We obtain, for example:

$$T_t = eT \bar{A}^{-\chi} K_t^{\alpha} L_t^{\delta} \qquad (2.8)$$

where $\alpha+\beta+\chi>1$ (increasing returns to scale, IRS).

In other words, given a suitable factor distribution, the larger the total amount of inputs, the higher their total productivity. What does that mean for migration? Imagine again two originally separate regions, R and Q which are identical in every respect but their size. Due to the simple difference in economic output produced and the existence of economy wide IRS, the compensation of input factors in the economically larger region R will be higher than in the economically smaller, peripheral region Q. If we now allow people to migrate from Q to R where they get better compensation for their work, migration will no longer even out differences in factor payments but increase the scope for returns to scale in the R economy even further. Migration makes the immigration region become the centre and emigration region the periphery, and once started, the process of widening wage and interest rate gaps between the emigration and immigration regions does not stop until scarce location specific factors $\bar{A}$ in the immigration region and corresponding redistribution effects eventually level out centre-periphery differences in mobile factor's return to an extent that mobile factors no longer consider it worthwhile to move. This implies that if an economy faces increasing returns to scale, international mobility of production factors allows their exploitation. This however widens the development gap between the economically more important and the less important integrating regions (Krugman and Venables 1994).

Secondly, who benefits from economies of scale depends on what region is economically more important initially. Immigration to the initially bigger region strengthens its position as the core economy, while the smaller economy loses competitiveness.

Thirdly, distributive effects benefit immobile factors in the immigration region but due to scale economies, also mobile ones win. The main losers are immobile factors in the emigrant economy.

However, while economies of scale at the firm level are intuitively convincing, the idea that, for example, West German labour and capital have become more efficient simply because there was a reunification of Eastern and Western Germany, seems somewhat more questionable.

Generally speaking, the beneficial effects of economies of scale are limited to factors that decrease efficiency with growing scale, for example, rising control and transaction costs. Beyond a critical point, scale economies may even turn from increasing to decreasing. One may therefore more naturally think about the development of an urban agglomeration or a local region rather than of a whole country. Also, the nature of the aggregate scale economies are likely to depend on the *absolute size* of the industry or economic production measures in labour inputs.

To conclude, situations where scale economies matter on the aggregate level may not enforce sustainable per capita growth in the long run, in the absence of technological change, due to the inescapable intervention of limitational factors. Nevertheless, they may be important in a setting of economic integration. If institutional changes, such as European Integration or technological changes, such as decreases in transport and transaction costs increase economic integration of markets and potential market size, these changes allow and stimulate the exploitation of additional scale economies through factor mobility.

The *initial* direction of migration flows determines which regions become periphery and which core. At the outset, it may depend on sheer coincidence, history, or people's expectations where to and to what extent factors of production move and hence which of two similar regions become 'core' and which 'periphery' (Krugman 1991c). To attract mobile production factors can thus become an issue of high political relevance on a regional or eventually on a locally concentrated industry level.

The importance of increasing returns to scale and its interplay with migration may not only explain different growth patterns of regional economies, it can also help us to understand what Krugman has labelled 'economic geography' (Krugman 1991a, b, 1993, 1994; Krugman and Venables 1994; Faini 1996). In the tradition of economic geography models, increasing returns to scale are typically industry specific. Firms will locate a) where there is scope for demand determined IRS, i.e. where there are concentrations of people who demand their products (Krugman 1991b), b) where a large cluster of specialists allows IRS due to local knowledge spillovers and/or c) where there is scope for IRS due to intermediate inputs being particularly cheaply supplied by other locally concentrated producers (Faini 1996). Newly entering firms will 'pull' even more people and other firms to the location, thereby increasing the prospects for further output expansions and further economies of scale. This leads to a self-sustaining agglomeration process until economies of scale cease to increase due to limitational factors like increasing agglomeration costs and negative congestion effects. This idea may prove particularly appealing to explain why and for whom migration in economically integrating regions matters (for a first attempt to model such effects see e.g. Rivera-Batiz and Romer 1991).

Historical experiences like the absence of development in the Italian Mezzogiorno demonstrate that there may be critical points in the economic history of regions where the presence or absence of a particular factor of production can determine the success or failure of the process. Case studies and empirical investigations of the consequences of economies of scale would require a micro foundation of the sketched IRS macro concept in order to explain the divergence process. Despite considerable measurement and identification problems, Caballero and Lyons (1990) found fairly robust evidence in favour of increasing returns to scale at a national level for the US and a couple of European countries. Krugman (1991a) presents some first empirical evidence for increasing returns to scale to shape the geographic patterns of industry location.

2.4.2 Departing from Classical Assumptions

Imperfect competition and externalities The assumption of increasing economies to scale implies that markets are no longer efficient in the classical sense because IRS precludes perfect competition between firms. Henceforth wages and interest rates will no longer correspond to the production factors' returns. One reason for the inefficiency of market solutions may be the existence of *externalities*. For a discussion on migration and growth, the often assumed positive externalities of the total stock of 'human capital' on the productivity of all production factor inputs are especially relevant.

To assume positive (social) externalities of human capital is an attempt to explain technological progress exogenously by changes in the total amount of (educated) knowledge accumulated in an economy. We may think of an aggregate production function:

$$Y_t = eT(HC_t^{1-\chi}) \, K_t^{\alpha} \, L_t^{\beta} \, HC_t^{\chi} \tag{2.9}$$

where $\alpha+\beta+\chi=1$ (CRS) and $dT/dHC > 0$. HC_t equals the total stock of human capital accumulated at time t. This kind of growth model provides one explanation for continuing endogenous growth (Lucas 1988, 1993).

Basically, it is argued that the technology which determines the productivity of input factors is dependent on the available amount of 'human capital'. The higher the human capital stock, the higher the input factors' output production (given an efficient distribution of inputs). Input factors exhibit constant private returns to scale and decreasing partial marginal productivity. They may substitute each other and are paid according to their marginal productivity. But in the specification above, the technological externality just compensates for the decreasing private marginal productivity of human capital in a sense that assures a constant aggregate human capital productivity of one. Given this set up, however, markets fail because they compensate people who invest in skill only for the partial marginal productivity of their human capital, and not for the collective external effect of their skills on technology. Why is this so important? In such a situation, the accumulation of 'human capital' may become an 'engine of growth' that explains persistent differences in growth paths.[18]

Lucas type models that explain growth in terms of human capital externalities derive specific implications with respect to the allocative impact of migration on growth. If technology depends on the locally available stock of human capital, then the 'skill content' of migration is of key importance to growth. Migration induces changes in the technology available in the immigration region and therefore accounts for different growth prospects in the immigration and emigration regions. To the extent that economic integration reduces the barriers to human capital mobility, it enforces the divergence impact of highly skilled migration.

In a situation where human capital determines technology, the private and social rates of return to human capital investments diverge. This makes the locational competition for human skills a policy issue that gains in importance when economic integration diminishes the obstacles to mobility.[19]

In a world of that given above, 'human capital' is unlikely to flow to where it is most scarce. The higher an already existing stock of human capital is, the higher the incentives for mobile factors to move there.

2.5   Conclusions and Implications for Migration Policy

The above discussion on whether, and for whom, migration matters derives somewhat ambiguous conclusions. They are ambiguous in the sense that there is no clear answer to whether migration *always* has certain allocational and distributional impacts. The theoretical allocation and distributional effects of migration heavily depend on the assumptions that describe the nature of the macroeconomic environment in which migration takes place. On the one hand, in a neoclassical setting, economic integration through migration tends to enhance convergence. On the other hand, allowing for technological differences, increasing returns to scale and imperfect competition identifies factor mobility as a potential driving force behind the emergence of diverging centre-periphery patterns.

We can nonetheless derive seven general conclusions:

1   Limited migration matters in a neoclassical world only in the short to medium term. Migration is one possible instrument for economic integration. It may *speed up* transition to a steady state, but in the long run intertemporal optimization behaviour will bring the economy to the very same steady state. *Speed, intensity* and *structure* of migration flows influence the transition and may be potential tools to minimize the costs of adjustment to the long run steady state.

2   The most commonly analysed effects of migration such as wage and employment effects, public transfer incidences, remittance, etc. are based on neoclassical comparative-static analyses that are valid in the short run only.

3   Regardless of whether we apply a short or a long term perspective, there are no allocative reasons why migration should not be welcome in a purely neoclassical world. In the short as well as in the long run the allocative effects of economically motivated migration increase total welfare in the immigration economy and do not lower it in the emigration economy. Economic integration eases migration and migration enforces economic integration. But migration is a pure arbitrage phenomenon. From this point of view, opposition to economic integration through free mobility can only be explained by distributional aspects. At least in the short run, native labour in the immigrant economy and capital owners in the emigration region may 'lose' from migration. In this sense, opposition to free migration represents group specific action to safeguard protectionist rents from the allocationally efficient pressure of comparative advantage and structural change. Activist 'losers' could, however, be compensated by the 'winners': capital owners in the immigration region and native labour in the emigration region. But in the medium term, dynamic allocative effects of migration are likely to transform those who eventually lost at the outset into beneficiaries anyway.

4   If neoclassical assumptions fit private markets, opposition to immigration may be further rooted in negative externalities of migration on the consumption of publicly provided 'club goods' (e.g. nature and recreation areas, political stability, etc.) whose consumption may become partly rival (see also Chapter 3 of this book).

5   Location specific immobile production factors may explain persistently different economic performance. If institutional settings or efficiency parameters generate persistently different total factor productivity, factor mobility may worsen the situation of immobile factor in the disadvantaged locations and speed up development in the technologically advanced ones. Once migration sets in, it may

59

become increasingly difficult for the disadvantaged region to catch up.

6   Potentials for increasing returns to scale as well as positive social externalities of population density or human capital strengthen the argument that allocational effects of migration can matter. Immigrants can promote growth, increase economic welfare and make at least the transition towards a new steady state less cumbersome. Migration may help a region to become centre rather than 'trapped' periphery, especially in the context of economic integration. The New Growth Theory provides theoretical tools to capture this effect. Further empirical scrutiny of these theories is still warranted.

7   If demand determined scale effects – scale effects that are dependent on the size of the local population – or local externalities are important, the mobility of people can represent a key determinant in shaping 'economic landscapes'.

In brief, the argument of this chapter is that for an answer on whether and for whom migration matters, it is crucial whether economies are open or not, how well they fit traditional assumptions on market organization, to what extent immigration and emigration regions differ in their relative endowment of production factors and their available technology. In *some* situations migration contributes to a diverging development while in others it enforces convergence. In *many* cases, migration will not matter that much, at least not for long run growth and development processes. In periods of international economic integration, however, the costs of regional labour mobility – especially of the labour that crosses national political borders – are decreasing. Simultaneously, the demand for migration is increasing. Therefore, it is in periods of intensified economic integration where migration is most likely to be important for the growth prospects of integrating regions and the emergence of new economic geography patterns. But limitational factors (including individuals' propensity to migrate) are bound to narrow the spatial scope of an eventual redrawing of the 'economic landscape'. Finally, it has to be emphasized that growth and development in general is subject to much more complex determinants than just the mobility of people and other production factors. Available empirical evidence suggests that in most situations, migration is likely to be of minor importance for development, although this may be partly due to the usually rather limited scale of migration that actually occurs, towards and within developed regions, in contemporary times.

References

Barro, R.J. (1990), 'Government Spending in a Simple Model of Endogenous Growth', *Journal of Political Economy*, vol. 98, pp. 103–25.

Barro, R.J. and Sala-i-Martin, X. (1991), 'Convergence across States and Regions', *Brookings Papers on Economic Activity*, pp. 107–82.

Barro, R.J. and Sala-i-Martin, X. (1992), 'Convergence', *Journal of Political Economy*, pp. 223–51.

Barro, R.J. and Sala-i-Martin, X. (1995), *Economic Growth*, Mc Graw-Hill, New York.

Barro, R.J., Mankiw, N.G. and Sala-i-Martin, X. (1995), 'Capital Mobility in Neoclassical Models of Growth', *American Economic Review*, vol. 84, pp. 103–15.

Bhagwati, J. and Hamada, K. (1974), 'The Brain Drain, International Integration of Markets for Professionals and Unemployment', *Journal of Development Economics*, vol. 1, pp. 19–24.

Bhagwati, J. and Rodriguez, C. (1975), 'Welfare – Theoretical Analyses of the Brain Drain', *Journal of Development Economics*, vol. 2, pp. 91–100.

Borjas, G.J. (1990), *Friends or Strangers? The Impact of Immigrants on the US Economy*, Basic Books, New York.

Borjas, G.J. (1994), 'The Economics of Immigration', *Journal of Economic Literature*, vol. 32, no. 4, pp. 1667–717.

Borjas, G.J. (1995), 'The Economic Benefits from Immigration', *Journal of Economic Perspectives*, vol. 9, no. 2, pp. 3–22.

Borjas, G.J., Freeman, R.B. and Katz, L.F. (1992), 'On the Labour Market Effect of Immigration and Trade', *Immigration and the Workforce: Economic Consequences for The United States and Source Areas*, An NBER Project Report, University of Chicago Press, Chicago and London.

Boyer, G.R., Hatton, T. and O'Rourke, K.H. (1993), 'The Impact of Emigration on Real Wages in Ireland 1850–1914, CEPR Discussion Paper, London.

Brecher, R. and Choudhri, E. (1987), 'International Migration versus Foreign Investment in the Presence of Unemployment', *Journal of International Economics*, vol. 23, nos. 3–4, pp. 329–42.

Caballero, R.I. and Lyons, R.K. (1990), 'Internal versus External Economies in European Industry', *European Economic Review*, vol. 34, pp. 803–26.

DeNew, J.P. and Zimmermann, K.F. (1994), 'Native Wage Impacts of Foreign Labour: A Random Effects Panel Analysis', *Journal of Population Economics*, vol. 7, pp. 177–92.

Decressin, J. and Fatas, A. (1995), 'Regional Labour Market Dynamics in Europe', *European Economic Review*, vol. 39, pp. 1627–55.

Dowrick, S. and Nguyen, D. (1989), 'OECD Comparative Economic Growth 1950–85, Catch-Up and Convergence', *American Economic Review*, vol. 79, pp. 1010–30.

Ekberg, J. (1983), 'Inkomsteffekter av invandering (with English summary), *Acta Wexionensia*, Tryck & Skrivservice Växjö.

Ethier, W. (1984), 'Higher Dimensional Issues in Trade Theory', in Jones, R.W. and P.B. Kenen, (eds), *Handbook of International Economics*, I, Elsevier Science Publishers.

Faini, R. (1996), 'Increasing Returns, Migrations and Convergence', *Journal of Development Economics*, vol. 378, pp. 1–16.

Franz, W. (1993), 'Zur ökonomischen Bedeutung von Wanderungen und den Möglichkeiten und Grenzen einer Einwanderungspolitik', CILE Diskussionspapier 3, Fakultät für Wirtschaftswissenschaften und Statistik, Universität Konstanz.

Friedberg, R.M. and Hunt, J. (1985), 'The Impact of Immigrants on Host Country Wages, Employment and Growth', *Journal of Economic Perspectives*, vol. 9, no. 2, pp. 23–44.

Gang, I.N. and Rivera-Batiz, F.L. (1994), 'Labour Market Effects of Immigration in the United States and Europe (Substitution and Complementarity), *Journal of Population Economics*, vol. 7, pp. 157–75.

Giersch, H. (ed.) (1989), *Economic Aspects of International Migration*, Springer: Berlin.

Grossman, J.B. (1982), 'The Substitutability of Natives and Immigrants in Production', *Review of Economics and Statistics*, vol. 64, no. 4, pp. 596–603.

Gross, J.B. and Helpman, E. (1994), 'Endogenous Innovation in the Theory of Growth', *Journal of Economic Perspectives*, vol. 8, no. 1, pp. 23–44.

Grubel, H.G. (1994), 'The Economics of International Labor and Capital Flows', in Giersch, H. (ed.), *Economic Aspects of International Migration*, pp. 75–92.

Hirschmann, A.O. (1958), *The Strategy of Economic Development*, Yale University Press, New Haven.

Krugman, P.R. (1991a), *Geography and Trade*, Leuven.

Krugman, P.R. (1991b), 'Increasing Returns and Economic Geography', *Journal of Political Economy*, vol. 99, no. 3, pp. 483–99.

Krugman, P.R. (1991c), 'History versus Expectations', *The Quarterly Journal of Economics*, vol. 106, pp. 651–67.

Krugman, P.R. (1993), 'On the Number and Location of Cities', *European Economic Review*, vol. 37, no. 1, pp. 293–98.

Krugman, P.R. (1994), 'Complex Landscapes in Economic Geography', *American Economic Review*, vol. 84, (Papers and Proceedings), pp. 412–16.

Krugman, P.R. and Smith, A. (1994), *Empirical Studies of Strategic Trade Policy*, University of Chicago Press: Chicago.

Krugman, P.R. and Venables, A.J. (1994), 'Globalization and the Inequality of Nations', Centre for Economic Policy Research Discussion Paper, 1015, September.

Koopmans, T.C. (1965), 'On the Concept of Optimal Economic Growth', in *The Econometric Approach to Development Planning*, North Holland, Amsterdam.

LaLonde, R. and Topel, R. (1991), 'Labour Market Adjustments to Increased Immigration', in J. Abowd, R. Freeman (eds), *Immigration, Trade and the Labour Market*, Chicago Press: Chicago.

Lucas, R.E. (1988), 'On the Mechanics of Economic Development', *Journal of Monetary Economics*, vol. 22, no. 1, pp. 3–42.

Lucas, R.E. (1993), 'Making a Miracle', *Econometrica*, vol. 61, pp. 251–72.

Mankew, N., Romer D. and Weil D. (1992), 'A Contribution to the Empirics of Economics Growth', *The Quarterly Journal of Economics*, vol. 107, pp. 407–37.

Martin, R. (1995), 'Determinants of Growth in European Regions', European Commission, DGII, mimeo, Brussels.

McDowell, J.M. and Singell, L.D. (1993), 'An Assessment of the Human Capital Content of International Migrants: An Application to US Immigration', *Regional Science*, vol. 27, pp. 351–63.

Mühleisen, M. and Zimmermann, K.F. (1994), 'A Panel Analysis of Job Changes and Unemployment', *European Economic Review*, vol. 38, pp. 793–801.

Myrdal, G. (1956), *Rich Lands and Poor*, Harper & Row, New York.

Neven, D.J. and Gouyette, C. (1994), 'Regional Convergence in the European Community', CEPR Discussion paper 914, London.

Pack, H. (1994), 'Endogenous Growth Theory: Intellectual Appeal and Empirical Shortcomings', *Journal of Economic Perspectives*, vol. 8, no. 1, pp. 55–72.

Papademetriou, D.G. and Martin, Ph.L. (eds) (1991), 'The Unsettled Relationship: Labour Migration and Economic Development', *Contributions in Labour Studies, 33*, Greenwood Press, Westport.

Pischke, J.-S. and Velling, J. (1994), 'Wage and Employment Effects of Immigration to Germany: An Analysis Based on Local Labour Markets', CEPR Discussion Paper 935, London.

Pope, D. and Withers, G. (1993), 'Do Migrants Rob Jobs? Lessons of Australian History 1861–1991', *Journal of Economic History*, vol. 53, pp. 719–42.

Ramsey, F. (1928), 'A Mathematical Theory of Saving', *Economic Journal*, vol. 38, pp. 543–59.

Razin, A. and Sadka, E. (1995a), 'Resisting Migration: Wage Rigidity and Income Distribution', CEPR Working Paper 1091, London.

Razin, A. and Sadka, E. (1995b), *Population Economics*, MIT Press: Cambridge, MA.

Rivera-Batiz, L.A. and Romer, P.A.(1991), 'Economic Integration and Endogenous Growth', *Quarterly Journal of Economics*, pp. 531–55.

Romer, P.M. (1994), 'The Origins of Endogenous Growth', *Journal of Economics Perspectives*, vol. 8, no. 1, pp. 3–22.

Schmidt, Ch. M., Stilz, A. and Zimmermann, K.F. (1994), 'Mass Migration, Unions and Government Intervention', *Journal of Public Economics*, vol. 55, pp. 185–201.

Siebert, H. (1994), *Migration: A Challenge for Europe*, Tübingen.

Simon, J.L., *The Economic Consequences of Immigration*, Blackwell and The Cato Institute, Oxford.

Simon, J.L. (1994), 'On the Economic Consequences of Immigration: Lessons for Immigration Policies', in Giersch, H. (ed.), *Economic Aspects of International Migration*, Berlin, pp. 227–48.

Smith, A. (1776), *An Enquiry into the Nature and Causes of the Wealth of Nations*, Edwin Cannan, London.

Smolny, W. (1991), 'Macroeconomic Consequences of International Labour Migration: Simulation Experience from an Econometric Disequilibrium Model', in Vosgerau, H.J. (ed.), *European Integration in the World Economy*, Springer-Verlag, Berlin, pp. 376–412.

Solow, R.M. (1956), 'A Contribution to the Theory of Economic Growth', *Quarterly Journal of Economics*, vol. 70, pp. 65–94.

Solow, R.M. (1994), 'Perspectives on Growth Theory', *Journal of Economic Perspectives*, vol. 8, no. 1, pp. 45–54.

Straubhaar, T. (1992), 'Allocational and Distributional Aspects of Future Immigration to Western Europe', *International Migration Review*, vol. 26, pp. 462–82.

Taylor, A.M. and Williamson, J.G. (1994), 'Convergence in the Age of Mass Migration', NBER Working Paper, no. 474.

Wallerstein, I. (1974), *The Modern World-System: Capitalist Agriculture and the Origins of the European World Economy in the Sixteenth Century*, Academic Press, New York.

Winkelmann, R. and Zimmermann, K.F. (1993), 'Ageing, Migration and Labour Mobility', in Johnson, P. and K.F. Zimmermann (eds), *Labour Markets in an Ageing Europe*, Cambridge, pp. 255–83.

Zimmermann, K.F. (1993), 'Industrial Restructuring, Unemployment and Migration', in Beckermans, L. and L. Tsoukalis (eds), *Europe and Global Economic Interdependence*, College of Europe and European University Press, Bruges, pp. 25–52.

Zimmermann, K.F. (1995), 'Tackling the European Migration Problem', *Journal of Economic Perspectives*, vol. 9, no. 2, pp. 45–62.

Notes

1. There already exist a sizeable number of surveys looking at the links between migration and development. We used some of them as helpful starting points for our analysis of the issue. To name just a few: Borjas (1995); Friedberg and Hunt (1995); Zimmermann (1995); Grubel (1994) and Siebert (1993) are comparatively short introductions. Giersch (1994) and Siebert (1994) are recent collections of papers with Siebert making special reference to the European dimension of the problem. Straubhaar (1992) provides an overview of the major European issues. An interdisciplinary book combining case studies and theoretical insights is Papademetriou and Martin (1991).

2. For a review see, for example, Bhagwati and Rodriguez (1975).

3. This would happen even without migration. With migration, it happens much faster.

4. Note that we assumed migrants not to carry any capital with them and ruled out remittances effects.

5. Provided that migrants net contribution to the financing of public goods in the immigrant society and that labour income is taxed progressively, this redistribution of benefits from free labour allocation often takes place via the public transfer effect of migration.

6. It is, however, cumbersome to argue about the scale of potential medium term dynamic allocative effects of free labour mobility. One could imagine them to surpass the scale of short term comparative-static effects, but it is hard to come up with any justifiable actual estimate. One could think of simply ex post calibrating the described model for observed labour market developments, but we do not know of such an exercise having been undertaken as yet.

7. For a profound survey of the early 'brain drain' literature, see Bhagwati and Rodriguez (1975).

8. Admittedly, a drawback of the described approach to introduce human capital into a neoclassical framework is that it implies skills and human capital to be more scarce in the immigration than in the emigration region. One could explain the supposed paradox in neoclassical terms by additionally introducing different sorts of capital and/or amenities and assuming them to complement human skills. Once could then explain why e.g. computer scientists are more scarce in the South than in the North but nevertheless will not migrate to the South - simply because they will not earn appropriate rents in a country without computers and because they find that amenities in the North are that much better for them than in the South. In general, however, it becomes easier to understand why human capital should flow from South to North once we assume differences in technology and increasing returns to scale, features which are central to the divergence school.

9. See also the review of effects on the European labour market by Zimmermann (1995).

10. For an appraisal see Solow (1994). An up to date introduction to modelling and empirical relevance of neoclassical growth theories is provided by Barro and Sala-i - Martin (1995), chapters 1–13.

11. Our explanation of steady state growth resulting from individual intertemporal optimization behaviour is associated with a more formal model originally formulated by Ramsey (1928) and developed by Koopmans (1965). For an introduction to its properties and modelling techniques, see e.g. Barro and Sala-i-Martin (1995).

12. Note that the described difference in factor returns follows from the neoclassical assumptions applied. If the potential immigration and emigration regions are not equal with respect to preferences for present consumption, technology or if differently distributed location specific fixed factors (like e.g. natural resource constraints) have to be taken into account, R and Q will no longer converge to the same steady state.

13. Indeed, modifications of these neoclassical assumptions have in recent years led to the emergence of new macroeconomic fields, often referred to as 'New Growth Theory', 'New Trade Theory' and 'New Economic Geography'. For review articles on New Growth Theory see e.g. Romer (1994), Grossman and Helpman (1994) and Pack (1994). Krugman's introduction in Krugman and Smith (1994) gives a good summary of the development of New Trade Theory. The pioneering work in 'New Economic Geography' is Krugman (1991a).

14. In growth theory, an approach to capture such differences has been pursued under the heading of 'local taxes'. There are models that assume net after tax productivity of production flows to equalize internationally due to economic integration, but locational specific tax differences to account for locational differences in gross productivity and steady state development (see e.g. Barro, Mankiw and Sala-i-Martin 1995:106 for a formal discussion of the idea).

15. One can imagine situations where due to different relative scarcities of production factors, one factor may be better paid in the technologically inferior location. But the more mobile both factors are, the less stable such a situation will be. Over time, both factors' payments will necessarily be smaller in the technologically inferior country than in the superior one.

16. Furthermore, it is likely that also relative factor endowments will remain persistently different, $K_R L_R > K_Q L_Q$, given that there are absolute technological differences $e_R T_R > e_Q T_Q$ and all production factors are mobile.

17. For illustration, one could, for example, think of highly skilled specialists being mobile originally and unskilled labour being location specific. If highly skilled specialists get paid international returns and unskilled labour faces wage declines, incentives for unskilled labour to exit, increase.

18. Whether it is human capital accumulation by schooling or by learning by doing that produces externalities and/or allows IRS has become a key issue in the human capital debate. However, we abstain here from any differentiation and do not enter into a discussion of whether externalities may be internalized. Note also that the assumption of the private and collective return on capital adding to an aggregate constant productivity of exactly 1, is crucial for explaining endogenous growth, but not for our general implications of the importance of migration in the context of economic integration when human capital exhibits positive externalities.

19. For example, the provision of public goods (arts and culture) or amenities which are especially attractive to the highly skilled may have an effect on future local growth prospects.

3 Welfare Effects of Immigration in the Presence of Public Goods: A Case for Entrance Fees?

NADINE LEINER

3.1 Introduction

The world is observing huge and increasing immigration flows to western industrialized countries. By entering these destination countries, immigrants automatically gain access to the supplied public capital stock. During their stay, they can take advantage of the national traffic system, can send their children to public schools and they visit public parks, gardens and swimming pools. Furthermore, migrants tend to settle in the immigration country's urban areas. For example, in the German city of Stuttgart the share of foreigners is 23.3 percent, in Frankfurt it is even 27.9 percent. Apart from a possibly better labour market situation or already existing family ties, migrants are also attracted to these urban areas, because they usually have a broader supply of infrastructure than rural areas. Therefore, analogous to the typical regional migration from rural to urban areas, international migrants also prefer to live in big cities with a broader infrastructure spectrum.

As far as Germany is concerned, a country which has experienced extraordinary immigration in the last few years, some authors argue, e.g. Gieseck et al. (1992), Koll (1993) (see also Borjas 1994 and Simon 1989 for the US) that the extensive migration movements and the observable clustering of immigrants in particular cities lead to an intensified use of public infrastructure and increased congestion. For example the above authors state that because of immigration the number of pupils per teacher in public schools has increased such that the quality of education might have decreased. Therefore, especially residents in densely populated urban areas are confronted with immigration induced infrastructure bottlenecks. And because of these, some public facilities might have to be enlarged (e.g. Franz 1994:139; Kronberger Kreis 1994:27).

In addition, migrants become part owners of the country's public capital stock. Due to these effects, the necessity of compensation for the resident population is derived. Weber and Straubhaar (1994:4) are quite precise:

[..] the immigrants' financial responsibilities regarding the already existing capital stock (infrastructure) would have to be met through an equal entrance fee or a similar levy.

On the other hand, immigrants also pay taxes and therefore contribute to the financing of all public goods, even pure public goods which are not subject to congestion, as for example national defense. They additionally participate in the financing of replacement investments which are necessary to sustain a stable public infrastructure capital stock. Consequently, the aggregate welfare change due to immigration is unclear.

Nevertheless, the fact that countries which have been target of huge migration flows actually experience immigration induced infrastructure congestion has led to a public discussion about whether immigration in the presence of public goods is welfare deteriorating. But although the question of how immigration affects the residents' welfare in the presence of public goods forms an important part of the current political debate on international migration, its discussion has largely gone without a theoretical foundation. However, in order to formulate migration policy, a clear identification of immigration-related costs and benefits in the presence of public goods seems necessary. Migration policy instruments which aim at compensating the resident population for incurred welfare losses can be appropriately discussed only on this basis. In this context, specifically the role of entrance fees will be analysed.

Since international migration is a phenomenon of increased globalization the analysis should take into account the increasing importance of trade relationships between countries. The identification of immigration costs in a trade theoretic context can then give one explanation for the observed fact that countries who mainly support free trade strongly resist a free immigration of foreigners. Therefore, the model to be presented analyses international migration in the presence of public goods with the help of neoclassical trade theory.

The question of how immigration in the presence of public goods affects the residents' welfare seems to have similarities with problems discussed in the Brain Drain literature. Specifically, problems connected with emigration of highly qualified migrants who have been educated in publicly provided schools are discussed in that literature. As a result, a clear loss is identified to arise for the emigration country whereas the destination country actually reaps the fruits of the education investments. As a consequence, Jagdish Bhagwati (1979:22f) demanded his famous tax on the Brain Drain:

It would then be appropriate to ask that some taxation should be levied on those who are allowed to migrate in pursuit of a humanistic world order for the compensatory benefit of those who are unwilling, or more often unable to migrate.

As the public sector is not made explicit, possible negative effects for the destination countries in form of congestion effects cannot be part of the analysis. Thus, the problems currently observed in immigration countries can therefore not be explained.

Usher (1977) confronted the Brain Drain literature with a challenging argument: immigration countries do not clearly gain from immigration, they automatically lose:

> When a man migrates from one country to another, he abandons his share of public property – the use of roads and schools, the rights to a share of revenue from minerals in the public domain, and so on – in the former country and acquires a share of public property in the latter, conferring a benefit upon the remaining residents of the country from which he comes and imposing a cost upon the original residents of the country to which he goes.

Usher reaches this result by arguing that immigrants earn more than the marginal product of labour as they cannot be excluded from the public sector and therefore automatically share in the accruing capital rents. As in the Brain Drain literature, public goods are not modelled explicitly.

However, for an analysis of the problems connected with an immigration in the presence of infrastructure bottlenecks, the public sector has to be modelled explicitly and public goods have to be introduced into a migration scenario. This can be done with the help of the Local Public Finance literature. Here, following Tiebout (1956), a predominant field of research is the analysis of efficiency aspects of free interregional migration in the presence of locally supplied public goods (for a survey, see Rubinfeld 1987 and Wildasin 1987). But whereas regions allow the free migration of people, nation states strongly restrict immigration. Therefore, the immigration country can be modelled as a club in the Buchanan (1965) sense, which can exclude migrants from crossing the border (e.g. Arad and Hillman 1979; Straubhaar 1992). As the Local Public Finance literature is mainly interested in efficiency aspects of migration equilibria the models' production structures are often quite simple, not seldom assuming the existence of only one private good. In frameworks like these, international trade is usually not possible. Nevertheless, a general consideration of international migration should incorporate international trade relations as these are an important feature through which countries are interrelated. The interactions between international migration and international trade through goods and factor prices is therefore not to be neglected. Additionally, huge immigration flows can have important consequences for the country's production structure as possible infrastructure enlargements necessitate a detraction of production factors from the private industries. Some authors considering migration equilibria have incorporated trade in goods, but with exogenous terms of trade (e.g. Berglas 1976; Wilson 1990). In the

71

trade literature, migration is also an important subject. There, distributional aspects and influences on a country's terms of trade are considered (e.g. Dixit and Norman 1980; Woodland 1982; Leiner and Meckl 1995).

The chapter proceeds as follows. After presenting the underlying model in Section 3.2, Section 3.3 discusses the welfare effects of immigration in a two country trade model with public goods. The whole analysis will concentrate on the immigration country but will also take effects concerning the country of emigration into account. At first, the welfare effects of the immigrants' participation in the nation's public capital stock are analysed. Then, the welfare effects of immigration induced enlargements of the public infrastructure are discussed. After a short note on the effects of immigration on the nation's production structure, Section 4.4 discusses the model's migration policy implications for the design of entrance fees. Section 3.5 concludes.

3.2   The Model

We consider a two country model with r goods, s factors and a public good g in each country. The public good is assumed to be a national public good which does not create international spillovers. As immigration countries usually control immigration they can exclude foreigners from consuming the public good. Consequently, the public capital stock is common to the members of the country in which it is supplied. People who are allowed to immigrate therefore automatically gain access to the country's public good supply. This can include a wide variety of public goods. Only some of them will be pure public goods like national defense. These are goods from which nobody can be excluded because of technical and cost reasons and which are not subject to congestion. The impossibility of exclusion gives rise to market failure where no incentive for private production exists because consumers hide their willingness to pay for the public good and act as free riders. Then, a provision can only be realized by the government which is able to finance the public good through levying taxes. However, many publicly provided goods show elements of private goods. For example, it is possible to restrict access to schools and roads which nevertheless may be congested. Because of different reasons these goods are nonetheless publicly supplied. The resident and immigrant population then both reap the consumption benefits. For example, a provision of goods like primary education can be seen as a fundamental governmental task. As congestion and exclusion of non-residents from public good consumption are both possible, the publicly provided goods considered here can therefore be called club goods.

The relationship between the supplied capacity of the public good g and the total number of users l specifies a level of (quality-adjusted) collective good consumption g:

$$\tilde{g} = f(g, l); \frac{\partial f}{\partial g} > 0; \frac{\partial f}{\partial l} \le 0 \tag{3.1}$$

As an example, g could be a highway, whereas $\tilde{g}$ gives the resulting level of consumption additionally dependent on the number of drivers using g (see Hillman 1978 and Arad and Hillman 1979.) Crowding is modelled by assuming $\tilde{g}$ to be decreasing in l.[1] In the case of pure public goods, a change in the number of users has no influence on the level of (quality-adjusted) public good consumption. Moreover, the actual level of (quality-adjusted) public good consumption increases as the supply of g increases.

Finally, because of Walras' law we choose one private good as a numeraire good and set its price equal to one such that **p** denotes the price vector of the non-numeraire private goods. In the following subsections, the behaviour of consumers, private producers and the government is described.

3.2.1 Consumer Behaviour

The demand side of the model can be formulated with the help of the expenditure function e(**p**,g,l,u) that defines the minimum expenditure for a private consumption vector **c**, which is necessary in order to reach a predetermined utility level u, given the price vector for private goods **p**, the supply of the publicly provided good g and a total population l consuming the public good. The expenditure function is therefore defined as:

$$\tilde{e}(\mathbf{p},g,l,u) := \min_{\mathbf{c}} \{\mathbf{p}^T\mathbf{c}: h(\mathbf{c},\tilde{g}) \ge u, f(g,l) = \tilde{g}, \mathbf{c} \ge 0\} \tag{3.2}$$

where h denotes a quasi-concave utility function. The expenditure function is concave in **p** and convex in g and l.[2] The partial derivative of the expenditure function with respect to g, $D_g e(.) < 0$, is equal to the demand shadow price of the publicly provided good. It is the value of private expenditure that the consumer is willing to give up for an additional unit of the publicly provided good, which at constant l leads to a utility increasing rise in g. Moreover, the partial derivative with respect to l, $D_l e(.) \ge 0$, can be interpreted as crowding costs incurred by consumers. These costs are defined as the compensating value of minimum expenditure necessary to reach a constant predetermined utility level as the total population consuming the publicly provided good increases. Crowding costs are zero if the public good is of the pure type; otherwise they are positive. In the following, we assume identical homothetic preferences in both countries. Therefore, the expenditure function is written as

$$\tilde{e}(\mathbf{p},g,l,u) = e(\mathbf{p},g,l) \cdot u$$

73

3.2.2 Firm Behaviour

The supply side is described by the social product function $y(\mathbf{p},g,\mathbf{v},l)$, which describes the maximum value of private production produced with a constant returns to scale technology at a given price vector $\mathbf{p}$, a given supply of g, a given supply of factors of production $\mathbf{v}$ and the number of residents l:

$$y(\mathbf{p},g,\mathbf{v},l) := \max_{\mathbf{v}^j, \mathbf{v}^g, l_j, l_g} \left\{ \sum_{j=1}^{\bar{r}} p_j \cdot f_j(\mathbf{v}^j, l_j) : f_g(\mathbf{v}^g, l_g) \geq g; \; l_j, l_g \geq 0; \right.$$

$$\left. \mathbf{v}^g + \sum_{j=1}^{\bar{s}} \mathbf{v}^j \leq \mathbf{v}; \; \sum_{j=1}^{\bar{s}} \mathbf{v}^j = \mathbf{v}^p; \; \mathbf{v}^g, \mathbf{v}^j, \mathbf{v}^p \geq \sum_j l_j + l_g \leq l \right\}$$

$$(3.3)$$

Here, the total population l is actually an element of $\mathbf{v}$ For reasons of clarity it is used as a separate variable. Its composition is described in more detail below. $\mathbf{v}^p$ ($\mathbf{v}^g$) denotes the vector of factors of production in the private (public) sector. The social product function is convex in $\mathbf{p}$ and concave in g. Its partial derivative with respect to the public good, $D_g y(.) < 0$, defines the supply shadow price of the public good, i.e. the value of private production that has to be given up in order to produce an additional unit of the publicly provided good.[3] The social product function is concave in $\mathbf{v}$ and its partial derivative with respect to factor endowments determines the vector of factor prices $\mathbf{w}$:

$$\mathbf{w}(\mathbf{p}, g, \mathbf{v}, l) = D_\mathbf{v} y(\mathbf{p}, g, \mathbf{v}, l) \qquad (3.4)$$

All private goods and the public good differ in their factor intensities of production. This is an assumption that matters quite a lot in trade theory but not in the local public finance literature where the private good is often used as the single input in the production of the publicly provided good.

3.2.3 Government Behaviour

The government's task is to supply an adequate amount of the public good. The decision on the amount of public good to be supplied can hinge on different intentions. On the one hand, the government could wish to bring about a welfare maximizing provision of the public good. On the other hand, public good supply could be led by the intention to enable a constant and exogenously given level of public good consumption g.

As we have seen, immigrants tend to settle in already densely populated urban areas such that congestion effects can arise.

Consequently, an adjustment of public good supply might become necessary. For a clear identification of immigration costs the production costs of the public good g and how these are financed have to be discussed.

Production costs are minimized as expressed by the linear homogeneous cost function of g:

$$C_g(\mathbf{w}) : \min_{a_{ig}} \{ \sum_{i=1}^{\bar{s}} a_{ig} \cdot w_i : f(\mathbf{a}^g) \geq 1 \}$$

(3.5)

with a_{ig} as input coefficient of factor i in the production of g. The public capital stock is assumed to depreciate at a constant rate θ. In the following, we will assume that the existing public capital stock is already completely financed such that only replacement investments have to be financed.[4] From this follow aggregate costs as

$$C_g(\mathbf{w}, g) \equiv C_g(\mathbf{w}) \cdot \theta \cdot g.$$

(3.6)

The government levies a proportional income tax for financing these public investments. The income tax is one of the most important sources of tax revenue countries raise for financing the provision of public services. With the total income for the domestic country being defined as

$$y^*(\mathbf{p}, g, \mathbf{v}, l) \equiv y(\mathbf{p}, g, \mathbf{v}, l) + C_g(\mathbf{w}, g)$$

(3.7)

the governmental budget constraint stating that tax revenues have to equal public provision costs can be written as

$$t \cdot y^*(\mathbf{p}, g, \mathbf{v}, l) = C_g(\mathbf{w}, g)$$

(3.8)

Income tax rates for the domestic and foreign country can then be easily derived as:

$$t = \frac{C_g(\mathbf{w}, g)}{y(\mathbf{p}, g, \mathbf{v}, l) + C_g(\mathbf{w}, g)}$$

(3.9)

$$T = \frac{C_G(\mathbf{W}, G)}{Y(\mathbf{p}, G, \mathbf{V}, L) + C_G(\mathbf{W}, G)}$$

(3.10)

where capital letters indicate foreign variables. Hence, the government adjusts tax rates such that the budget is always balanced. Note that a situation with free trade is assumed, such that $p = P$. Furthermore, labour is in inelastic supply such that the consumption-leisure decision is not distorted by the income tax system.

3.2.4 Income Distribution

The following welfare analysis of an international migration in the presence of public goods will be restricted to a consideration of relatively low skilled migrants. As far as for example Germany is concerned, immigrants are observed to possess lower skills than the average indigenous population and therefore also earn relatively less. Pischke (1992) finds that foreigners earn on average about 20–25% less that Germans because they are mostly blue collar workers. The German Research Institute DIW (1994) finds that foreign incomes are on average 10% lower than that of an average German. It has to be pointed out that this wage differential does not exist because of wage discrimination but because of different skills and therefore working positions. This observed pattern is due to the fact that the former German guest worker programmes and the present working contracts with workers from Central and Eastern Europe have traditionally targeted low skilled people. But also for the U.S., Borjas (1991) warns that as a consequence of changes in the immigration policy the more recent immigration waves consist of a significantly increased number of unskilled workers than earlier ones. Although an analysis which is restricted to lower income immigrant groups does not cover the whole range of possible migration scenarios it represents a very typical form of international migration.[5]

Therefore, we assume that the total population l(L) in the two countries considered consists of two income classes, with n (N) being the high and m(M) being the low income group, i.e l(L)=m+n (M+N). One can imagine that the first group (called capitalists) possesses one unit of labour and additionally all the other factors of production, whereas the other group (called labourers) only possesses labour. Under the assumption of identical homothetical preferences it follows that capitalists receive higher factor incomes than workers such that $u_n > u_m$. Following this distribution of production factors among the two income classes considered it is possible to argue that low income group members are unskilled workers and high income group members are skilled workers with one production factor other than labour being human capital. We can now specify the vector of factors of production v(V) such that v_1(V_1) describes the amount of labour available in the economy, which is equal to the total number of resident population l(L). The vector of factor prices has to be standardized such that w_1(W_1) describes the domestic (foreign) wage rate. The budget restrictions of the different income classes can then be written as:

$$m \cdot e(\mathbf{p}, g, l) \cdot u_m = m \cdot (1 - t) \cdot w_1 (\mathbf{p}, g, v, l) \qquad (3.11)$$

$$n \cdot e(\mathbf{p}, g, l) \cdot u_n = y(\mathbf{p}, g, v, l) - m \cdot (1 - t) \cdot w_1(\mathbf{p}, g, v, l) \qquad (3.12)$$

$$M \cdot e(\mathbf{p}, G, L) \cdot U_M = M \cdot (1 - T) \cdot W_1(\mathbf{p}, G, V, L) \qquad (3.13)$$

$$N \cdot e(\mathbf{p}, G, L) \cdot U_N = Y(\mathbf{p}, G, V, L) - M \cdot (1 - T) \cdot (\mathbf{p}, G, V, L) \qquad (3.14)$$

where equal expenditure functions in both countries arise from identical preferences.

With the help of Equations (3.11) and (3.13) it is now possible to discuss the migrants' incentive to move. An international migration is based on a comparison of welfare levels which can be obtained in the potential immigration country and in the emigration country. For a comparison like this, a worker not only compares wage rates and income tax levels, he also takes the countries' public capital stocks and related congestion problems into account. In our model, free trade may not have equalized wage rates, for example because factor endowments differ too much. And although preferences are assumed to be identical worldwide the public good supply will differ in both countries when population sizes differ. If the migrant considers the quality associated with the public good to be equal in both countries, i.e. $\tilde{g} = G$, then Equations (3.11) and (3.13) show that a migration incentive exists until net incomes are equalized internationally, i.e., for example, $(1-t) \cdot w_1 = (1-T) \cdot W_1$. If the quality of public good consumption differs in both countries an elimination of migration incentives will be connected with unequal incomes after taxes. Then, a migration equilibrium will be associated with a higher (lower) net income in the country with the lower (higher) quality of public good consumption g.

From (3.11) and (3.12) or (3.13) and (3.14) respectively follow the national budget restrictions:

$$(m \cdot u_m + n \cdot u_n) \cdot e(\mathbf{p}, g, l) = y(\mathbf{p}, g, v, l) \qquad (3.15)$$

$$(M \cdot U_M + N \cdot U_N) \cdot e(\mathbf{p}, G, L) = Y(\mathbf{p}, G, V, L), \qquad (3.16)$$

Furthermore, we need the condition for the clearing of the world private goods markets:

$$x(\mathbf{p}, g, v, l) + X(\mathbf{p}, G, V, L) = 0 \qquad (3.17)$$

with

$$x(\mathbf{p},g,\mathbf{v},l) = D_p y(\mathbf{p},g,\mathbf{v},l) - \frac{D_p e(\mathbf{p},g,l)}{e(\mathbf{p},g,l)} \cdot y(\mathbf{p},g,\mathbf{v},l)$$

denoting the vector of excess supply. The derivation is simplified by recognizing that $(u_m \cdot m + u_n \cdot n) = y/e$ as we see from (3.15). With the help of (3.15), (3.16) and (3.17) the condition for an optimal public good supply can now be analytically formulated. By totally differentiating (3.15) and (3.16) respectively and setting changes in utility following a change in public good supply equal to zero we receive:

$$\frac{y(\mathbf{p},g,\mathbf{v},l)}{e(\mathbf{p},g,l)} \cdot D_g e(\mathbf{p},g,l) = D_g y(\mathbf{p},g,\mathbf{v},l) \tag{3.18}$$

$$\frac{Y(\mathbf{p},G,V,l)}{e(\mathbf{p},G,L)} \cdot D_G e(\mathbf{p},G,L) = D_G Y(\mathbf{p},G,V,L). \tag{3.19}$$

where we have assumed that countries do not strategically influence the terms-of-trade such that $d\mathbf{p}/dg = d\mathbf{p}/dG = 0$. Equations (3.18) and (3.19) then give the Samuelson conditions, stating that the sum of the demand shadow prices for the public good have to equal its supply shadow price. In principal, for large open economies a deviation of public provision from allocative efficiency implied by the Samuelson condition can be rational. With $d\mathbf{p}/dg = 0$ the maximization calculus is combined with a maximization of world welfare.

Summarizing, the model can be expressed through equations (3.9) and (3.10), (3.11)–(3.14), (3.18), (3.19) and (3.17). This determines t,T,u_m,u_n,U_M,U_N,g,G and $\mathbf{p}$. In the following, distributional aspects between income groups within one country are not considered, i.e. only aggregate national utilitarian welfare, defined as $m \cdot u_m + n \cdot u_n$ and $M \cdot U_M + N \cdot U_N$ respectively, matters.[6,7] The resulting welfare changes for non-migrants can now be considered.

3.3 Welfare Effects of Migration in the Presence of Public Goods

This section lays the theoretical foundation for a suitable discussion of entrance fees for immigrants. Additionally, we will briefly look at compensation schemes for the country of emigration. Therefore, the residents' welfare change in the immigration and the emigration country is considered. As it illustrates our model and as it is an actual international migration pattern which we can observe, we will call the immigration country North and the emigration country South, such that migration goes from the southern to the northern part of the world. The following analysis explicitly considers the residents' welfare change in

78

the North by excluding the immigrants. This is because it is the group of non-migrants that actually decides on migration policy measures. Generally, it is the non-migrants' welfare change that matters for an adequate implementation of entrance (or exit) fees as a compensation for incurred welfare losses.

The comparative static analysis proceeds from the initial equilibrium described in Section 3.2. By total differentiation of (3.15) and (3.16) we get with dm = –dM = dl = -dL:

$$\phi = x \cdot \frac{d\mathbf{p}}{dl} + \delta \cdot \frac{dg}{dl} - (m \cdot u_m + n \cdot u_n) \cdot D_l e + t \cdot w_1 \quad (3.20)$$

$$\psi = -x \cdot \frac{d\mathbf{p}}{dl} + \Delta \cdot \frac{dG}{dl} + (M \cdot U_M + N \cdot U_N) \cdot D_L e - T \cdot W_1 \quad (3.21)$$

where ϕ = (m · du$_m$/dl + n · du$_n$/dl) · e($\mathbf{p}$,g,l) describes the domestic, non - immigrants, and ϕ = (M · dU$_M$/dl + N · dU$_N$/dl) · e($\mathbf{p}$,G,L) the foreign, non-emigrants'' aggregate welfare change following an international migratory movement of workers. δ = D$_g$y-(m · u$_m$ + n · u$_n$) · D$_g$e and δ = D$_G$Y – (M · U$_M$ + N · U$_N$) · D$_G$e describe the degree of optimality in public good supply (i.e. optimal, over or undersupply) in both countries. As (3.20) and (3.21) show, international migration affects the North's as well as the South's welfare level through a change in the terms-of-trade (d$\mathbf{p}$), a change in public good supply (dg), a congestion cost effect (dl) and a change in tax revenue. As the government decides on changes in public good supply and simultaneously adjusts tax rates such that the budget is balanced, tax rate changes are not explicit. That is, the interactions between additional tax revenue, additional public good provision and possible tax rate changes are not visible.

We can now discuss the conditions under which the non-migrant population in each country wins or loses following an international migratory movement of workers. The procedure is as follows: at first, we will discuss the welfare effects by abstracting from possible adjustments in public good supply. This will enable a valuation of migration-induced welfare effects for the resident population in the North connected with the immigrants' use of a given public capital stock. Afterwards, the effect of a change in public good supply is introduced such that an analysis of the costs and benefits associated with immigration-induced public capital enlargement investments becomes possible.

3.3.1 Consequences of the Migrants' Participation in the Natives' Public Capital Stock

Due to their presence in the host country immigrants automatically participate in the nation's public capital stock and therefore gain a share of it. This becomes most obvious when migrants not only stay temporarily. But is this participation in a given public good supply which can be already completely financed connected with welfare losses for the resident population in the North? Clarke and Ng (1993:261) point out:

> [..] to the extent that current publicly available benefits (e.g. roads, libraries) are funded out of past community savings rather than current taxes, public expenditures themselves represent a redistribution from existing to new residents.

With the help of our model we can now discuss the welfare changes for residents in the North resulting from the fact that immigrants automatically gain a share of the nation's capital stock.

The model assumes the public capital stock to be already completely financed such that the income tax is only needed for replacement investments. Consequently, immigrants are instantly able to consume a public good which has been supplied without their financial help. As we intend a consideration of a public capital stock already in existence, we first abstract from a potential change in public good supply such that dg/dl in (3.20) equals zero. Thus, in the North a given public capital stock is now consumed by more persons whereas in the South the number of users has decreased. If the North is a small open economy with a pure public good, i.e. $dp/dl = (m \cdot u_m + n \cdot t \, u_n) \cdot D_l e = 0$, Equation (3.20) then shows that the mere existence of additional users does not hurt residents but clearly improves their welfare. This is because immigrants now share in the tax burden for financing necessary replacement investments. At constant goods and factor prices we yield for the change in the income tax rate:

$$\frac{dt}{dl} = -\frac{t \cdot w_1}{y^*} < 0$$

(3.22)

However, the South suffers a clear welfare loss from an emigration as the necessary replacement investments have now to be financed by a smaller group of residents which at constant goods and factor prices clearly leads to an increased tax rate for those left behind:

$$\frac{dT}{dl} = \frac{T \cdot W_1}{Y^*} > 0$$

(3.23)

In the case of impure public goods the resulting welfare effects are ambiguous. Contrary to the positive cost sharing effect an increased usage of the public good creates a welfare loss equal to arising congestion costs. If the congestion costs outweigh the cost sharing effect an immigration is actually welfare deteriorating. Nevertheless, in the

South existing infrastructure bottlenecks are reduced, thereby enhancing the residents' welfare. Moreover, if the immigration country is a large open economy, a migration induced increase (decrease) in the terms-of-trade would improve (lower) its welfare.

It is at this stage of analysis where the differences between our analysis and the literature on the Brain Drain come out most clearly. There, an emigration of high-skilled leaves those left behind worse off, whereas in our analysis the non-emigrants' welfare can possibly increase. This is because the literature on the Brain Drain is concerned with a special public good, education, which creates positive human capital externalities. Instead, we are concerned with a public capital stock which can be subject to congestion that is reduced by an emigration.

Thus, the fact that migrants automatically gain a share of the public capital stock by entering the host country does not affect residents if the good under consideration is of the pure type and the terms-of-trade do not worsen. This is because the costs for public provision are sunk: in the absence of congestion and decreased terms-of-trade the resident population in the North would have supplied the public good independently of immigration. Analogously, the non-emigrant population does not automatically gain from an emigration of nationals as the share of public capital per capita increases. Consequently, the fact that immigrants theoretically gain a share of the immigration country's capital stock is not associated with economically explainable costs. Therefore, the immigration-induced redistribution from existing to new residents mentioned by Clarke and Ng (1993) is actually welfare-neutral. And additionally it is already obvious from this analysis that the entrance fees demanded by Weber and Straubhaar (1994) for financial responsibilities regarding an already existing infrastructure cannot be based on a cost argument but must derive from other aspects. These will be discussed in connection with a more general analysis of entrance fees in Section 3.4.

The results can be summarized in

Proposition 1. Immigrants automatically gain a share of the immigration country's public capital stock. Although it may have been already completely financed, the resident population suffers no welfare loss as these costs are sunk. The non-immigrants only incur a welfare loss, if

1 the public good under consideration is of the impure type such that congestion occurs or
2 the country's terms-of-trade worsen.

However, the North clearly gains from a participation of immigrants in financing necessary replacement investments. Though the emigration country experiences decreased congestion it suffers from the fact that the tax burden now has to be financed by a smaller group.

81

3.3.2 Consequences of Migration-Induced Enlargements of the Public Capital Stock

As was pointed out at the beginning, large migration flows to urban centres can lead to infrastructure bottlenecks which may necessitate enlargement investments. Let us therefore analyse the conditions under which a migration induced adjustment of public good supply is connected with pure immigration costs which might have to be compensated for by entrance fees. In discussing immigration costs, Simon (1989:153) points out:

> [..] if all construction were paid for on current account, immigrants would underpay for the structures they use, because they would then be paying only a part [..] for the new construction necessary for them (causing increased expenditure by natives for the new construction), while not paying at all for the existing structures they would be using.

That is, he mentions that immigrants do not pay for the existing public capital stock but additionally he argues that the non-migrant population suffers a loss if a migration-induced enlargement of public good supply becomes necessary: as additional costs are split among residents and immigrants the latter then only pay part of it, although expansion is exclusively due to them.

Let us first consider briefly the conditions under which the government decides to enlarge the public capital stock in reaction to an immigration flow. If the government wishes to supply a constant level of quality adjusted public good consumption g to its residents it follows that its supply has to be enlarged as soon as congestion occurs.[8] With pure public goods no congestion occurs such that no adjustment needs to be undertaken. That is only in the presence of impure public goods does immigration automatically lead the government to enlarge public provision such that a constant g can be attained. If the government instead follows an optimization calculus aiming at maximizing welfare without strategically influencing the terms-of-trade, then (3.18) shows that the supply decision is also influenced through goods and factor price changes. Consequently, an immigration does not necessarily lead to an enlargement of public good supply, also a shrinkage is possible. Moreover, also a stock of pure public goods might have to be enlarged. Nevertheless, in the following we will always consider the case in which the government in the North will enlarge public good supply as a result of infrastructure bottlenecks. At this stage of analysis we can work out which public provision adjustment costs are actually welfare deteriorating. Therefore, we analyse how the degree of optimality in public good provision in the initial equilibrium, combined with a migration-induced change, affects residents' welfare. Thus, we first analyse the combined effect $\delta \cdot dg/dl$ in (3.20) for the North. An optimal provision of public good supply, i.e. $\delta = 0$, means that the

82

individuals' marginal willingness to pay for the public good equals its marginal costs. Instead, an underprovision (overprovision) of the public good, $\delta > 0$ ($\delta < 0$), implies that the individuals' marginal willingness to pay for the public good is larger (smaller) than marginal costs, such that the level of public good supply is actually too low (high).

As soon as the government has full information about tastes and costs, a welfare maximizing amount of g could be supplied. Then, if the public good is optimally supplied in the initial equilibrium it follows that $\delta \cdot dg/dl=0$. Consequently, an optimal adjustment in its provision leaves the resident population unaffected – additional costs for the public good g are just internalized through the demand shadow prices. On the other hand, if an under- or oversupply exists in the initial equilibrium due to unobservable preferences, a welfare maximizing adjustment in public provision following (3.18) is impossible. In that case, government behaviour is assumed to be led by the simple aim of maintaining the initial equilibrium's quality adjusted level of public provision g. Such an adjustment is then undertaken without recognition of a possible non-optimal supply in the initial equilibrium. An underprovision of public good supply in the initial equilibrium then implies $\delta \cdot dg/dl>0$, such that a marginal increase in public good supply does not lead to immigration costs but to a clear gain to residents as their marginal willingness to pay for the additional unit is larger then marginal costs. But if g is initially oversupplied, a marginal enlargement of public provision is connected with immigration costs which leave the resident population worse off as their willingness to pay for an additional unit is smaller than marginal production costs, i.e. $\delta \cdot dg/dl<0$. They would prefer a shrinkage in public good supply.

We can summarize these conclusions in terms of

Proposition 2. Migration induced investments for an enlargement of the public capital stock do not necessarily create immigration costs. If the public good is initially undersupplied an immigration - induced enlargement is actually welfare enhancing. Thus, costs for public investments always have to be interpreted in relation to the residents' aggregate willingness to pay for the public good.

Let us now follow the argument proposed by Simon (1989), who argues that immigrants only pay a part of the migration-induced public provision costs as these additional costs are also spread among residents. It should be pointed out that considerations like these only make sense if no taxes are levied in the initial equilibrium, i.e. if public capital costs are already completely financed. In the more realistic case in which public replacement investments are undertaken and which are financed with current tax revenue, the directions of welfare changes are not obvious anymore. Since in such a situation tax rates are given, one has to compare additional tax revenue with additional costs of public provision – and why should the latter necessarily be larger?

83

Hence, we obtain

Proposition 3 If public good supply is financed with the help of current tax revenue, i.e. taxes are levied in the initial equilibrium, the residents' welfare in the North is improved (worsened) if the immigration induced change in tax revenue is larger (smaller) than additional costs.

It has to be pointed out that Equation (3.20) does not give the complete welfare effect associated with an immigration-induced enlargement of the public good. This is due to the fact that in this framework enlargement and therefore increased replacement investments cannot simultaneously be considered. Consequently, we discussed necessary enlargement investments without taking into account that these necessitate further replacement investments. This modelling was needed because we had to model a given stock of public goods and a given flow of public expenditures as in a framework which also aims at a discussion of entrance fees for a public good which is already in existence it makes no sense to assume that the public good is destroyed after one period. Thus, our analysis compares immigration induced enlargement investments with additional tax income by actually understating incurred public expenditures. Nevertheless, the welfare effects derived here address fundamental costs and benefits of an international migration. This analysis as well as a more-period-model which simultaneously includes enlargement and replacement investments show that the welfare change in the presence of induced enlargements of the public capital stock is ambiguous as additional tax income can always outweigh immigration costs.

3.3.3 Effects of Migration on the Production Structure

Large immigration flows which, for example in Israel, necessitate important infrastructure investments can be imagined to influence the countries' production structures of private goods z. In the following, it will therefore shortly be demonstrated how a marginal immigration to the North that is followed by an enlargement of public good supply affects the production structure of traded goods. In our model this effect is part of the terms of trade effect as this is determined through the migration induced change in worldwide production and consumption of private goods. The change in p is given by the total differential of (3.17):[9]

84

$$S \cdot \frac{dp}{dl} = \underbrace{-D_{pl}y - D_{pg}y \cdot \frac{dg}{dl}}_{\text{equals } \frac{dz}{dl}} + \underbrace{D_{pL}Y - D_{pG}Y \cdot \frac{dG}{dl}}_{\text{equals } \frac{dZ}{dl}} +$$

$$\frac{D_p e(p,g,l)}{e(p,g,l)} \cdot \left[w - W\, D_g y \cdot \frac{dg}{dl} + D_G Y \cdot \frac{dG}{dl} \right] \qquad (3.24)$$

The first line in (3.24) gives the effect of a migratory movement on world supply, the second line gives its effect on world demand. As we are interested in the immigration country's production structure, only the effect dz/dl needs to be considered. Terms-of-trade effects can only be derived for some special cases with two private goods, one public good and two factors of production, for example labour and capital. Under these assumptions, the stability condition $S^{-1} = D_p x + D_p X$ is a positive scalar such that the right hand side of (3.24) is sufficient for the sign of dp/dl. The first effect in the term dz/dl, $-D_{pl}y$, describes the pure Rybczynski effect of a labour movement on traded goods' outputs as the government leaves public good supply unchanged. Consequently, with $dg/dl = 0$ immigration always increases the output of the labour intensive traded good; the output of the capital intensive traded good decreases. The second effect in the term dz/dl, $-D_{pg}y$, shows for $dg/dl>0$ how an immigration-induced enlargement of public supply directly affects the production of private goods via a detraction of production factors from the private industries proportional to the scale of growth dg/dl. One can now also imagine the counterintuitive effect that an immigration of workers leads to decrease in the production of the tradable labour intensive good. This is the case, if an enlargement of a very labour intensive public good leads to a detraction of a very labour intensive factor bundle from the private industries, such that the pure Rybczinski effect of an immigration is outweighed.

3.4 Implications for Migration Policy

After we have identified fundamental costs and benefits of immigration in the previous section, this section is concerned with a thorough discussion of the role and suitable design of entrance fees as a migration policy instrument. This analysis therefore pays attention to the fact that nation states generally control the immigration of foreigners whereas the emigration of their own people is usually not restricted. As the former existence of the Iron Curtain shows, the decision to not control emigration hinges on moral or political motives (for a discussion of this aspect see Bhagwati 1984; Krugman 1991), but there could also be an economic reason for restricting emigration. For example, the Berlin

Wall was built because the former GDR feared the mass exodus of workers to the West and the related labour scarcity. Although controlled, a legal immigration is often viewed with scepticism. An adequate implementation of entrance fees for a suitable compensation of possibly incurred welfare losses could then be helpful to increase the residents' acceptance towards immigration. Alternatively, if the additional benefit of an immigration outweighs potential costs, the government could use immigration as an instrument to increase the residents' welfare. We will now discuss these two policy objectives in connection with the existence of publicly provided goods.

3.4.1 Compensating Migration Policy

As was demonstrated, the pure participation of immigrants in an already completely financed public capital stock does not create immigration costs. This is due to the fact that in the absence of congestion and a decrease in the country's terms-of-trade the residents' welfare is completely left unaffected as the costs for the existing public capital are sunk. Therefore, it was concluded that the 'redistribution from existing to new residents' mentioned by Clarke and Ng (1993:261) is actually welfare-neutral to the resident population in the North. If the North follows a compensation for welfare losses accruing to non-immigrants through an exogenous marginal inflow of workers such that their initial utility level can be attained, no migration policy measures would have to be implemented. This reasoning obviously assumes that the design of entrance fees is based on actually incurred welfare losses. On the other hand, the proposal by Weber and Straubhaar (1994) that immigrants should pay entrance fees for the participation in the nation's public capital stock is not related to actual costs. It is mainly based on the argument that the membership in a society and the associated right to use the welfare enhancing public goods is a value itself for which an entrance fee could be levied. Nevertheless, this argument leads to the question why members of the young indigenous population like children do not have to pay for the public goods as they as well as foreigners have not shared in public provision costs.

Additionally, entrance fees as a compensation for a given capital stock might be justified if immigration is connected with psychological costs or negative externalities. These can result because the resident population in the immigration country has the feeling migrants participate in their public capital stock although they have not adequately helped finance it. Consequently, based on an argument of justice, a fair contribution could be demanded as an entrance fee. However, the aim of this chapter is to identify economic costs and benefits of immigration in the presence of public goods. Although an argument for entrance fees is generally that they increase the residents' acceptance, here only a compensation of economic costs is considered.

Following a pure cost reasoning migration induced increased congestion is associated with pure immigration costs.[10] Generally, following (3.20) immigrants would have to pay an entrance fee ζ equal to

$$\zeta = - x \cdot \frac{d\mathbf{p}}{dl} - \delta \cdot \frac{dg}{dl} + (m \cdot u_m + n \cdot u_n) \cdot D_l e - t \cdot w_l. \qquad (3.25)$$

Thus, if the public good is financed by current tax revenues in which the migrants participate, and if furthermore the public capital stock does not need to be adjusted, the difference between potential congestion costs and the tax price would have to be levied as an entrance fee. More interesting is the case where the government has to adjust public good supply following immigration. A discussion of the welfare effects of migration has shown that in the case of an optimal public good supply no welfare losses occur. An entrance fee as a compensation for actual welfare losses is justified only if a migration induced adjustment in public good supply is combined with overprovision. This implies that additional production costs of g are larger than the residents' willingness to pay for them. The maximum possible entrance fee needed for compensation would have to be levied if the aggregate welfare loss to residents is balanced with the help of additional investments in public provision such that the initial utility level and the combined level of g are reestablished. If, on the other hand, non-immigrants wish to substitute private for public consumption in order to attain their initial utility level, dg/dl will be smaller than in the previous case. Consequently, entrance fees would have to be lower. This is because, by revealed preferences, a situation in which consumers wish to substitute private for public consumption must be relatively welfare improving; otherwise they would not have done it. Moreover, a positive (negative) terms of trade effect would lead to a lower (higher) entrance fee in the presence of public goods. If a country's migration policy is solely based on a compensation of welfare losses for non-migrants this would actually give rise to an exit fee for emigrants. This would have to be equal to:

$$\zeta^* = x \cdot \frac{d\mathbf{p}}{dl} - \Delta \cdot \frac{dG}{dl} - (M \cdot U_M + N \cdot U_N) \cdot D_L e + T \cdot W_l. \qquad (3.26)$$

with dG/dl<0. Thus, the exit fee would have to compensate the resident population in the South for the fact that tax payments for replacement investments of a given public capital stock now have to be borne by a smaller group of tax payers. If the government reduces the supply of the public good by not realizing that it is already undersupplied this would also have to be compensated as well as a possible decrease in the terms-of-trade. Nevertheless, these effects are partly outweighed by the welfare increasing diminished congestion which would lead to a relatively lower exit fee.

87

Consequently, if the North as well as the South follow migration policies which completely compensate the non-migrants for incurred welfare losses, an international migration of workers is associated with a maximization of world welfare as all associated externalities are internalized.

3.4.2 Welfare Maximizing Migration Policy

So far we have discussed entrance fees as a compensation of incurred welfare losses. Thus, the implementation of an adequate entrance fee implies that immigration costs exceed the associated benefits. On the other hand, as soon as immigration of workers is connected with a net gain, the North could follow a welfare maximizing migration policy aiming at maximizing the residents' welfare. Consequently, the government could now use immigration as a measure to reach its optimal club size, i.e. population (membership) size.[11] For an optimal club size, the Samuelson condition (3.18) and the condition for an optimal membership size have to be fulfilled. The latter is reached by setting φ in (3.20) equal to zero:

$$t \cdot w_1 = - x \cdot \frac{dp}{dl} + (m \cdot u_m + n \cdot u_n) \cdot D_l e \tag{3.27}$$

For a small open economy with pure public goods, the optimal rate of immigration is reached when the wage rate is driven down to zero such that no additional tax revenue is raised through immigration. For impure public goods the optimal membership size is attained when additional tax income equals marginal congestion costs. If a positive (negative) terms-of-trade effect additionally benefits (hurts) the non-immigrants, the optimal population size would be larger (smaller) than with $dp = 0$.

Consequently, the North could increase its welfare through adequately controlling immigration although the tax system does not discriminate between the resident and the immigrant population as both parties have to pay the same income tax rate. The existence of a positive immigration gain will probably increase the acceptance towards an inflow of foreigners. If instead a migration policy is pursued which intends to further increase the immigration gain, this would imply the implementation of entrance fees which are not directly related to immigration-induced costs. A migration policy like this would correspond to an auction of immigration licences as recommended for example by Simon (1989:329) and Chiswick (1982:308ff). In the very extreme case the whole migration gain in form of the net income differential could be taxed away. Obviously, moral restraints against taxing immigrants have then to be weighed against the positive effect of increasing the indigenous population's acceptance towards an immigration of foreigners.

88

Generally, (3.27) shows that it is always better to attract high income immigrants as incurred congestion costs are independent of the type of immigrants but additional tax income raised is then higher. If the income taxation was designed in a progressive way it would reinforce the demand for high income migrants as these then pay relatively more taxes than on the basis of a proportional income taxation. The conclusion that an immigration of high skilled persons, which are usually observed to earn high incomes, is desirable is also shared by Layard et al. (1992:50) with regard to the observed East-West migration:

> [..] controlled admission to the West of well educated fellow Europeans ought not to be a source of tension. It could only be achieved in a non-racist way by an immigration policy based on skill [..]. It would be shameful to reerect the Berlin wall.

Nevertheless, it is important to recognize that it is this group of persons which is strongly needed by the emigration countries in the eastern part of Europe as these persons importantly share in the financing of public duties. A controlled immigration of highly skilled workers with high income could therefore considerably increase the emigration pressure of those left behind.

3.5   Conclusion

The aim of the chapter was to identify costs and benefits of immigration with regard to the fact that migrants tend to cluster in the destination country's densely populated urban areas. From this, immigration costs were identified in connection with increased public good congestion, migration induced infrastructure enlargements in the presence of an initial oversupply and a decrease in the terms-of-trade. Nevertheless, the fact that immigrants automatically gain a share of the destination country's public capital stock was found to be welfare-neutral to residents as the costs for an already completely financed public capital stock are sunk. These basic results then enabled a discussion of the possible role and design of entrance fees. As a migration policy instrument they could help to increase the residents' acceptance towards an immigration of foreigners. It was worked out that a compensation scheme through entrance fees can be based on different arguments. If it is derived from actually incurred costs no entrance fee for the migrants' participation in the public capital stock needs to be implemented but only for congestion and enlargement investments. This analysis makes clear that entrance fees proposed by Weber and Straubhaar (1994) which are founded on the opinion that membership in a society and the associated right to use the public capital stock is a value itself, is not related to actually incurred costs. Thus, this discussion more sharply outlines different reasons for implementing entrance fees. These considerations also gave rise to a discussion of exit fees as a compensation for those left behind. It was further worked out that the immigration country can use immigration as a measure to maximize its national welfare if there is a net benefit to be reaped. Finally, it became obvious that an immigration of high-skilled high income groups is preferable as they then share more in public provision costs. Nevertheless, a migration policy based on skill can dangerously harm the emigration country which strongly depends on this group such that the emigration pressure could be considerably increased.

Consequently, by identifying immigration costs in the presence of public goods this paper is also a first step to a deeper understanding of why countries who pursue free trade resist immigration. The implementation of adequate entrance fees as a compensation for clearly identifiable costs could help to increase the residents' acceptance towards foreigners if it is impossible otherwise.

References

Arad, R.W. and Hillman, A.L. (1979), 'The Collective Good Motive for Immigration Policy', *Australian Economic Papers*, pp. 243–57.

Berglas, E. (1976), 'Distribution of Tastes and Skills and the Provision of Local Public Goods', *Journal of Public Economics*, vol. 6, pp. 409–23.

Berry, R.A. and Soligo, R. (1969), 'Some Welfare Aspects of International Migration', *Journal of Political Economy*, vol. 77, pp. 778–94.

Bhagwati, J.N. (1979), 'International Migration of the Highly-Skilled: Economics, Ethics and Taxes', *Third World Quarterly*, vol. 1, pp. 17–30.

Bhagwati, J.N. (1984), 'Incentives and Disincentives: International Migration', *Weltwirtschaftliches Archiv*, vol. 1, no. 20, pp. 678–701.

Borjas, G.J. (1991), 'Immigration Policy, National Origin and Immigrant Skills: A Comparison of Canada and the United States', NBER Working Paper No. 3691, Cambridge.

Borjas, G.J. (1994), 'The Economics of Immigration', *Journal of Economic Literature*, vol. 32, pp. 1667–717.

Buchanan, J.M. (1965), 'An Economic Theory of Clubs', *Economica*, vol. 32, pp. 1–14.

Chiswick, B.R. (1982), 'The Impact of Immigration on the Level and Distribution of Economic Well-Being', in Chiswick, B.R. (ed.), *The Gateway: U.S. Immigration Issues and Policies*, American Institute for Public Policy Research, Washington, pp. 289–313.

Clarke, H.R. and Ng, Y.-K. (1993), 'Immigration and Economic Welfare: Resource and Environmental Aspects', *The Economic Record*, vol. 69, pp. 259–73.

Deutsches Institut für Wirtschaftsforschung (DIW) (1994), Ausländerintegration und Bildungspolitik, Wochenbericht des DIW, vol. 61, pp. 33–8.

Dixit, A. and Norman, V. (1980), *Theory of International Trade*, Cambridge University Press, Cambridge.

Flatters, F., Henderson, V. and Mieszkowski, P. (1974), 'Public Goods, Efficiency and Regional Fiscal Equalization', *Journal of Public Economics*, vol. 3, pp. 99–112.

Franz, W. (1994), 'Ökonomische Aspekte der internationalen Migration', *Hamburger Jahrbuch für Wirtschafts-und Gesellschaftspolitik*, vol. 39, pp. 117–44.

Gieseck, A., Heilemann, U. and von Loeffelholz H.D. (1992), 'Implikationen der Zuwanderung aus Ost- und Südosteuropa für die öffentlichen Finanzen und das Wirtschaftswachstum in der Bundesrepublik', *Sozialer Fortschritt*, vol. 41, pp. 271–74.

Hillman, A.L. (1978), 'The Theory of Clubs: A technological Formulation', in Sandmo, A. (ed.), *Essays in Public Economics*.

Kronberger Kreis (1994), *Einwanderungspolitik-Möglichkeiten und Grenzen*, Frankfurter Institut, Stiftung Marktwirtschaft und Politik: Bad Homburg.

Krugman, P. (1991), *Geography and Trade*, Leuven University Press: Leuven, Belgium and The MIT Press, Massachusetts.

Koll, R. (1993), 'Auswirkungen der internationalen Wanderungen auf Wohnungsmarkt, Infrastruktur und Flächenverbrauch in Bayern', *ifo-Schnelldienst*, pp. 11–23.

Layard, R., Blanchard, O, Dornbusch, R. and Krugman, P. (1992), *East-West Migration*, MIT Press, Cambridge.

Leiner, N. and Meckl, J. (1995), 'Internationale Migration und Einkommensverteilung – eine aussenhandelstheoretische Analyse', *Jahrbücher für Nationalökonomie und Statistik*, vol. 214, pp. 324–41.

Pischke, J.-S. (1992), 'Assimilation and the Earnings of Guestworkers in Germany, Zentrum für Europäische Wirtschaftsforschung', (ZEW), Mannheim.

Rubinfeld, D.L. (1987), 'The Economics of the Local Public Sector', *Handbook of Public Economics*, vol. II, North-Holland, Amsterdam.

Schweinberger, A. (1994), 'Public Goods and Commercial Policy in More or Less Populous Economies', University of Konstanz, Sonderforschungsbereich 178, Discussion Paper No. 219, Series II.

Simon, J.L (1989), *The Economic Consequences of Immigration*, Basil Blackwell, Oxford.

Straubhaar, T. (1992), 'Migration und öffentliche Glüter', *Acta Demographica*, pp. 177–88.

Tiebout, C.M. (1956), 'A Pure Theory of Local Expenditure', *Journal of Political Economy*, vol. 64, pp. 414–24.

Usher, D. (1997), 'Public Property and the Effects of Migration upon other Residents of the Migrants' Countries of Origin and Destination', *Journal of Political Economy*, vol. 85, pp. 1001–1026.

Weber, R. and Straubhaar, T. (1994), 'Budget Incidence of Immigration into Switzerland: A Cross-Section Analysis of the Public Transfer System', CEPR Discussion Paper No.924.

Wildasin, D.E. (1987), 'Theoretical Analysis of the Local Public Sector', *Handbook of Regional and Public Economics*, vol. II, North-Holland, Amsterdam.

Wilson, J.D. (1987), 'Trade in a Tiebout Economy', *American Economic Review*, pp. 431–41.

Wilson, J.D. (1990), 'Trade and the Distribution of Economic Well-Being in an Economy with Local Public Goods', *Journal of International Economics*, vol. 29, pp. 199–215.

Woodland, A.D. (1982), *International Trade and Resource Allocation*, North-Holland, Amsterdam.

Notes

1. Note that $\partial f/\partial l > 0$ may be possible for some public goods. For example, immigration can confer external benefits on human capital accumulation or cultural assets.

2. For the properties of the expenditure function with pure public goods see Schweinberger (1994:4). Congestion in a duality framework is modelled in Wilson (1990).

3. See Schweinberger (1994:6).

4. This is equal to considering steady-states in which only replacement investments are necessary for a constant public good supply.

5. For a more complete analysis one could also consider an international movement of persons who take capital with them (see Berry and Soligo 1969).

6. The choice of this simple social welfare function makes sense if it is assumed that each individual has exactly one vote in a hypothetical political process.

7. For a detailed discussion of distributional aspects of international migration in a trade-theoretic context see Leiner and Meckl (1995).

8. From $e(\mathbf{p},g,l) = e(\mathbf{p},g)$ we get: $D_g e \cdot dg + D_l e \cdot dl = D_g e \cdot dg = 0$. It follows that: $dg/dl = -D_l e/D_g e > 0$.

9. It is assumed that the fractions of consumption spent on private goods are independent of g and l such that $D_p e/e$ is not derived. As a further simplification, identical levels of quality adjusted public good consumption, i.e. $g = G$, are assumed in both countries such that $e(\mathbf{p},g,l) = e(\mathbf{p},G,L)$.

10. This is because residents would need more private consumption in order to attain their initial utility level, i.e. $(m \cdot u_m + n \cdot u_n) \cdot D_I e > 0$.

11. See also the discussion in Arad and Hillman (1979) and Straubhaar (1992).

4 Causes of International Migration: A Survey

THOMAS BAUER AND KLAUS ZIMMERMANN

4.1 Introduction

The migration question seems to be one of the most demanding social issues for Europe at the turn of the century. Large migration pressures are expected from developing countries, especially from North Africa, and from East Europe. Driving forces are economic and political motives. (An analysis of the empirical dimension of future European migration issues is given by Zimmermann, 1995.) In comparison, internal European migration seems to be rather unimportant in relative and absolute terms. The motives of migration decisions are largely unexplored at the empirical level. There is also an excess demand for good economic theories. Currently, no up-to-date survey paper of empirically oriented economic studies is available. (An earlier evaluation is Krugman and Bhagwati 1976.)

Economists generally support the view that formal methods are useful to structure the empirical analysis even if not all model implications can be tested. On the other hand, more explorative approaches are useful to stimulate theoretical modelling. At present, most applied research of economists is devoted to issues of assimilation of migrants and their effects on the receiving country. (See for an overview Simon (1989), Borjas (1990) and Zimmermann (1994).) The problems of the sending countries, which were much discussed for instance in the brain drain debate two decades ago, are mostly ignored. There is however a rich set of new theoretical ideas (Stark 1991) that were not yet implemented in practice.

The empirical analysis of international migration is a black hole in economics. As in other disciplines this can be explained in part by the poor quality of time-series data and the lack of appropriate individual data. However, it is also caused by an insignificant interest of applied economists in the migration question per se. Since a large part of the migration decision is about geographical mobility, whether within a country or across the borders, we think that it is justified to survey also empirically oriented internal migration studies as long as we can learn from their findings for a promising approach to international migration. This is especially of value for problems dealing with the European Union (EU). Because of the free movement of people, which was established by the Treaty of Rome of 1957 and the Single European

Act of 1993, it is possible to consider international migration between EU member states as internal migration.

The outline of the chapter is as follows: Section 4.2 provides a review of the various individual economic approaches that were suggested in the literature, namely the standard neoclassical framework, the human capital approach, asymmetric information, family migration, and network migration. Section 4.3 investigates econometric issues, among them data availability and data quality and methodological problems like time-series estimation with data and limited dependent variable estimates with individual data. Section 4.4 surveys the empirical findings for internal and international migration. Section 4.5 evaluates the state of the art and provides an outline of new research issues.

4.2 Theoretical Approaches to the Migration Decision

This section reviews theories concerning the economics of labour migration. Recent surveys are given by Stark (1991), Greenwood (1985), Massey et. al. (1993), Molho (1986), Shields and Shields (1989) and Straubhaar (1988). In the following internal as well as international migration theories are considered, because the only basic difference between these two approaches are the legal restrictions of the latter. An overview of the immigration policies in Europe is given by Straubhaar and Zimmermann (1993) and Zimmermann (1993, 1994).

4.2.1 The Neoclassical Approach

The neoclassical approach to migration analysis can be traced back to Smith (1776) and Ravenstein (1889). The basic assumption of this model is utility maximizing of individuals subject to a budget constraint. The central argument to reach this maximum are wages. Migration mainly takes place because of geographical differences in demand and supply on labour markets. Regions with a shortage of labour relative to capital have a high equilibrium wage, whereas regions with a large supply of labour relative to the endowment of capital are faced with low equilibrium wages. This wage differential causes a migration flow from low wage to high wage regions. In response to the migration flow the wages in the high wage region will fall, while the wages in the low wage region will rise. The migration flow will end as soon as the wage differential between the two regions reflects the costs of movement from the low wage to the high wage region. As a result, labour migration emerges from actual wage differentials between regions, i.e. the larger the wage differential the larger the migration flow. Hicks (1932, p. 76) concludes that '... differences in net economic advantages chiefly in wages are the main causes of migration'. The costs of movement between two regions can be proxied by distance. It is suggested that the migration probability of individuals is decreasing with rising distance.

96

This early approach was extended in various ways. In order to explain rural-urban migration in less developed countries Todaro (1968, 1969) and Harris/Todaro (1970) dropped the neoclassical assumption of full employment and included the probability to find employment in the destination region in the utility function of migrants. (A review of this framework and its empirical evidence is given by Todaro (1980).) With this extension it is possible to explain the observed large migration flows from rural to urban regions, although the urban regions are characterized by a scarcity of jobs. Exclusively the prospect to find a high-paid job in the urban region causes labour migration out of the rural areas even though this migration could lead to unemployment. Contrary to the pure neoclassical theory migration is determined by expected rather than actual earnings differentials. The key variable for migration are earnings weighted by the probability to find employment in the destination region.

Several modifications of the basic Harris-Todaro-model have been developed to make it more realistic. Bhagwati and Srinivasan (1974) introduced wage and production subsidy programs. Cordon and Findlay (1975) considered capital mobility between the rural and urban regions, Fields (1975) used quantity instead of wage adjustments in the urban labour market, Stiglitz (1974) studied endogenous wage determination, and Calvo (1978) introduced trade unions in the urban labour market. Schmidt, Stilz and Zimmermann (1994) investigated more closely how the process of wage and employment determination is influenced by a labour union in the receiving country. However, these modifications do not change the basic findings of the original model.

4.2.2 Human Capital Theory

Following the work of Becker (1962) the human capital model was introduced to migration research by Sjaastad (1962). This model, which became probably the most influential and widely used approach, treats migration as an investment decision. Depending on their skill levels, individuals are calculating the present discounted value of expected returns in every region, including the home location. Migration occurs, if the returns in a potential destination region net of the discounted costs of movement are larger than the returns in the country of origin. The costs of movement not only include money costs like travel expenses, differences in the costs of living and foregone earnings while moving, but also psychological costs arising from the separation from family and friends. It should be noted, that every individual evaluates the returns and costs in a different way, depending on personal characteristics like age, gender and schooling. According to the human capital model, the likelihood of migration is decreasing with age, reflecting the smaller expected lifetime gain from moving for older people. Individuals with higher education should exhibit a higher migration probability, because higher education reduces the risks of migration through a higher ability to collect and process information.

97

The risks and costs of movements are expected to rise with distance, because information about labour market conditions is expected to be better for closer locations.

In two recent papers, Burda (1995) and Bauer (1995) have extended the human capital model of migration by introducing uncertainty about the wage differential between sending and receiving country and the costs of migration, respectively. According to Burda (1995) and Bauer (1995) existing models of migration ignore an important aspect of the migration decision; that is, if the decision to migrate can be postponed, and given an uncertain economic environment, a potential migrant has the opportunity to wait for new information about the real costs and returns of the migration project. The option of delaying migration may have some value which has to be taken into consideration when modelling migration behaviour. Originally, this approach was developed to provide a better understanding of the investment behaviour of firms (see Dixit and Pindyck, 1994 for an overview). Burda (1995) and Bauer (1995) conclude that with uncertainty about the real gains of migration, it may be rational for an individual to delay migration and to wait for new information even in a situation where the expected migration income gain is greater than the costs of moving. Therefore these models could give a theoretical explanation of the coexistence of large income differentials and low migration flows.

The human capital model is not only helpful to model permanent migration, but also to deal with temporary migration which is very important for countries with a guest worker system like Germany or Switzerland. There are several explanations for temporary migration. (See Dustmann, 1996 for an overview.) Subsequent migration could be the result of decreasing costs due to information obtained from the first move. Djajic and Milbourne (1988) and Dustmann (1994) assumed that different preferences for consuming at home and at the destination may be responsible for temporary migration. Repeated moving may be also determined by an unsuccessful prior move (Grant and Vanderkamp, 1985). The theoretical and empirical research of the economic success of immigrants in the receiving country have become one of the dominant microeconomic topics in the migration literature. (An overview of this literature is given by Greenwood and McDowell (1986), Simon (1989) and Borjas (1990).) Following the work of Chiswick (1978), the performance of migrants is a positive function of the transferability of human-capital between regions and the willingness of immigrants to invest in destination specific human capital. The transferability of human-capital between two areas is important only in the international framework. It is assumed that the transferability is the better the more similar are the labour markets of the destination and the origin. Furthermore, the transferability is expected to be highest for economically motivated migrants and lowest for asylum seekers and chain migrants, because the latter can not plan their movement in an efficient way. The incentive to invest in destination specific human capital depends on the socioeconomic characteristics of the migrants.

A further cause of large subsequent migration could be that the economic conditions in other locations have improved. In general, it is expected that an increase in immigration would cause a decline in labour force's wages of the receiving country. In the case of rigid wages due to the behaviour of unions immigration could lead to increased unemployment in the destination country, but this is not necessarily the case. (See Schmidt, Stilz and Zimmermann (1994) and Zimmermann (1994, 1995) for a theoretical treatment of this issue.) Both, declining wages and increasing unemployment in the receiving country could make it beneficial for the individuals to move to another region or to return back home. On the other hand, the wage and employment possibilities in the sending countries rise due to the emigration of labour which may also improve the incentives for return migration. Only in the case of free labour mobility with perfectly competitive labour markets, wages in the sending and receiving regions will perfectly adjust and there is no unemployment.

In his contribution to the discussion about the labour market success of immigrants, Chiswick (1978) did not only show that the transferability of skills plays an important role, but also that immigrants are positively self-selected, which means that they are more motivated than the average individual. Extending the work of Chiswick (1978), Borjas (1987, 1990) applied the model by Roy (1951) to find that the direction of self-selection of immigrants depends on differences in the economic situation and the income distribution in the countries of destination and origin. According to Borjas (1987, 1990) a high income inequality in the destination country leads to a positive self-selection of the migrants. The opposite could be shown for a comparatively high income inequality in the sending country. According to these theories, immigrants cannot be treated as a representative group of the population of the origin. This conclusion raises doubts that aggregate data is useful for modelling migration decisions.

In essence, the main contribution of the human capital approach is that one should not only pay attention to aggregate labour market variables like wage and unemployment differences, but should also consider the importance of the heterogeneity of individuals for the migration decision. Therefore, socioeconomic characteristics of migrants should be taken into consideration in empirical studies. In contrast to the standard neoclassical framework, the individuals within the same country can display very different propensities to migrate, because the rate of remuneration on specific human capital characteristics could be different in the destination and receiving country. The human-capital approach concludes, that the probability to obtain a job in the destination country depends on the skill levels of the migrants and their incentives to invest in destination specific human capital. This implies that the Harris-Todaro-model can be considered in a human capital framework which indicates that there might be problems to discriminate between both approaches in empirical work.

99

4.2.3 Asymmetric Information about Worker Skills

So far, we considered only models with a symmetric information regime. In such a regime it is assumed that the employers in the destination region have all relevant information about the skills of the immigrants. However, with asymmetric information the theoretical propositions may change substantially (Stark 1991). A possible asymmetric information regime is where migrants have full information about their skills but employers of the destination region cannot observe the true levels of skills of the immigrants. In this case it is efficient for the employers to offer all immigrants a wage reflecting the productivity of the average immigrant. If the assumption of imperfect information on the part of employers is combined with the assumption of heterogeneous workers, the following two polar cases are obtained. The first one is characterized by a positive discounted wage differential for migrants with low skill levels. In contrast to a symmetric information regime, asymmetric information results in a migration pattern which is characterized by a reduction of the quantity and quality of migration or has no effect at all. Contrary, the situation of a migration incentive for high skilled persons through a positive wage differential for this group is marked by either migration of all persons in a region or migration by none when introducing asymmetric information.

In the long term it is realistic to assume that the employer will learn about the true skill level of the immigrants so that the immigrants will receive a wage reflecting their true productivity. This leads to an increasing quantity and quality of migrants. Furthermore, the wages of low-skilled migrants will increase, because the prospect of higher wages in the future results in a rising migration of high-skilled individuals and therefore in a rising short-term wage for the low-skilled persons. A turnover of the migration flows could also be observed, if the employers of the destination country make efforts to get more information about the skill levels of the immigrants. Alternatively it is possible that migrants may invest in signalling devices like certificates. It can be shown that the most skilled migrants have the highest probability to invest in such signals. Furthermore, signalling results in an U-shaped migration pattern with respect to skill levels, that means only the lowest and the highest skilled individuals will migrate.

To summarize, allowing for asymmetric information in models of labour migration results in an unclear structure of migration depending on differences of initial migration incentives for persons with different skill levels, the time horizon of the analysis and investments of employers in information gathering as well as investments of migrants in signalling their true skill level. Though investment in signalling can be optimal from an individual point of view, it might be inefficient for the whole economy.

4.2.4 Family Migration

In the theories discussed above, the focus of migration theory was on treating migration as a problem of individual decision making. Recently a new approach challenges many of the conclusions of the previous approaches by postulating that migration decisions are typically made by families or households.

Mincer (1978) has examined the influence of increased labour force participation of wives on the migration decision of families. The household size and the number of working family members increases the sources of costs and benefits from migration. Those family members who do not move on their own initiative often have to expect reduced earnings and employment possibilities in the labour market of the destination country. Therefore, a family will only migrate, if the gains of one family member internalizes the losses of other family members. Mincer (1978) showed that increased labour force participation rates of women leads to increased interdependence of the partner's migration decision, which results in both less migration and more marital instability. Increased marital instability in turn encourages migration as well as increased women's labour force participation. Furthermore, migration should be a decreasing function of family size.

A different starting point was chosen by the new economics of migration. (See Stark (1991) for an overview.) This approach models migration as risk-sharing behaviour of families. In contrast to individuals, households are able to diversify their resources like labour in order to minimize risks to the family income. This goal can be reached by sending some family members to work in foreign labour markets where wages and employment conditions are negatively or weakly correlated with those in the local region. This strategy enables a family to secure their economic well-being in the case of an economic deterioration in the local labour market by remittances of family members working abroad. With this kind of model it is possible to explain migration flows in the absence of wage differentials.

Another feature of this new approach can be seen in the assumption that families not only evaluate their income in absolute terms but also relative to other households (Stark, 1991). In the relative deprivation approach, migration occurs in order to improve the income of the household relative to a reference household. Therefore, not only income differentials between the regions of origin and destination matter for the migration decision, but also the income distribution in the original location. According to this theory, high income inequality results in stronger relative deprivation which itself causes higher migration rates in this group. This approach is also applicable to models with individual decision making.

The new economics of migration changed the evaluation of the migration decision in emphasizing the family as a decision making unit, which not only wants to maximize income, but also minimizes risks to the family income and to overcome labour market restrictions in the country of origin, even if this is not combined with a higher total family income. It should be noted that these models are mainly applicable in developing countries where it is not possible to secure the family income through private insurance markets or governmental programs like in developed countries. Furthermore, it is impossible to test the approaches of the new migration theory without micro data, because detailed information about the family structure is needed.

4.2.5 Network Migration

A dynamic view of migration is given by the network approach (Hugo 1981; Massey 1990a, 1990b; Massey and España 1987; a formal treatment is given by Bauer 1995). According to this framework migration may become a self-perpetuating process because the costs and risks of migration are lowered by social and informational networks. Due to a lack of information about the labour market at the region of destination the first person moving is faced with high costs and risks. After the migration of the first individual the monetary and psychological costs of migration are substantially lowered for relatives and friends of this individual in the original location. Furthermore, existing network ties lower the risks associated with migration to a foreign region because individuals can expect help from previously migrated people to find a job in the destination country. This reduction of the costs and risks leads to a higher net return of mobility and therefore to a higher migration probability. A new migrant raises the number of persons in the region of origin with social ties to the destination country, which may result in a self-perpetuating migration process. However, not all people in the sending region may be affected, and hence this process may eventually stop. Another reason which weakens the self-feeding process are the rising wages in the sending and the falling wages in the receiving country in the process of outmigration lowering the possible benefits of moving. These diminishing effects on the self-perpetuating process are very important for the stability of this model, because otherwise it would predict unrealistically the migration of whole countries.

This model also suggests a smaller direct correlation between factor price differentials, employment prospects and the migration decision than the neoclassical model through growing network relationships and the associated reduction in costs and risks. Furthermore, it should be expected, that the self-selective effect of migration diminishes over time and that the migrants will become a more representative sample of the sending region. This approach relies not only on the migration decision of individuals or families at one point in time, but also considers that every migration decision of a person alters the economic and social situation in which subsequent decisions are made. On the other hand, a change in relative economic conditions at one point in time has effects on migration decisions in all future periods by starting additional network migration.

102

4.2.6 A General View: Push- and Pull-Migration

A general view of labour migration can be given in the push and pull framework, which integrates the previously discussed theories. Zimmermann (1994) defines demand-pull migration and supply-push migration in line with shifts in the aggregate demand and supply curves of the receiving economy. Assume a standard price-output diagram like Figure 4.1(a) with an upward-sloping supply curve. If aggregate demand increases, output and prices are rising. With rising wages, it is beneficial to allow for immigration to avoid inflation and to obtain a further increase in output. Hence, the supply curve shifts downwards and AB in Figure (4.1a) is pull migration. Conversely, an inflow of migrants without a change in demand shifts the supply curve downwards and prices fall while output rises. Hence AC in Figure (4.1a) is push migration. A different case of push migration occurs if the supply curve shifts upwards (say from equilibrium point C to A in Figure (4.1a)) due to a supply shock, for instance by a reduction of native labour supply, and this is (at least partly) compensated by immigration so that the equilibrium moves again down on the aggregate demand curve.

To summarize, push-supply migration affects the aggregate supply curve alone while pull-demand migration deals with migration (and hence a shift of the supply curve) that responds to a shift in the demand curve. All internal factors affecting aggregate demand causing migration are considered to be determinants of pull migration while all internal or external factors affecting the aggregate supply and are associated with migration are defined to be determinants of push migration. This is a particular way to define push and pull, namely to stress the economic context of the inflow of workers.

In the case of a vertical aggregate supply curve (see Figure (4.1b)) the supply and demand curves of labour are only affected by real wages. If the trade unions (or other institutional constraints) fix real wages above the equilibrium level, for instance at A_1 in Figure (4.1c), this results in unemployment of about A_1A_2. Immigration (or push migration) shifts the labour supply curve and increases unemployment and government deficits due to payments of unemployment compensation. This in turn affects aggregate demand and increases prices while leaving output constant. Hence, there is stagflation caused by immigration of workers or (more precisely) by push migration.

In practice, push migration may occur from various sources. Among them are positive economic conditions in the receiving countries relative to the sending regions measured by variables like unemployment, wages, work conditions, social security benefits and the structure of the economy. Demographic determinants like the size and the age distribution of the labour population also effect the labour supply decisions of migrants. Family migration and inflow by asylum seekers and refugees are also considered to be push migration. Family migration is chain migration and may also be affected by family reunification policies in destination countries. In a certain sense, this could be considered as pull migration. However, it affects the supply curve of the receiving economy alone, and hence this is defined to be push-supply migration. Only if reunification policies would be changed in response to changes in aggregated demand, this would be pull demand migration.

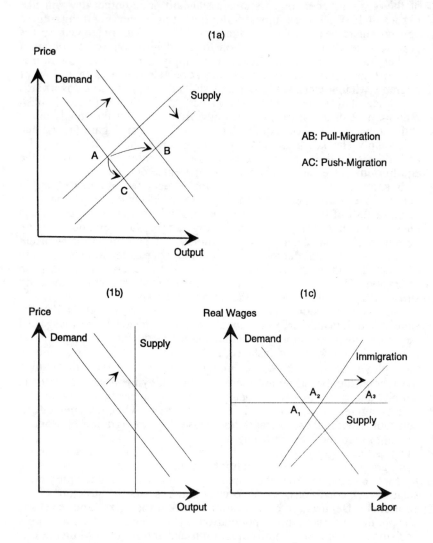

Figure 4.1   Migration push and pull and the economy

4.3   Econometric Issues

4.3.1   Data Availability and the Case for Econometrics

The key source of statistical analyses in migration research in the last decades has been aggregated data, either in form of time-series or by use of regionally aggregated variables. Time-series studies were supported by inexpensive usable sources provided by the statistical offices in the respective countries and the econometric methods were sufficiently developed to do a sound analysis. Since the last decade there is some tradition in the analysis of individual data, which is much stronger in the US than in Europe. This can be explained by the availability of the necessary data as the proper methods to analyse them. The investigation of individual data was hindered so far by limited computer facilities and non-existing econometric techniques to deal with specific problems of such data like their often discrete or only partly continuous nature, if such data was available at all. Even computer centres were hardly able to deal with the large data sets or the very time-consuming computer programs that were already available to apply some of the newly developed microeconometric techniques.

Since the 1980s, the situation has changed dramatically due to the tremendous speed in the improvement of the main frame and micro computer technologies. Most individual data problems including the handling of the data are now possible to execute on PCs or workstations. Now the provision of such data remains more and more the real problem, at least in Europe, since Statistical Offices and other public producers of such data often refuse to make their data available to researchers with the argument that this would endanger the privacy of respondents. This corresponds to an increasing resistance in the public to create such data, for instance census data became much more difficult to create. An important alternative is the provision of sample survey data that could also be better tailored to the problems under study.

The future of time-series analysis of migration is hindered by the low quality of such data in Europe. This is even true in single countries where the material is often flawed by measurement problems. For instance, it is often difficult to obtain reliable numbers for out-migration due to the poor monitoring process of deregistration. The real problem for cross-country studies is data comparability, since official statistics show large differences in the measured migration streams between the countries. Long run consistent time-series of stock and flow data of migrants are not available in Europe. There are also methodological problems for time-series studies that are discussed in the next section. The analysis of the theoretical developments in the previous sections also showed that there is particular interest in the microeconomic differences of the decision making process which can only be investigated at the level of individual data.

A further data problem is the definition of a migrant, which largely differs between the countries. Migrants measured in Europe are typically foreign nationalities, there is no separate statistic on foreign born people. Naturalizations as well as ethnic migrants are not properly covered, at least not in stock statistics. For instance, Germany has received millions of ethnic German migrants in the last decades, which are all not covered in the official stock statistic of migrants. German born individuals are still foreigners, if their parents are, and a substantial share of the foreigners live for more than 20 years in Germany. There are similar problems in many other European countries.

Despite the substantial problems in the provision of a data base of sufficient quality and the development of convincing theories to explain and predict migratory movements, a sound econometric analysis is the only way to make substantial progress in our understanding of this demographic process. This has to be kept in mind if we qualify the current advances of applied research. More experience is the only way to discriminate between alternative theories and to concentrate on the more promising ones, to learn for the improvement of the theoretical models, and to obtain a clear picture of the sizes of the driving forces. The remainder of Section 4.3 therefore deals with recent advances in the econometrics of time-series and individual data.

4.3.2   Time-Series Issues

Recent methodological developments in time-series analysis deal with the proper treatment of trended variables. Most time-series are not stationary as required by standard econometric theory, which may generate biased conclusions. (See Greene (1993) for an outline of the basic problems.) A particular issue of non-stationarity is the problem of spurious regressions: This suggests for example that with trends in the data, it is easy to find significant relationships between variables even if the true effect parameters are zero. While the standard t-test suggests significance at a standard normal value of 1.96, one cannot be sure that this is actually true if the t-statistic is not larger than 6 times of this size.

So at least, the time-series analysis used must be carefully examined to identify possible unit roots (or non-stationarity). The non-stationarity indicates problems for the application of traditional econometrics because the error structure of the regression equation must be stationary. A sufficient condition to achieve stationarity of the error term is that all variables in the equation are stationary. This is often achieved by reformulating the model in first differences. This, however, normally implies that the dynamic version of the model is not consistent with the long run solution, and even worse, this long-run relationship between the levels of the variables under study cannot be identified.

Recently developed co-integration theory suggests a method to test for and to estimate this long-run relationship as well as the dynamic process around it. The accumulated sum of a stationary series is called integrated of order 1. If a linear combination of some of the integrated series is stationary, it is said to be co-integrated. It is then possible to estimate the long-run relationship by means of a simple OLS regression

106

independently from the dynamic process, because its error term is now stationary. These estimates are super-consistent. The dynamics can then be estimated consistently with the long run solution by modelling an error correction model including the (past) error term of the co-integrating regression as a separate variable along with changes of the exogenous and past endogenous variables.

A valuable strategy to analyse the data is then: first, to investigate the stationary of each series; second, to run co-integration regressions between the variables if they are all integrated of order 1; and third, to fit an error correction model around this long-run solution which captures the short run dynamic process. This procedure also requires the availability of longer time-series (say larger than 40). Currently, most time-series applications in the field of migration do not properly deal with the issues raised in this section.

4.3.3 Individual Data Analysis

Individual data analysis typically relies on cross-section sample surveys of individuals. Sometimes the same group of individuals or households are followed over time so that one obtains a panel study. Panel studies are extremely helpful for testing hypotheses, since they allow to statistically control for unobserved heterogeneity. A disadvantage is that individuals may systematically drop out over time and create sample attrition. The consequences are biased estimates. An alternative is to pool independent cross-sections, surveys with a similar questionnaire but with different individuals, in a pseudo-panel analysis. Most microeconometric investigations are actually pure cross-section studies, mainly because panel surveys are rather rare, but also because the methodology for the analysis of panel data is not yet fully developed. The problem for the analysis of international migration is that a migrant can never be observed before and after migration in one national survey, which hinders the potential for applications considerably, since we do not have international migration surveys. Another problem with the sampling scheme is that migrants are only a small fraction of the population, and hence have to be stratified to receive usable sizes in samples. For the analysis of the migration decision we then have a choice-based sampling problem, which has to be addressed in the econometric analysis.

However, already cross-section samples raise a couple of specific questions for which modern econometric textbooks (Greene 1993, for instance) provide clear answers: One has to deal with unobserved heterogeneity which may generate inefficient estimates (with too high standard errors). Mostly, the migration analysis deals with non-continuous dependent variables, like the migration event (0, 1), the number of migrants in a family (0, 1, 2, ..), the duration of stay in a country, etc. Here, standard regression analysis is no longer applicable and one has to rely on more advanced classes of econometric methods for limited-dependent variables that are based on the maximum likelihood-principle. For example, we deal with the probability of an event (0, 1) in a Logit or Probit approach, where the former method assumes a logistic distribution and the latter a standard normal distribution of the error term. Both approaches provide us with quite similar qualitative results, although the size of the parameters are different. The number of migrants of a family (or the number of migrations in persons live) can be investigated with count data models, and the duration of an event can be studied by duration models. All usual testing procedures are available. Given the rich body of econometric methods developed in the last decade for the individual data situation, it is fair to say that micro surveys can be analysed by any moderately educated applied researcher. Currently, the methods discussed in this section are not yet sufficiently used.

4.4 Empirical Findings

Over the past decades extensive econometric investigations of the determinants of migration and return migration have been undertaken for developed and developing countries. For a survey of the earlier literature see Krugman and Bhagwati (1976). Greenwood (1985) reviewed the empirical findings for the developed countries and Todaro (1980) for the developing countries, the latter especially those papers related to the Harris–Todaro model. We will review only studies not surveyed in the above articles and point out the most important general common findings and differences with the work summarized in these papers. In the sequel, we will distinguish between research using aggregate data and micro data.

4.4.1 Aggregated Data Research

Most empirical studies of migration use aggregate data due to a lack of available micro data sets or insufficient computer facilities. Typically, this is either cross-section data or time-series data. Cross-section studies are mainly applied to internal migration research, whereas international migration research concentrates on time-series data. This is hardly surprising, since, as was outlined in the previous section, international migration can hardly be studied by national surveys.

Before presenting the main results with regard to the most important determinants of migration, we will discuss some problems of the measurement of migration. Commonly used definitions of the dependent variable are net migration, gross migration and the rate of migration. A discussion about the right choice of the dependent variable is given by Krugman and Bhagwati (1976). The rate of migration is the number of migrants from the origin to the destination country weighted by the population living in the sending region at the beginning of the period. This concept takes into account that countries with a large population have also a higher number of potential migrants. Net migration is defined as absolute difference between emigration and immigration in a region. Gross migration for two regions is either the number of out-migrants in the country of origin or the number of inmigrants in the destination regions. The use of the net migration measure is compounded with problems, if emigration and immigration flows are correlated. In other words, a migration model using net migration flows as dependent variable cannot separate the various push and pull factors which are responsible for the gross migration flows in ·both directions. This will result in upward-biased coefficients of variables which have the same effects on the flows in both directions and in downward-biased coefficients of variables with different effects on the flows (Brosnan and Poot 1987). In the case of correlated migration flows between two regions it seems to be useful to estimate two different models using gross migration flows or gross migration rates as dependent variable.

Migration studies using time-series data are often faced with the problem that they are unable to discriminate between labour migrants and non-labour migrants. Because the latter are not motivated by economic reasons, the inclusion of both types of migrants could lead to biased estimation results. Graves (1979) showed in a study of internal migration in the US that the income effect is significantly negative for retirees, which can be explained by a positive correlation with unmeasured prices. This result indicates that the positive effects of income on migration for labour-migrants may be weakened by a conflicting behaviour of non-labour migrants.

To summarize the main results of all studies included in this survey, we put together the signs of the coefficients of the most common variables in Table 4.1. It is striking, that nearly all studies have found a statistically significant positive effect of income or wages in the destination region, and a negative effect of wages and income in the sending country. When income differentials are combined to a single variable, migration increases with the size of the differential. Allowing for a non-linear influence on migration of the income level Faini and Venturini (1994) found a positive coefficient on the income level of the sending country and a negative influence of its square, suggesting the existence of a hump-shaped pattern of migration in response to the home country's income. This result seems to indicate that, in the early stages of development, increases in the sending country's economic well-being lead to more, rather than less migration, to the extent that they help relaxing the financial and educational constraints which prevented many would-be migrants from moving abroad. However, these results confirm the findings of earlier empirical studies and hold for internal as well as international investigations. Furthermore, they are in line with most of the theoretical models considered in Section 4.2. It should be noted that income or wage variables should be measured at the beginning of the period, since migration affects the income and the wages in the receiving as well as in the sending regions and therefore could lead to downward biased estimates if one would use end-of-period measures (Greenwood and Sweetland 1972).

Findings with regard to the unemployment or employment rates as proxies for the employment opportunities in the regions of destination and origin are a little bit more ambiguous. Contrary to what is expected from the theory, some studies found a negative correlation between the employment opportunities in the destination region and the size of the migration flow indicating that individuals are attracted by regions with a shortage of jobs (Kau and Sirmans 1976; Fields 1991; Katseli and Glytsos 1989; Poot, 1995). Likewise, the employment opportunities in the sending regions have no clear effect on the migration decision. Fields (1991) tried to overcome these conflicting results by introducing turnover variables like the rates of new hires, resignations and layoffs in the specification of the migration equation. His findings show that individuals are attracted by regions with high rates of new hires and low rates of quits and layoffs, which is in line with neoclassical and human capital theory. Furthermore, there is some other empirical evidence that employment rates are more important in determining the migration decision than are wages or income levels (Levy and Wadycki 1973; Greenwood 1975, 1981; Waldorf and Esparza 1988). Another reason for the ambiguous results of unemployment variables could be due to the use of aggregate data. Imagining this argument, Greenwood (1985, p. 532) concluded: 'Since higher unemployment rates are likely to be of most concern to the unemployed and perhaps of little or no concern to those who have a job when they move, the effects of higher unemployment rates may well not be apparent in studies that attempt to explain population or labour force migration with aggregate data'.

As outlined in the theoretical section, the Harris-Todaro-model concludes that the most important determinant of migration are expected income gains. The easiest way to test this hypothesis is to introduce income or wages in the regression which are weighted by the inverse of the unemployment rates rather than using this variables linearly. Confirming former studies, Bowles (1970), Straubhaar (1988) and Fields (1991) have found a high statistically significant influence of expected income gains on the migration flow supporting the approach of Harris and Todaro.

In nearly all studies the distance from the origin to the destination country shows a statistically significant negative influence on migration flows, supporting the theoretical considerations of the costs and risks of movement on the migration decision (Greenwood 1970; Fields 1991; Molle and van Mourik 1989). Schwartz (1973) analysed the effect of age and education on the distance elasticity of migration for internal migrants in the US. His results indicate that there is no effect of age on the distance elasticity of migration whereas the level of education diminishes the distance elasticity. This result suggests that the generally expected negative influence of distance on migration is basically due to decreasing information. As expected from the network approach, the stock of migrants from a particular origin in a destination region have a positive effect on subsequent migration.

Predominantly, the findings with respect to the influence of mean education and age of the total population on migration flows are in line with the human capital theory. More sophisticated analyses of the effect of these variables showed increased migration with higher mean education and a negative influence of mean age of migrants (Bowles 1970; Lundborg 1991b; Schwartz 1976). However, these results should be treated with care. According to the human capital model migration is typically an individual decision depending on the expected benefits of moving given his or her own specific socioeconomic characteristics like age, schooling and work experience. Using aggregate data may mask important parts of the individual migration decision.

Zimmermann (1994) tried to explore the strength of push- and pull-migration to Germany from the major recruitment targeting countries. He argued that determinants of migration decisions like relative wages and relative unemployment rates should not matter when immigration is largely driven by policy measures that account for economic motives of the receiving countries like in the case of Europe. In such a framework, migration flows should be determined by labour demand and not by labour supply factors. Zimmermann (1994) estimated standard OLS regressions of net immigration from the main recruitment countries Italy, Greece, Portugal, Spain, Turkey and Yugoslavia to Germany including a constant, real growth rates of German gross national product, lagged net immigration and a time trend. Real growth was assumed to capture the pull factors, whereas lagged net immigration as a measure of persistence and network migration, and the time trend as a proxy of unobserved variables operating in the sending and receiving country are assumed to capture the push factors. Since regression results are likely to change with the German recruitment stop in 1973, the paper allows for different parameters until and after 1973.

Measured by the respective coefficient, immigration responded strongly to the German business cycle and became lower after 1973. Using micro data on German firms, Bauer and Zimmermann (1996) have shown that this finding can be explained by the increased employment adjustment costs of guest worker employment due to the recruitment stop in 1973. According to their findings the temporary employment of guest workers acts as an buffer for native employment. This buffer function of the guest worker employment decreased after the recruitment stop due to the increased adjustment costs of guest worker employment. Furthermore, the analysis of Zimmermann (1994) revealed that the coefficients for lagged migration were significant for all sending countries and remained mostly stable after 1973. The constant has not changed after 1973 for all countries indicating that the switch in the immigration policy was either neutralized by other factors or is operating only through changes in the other coefficients. These results indicate that there are elements of push and pull migration

111

before and after the policy change. Nevertheless, this distinction was confirmed by the fact that the cyclical variability of immigration has largely decreased after 1973 in most of the analysed sending countries. For Yugoslavia and Turkey which are not members of the EU, Zimmermann (1994) showed that the lagged migration coefficient dominates the immigration process to Germany. Using German data on new entrants from 1957-1968, Böhning (1970) showed that labour demand pressure in the receiving country is the most important determinant as long as there is large unemployment in the sending country. On the other hand, wage differentials became the main determinant when labour demand pressure is roughly the same in the sending and receiving country. Furthermore Böhning (1970) showed that the inflow of migrants in Germany from developed countries is less sensitive to the business cycle than the inflow of migrants from less developed countries.

4.4.2 Micro Data Analysis

Since the early 1980s several micro surveys have been created. This data open the possibility to overcome the problems of aggregate data and to test the relevance of individual and local characteristics. Navratil and Doyle (1977) analysed the influence of aggregation of census data on the regression results of empirical migration research. Their results indicate that studies using aggregate data underestimate the elasticities of variables reflecting personal characteristics. Furthermore, their estimates reveal that personal characteristics are much more important for the migration decision of individuals than the characteristics of the destination areas. These findings emphasize the important role of microdata for applied migration research.

Among the mostly used data sets in migration research are the Panel Study of Income Dynamics (PSID), the National Longitudinal Surveys (NLS) and the Census Public Use Microdata Samples (PUMS) for the US or the Sozioökonomische Panel (SOEP) for Germany. Since these data sets in general have no information about the economic and social situation of immigrants before their emigration, it is not surprising that most of the empirical research concentrates on internal migration. There are only a few data sets which have been collected in the sending countries and could identify the destination country of immigrants (Lucas 1985; Taylor 1986; Ó Gráda 1986; Stark and Taylor 1991 and Adams, 1993). Normally the dependent variable is constructed as a discrete variable which takes the value 1 if an individual changes the location between two censuses and 0 otherwise. This construction requires the use of binary choice models for estimation like the probit or the logit model.

The main results are summarized in Table 4.2 by providing the signs of the estimated coefficients. Furthermore, we will discuss studies not mentioned in Table 4.2 which analysed some of the determinants in a more detailed way. All studies which allowed only for a linear relationship between age and the probability of a geographical move have found a significantly negative coefficient for the age variable. By considering a nonlinear relationship between age and migration Taylor (1986), Stark and Taylor (1991) and Adams (1993) have received an inverted U-shaped age-migration pattern, with individuals between 20 and 33 years of age having the highest probability to emigrate. Goss and Paul (1986) demonstrated that it may be very important to control not only for age but also for general job skills. As proxy for these skills the authors included the years of labour market experience in the regression equation and found a highly significant coefficient. Goss and Paul (1986) concluded that studies which do not control for the general labour market experience may underestimate the negative impact of age on the migration decision.

Education exhibited a positive correlation with the probability of migration in all studies of internal migration. In contrast to these results, and with the exception of Ó Gráda (1986) insignificant or significantly negative coefficients have been found in the international migration context. For migrants from Botswana to South Africa this could be traced back to the apartheid system which reserved skilled jobs to white persons and therefore reduced the returns on schooling for skilled black migrants (Lucas 1985). The explanation for the migration from Mexico to the US and out of Egypt is similar. Due to the prevalence of low-skilled labour markets for migrants in the destination countries migration for high-skilled individuals is not beneficial (Adams 1993; Stark and Taylor 1991).

Other important personal characteristics explaining the migration of individuals are marital status, house ownership and the existence of a network in the receiving country. The empirical findings support the proposition of Mincer (1978) that married persons should exhibit a smaller migration probability than unmarried individuals. Unexpected results have been found with respect to the variables indicating whether or not an individual owns a house. Only Goss and Schoening (1984) and Goss and Paul (1986) have obtained the expected negative coefficient reflecting the higher costs of movement for these migrants. Contrary to the findings of studies using aggregate data, the network variable seems to be only important for international migration. Nevertheless, more detailed studies support the conclusion, that the network variable is one of the most important determinants of migration decisions. A survey of empirical studies regarding network migration is given by Gurak and Caces (1992). In an empirical analysis of the network migration of ethnic Germans Bauer and Zimmermann (1997a) have shown that the probability to have connections to friends from the same country of origin strongly declines with duration of residence and the presence in rural areas. Furthermore, they have found that older people are more likely to settle close to friends or relatives at the time of immigration. Population density increases, while education, length of stay in a reception camp and per capita government expenditures decreases the likelihood of such a settlement.

Table 4.1   Signs of the coefficients in econometric studies using aggregate data*

	Country	Y in j	Y in i	rel Y	U in j	U in i	rel U	S	Age	D	MS in j
Internal Migration	i n										
Greenwood (1970	U.S.			+					-	-	+
Bowles (1970)	U.S.	+						+	0	0	
Navratil and Doyle (1977)	U.S.	0			-			+	0	0	
Kau and Sirmans (1976)	U.S.	+		+	+	+		0	0	0	+
Eriksson (1989)	Finland			+	+	+					+
Fields (1991)	U.S.	+	0		+	0	-			-	
International Migration	t o										
Lundborg (1991a)	Sweden	+			-	0					+
Waldorf and Esparze (1998)	Germany			0			-				
Molle and van Mourik (1989)	Europe	+		+	0					-	
Geary and Ó Gráda (1989)	U.S.			+			+				
Eriksson (1989)	Sweden			+		+					+
Hartog and Vriend (1989)	Netherlands	+		+	-						
Katseli and Glytsos (1989)	Germany	+	-	+	+	-			-		
Faini and Venturini (1994)	Europe		+	+	-	+					
Poot (1995)	Australasia			+	-	+			-	-	+

* Y: Income or wages; U: Employment opportunities; S: Education; D: DIstance between destination and sending country; MS: Network variables; j: Receiving country; i: Sending country. If a veriable encourages statistically significant migration from i to k, it receives a + sign; if it discourages at a significant level, it receives a – sign; if the effect is insignificant, 0 is used.

114

Table 4.2 Signs of the coefficients in econometric studies of individual migration*

	Country	Age	Age squ'd	S	M	U	PM	Net	HO	HH	HY	HS
Internal Migration	**in**											
Navratil and Doyle (1977)	U.S.	−		+	−	+	+					
Schlottmann and Herzog (1981)	U.S.	−		+								
Herzog and Schlottmann (1984)	U.S.	−		+	−	+	+					
Goss and Schoening (1984)	U.S.	−		+		+	0		−			
Goss and Paul (1986)	U.S.	−		+			+		−			
Hunt and Kau (1985)	U.S.	−		0	0							
Taylor (1986)	Mexico	+	−	+			+	0	0	0	−	0
Stark and Taylor (1991)	Mexico	+	−	+			+	0	0	0	0	0
Molho (1987)	Britain	−		0	−				0	−		
Burda (1993)	Germany	−		+	−	0			0	−	+	
International Migration	**from**											
Lucas (1985)	Botswana	−		−	−				−	−	0	
Ó Gráda (1986)	Ireland	0		+								
Taylor (1986)	Mexico	+	−	0			+	+	0	−	+	0
Starl and Taylor (1991)	Mexico	+	−	−			+	+	0	−	+	0
Adams (1993)	Egypt	+	−	0								

* S: Years of schooling; M: Married; U: Unemployed before moving; PM: Prior migration experience; Net: Network variables; HO: Home owner; HH: Household head; HY: Household income; HS: Household size. If a variable encourages statistically significant migration from i to j, it receives a + sign; if it discourages at a significant level, it receives a − sign; if the effect is insignificant, 0 is used.

115

Compared with employed persons, unemployed individuals do not suffer an earnings loss while moving. Therefore, a higher likelihood of migration for the unemployed can be derived due to the smaller monetary costs of movement. This prediction have been strongly supported by the significantly positive coefficient of pre-move unemployment in the works of Navratil and Doyle (1977), Schlottmann and Herzog (1984) and Goss and Schoening (1984). The insignificant coefficient in the study of Burda (1993) on the readiness of migrating from East Germany to West Germany may be attributed to the socialist system in the former German Democratic Republic where full employment was secured by the government.

The unemployment-migration relationship was the subject of detailed studies by Da Vanzo (1978); Goss and Schoening (1984) and Herzog and Schlottmann (1984). Using data from the first five waves of the PSID, Da Vanzo (1978) showed that families whose heads are unemployed are more likely to migrate. The estimates indicate that local economic conditions mainly determine the migration decision of the unemployed, but have no impact on employed persons. Furthermore, relative to persons holding a job, the unemployed are more responsive to economic determinants of the migration decision like local unemployment rates. This result may explain the ambiguous findings with regard to local unemployment rates in studies using aggregate data. Herzog and Schlottmann (1984) have found that pre-move as well as post-move unemployment rates of migrants exceeds those of stayers with the highest probability of post-movement unemployment for blue-collar workers. Da Vanzo (1978) and Herzog and Schlottmann (1984) have calculated that individual unemployment doubles the likelihood of internal migration. Controlling for unemployment duration Goss and Schoening (1984) have found a decreasing migration propensity with time suggesting that regressions that exclude this variable will overstate the migration probability of unemployed persons.

Investigations of repeat migration by Da Vanzo (1983) and Grant and Vanderkamp (1985) have shown that return migration is a positive function of the location-specific capital a person left behind in his original location. Using education as a proxy for the ability of individuals to process information about employment opportunities elsewhere, Da Vanzo (1983) estimated that more educated people are less likely to return and that the most educated people more often move to a third location. Similar results were obtained by Herzog, Hofler and Schlottmann (1985) and Schmidt (1994) strongly supporting the human-capital model which constitutes that more educated persons are more able to plan migration in an efficient way. The results of Da Vanzo (1983) that the distance of the initial move is positive related to subsequent movements was not confirmed by the work of Grant and Vanderkamp (1985) who have found a insignificant coefficient for this variable. The hypothesis, that the information about foreign labour markets is decreasing with distance, and that therefore moving to more distant areas results in increasing repeat migration, could not be uniformly confirmed.

Grant and Vanderkamp (1985) used a direct measure of disappointment, calculated as the difference between actual and expected income in the destination region, and found a highly significant coefficient for this variable, supporting the view that an unsuccessful first move is one of the most important determinants of repeat migration. The results of Da Vanzo (1983) indicate that the probability of return migration is decreasing with the time of residence in the destination area which could be due to decreasing ties to the sending and increasing ties to the receiving regions. On the contrary Schmidt (1994) found no significant influence of time spent in the receiving country on the return probability of German guest workers. Bad economic conditions in the region of origin have a negative influence on the return probability of migrants (Da Vanzo 1983; Schmidt 1994) and a positive impact on onward migration within the first year after the initial move (Da Vanzo 1983).

As outlined in the theoretical part of this chapter, the two dominant microeconomic topics of migration are the performance of immigrants on the labour market of the receiving country and the consequences of immigration on the labour market of the destination (For an overview see Greenwood and McDowell (1986), Simon (1989), and Borjas (1990) for studies about North America and Zimmermann (1994, 1995) for Europe). Studies on earnings assimilation of permanent migrants in Canada, the United States and Australia had shown that an initial earnings gap between immigrants and native labour decrease strongly over time indicating the willingness of foreign labour to invest in destination specific human capital. The results for immigrants in Europe are not as clear (Dustmann 1993; Schmidt 1992; Granier and Marciano 1975; Hartog and Vriend 1990; Kee 1993; Aguilar and Gustafsson 1991; Chiswick 1980; Bauer and Zimmermann 1997b). The unemployment effects of immigration have shown to be small or statistically insignificant in the available European studies (Winkelmann and Zimmermann 1993; Mühleisen and Zimmermann 1994; Hunt 1992). Furthermore, empirical evidence for Germany (De New and Zimmermann 1994a, 1994b) and France (Hunt 1992) imply modest wage reductions in the receiving countries due to the immigration of labour.

Since the 1980s several empirical studies have included household variables in their regression equations to test some propositions of the family migration approach. None of the studies which considered household size as an independent variable have found a significant influence on the migration decision. This finding is not compatible to the approach of Mincer (1978). However, in a detailed analysis of internal family migration in the U.S. Shields and Shields (1993) have obtained some interesting results which strongly support the theory of Mincer (1978). They revealed that the higher the wife's wage rate the lower the family migration propensity. Furthermore, the authors have

117

estimated a positive impact of the education of the wife on migration. This is just what the theory predicts, since higher general human capital implies that migration will less likely lead to a loss in household income. Household heads are less likely to migrate than other family members particularly in the case of international migration. This result does not only reflect different opportunity costs between international and internal migration of the heads of families, but also suggests that there are larger moving costs due to family responsibilities (Stark and Taylor, 1991). Taylor (1986), Stark and Taylor (1991) and Bilsborrow, McDevitt, Kossoudji and Fuller (1987) have estimated a positive impact of the number of adults in a family on the migration probability of an individual. An extensive analysis of internal and international migration in Ilocos Norte, a rural province in the Philippines, gave further support for the new economics of migration (Root and Jong 1991). They found that higher education of adult members of the family combined with few real estate results in increased migration of some family members, whereas network relationships are more important for families who migrate as a whole.

However, Bilsborrow, McDevitt, Kossoudji and Fuller (1987) obtained different results for the impact of migration for rural-urban migration in Ecuador. They estimated a negative impact of education on the migration pattern. Three reasons could be responsible for this result. First, the urban employment opportunities in Ecuador are concentrated in the services sector mainly attracting less educated people. Second, it could be argued that less educated people are constrained to move. Furthermore, Bilsborrow, McDevitt, Kossoudji and Fuller (1987) excluded individuals in their sample which do not move for economic reasons. Therefore, a third explanation for the negative correlation between education and migration might be the result of this sample creation, because in developing countries one reason for the migration of more educated people from rural to urban areas could be found in the desire to obtain more education, since post primary schools are concentrated in urban areas. In essence, all the results obtained by considering household variables are in line with a risk-diversifying behaviour of families.

Stark and Taylor (1991) used a measure of the relative deprivation of households. This variable had a significant positive impact on migration from Mexico to US destinations, but did not have any significant effect on internal migration. With everything else held constant, relatively deprived households are more likely to participate in Mexico-US migration than less relatively deprived households. Furthermore Stark and Taylor (1991) demonstrated, that the influence of relative deprivation on international migration is not the same at all points in the income spectrum of a village. Relative income motives for Mexico-U.S. migration are lower in the most relatively deprived households. This result supports the conclusion of the relative deprivation approach that households want to increase their absolute and relative income. However, with household incomes very near or below subsistence, relative income considerations do not matter as much as concerns of mere survival.

4.5 Summary and Conclusions

It has been shown that empirical studies using aggregate data have substantial problems in identifying the determinants of the migration decision. These problems are mainly caused by the inaccuracy of the aggregated measures to account for the important factors in the individual decision making. Nevertheless, there is strong empirical evidence that migration is largely determined by the search of individuals for better economic conditions. Micro data may help to shed more light on the complex individual decision making process. However, despite the growing number of micro data sets it seems to be very difficult to discriminate between alternative theories. This follows from similar predictions about important determinants of migration of different theoretical approaches, but it is also due to missing data especially in an international framework.

This review has made obvious that the international migration issue is not yet sufficiently empirically analysed. Economic research papers are scarce and rather selective in their treatment of the relevant questions. At best, they deal with a two-country framework and make no attempt to investigate the common problems of a group of countries such as the European Union. There is a strong need for comparative research, either by testing similar hypotheses for various countries or by dealing with specific interrelationships within a certain group of countries. The latter could include the internal migration within the European Union. Since there are no more barriers to mobility within the European Union for natives of the member states, it deals with the issue of a common labour market, although it is still international migration between independent states.

A problem so far is that not many survey data sets can be used for the analysis of the international migration decision. These data are either created in the country of origin or destination. Hence, the groups of migrants and non-migrants are exactly separated. One way out is to merge comparable surveys across countries or to create new panel data that follow people of one nation across time, where one would eventually observe migrants and return migrants. An issue for the latter case is that one would need a quota for migrants since they are only a smaller fraction of the population. This ends with a choice-based sampling problem for the econometric analysis. Nevertheless, the paper has shown that the econometric techniques are available to deal with the particular nature of the micro data that are often discrete or only continuous over a certain range of values. Various models like Probit, Logit, Tobit or count data approaches are available.

Most papers use time-series data in the various countries or regions. There are doubts about the quality of the data even at the national level.

Even more, there are problems with the availability and comparability when dealing with a cross-country framework. It is obvious that there are large measurement problems given the well known differences between inflow and outflow of migrants between countries. This is reinforced by recent methodological developments concerning the proper treatment of trended time-series variables in the regression analysis. Most time-series are not stationary as required by statistical theory, which may generate biased conclusions. Simple differencing may not help, and the relationship to the long-run solution between the variables under study might get lost. A proper treatment of the situation includes careful testing for deterministic and stochastic trends, and a distinction between short-run and long-run relationships that have to be consistent with each other. All this requires longer time-series (at least more than say 40), which are often not available.

We do not know much about the effects of country differences on migration, which is due to the fact that there are not sufficiently many papers written in this area. These differences could be either national characteristics or policy differences. It is of large interest to study the effects of differences in policies (for instance in the transfer systems across states) or regime changes within countries across time, which might be common to some countries. An example for the latter case is the stop in labour hiring policies in western Europe (especially in France and Germany) in 1973. Most recently developed theories require the use of micro data to cover individual differences. Since this data was until recently largely not available, most of these theories are not yet proper tested.

Another underresearched area is network migration. Large differences between the micro and the macro approach can be observed: In a time series context, network variables like lagged migration usually exhibit a strong positive effect, whereas in a micro data context such variables are much less relevant. This might be caused by measurement problems with opposite directions at both levels. A better way of measuring the network at the micro level is to improve the questionnaires by requesting more detailed information, whereas at the macro level one needs a better treatment of the stochastic properties and to deal with the correlation with other variables. In this field, time-series and micro data analyses are complements.

In general, we opt for a better use of micro data, especially in the context of international migration research. One simple solution is to pool comparable micro surveys across countries. Another is to enrich national surveys, for instance by adding a question on migration intentions in surveys of emigration countries, and a question on return intentions of migrants or about the characteristics of their family members who remained in the country of origin in surveys of immigration countries. It is also possible to ask retrospective questions to cover differences in past experience with migration as well as their driving forces across time. On top of that, more attempts have to be made to obtain comparable micro surveys across the countries of the

European Union, which should have a panel character. It is important to follow individuals that cross borders. Micro data should be merged with macro data from the respective regions or countries covering economic differences as well as different policy approaches. The merging of both levels however creates new demands on the methodology to analyse the data.

Last but not least, one should examine whether or not we are currently asking the right questions. The migration decision is based on more than on a comparison of the differences in potential wages. At first, more has to be done to test the recently advanced theories of individual and family migration. A promising additional area of research seems to be network migration. The stock of migrants across Europe exhibits a significant ethnic and national pattern that support the conjecture that network migration is a dominant factor. Uncertainty about the advantages of mobility contributes to this approach. It is not only the employer who has to learn about the migrant, but also the worker, who has to learn about the labour market of the receiving country. Of further importance is that most economic models investigate labour migration, whereas in practice we often deal with political and war refugees. These groups deserve further attention. As Zimmermann (1994) has shown, the flow of those migrants is also affected by economic differences between the receiving countries.

References

Adams, R.H. Jr. (1993), 'The Economic and Demographic Determinants of International Migration in Rural Egypt', *The Journal of Development Studies*, vol. 30, no. 1, pp. 146–67.

Aguilar, R. and Gustafsson, B. (1991), 'The Earnings Assimilation of Immigrants', *Labour*, vol. 5, no. 2, pp. 3–58.

Bauer, T. (1995), 'The Migration Decision with Uncertain Costs', *Münchener Wirtschaftswissenschaftliche Beiträge,* no. 95-25, Munich.

Bauer, T. and Zimmermann, K.F. (1996), 'Konjunktur, Migration und Beschäftigung: Erfahrungen aus dem Gastarbeiterregime', Helmstädter, E., Poser, G. and H.J. Ramser (eds), *Beiträge zur angewandten Wirtschaftsforschung*. Berlier Humblot: Berlin, pp. 83–96.

Bauer, T. and Zimmermann, K.F. (1997a), 'Network Migration of Ethnic Germans', *International Migration Review*, vol. 31, pp. 143–49.

Bauer, T. and Zimmermann, K.F. (1997b), 'Unemployment and Wages of Ethnic Germans', *Quarterly Review of Economics and Finance*, vol. 37, pp. 361–77.

Becker, G.S. (1962), 'Investments in Human Capital: A Theoretical Analysis', *Journal of Political Economy*, Supplement, vol. 70, pp. 9–49.

Bhagwati, J.N. and Srinivasan, T.(1974), 'On Reanalyzing the Harris-Todaro Model: Rankings in the Case of Sector Specific Sticky Wages', *American Economic Review*, vol. 64, pp. 502–08.

Bilsborrow, R.E., McDevitt, T.M., Kossoudji, S. and Fuller, R. (1987), 'The Impact of Origin Community Characteristics on Rural-Urban Out-Migration in a Developing Country', *Demography*, vol. 24, no. 2, pp. 191–210.

Böhning, W.R. (1970), 'The Differential Strength of Demand and Wage Factors in Intra-European Labour Mobility: with Special Reference to West Germany, 1957–1968', *International Migration*, vol. 8, no. 4, pp. 193–202.

Borjas, G.J. (1987), 'Self-Selection and the Earnings of Immigrants', *American Economic Review*, vol. 77, pp. 531-553.

Borjas, G.J. (1990), *Friends or Strangers: The Impact of Immigrants on the U.S. Economy*. Basic Books: New York.

Bowles, S. (1970), 'Migration as Investment: Empirical Tests of the Human Investment Approach to Geographical Mobility', The *Review of Economics and Statistics*, vol. 52, pp. 356–62.

Brosnan, P. and Poot, J. (1987), 'Modelling the Determinants of Trans-Tasman Migration after World War II', *The Economic Record*, vol. 63, pp. 313–29.

Burda, M.C. (1993), 'The Determinants of East-West German Migration', *European Economic Review*, vol. 37, pp. 452–61.

Burda, M.C. (1995), 'Migration and the Option Value of Waiting', *Economic and Social review*, vol. 27, pp. 1–19.

Calvo, G.A. (1978), 'Urban Unemployment and Wage Determination in LDC's: Trade Unions in the Harris-Todaro Model', *International Economic Review,* vol. 19, pp. 65–81.

Chiswick, B.R. (1978), 'The Effect of Americanization on the Earnings of Foreign - Born Men', *Journal of Political Economy*, vol. 86, pp. 897–921.

Chiswick, B.R. (1980), 'The Earnings of White and Coloured Male Immigrants in Britain', *Economica*, vol. 47, no. 1, pp. 81–7.

Cordon, W.M. and Findlay, R. (1975), 'Urban Unemployment, Intersectoral Capital Mobility and Development Policy', *Economica*, vol. 42, pp. 59–78.

DaVanzo, J. (1978), 'Does Unemployment Affect Migration? – Evidence from Micro Data', *The Review of Economics and Statistics*, vol. 60, pp. 504–14.

DaVanzo, J. (1983), 'Repeat Migration in the United States: Who Moves Back and Who Moves On?', *The Review of Economics and Statistics*, vol. 65, pp. 552–59.

De New, J.P. and Zimmermann, K.F. (1994a), 'Blue Collar Labor Vulnerability: Wage Impacts of Migration', in Steinmann, G. and R. Ulrich (eds), *Economic Consequences of Immigration to Germany*. Heidelberg, Physica-Verlag, pp. 81–99.

De New, J.P. and Zimmermann, K.F. (1994b), 'Native Wage Impacts of Foreign Labor: A Random Effects Panel Analysis', *Journal of Population Economics*, vol. 7, no. 2, pp. 177–92.

Djajic, S. and Milbourne, R. (1988), 'A General Equilibrium Model of Guest-Worker Migration', *Journal of International Economics*, vol. 25, pp. 335–51.

122

Dixit, A.K. and Pindyck, R.S. (1994), *Investment under Uncertainty*, Princeton University Press, Princeton.

Dustmann, C. (1993), 'Earnings Adjustment of Temporary Migrants', *Journal of Population Economics,* vol. 6, no. 2, pp. 153–86.

Dustmann, C. (1994), 'Returns Intentions of Migrants: Theory and Evidence', CEPR Discussion Paper No: 906, London.

Dustmann, C. (1996), 'Return Migration: The European Experience', *Economic Policy*, vol. 22, pp. 215–49.

Eriksson, T. (1989), 'International Migration and Regional Differentials in Unemployment and Wages: Some Empirical Evidence from Finland', in Gordon, I. and A.P. Thirlwall (eds), *European Factor Mobility*, St. Martin's Press, New York pp. 59–73.

Faini, R. and Venturini, A. (1994), 'Migration and Growth: The Experience of Southern Europe', CEPR Discussion Paper No. 964, London.

Fields, G.S. (1975), 'Rural-Urban Migration, Urban Unemployment and Underemployment, and Job Search Activity in LDC's', *Journal of Development Economics*, vol. 2, no. 2, pp. 165–88.

Fields, G.S. (1991), 'Place-To-Place Migration: Some New Evidence', *The Review of Economics and Statistics*, vol 61, pp. 21–32.

Geary, P. and Ó Gráda, C. (1989), 'Post-war Migration between Ireland and the United Kingdom: Models and Estimates', in Gordon, I. and A.P. Thirlwall (eds), *European Factor Mobility*, St. Martin's Press, New York, pp. 53–8.

Goss, P. and Schoening, N.C. (1984), 'Search Time, Unemployment, and the Migration Decision', *The Journal of Human Recources*, vol. 19, no. 4, pp. 570–79.

Goss, P. and Paul, C. (1986), 'Age and Work Experience in the Decision to Migrate', *Journal of Human Resources*, vol. 11, no. 3, pp. 397–405.

Granier, R. and Marciano, J.P. (1975), 'The Earnings of Immigrant Workers in France', *International Labour Review*, vol. 111, no. 2, pp. 143–65.

Grant, E.K. and Vanderkamp, J. (1985), 'Migrant Information and the Remigration Decision: Further Evidence', *Southern Economic Journal*, vol. 51, pp. 1202–215.

Graves, P.E. (1979), 'A Life-Cycle Empirical Analysis of Migration and Climate by Race', *Journal of Urban Economics*, vol. 6, pp. 135–47.

Greene, W.H. (1993), *Econometric Analysis*, Macmillan, New York.

Greenwood, M.J. (1970), 'Lagged Response in the Decision to Migrate', *Journal of Regional Science*, vol. 10, no. 3, pp. 375–84.

Greenwood, M.J. (1975), 'Research on Internal Migration in the United States: A Survey', *Journal of Economic Literature*, vol. 13, pp. 397–433.

Greenwood, M.J. (1981), *Migration and Economic Growth in the United States*, Academic Press, New York.

Greenwood, M.J. (1985), 'Human Migration: Theory, Models, and Empirical Studies', *Journal of Regional Science*, vol. 25, no. 4, pp. 521–44.

Greenwood, M.J. and McDowell, J.M. (1986), 'The Factor Market Consequences of U.S. Immigration', *Journal of Economic Literature*, vol. 24, no. 4, pp. 1738–772.

Greenwood, M.J. and Sweetland, D. (1972), 'The Determinants of Migration between Standard Metropolitan Statistical Areas', *Demography*, vol. 9, pp. 665–81.

Gurak, D.T., and Caces, F. (1992), 'Migration Networks and the Shaping of Migration Systems', in Kritz, M. Lim, L.L. and H. Zlotnik (eds), *International Migration Systems: A Global Approach.*, Clarendon Press, Oxford, pp. 150–76.

Harris, J. and Todaro, M.P. (1970), 'Migration, Unemployment, and Development: A Two-Sector Analysis', *American Economic Review*, vol. 60, no. 1, pp. 126–42.

Hartog, J. and Vriend, N. (1989), 'Post-War International Labour Mobility: The Netherlands', in Gordon, I. and A.P. Thirlwall (eds), *European Factor Mobility*, St. Martin's Press, New York, pp. 74–94.

Hartog, J. and Vriend, N. (1990), 'Young Mediterraneans in the Dutch Labour Market: A Comparative Analysis of Allocation and Earnings', *Oxford Economic Papers*, vol. 42, no. 2, pp. 379–401.

Herzog, H.W. and Schlottmann, A.M. (1984), 'Labor Force Mobility in the United States: Migration, Unemployment, and Remigration', *International Regional Science Review*, vol. 9, no. 1, pp. 43–8.

Herzog, H.W., Hofler, R.A. and Schlottmann, A.M. (1985), 'Life on the Frontier: Migrant Information, Earnings and Past Mobility', *The Review of Economics and Statistics*, vol. 67, pp. 373–82.

Hicks, J. (1932), *The Theory of Wages*, Macmillan, London.

Hugo, G.J. (1981), 'Village-Community Ties, Village Norms, and Ethnic and Social Networks: A Review of Evidence from the Third World', in De Jong, G.D. and R.W. Gardner (eds), *Migration Decision Making: Multidisciplinary Approaches to Microlevel Studies in Developed and Developing Countries*, Pergamon Press, New York, pp. 186–225.

Hunt, J.C. (1992), 'The Impact of the 1962 Repatriates from Algeria on the French Labor Market', *Industrial and Labor Relations Review*, vol. 43, no. 3, pp. 556–72.

Hunt, J.C. and Kau, J.B. (1985), 'Migration and Wage Growth: A Human Capital Approach', *Southern Economic Journal*, vol. 51, pp. 697–710.

Katseli, L.T. and Glytsos, N.P. (1989), 'Theoretical and Empirical Determinants of International Labour Mobility: A Greek-German Perspective', in I. Gordon and A.P. Thirlwall (eds) *European Factor Mobility*, St. Martin's Press, New York, pp. 95–115.

Kau, J.B. and Sirmans, C.F. (1976/77), 'New, Repeat, and Return Migration: A Study of Migrant Types', *Southern Economic Journal*, vol. 43, pp. 1144–48.

Kee, P. (1993), 'Immigrant Wages in the Netherlands: The Valuation of Pre- and Postimmigration Human Capital', *De Economist*, vol. 141, no. 1, pp. 96–111.

Krugman, P. and Bhagwati, J. (1976), 'The Decision to Migrate: A Survey', in Baghwati, J.N. (ed.), *The Brain Drain and Taxation II: Theory and Empirical Analysis*, North-Holland, Amsterdam, pp. 31–51.

Levy, M.B. and Wadycki, W.J. (1973), 'The Influence of Family and Friends on Geographic Labor Mobility: An International Comparison', *The Review of Economics and Statistics*, vol. 55, pp. 19–203.

Lucas, R.E.B. (1985), 'Migration Amongst the Batswana', *The Economic Journal*, 95, pp. 358–82.

Lundborg, P. (1991a), 'Determinants of Migration in the Nordic Labor Market', *Scandinavian Journal of Economics*, vol. 93, no. 3, pp. 363–75.

Lundborg, P. (1991b), 'An Interpretation of the Effects of Age on Migration: Nordic Migrants' Choice of Settlement in Sweden', *Southern Economic Journal*, vol. 58, pp. 392–405.

Massey, D.S. (1990a), 'The Social and Economic Origins of Immigration', *Annals of the American Academy of Political and Social Sciences*, vol. 510, pp. 60–72.

Massey, D.S. (1990b), 'Social Structure, Household Strategies, and the Cummulative Causation of Migration', *Population Index*, vol. 56, pp. 1–26.

Massey, D.S. and España, F.G. (1987), 'The Social Process of International Migration', *Science*, vol. 237, pp. 733–38.

Massey, D.S., Arango, Hugo, J.G., Kouaouci, A., Pellegrino, A. and Taylor, J.E. (1993), 'Theories of International Migration: A Review and Appraisal', *Population and Development Review*, vol. 19, no. 3, pp. 431–66.

Mincer, J. (1978), 'Family Migration Decisions', *Journal of Political Economy*, vol. 86, pp. 749–73.

Molho, I. (1986), 'Theories of Migration: A Review', *Scottish Journal of Political Economy*, vol. 33, no. 4, pp. 396–419.

Molho, I. (1987), 'The Migration Decision of Young Men in Great Britain', *Applied Economics*, 19, pp. 221–43.

Molle, W. and van Mourik, A. (1989), 'A Static Explanatory Model of International Labour Migration to and in Western Europe', in Gordon, I. and A.P. Thirlwall (eds), *European Factor Mobility*, St. Martin's Press, New York, pp. 30–52.

Mühleisen, M. and Zimmermann, K.F. (1994), 'A Panel Analysis of Job Changes and Unemployment', *European Economic Review*, vol. 38, no. 3/4, pp. 793–801.

Navratil, F.J. and Doyle, J.J. (1977), 'The Socioeconomic Determinants of Migration and the Level of Aggregation', *Southern Economic Journal*, vol. 43, pp. 1547–559.

Ó Gráda, C. (1986), 'Determinants of Irish Emigration: A Note', *International Migration Review*, vol. 20, no. 3, pp. 651–56.

Poot, J. (1995), 'Do Borders Matter? A Model of Interregional Migration in Australasia', *Australasian Journal of Regional Studies*, vol. 1, pp. 159–82.

Ravenstein, E. (1889), 'The Laws of Migration', *Journal of the Statistical Society*, vol. 52, pp. 214–301.

Root, B.D. and De Jong, G.F. (1991), 'Family Migration in a Developing Country', *Population Studies*, vol. 45, pp. 221–33.

Roy, A.D. (1951), 'Some Thoughts on the Distribution of Earnings', *Oxford Economic Papers*, vol. 3, pp. 135–46.

Schlottmann, A.W. and Herzog, H.W. Jr. (1981), 'Employment Status and The Decision to Migrate', *The Review of Economics and Statistics*, vol. 63, pp. 590–98.

Schmidt, C.M. (1992), 'The Earnings Dynamics of Immigrant Labor', Universität München Discussion Paper No. 92-28, Munich.

Schmidt, C.M. (1994), 'The Country of Origin, Family Structure and Return Migration of Germany's Guest-Workers', *Vierteljahreshefte zur Wirtschaftsforschung*, vol. 63, no. 1/2, pp. 119–25.

Schmidt, C.M., Stilz, A. and Zimmermann, K.F. (1994), 'Mass Migration, Unions and Government Interventions', *Journal of Public Economics*, vol. 55, pp. 18–201.

Schwartz, A. (1973), 'Interpreting the Effect of Distance on Migration', *Journal of Political Economy*, vol. 81, pp. 1153–169.

Schwartz, A. (1976), 'Migration, Age, and Education', *Journal of Political Economy*, vol. 84, no. 4, pp. 701–19.

Shields, G.M. and Shields, M.P. (1989), 'The Emergence of Migration Theory and a Suggested New Direction', *Journal of Economic Surveys*, vol. 3, no. 4, pp. 277–304.

Shields, M.P. and Shields, G.M. (1993), 'A Theoretical and Empirical Analysis of Family Migration and Household Production: U.S. 1980-1985', *Southern Economic Journal*, vol. 59, no. 4, pp. 768–82.

Simon, J.L. (1989), *The Economic Consequences of Immigration*, Basil Blackwell, Cambridge.

Sjaastad, L.A. (1962), 'The Costs and Returns of Human Migration', *The Journal of Political Ecomomy*, vol. 70, pp. 80–93.

Smith, A. (1776), *Inquiry into the Nature and Causes of the Wealth of Nations*, Strahan/Cadell, London.

Stark, O. (1991), *The Migration of Labor*, Basil Blackwell, Cambridge.

Stark, O. and Taylor, J.E. (1991), 'Migration Incentives, Migration Types: The Role of Relative Deprivation', *The Economic Journal*, vol. 101, pp. 1163–78.

Stiglitz, J.E. (1974), 'Alternative Theories of Wage Determination and Unemployment in LDC's: The Labor-Turnover Model', *Quarterly Journal of Economics*, vol. 88, pp. 194–227.

Straubhaar, T. (1988), *On the Economics of International Migration*, Verlag Paul Haupt, Bern and Stuttgart.

Straubhaar, T. and Zimmermann, K.F. (1993), 'Towards a European Migration Policy', *Population Research and Policy Review*, vol. 12, no. 3, pp. 225–41.

Taylor, J.E. (1986), 'Differential Migration, Networks, Information and Risk', *Research in Human Capital and Development: Migration, Human Capital and Development*, vol. 4, pp. 147–71.

Todaro, M.P. (1968), 'An Analysis of Industrialization, Employment and Unemployment in LDC's', *Yale Economic Essays*, vol. 8, no. 2, pp. 329–402.

Todaro, M.P. (1969), 'A Model of Labor Migration and Urban Unemployment in Less Developed Countries', *American Economic Review*, vol. 59, no. 1, pp. 138–48.

Todaro, M.P. (1980), 'Internal Migration in Developing Countries: A Survey', in R.A. Easterlin, R.A. (ed.), *Population and Economic Change in Developing Countries*. Chicago, NBER, pp. 361–402.

Waldorf, B.S. and Esparza, A. (1988), 'Labor Migration to Western Europe: A Commentary on O'Loughlin, 1986', *Environment and Planning A*, vol. 20, pp. 1121–24.

Winkelmann, R. and Zimmermann, K.F. (1993), 'Ageing, Migration and Labour Mobility', in P. Johnson and K.F. Zimmermann (eds), *Labour Markets in an Ageing Europe*. Cambridge, Cambridge University Press, pp. 255–83.

Zimmermann, K.F. (1993), 'Immigration Policy in Europe – An Overview', Siebert, H. (ed.), *Migration – A Challenge for Europe*, JBC Mohr (Paul Siebeck), Tübingen, pp. 227–58.

Zimmermann, K.F. (1994), 'European Migration: Push and Pull', *Proceedings of the World Bank Annual Conference on Development Economics 1994. Supplement to The World Bank Economic Review and the World Bank Research Observer*, pp. 313–42.

Zimmermann, K.F. (1995), 'Tackling the European Migration Problem', *Journal of Economic Perspectives*, vol. 9, pp. 45–62.

5 The Impact of Immigration on Labour Markets and Urban Infrastructure in Australia and New Zealand

JACQUES POOT

5.1 Introduction

This chapter surveys recent findings regarding the impact of immigration on labour markets and urban infrastructure in Australia and New Zealand. While some of the issues identified in the previous chapter re-emerge, the case of Australia and New Zealand deserves separate attention for several reasons. Firstly, unlike many other developed countries, the governments of Australia and New Zealand actively encourage immigration as a means of increasing population growth. Secondly, the proportion of the population born overseas is higher than in most other developed countries. Thirdly, the empirical findings on the impact of immigration in Australia and New Zealand have not permeated the international literature as much as those for North America and, more recently, Europe.

The chapter highlights differences and similarities between the findings for the two countries, also in relation to the experience of other high-income countries. The next section provides some brief background information on immigration levels and policies in Australia and New Zealand since the end of World War II. Section 5.3 addresses the issue of how migration affects labour market conditions. It is noted that the distinction between micro and macro level approaches, and between short-run and long-run impacts, is important. There appears to be little evidence of immigration affecting wage levels and unemployment rates at the macro level.

Section 5.4 considers changes in the migrants' position in the labour market over time. While analyses of migrant earnings show a process of generally successful adaptation, although not necessarily catch-up, there are clear differences between migrant groups - related to characteristics such as birthplace, ethnicity and occupation.

Section 5.5 focuses on the impact of immigration on spatial population distribution and urban conditions. With respect to the spatial impact, immigrants are disproportionately attracted to certain regions and to the largest cities. The Australian and New Zealand evidence suggests that their presence may lead to short run upward pressure on house prices and rents. Moreover, urban population growth due to immigration generates both positive and negative externalities. However, these are difficult to identify empirically. The final section points to gaps in the existing literature, particularly in the New Zealand case.

5.2   Immigration Policies and Immigration Levels

Immigration has played an important role in shaping the Australian and New Zealand societies of today. Both are relatively young nations with Australia having celebrated its bicentennial in 1988 and New Zealand its sesquicentennial in 1990, although European settlement was of course preceded by the much earlier settlement of the indigenous people.[1] Following 19th century colonialization and relatively low levels of immigration during the early 20th century, both countries embarked on government-sponsored recruitment of new immigrants after World War II. The Australian population grew from 8.2 million in 1950 to 18.0 million in 1995, which implies an average annual growth rate of 1.76 percent. The New Zealand population grew from 1.9 million in 1950 to 3.6 million in 1995, that is, at an average annual growth rate of 1.43 percent.

Immigration has played a greater role in this post-war population growth in Australia than in New Zealand. For example, over the period 1950-84, net immigration contributed 39 percent to total population growth in Australia, but only 15.9 percent in New Zealand (Poot 1986). Three factors are responsible for this difference. First, the immigration targets tended to be higher in Australia. Immigration policy in Australia was driven by the view that the continent could sustain a much larger population and that an underpopulated country was not only detrimental to economic development, but also to the security of the nation. In the New Zealand case, immigration was seen as a means to overcome labour shortages resulting from an import-substitution oriented industrial development and rapid population growth was not a goal. At least until the 1980s, the New Zealand approach to immigration may be interpreted as having some similarity to the policies of Western European countries at the time, particularly since also a guest-worker type of temporary recruitment of unskilled workers (particularly from the Pacific Islands) took place.

The second reason for the lower contribution of immigration to total population growth in New Zealand is that New Zealand had a higher rate of natural increase than Australia. Thirdly, New Zealand net migration has been greatly affected by the unrestricted movement of people between the two countries. Since 1967, this movement has tended to fluctuate strongly, but the net balance was mostly in the direction of Australia. Factors responsible include a higher average rate of economic growth in Australia – leading to higher real earnings and employment growth – and large cohorts of New Zealanders in the mobile age groups (Brosnan and Poot 1987). At the time of the census

130

in 1991, about 11.1 percent of the New Zealand population of Australasia (i.e. Australia and New Zealand together) lived in Australia, if the second generation is included (Poot 1995).

The outcome of the extensive Australian post war immigration program was that, in the mid 1990s, just under one in four of the Australian population is an immigrant, the majority from non-English speaking countries (McAllister 1995). Although the United States has been the recipient of a much larger absolute number of migrants, Australia's experience among Western countries is in relative terms only surpassed by Israel. In New Zealand, the foreign born account for about 16 percent of the population.

Although immigration selection in both countries was initially highly restrictive, and primarily aimed at recruitment of persons from the United Kingdom, there were simply not enough potential immigrants from that source to meet the demand, and recruitment was broadened to include, first, other Northern Europeans in the 1950s and later Southern Europeans in the 1960s. However, immigration from Southern Europe was much more important in Australia than in New Zealand. Instead, New Zealand experienced since the 1960s a growing influx from the Pacific Islands. Since the mid 1970s, migration from Asian countries started to become prominent in both countries but initially again more so in Australia.

In both countries, immigration policy has tended to be pro-cyclical. Political pressures tended to force the governments to reduce the intake during recessions, and relax the regulations during times of labour shortages. Ironically, research has shown that the opposite would have been a more prudent policy: immigration tended to generate an excess demand effect during booms (e.g. McGill 1981) which exacerbated rather than alleviated labour shortages.

Since the late 1980s, Australia and New Zealand have in common with the United States and Canada that immigration policy shifted towards accepting larger numbers (Rod and Williams 1996). However, New Zealand lagged somewhat behind the others. While a new policy, which broadened the criteria and removed a preference for persons from traditional source countries, was introduced in 1986, sharp increases in immigration have been recorded from 1993 until 1995 after the full implementation of the 1991 policy which targeted skilled persons and business immigrants by means of a points system.[2] The original target was to grant permanent residence to 25,000 persons per year, but in the 1993–95 period this target was greatly exceeded. Hence, at a time when immigration in Australia was much lower than in the late 1980s, immigration in New Zealand increased. During 1995, as many as 55,325 persons were approved for permanent residency in New Zealand.

The high level of residency approvals led to a political backlash which forced the New Zealand government to reconsider its immigration policy. Consequently, requirements were introduced in late 1995. These led to sharp declines in the 'general immigrant' and 'business investor' categories of applications. The level of immigration is therefore likely to have peaked during 1995.

Table 5.1 shows new settlement in the two countries, in terms of a rate per thousand of the population. It should be noted that the Australian figures refer to actual settler arrivals in years ending 30 June, while the New Zealand figures refer to persons approved for residency rather than actual arrivals.[3] Table 5.1 clearly shows that Australian immigration dropped sharply since 1992, at a time when New Zealand's intake increased. In peak years, new settler arrivals added close to 1 percent to the population growth rate in both countries, although trans-Tasman migration (the population movement between Australia and New Zealand across the Tasman Sea) has always been an offsetting factor in the New Zealand case. Trans-Tasman migration has led in some years, particularly in the late 1970s and 1980s, to a significant overall net migration loss there. Immigration has been on average at a higher level in Australia than in New Zealand until the 1990s, but the rapid growth in immigration in the latter country in recent years resulted in a somewhat higher average rate for the 1983–95 period, 6.27 versus 6.09 per thousand of the mid-point population respectively (see Table 5.1).

Table 5.1 Immigration to Australia and New Zealand, 1983–1995

Year Ending June	Australia[1]	New Zealand[2]
	Rate per 1000 of mid-point population	
1983	6.07	3.29
1984	4.49	2.57
1985	4.96	2.36
1986	5.79	2.89
1987	6.99	4.35
1988	8.71	5.92
1989	8.67	7.42
1990	7.13	6.39
1991	7.06	7.44
1992	6.15	6.42
1993	4.33	9.04
1994	3.92	9.36
1995	4.86	14.11
Average 1983–95	6.09	6.27

Notes:
1. All settler arrivals in Australia recorded from arrival card information.
2. All persons approved for residency in New Zealand (total of visas and permits) as recorded by the New Zealand Immigration Service.

Source: Rod and Williams (1996), Australian Bureau of Statistics, New Zealand Immigration Service, Statistics New Zealand.

Table 5.2   The composition of Australasian immigration

A. Birthplace of settler arrivals in Australia

	1989–90 Average Number per Year	Percentage	1991 Number	Percentage
UK & Ireland	25000	19.8	18900	16.2
New Zealand	13150	10.4	6700	5.7
Vietnam	11900	9.4	10700	9.2
Hong Kong	8950	7.1	14500	12.4
Philippines	6550	5.2	6500	5.5
Malaysia	6550	5.2	4400	3.8
India	3400	2.7	5800	5.0
China PRC	3350	2.7	3400	2.9
Taiwan	3000	2.4	3700	3.2
Fiji	2500	2.0	2500	2.1
South Africa	2450	1.9	1700	1.5
Lebanon	2450	1.9	2400	2.0
USA	2000	1.6	1700	1.5
Yugoslavia	2000	1.6	2300	2.0
Poland	1600	1.3	1800	1.5
Others	31500	24.9	29600	25.4
Total	126350	100.00	116600	100.00

Note: Based on arrival card information. New Zealanders wishing to settle permanently are included.

Source: Year Book Australia 1994.

Table 5.2 continued
B. Source country of persons approved (visas and permit) by the
    New Zealand Immigration Service

	1988–92 Average Number per Year	Percentage	1993 Number (June)	Percentage
Great Britain	3784	15.7	3766	13.9
Hong Kong	3097	12.9	2780	10.3
Fiji	2092	8.7	857	3.2
Western Samoa	2002	8.3	1471	5.4
Malaysia	1812	7.5	1116	4.1
Taiwan	1806	7.5	2666	9.8
China PRC	1205	5.0	1985	7.3
Tonga	1037	4.3	1356	5.0
Philippines	700	2.9	539	2.0
India	650	2.7	1031	3.8
USA	588	2.4	609	2.3
Korea Rep of	579	2.4	3085	11.4
Netherlands	552	2.3	551	2.0
South Africa	319	1.3	960	3.5
Sri Lanka	270	1.1	484	1.8
Others	33594	14.9	3843	14.2
Total	24087	100.00	27099	100.00

Note: Australian residents are not included as they have unrestricted entry to
New Zealand
* Excluding a remainder of persons approved under the pre-1991 policy
regulations
Source: Quirk (1994).

Table 5.2 continued
C: Composition of the intake by category

AUSTRALIA		NEW ZEALAND	
Year ending June 1993		1994	
Family	48.2	Family	15.5
Skill		General	68.6
	18.3	Business	3.3
Humanitarian	16.3	Humanitarian	1.4
Other viased	1.0	Refugees	2.0
Non-viased	16.2	Other	9.2
Total	100.0	Total	100.0

Source: Rod and Williams (1996).

In addition to differences in the level of the intake, there are also differences between Australia and New Zealand in the composition of immigration. Table 5.2 shows immigration by country of birth and by immigration approval category. Immigration to Australia is spread over a wider range of source countries. Family migration is considerably more important in Australia. In New Zealand, family migration tended to take a large share under previous policies, but under the new policy the vast majority of immigrants are skilled workers and entrepreneurs. It can be noted from Table 5.2 that New Zealanders are the second largest immigrant group in Australia. The Australian born are not included in the New Zealand statistics, which refer to residency approvals rather than arrivals. However, the trans-Tasman movement in both directions is dominated by New Zealanders and many Australian born emigrants to New Zealand are in fact dependents of New Zealanders returning (Carmichael 1993). It can also be noted from Table 5.2 that both countries have in common that the single largest source country remains the United Kingdom although the flows from this source have become much less important in percentage terms when compared with previous decades. Moreover, as noted earlier, migration from Asian sources has been growing rapidly in both countries, accounting now for about half of total immigration.

Being island nations, illegal entry has not been a problem, except for the arrival of some so-called 'boat people' on Australia's northern shores.[4] The number of visa overstayers has been a bigger issue in both countries, although relative to population size the problem is far less significant than in the USA.

It is not surprising that much more research on the impact of immigration on society has been carried out in Australia than in New Zealand. Immigration contributed more to post World War II population growth in the former country than in the latter. Moreover, Australia – being the country with the much larger population and economy – has had more funds available for carrying out immigration related research. This has been particularly so since the government of

135

Australia established an agency formally commissioned to carry out and sponsor research on all aspects of international migration in 1989.[5] In New Zealand, no such agency has existed and much of the literature consists of subjective accounts without formal empirical analysis. However, some substantive work has been carried out. An extensive review of the economic impact of immigration, with emphasis on Australian and New Zealand literature, can be found in Chapple et al. (1994).

Given that there are many aspects of the economics of immigration of interest for research and policy formulation, this short paper does not aim to give a complete overview.[6] Instead, the objective will be to summarize the Australian and New Zealand research findings in two areas, namely the labour market and urban infrastructure. Both areas feature strongly in the debates about the desirability of current policy, with critics of the immigration policies pointing to the perceived detrimental effect of immigration on employment conditions of natives (wages and the likelihood of unemployment) and to a detrimental impact on urban areas due to greater congestion, social unrest and lower housing affordability due to sharply rising prices.

5.3   The Impact of Immigrants on the Host Labour Market

When considering the impact of immigration on the labour market, it is useful to make a distinction between micro-level and macro level studies. As Foster and Withers (1992) noted, Australian research has – at least until recent years - tended to focus on the macro level. The same is true in New Zealand. Of particular interest has been the relationship between migration and aggregates such as GDP, investment, balance of payments, real wages and unemployment. In contrast, studies in the United States have tended to focus on the micro level: migrants in specific regions, occupations and industries. Such studies have tended to investigate the behaviour of migrants, the degree of substitution between migrants and natives and the assimilation of migrants in the host labour market.

The reasons for the interest in macro aspects in Australasia are straightforward. Immigration had a significant impact on national population growth in both countries so that its impact on macro aggregates is naturally of interest. However, another reason is a lack of rich micro-level data sets, so that researchers had primarily only aggregate statistics available for empirical work.

Another fruitful distinction is that between short run analyses, where the focus is on the immediate impact of immigration on conditions in the host country and the experiences of immigrants themselves, and long-run analyses in which both markets and migrants themselves had the time to adjust to the new circumstances and in which the path of the economy may have changed. Combining the micro/macro distinction with the short-run/long-run distinction leads to a two by two matrix.

136

Table 5.3 provides examples of Australian and New Zealand research of the last decade which contributed new empirical findings to the stock of knowledge on the economics of immigration.

Table 5.3 A selection from the Australian and New Zealand empirical literature of the last decade on the economic impact of immigration

	SHORT RUN	LONG RUN
MICRO	*Housing* A: Burnley and Murphy (1994) *Infrastructure* A: Murphy et al. (1990) *Education and Training* A: Baker and Wooden (1992) *Social Security* A: Whiteford (1991) *Initial Location* A: Tonkin (1993) *Business Immigration* NZ: Trlin and Kang (1992)	*Public & Private Sectoral Reallocation* A: Norman and Meikle (1985) NZ: Poot et al. (1988) *Migration Adaptation* A: Beggs and Chapman (1988,1990) NZ: Poot (1993b) *Migration Occupational Mobility* A: McAllister (1995) *Externalities* A: Baker and Wooden (1992)
MACRO	*Aggregate Demand* NZ: McGill (1981) *Unemployment* A: Withers and Pope (1985) *Inflation* A: Junankar and Pope (1990) *Aggregate Wages* A: Withers (1987) *Migrant Experience over the Business Cycle* A: Brooks and Williams (1995) *Total Factor Productivity* NZ: Poot (1993a)	*Technological Change and Economies of Scale* A: Norman and Meikle (1985) NZ: Poot et al. (1988) *Balance of Payments* A: Junankar et al. (1993) *Native's Income per Head* A: Peter (1993) *Income Distribution* A: Saunders and King (1994) *Growth* A: Gruen (1986) NZ: Easton (1991)

Note: 'A' and 'NZ' refer to empirical research carried out with Australian and New Zealand data respectively.

Source: Modified and updated from Chapple et al. (1994).

Table 5.3 shows that a wide range of economic aspects of immigration has been researched in both countries. However, the range of issues addressed in Australia is much greater and the research activity has been much more dispersed among the research community. The availability of a significant amount of public funding, particularly since the establishment of the Australian Bureau of Immigration Research in 1989 has been an important contributing factor. However, although this cannot be seen from Table 5.3, it should be again noted that the volume of papers on macro issues is in both countries much greater than those on micro issues.

The discussion of the impact of immigration on the labour market is therefore started with macroeconometric research findings. The central question in this context is whether immigration in Australia and New Zealand has affected the rate of unemployment and the real wage in the economy. Since immigrants affect both the demand for labour (due to their own demand for domestic goods and services) and the supply of labour (by their own labour force participation), the effect on labour market equilibrium cannot be established a priori. A popular way in Australasia to address this issue has been the use of a-theoretic Granger causality tests. It is said that if in a bivariate time-series model of x and y, y can be better predicted using past values of x than by not doing so, x is said to Granger cause y (for a survey of the scope and limitations of this approach, see e.g. Bishop 1979). Note that it is statistically possible for both x to cause y and y to cause x, in which case there is said to be feedback.

The seminal work on testing for causality between unemployment and immigration was done by Withers and Pope (1985) for Australia and was partially replicated for New Zealand by Poot (1986). For illustration, consider the following two regression equations:

$$\Delta(U/LF)_t = \alpha_0 + \alpha_1 T + \beta_1 \Delta(U/LF)_{t-1} + \beta_2 \Delta(U/LF)_{t-2} + \beta_3 \Delta(U/LF)_{t-3}$$
$$+ \gamma_0(M/P)_t + \gamma_1(M/P)_{t-1} + \gamma_2(M/P)_{t-2} + \gamma_3(M/P)_{t-3}$$

and

$$(M/P)_t = \delta_0 + \delta_1 T + \varepsilon_1(M/P)_{t-1} + \varepsilon_2(M/P)_{t-2} + \varepsilon_3(M/P)_{t-3}$$
$$+ \phi_0\Delta(U/LF)_t + \phi_1 U(Y/LF)_{t-1} + \phi_2\Delta(U/LF)_{t-2} + \phi_3\Delta(U/LF)_{t-3}$$

where Δ = change operator, U = registered unemployment, LF = estimated fulltime labour force, T = deterministic linear time trend, M = net permanent and long-term migration, and P = population.[7]

The first equation permits a test of the hypothesis that the aggregate rate of unemployment has been affected by an immigration effect (measured by net permanent and long-term migration as a proportion of population size). If the estimates of γ_1, γ_2 and γ_3 are statistically insignificant, immigration does not 'Granger cause' the unemployment rate.[8] The second equation can be used to test a hypothesis about the behaviour of migrants, namely whether they are themselves responsive to changes in the rate of unemployment. Alternative specifications for causality testing are possible, for example equations which include future rather than past values on the right hand side (with the associated tests referred to as future F-tests) (see e.g. Greenberg and Webster 1983 for details).

Estimates of equations such as those presented above suggested that the immigration rate did not Granger cause the unemployment rate (or, alternatively, a ratio of unemployment to vacancies). However, unemployment did Granger cause immigration. It is particularly interesting that this pattern of conclusions was repeated in other Granger causality analyses. Withers (1987) carried out a Granger-causality test of the relation between immigration and the real wage in Australia. Junankar and Pope (1990) studied the links between immigration and inflation in Australia and a New Zealand analysis of Granger causality between total factor productivity growth and immigration can be found in Poot (1993a).

In all cases, the general conclusion is that immigration has no strong short-run influence on the macroeconomic variables. In contrast, immigration itself is highly endogenous and tends to be Granger caused by macroeconomic conditions. The first reason for this causality from the macroeconomy to immigration is that, as the human capital model of migration would suggest, the pool of applicants will vary with signals regarding the economic returns to migration and published macroeconomic statistics are a source of such signals. Secondly, the immigration targets set by government are themselves endogenous as the policy response has been to reduce the intake during recessions. Finally, an important factor in the Australasian case is the free movement of Australians and New Zealanders, who are a part of the observed international migration flows and who have been shown to be highly responsive to relative economic conditions (e.g. Brosnan and Poot 1987).

It should be noted that the 'black-box' causality tests have certain weaknesses. Firstly, the relationship may have been unstable over the sample period. Secondly, relevant variables may have been omitted from what is essentially a vector autoregression (VAR) model. Thirdly, spurious correlations may be the result of the shortness of the available time series.

To overcome these deficiencies, the Australian studies have also estimated several structural models. For example, Withers and Pope (1985) estimated an unemployment equation which incorporated variables explaining the frictional, structural and cyclical components of unemployment. Independent variables included real wages (in levels and rate of change form), capacity utilization, real unemployment benefits, demand dispersion and various measures of migration rates. Given that the migration measures had negative signs, this analysis suggested that immigration may in fact reduce unemployment slightly. Thus, the general conclusion is that 'migrants have created at least as many jobs as they have occupied' (Withers and Pope 1985, p. 562). While this conclusion appears robust across studies, Chapple et al. (1994) noted that the structural unemployment equation is likely to have been misspecified. An alternative approach would be to estimate a reduced-form labour market model such as proposed by Layard and Nickell (1986). Such a model would include a set of wage push variables, such as the wedge between consumer and product wages, the benefit replacement rate, and measures of union power, immigration rates and price surprises.

Because immigration increases the size of the labour force (due to the labour force participation of the immigrants themselves)[9] and empirical research suggests that immigration does not affect the rate of unemployment, it follows that the number of unemployed does increase with a wave of immigration. Whether there will be a net inflow of native workers to the stock of unemployed depends on the unemployment rates of migrants versus natives. Because migrants do tend to have a higher propensity to be unemployed upon arrival than comparable native workers and immigration leaves the aggregate unemployment rate unaffected, it follows logically that immigration does reduce the unemployment rate of natives.

This macro analysis, however, ignores the possible segmentation of the labour market. Moreover, migrants are not a homogeneous group but represent a wide range of occupations, skills and experiences. Migrants with relatively low reservation wages may be substitutes for native workers in certain segments of the labour markets and increase the unemployment rate of the latter, or reduce the wage level.

For a better understanding of the impact of immigration on the labour market, the macro level analyses in Australasia have been supplemented by extensive sectoral studies. Both countries have a tradition of carrying out such sectoral studies by means of a Computable General Equilibrium (CGE) model. The CGE models developed in Australia and New Zealand are similar in nature and have their roots in the work of Johansen (1960). The models are designed to carry out a long-run comparative static analysis with all variables expressed in percentage changes relative to pre-shock levels. Hence the models do not generate forecasts of the variables of interest, but show instead how endogenous variables would change relative to what they would be otherwise after markets have had time to adjust to an exogenous shock. In the case of studies of the impact of immigration policy, the shock was of course a change in the level and composition of immigration. Sensitivity analyses, both in terms of varying the assumed immigration scenarios and varying the wide range of model parameters, are an important part of CGE modelling. Extensive CGE analyses of the economic effects of immigration in Australia can be found in Norman and Meikle (1985) and CAAIP (1988). Both reports present results derived with the popular Orani model. In New Zealand, the CGE model used for immigration policy simulation is called Joanna and the sectoral consequences of various immigration scenarios are discussed in detail in Poot et al. (1988). The latter book also provides a comparison of the Australian and New Zealand results.

Orani and Joanna differ primarily in sectoral disaggregation, 112 versus 22 sectors respectively, and in assumptions about the capital stock and investment. The time horizon considered in CGE immigration studies tends to be fairly long, namely 15 years. The strength of the CGE model approach is that a considerable amount of detail is generated ranging from national account statistics to the composition of exports, output and employment by industry and employment by occupation.

However, this type of approach has two weaknesses. First, as the authors of the above reports acknowledge, the macro results are primarily driven by assumptions fed into the CGE models regarding technology and overall resource endowment (capital, labour). Thus, to have confidence in the macro results of the CGE models these must have been verified by independent analysis. In the case of New Zealand, this independent verification consisted of research into economies of scale at the sectoral level and an analysis of the Denison-residual in growth accounting at the macro level (Poot et al. 1988, Chapter 5.4).[10] Subsequently, the assumptions of the original scenarios were reinforced by the positive, albeit weak, causal relationship between immigration levels and total factor productivity growth found in Poot (1993a).

An additional weakness is that Orani and Joanna are not dynamic models. They generate estimates of long run general equilibrium effects and neither consumers nor producers exhibit explicit forward looking behaviour. Moreover, the models do not permit the possibility of a path dependency in the way in which economies adjust to short-run disequilibria. Both in Australia and New Zealand, new CGE models have been developed which are truly dynamic and incorporate forward looking behaviour of consumers and producers (Malakellis 1993; Nana 1995). Such models face considerable technical difficulties at present, but it may be possible in due course to carry out a dynamic CGE analysis of the economic consequences of immigration.

In a critique of CGE modelling, Peter (1993) also pointed to the need to explicitly distinguish between natives and immigrants in studying the outcomes. In particular, the impact on the distribution of income between these groups is of interest. While employment of an immigrant worker will lead to a higher income for this worker, for the owners of capital and for native workers who are complements in production to immigrant workers, native workers who are substitutes for immigrants may find that their wages decrease unless there are significant positive externalities. Thus, the absence of adverse effects on the income distribution in the Orani and Joanna simulations are due to the assumed productivity improvements (economies of scale and a Verdoorn-type increase in the rate of technical change) which filter through to all occupations, while occupational wage relativities are assumed fixed (Poot et al. 1988, p.124).

While the Australian and New Zealand CGE analyses generate similar results at the macro level, at the sectoral level there are important differences due to differences in natural resource endowments, the sectoral composition, the inter-industry relations, international trade, the composition of domestic demand and the composition of international migration flows. Detailed comparisons have been made of a New Zealand scenario, in which the assumed level of net immigration was 15,000 persons per year between 1985 and 2001 rather than a 'control' level of zero net migration, with an Australian scenario of net immigration of 100,000 persons per year between 1981 and 2001 rather than a control level of 50,000 persons (Poot et al. 1988, pp. 122–30).

In Australia, such immigration generates considerable growth in the mining and basic metals industries and the resources drawn to these sectors limit the growth of sectors such as agriculture and the food, beverages and tobacco industry. The same sectors are also declining relatively in New Zealand, but a general sectoral expansion is more evenly spread in that country. In both countries there is a relative reallocation of resources from the public to the private sector, but more so in New Zealand. Industries which particularly benefit from immigration in New Zealand are forestry and logging, wood and related products, paper products, non-metallics (glass, cement etc.), basic metals and fabricated metals. In addition to export-led growth (following improvements in international competitiveness), a sharp increase in housing investment and housing consumption also drives these results.

The results show that plausible levels of immigration (based on historical experience) generate rather benign labour market outcomes even in the absence of positive externalities. For example, in the New Zealand case, the increase in immigration of the magnitude specified above, would lead without positive externalities to an increase in the unemployment rate of less than 0.17 percentage points if the aggregate real wage remained unaffected, while the increase in labour supply could alternatively be fully absorbed by a decrease in the real wage of no more than 0.3 percent. However, there are marked differences between the two countries in outcomes for occupation-specific labour markets. Immigration benefits particularly professional employment in Australia, but not in New Zealand. With respect to other white collar employment, skilled and unskilled, the opposite in true. Blue collar employment grows disproportionately with immigration, but more so in Australia. Finally, both countries have in common an increase in the demand for building-related trades and a relative fall in the demand for rural workers.

Despite the wealth of sectoral details, CGE analyses of immigration are still too aggregate to take into account the differences in productivity between immigrant workers of specific human capital characteristics and comparable natives. Nor can the effect on productivity of post-

142

immigration skill acquisition be taken into account. These issues have been addressed in Australasia by means of micro-level studies of migrant adaptation and labour mobility, to which we now turn in the next section.

5.4 Migrant Adaptation

Research on labour market adaptation is confronted with numerous methodological issues. First, such research is ideally based on longitudinal data, yet cross-section data have been far more readily available in Australasia and elsewhere.

Cross-section data tend to show evidence of a successful adaptation through revealing steeper experience-earnings profiles for migrants than for native-born workers. A well known example is Chiswick's (1978a) study, which showed that – based on 1970 US Census data – US immigrants entered the labour market with 15 percent lower earnings than the native born, but their earnings grew at a more rapid rate, overtaking natives in fourteen years.

However, as put forcefully by Borjas (1989), the cross-section earnings profile of a mix of recent and more established migrant groups may not reflect the actual life cycle experience of any of these groups. The reason is that the composition of the annual migrant intake is affected by changes in immigration policies and by changes in the conditions in source and host countries. Although cross-sections observed repeatedly allow us to follow a cohort over time, problems remain because return and repeated migration affect the cohorts non-randomly. Moreover, the process of adaptation is affected by the business cycle and by structural changes in the labour market. Thus, when a recent cohort of immigrants takes longer to successfully integrate into the host labour market, this may be due to factors influencing labour demand rather than due to qualitative changes in the immigrant intake. For example, Brooks and Williams (1995) recently studied the variations over the business cycle in labour force participation and unemployment among immigrant groups in Australia. They found that migrants from non-MES (Main English Speaking) countries were most affected by recessions.

It should also be noted that after controlling for all measurable factors influencing differences in productivity between natives and migrants, there may still be a residual gap in observed earnings. This gap is often related to ethnicity as a structural factor in determining earnings and can have its causes both on the demand side (discrimination) and on the supply side (differences in preferences).

Another problem is the lack of micro level data in Australia and New Zealand. In the latter country, census data were not accessible until recently at the unit record level out of a concern for confidentiality of the information provided by individuals. Micro analyses could therefore be based only on multi-way cross tabulations and resulting group averages. There are few surveys and the sample sizes used for the

143

official nationwide household surveys (e.g. the Household Expenditure and Income Survey and the Household Labour Force Survey) are too small to allow a detailed study of migrants.

In Australia, micro level data availability is better. Occasionally, samples of census unit records were made available for micro level analysis. Moreover, some important surveys have been conducted. One is the Multicultural Australia Survey, which was carried out in two waves (1988 and 1989), but individuals were interviewed once and no panel data were generated. Another survey is the September 1993 ABS survey of Labour Force and Other Characteristics of Migrants.

A very promising development is the commencement of the Longitudinal Survey of Immigrants to Australia (LSIA), of which the first wave was carried out in 1993–94. Some preliminary results concerning the use of social networks show that kinship networks and friendship networks were extremely important in providing assistance to recently arrived immigrants (Shu 1995). Which network was used, the nature of assistance provided, and the degree of reliance on networks were dependent on migrant characteristics such as birthplace and immigration category.

Another problem in migrant adaptation studies is that if the analysis is based on birthplace, a distinction must be made between those who migrate as adults and those who migrate as children. Kossoudji (1989) found evidence in the United States that pre-labour market experience in schools etc. is often the factor responsible for observed labour market assimilation, rather than human capital investments of workers who migrated as adults.

A final point to note is that adaptation research often does not link pre- and post-migration experience. Yet the impact of migration on, for example, occupational mobility is an interesting aspect of the experience of migrants. Chiswick (1978b) showed by means of US census data based on a question on 'occupation five years ago' that migration often involves the acceptance of a job in an occupation with lower status, seniority and earnings than before the move and that subsequent upward mobility is associated with length of stay in the adopted country.

Recent research in Australia reconfirmed this finding. McAllister (1995) used the Multicultural Australia Survey to link the occupation of a migrant's father, the migrant's occupation prior to migration, the first occupation in Australia and the current occupation. He detected a sharp drop in a quantitative measure of occupational status following migration. This sharp drop applied to both migrants from English speaking backgrounds and to those from non-English speaking backgrounds. The explanations put forward are similar to those in other adaptation research, namely: problems in the transferability of skills to jobs in the host country, the impact of cultural differences and discrimination on the level of the initial job, and lower productivity due to claims on time and resources associated with the act of settlement itself.

144

There are also several Australian studies, and one New Zealand study, on earnings catch-up of immigrants. For example, Beggs and Chapman (1988) find that there is no evidence for earnings catch-up between 1973 and 1981 in Australia of migrants from non-English speaking countries and only very slow catch-up for English speaking immigrants. In addition, their results provide indirect evidence that there had been an improvement in the unobserved dimensions of ability of non-English speaking migrants to Australia over this period.

Unobserved ability can be inferred from the residuals of regression equations explaining migrants' earnings. An important point in this context is that the comparison of earnings of immigrants and natives by means of estimating earnings functions is affected by the extent to which migrants are self-selected. Borjas (1989, 1994) shows that such self-selection depends on the difference in the rate of return to human capital between the source and the host country and the difference in the variance of the income distributions. The incidence and nature of self-selection also depends on the correlation between the income distribution in the source and host countries. Migrants are negatively self-selected when human capital investments get a higher return in the source country than in the host country. They are also negatively self-selected when immigrants would take similar relative positions in the income distribution of the source country and of the host country, while the former distribution has a greater variance. Borjas (1994) argues that all these conditions are satisfied to explain a negative self-selection of migrants from Mexico to the United States.

These ideas have been applied to an analysis of the composition of migration between Australia and New Zealand in Poot (1993a). It was found that the rate of return to investments in post-compulsory education were higher in Australia than in New Zealand, while the income distribution in the former country also had a greater standard deviation. Moreover, given that the countries had qualitatively similar labour markets, it was assumed that the earnings of an individual migrant in the host country would be highly correlated with the earnings of similar workers in the source country. Consequently, there appears to have been some positive self-selection among migrants from New Zealand to Australia.

How is catch-up detected? Beggs and Chapman (1988) explain the logarithm of earnings of natives (WN) and immigrants (WI) – by means of a regression analysis – in terms of years of schooling (YOS), years in the labour force (YLF) and immigrants' years in the host country (YCM). The following earnings functions emerge:

$$WN = a_0 + a_1 \, YOS + a_2 \, YLF$$

$$WI = b_0 + b_1 \, YOS + b_2 \, YLF + b_3 \, YCM$$

Immigrant wages are said to catch up when WI<WN for YCM=0 and b2+b3>a2. The problem with this approach is that when observed immigrant ability varies across cohorts, estimates of b3 using cross-sectional data are biased. Beggs and Chapman (1988) solve this problem by estimating cross-sectional earnings equations for two successive censuses. If the wage catch-up predicted from the first cross-section regression exceeds that observed by comparing the wage growth of the cohort during the time between the first and second census, this indicates that earlier immigrants had greater unobserved ability than more recent immigrants and vice versa.

Using group averages in earnings rather than a regression equation, similar work was carried out in New Zealand by Poot (1993b). Data were obtained from the 1981 and 1986 census to compute earnings of migrants by birthplace (Australia, UK and Pacific Islands), by the three occupational groups to which New Zealand migrants are most likely to belong (professional white-collar, semi- and unskilled white collar, and blue collar workers) and by years lived in New Zealand. Comparisons were then made with the earnings of comparable New Zealand-born persons.

The results in Poot (1993b) show that the adaptation effect is very strong for the Pacific Island born immigrants, but the cross-section evidence suggested that catching up could take an entire working life. Moreover, additional work with cohort data showed that the earnings catch-up as suggested by the 1986 cross-section 'earnings by experience profile' was quicker than was actually the case for recent cohorts of immigrants. Although the Pacific Island immigrants in the early 1980s may have had lower qualifications and abilities than their predecessors, a more likely reason for the slower earnings convergence can be found on the demand side of the labour market: a decline in the number of job opportunities in blue collar employment in manufacturing, which was the traditional labour market segment for these workers.

It was also found that the cohort-based income gradient was steeper for Australian and United Kingdom-born migrants than for comparable New Zealand-born workers, whereas this could not be detected in the cross-sectional data. This suggested that the average level of abilities of English speaking immigrants increased over time, which is plausible given rising vacancies for skilled workers in the early 1980s and the gradually more responsive immigration policy.

In summary, despite the absence of a full catch-up of earnings, immigrants have been successfully absorbed in the labour markets of Australia and New Zealand. Before the late 1970s this was due to a set of economic conditions which generated economies with high levels of vacancies and low unemployment rates overall. Since unemployment rates increased, immigration policies were initially tightened and when they were again subsequently relaxed, the policies targeted higher skilled workers. The average skill level of immigrants coming to Australia and New Zealand since the early 1980s has increased and this has, in addition to the demand effect discussed in the previous section, also cushioned the impact on the labour market.

5.5   Immigration and Urban Infrastructure

Information about the geographic distribution of immigrants in Australia and New Zealand is readily available from the population census, which in both countries is conducted every five years. Thus, it is not surprising that there have been many descriptive studies of the settlement patterns and the subsequent mobility of the overseas born. Such studies show that immigrants are disproportionately attracted to the largest cities, that is, Sydney, Melbourne and Brisbane on the East Coast of Australia, Perth on the West Coast, and Auckland in New Zealand (e.g. Bell and Cooper 1995, Zodgekar 1986). Murphy (1995) notes that Sydney, Melbourne, Perth and Brisbane together account for 53.6 percent of Australia's population, but 79.7 percent of recent immigrants (i.e. overseas born who have been resident of Australia for less than five years).

Both the interregional distribution of immigrants and the intra-urban distribution vary considerably by birthplace (or ethnicity). These differences tend to be studied by means of indices of dissimilarity. For example, Zodgekar (1986) computed the proportion of immigrants of specific birthplaces who would need to be redistributed to match the geographic distribution of the New Zealand born across Statistical Areas. Given his choice of regional boundaries, he found that the dissimilarity index for all overseas born was 19 percent. With the exception of the Netherlands-born, the dissimilarity index was higher than average for non-English speaking migrants to New Zealand.[11] Waves of Pacific Island immigrants during the 1970s and early 1980s and of Asian immigrants subsequently have contributed to a concentration of these ethnic groups in the two largest cities, Auckland and Wellington. However, it should be noted that statistical information on the dissimilarity of the geographical distribution between population groups does not provide any information about actual social segregation, i.e. the absence of social interaction (Grimes 1993).

After arrival, geographic mobility and labour mobility among migrants are initially high and subsequently subject to cumulative inertia. However, there appears to be a process of convergence to the geographic mobility patterns of the host population over time and interregional migration leads to a diffusion of the initial impact by partially offsetting the high geographic concentration of recently arrived migrants. Bell and Cooper (1995) found that, while the immigrants in Australia initially settle in the large cities, after some years they show the same tendencies as Australians to move north and into non-metropolitan areas such as coastal towns. It is therefore no paradox that, while the share of immigrants arriving in New South Wales (with Sydney being the dominant destination) is increasing, the internal net migration loss of this State is increasing as well. However, certain Asian groups – such as the Vietnamese, are less geographically mobile due to strong community networks. New Zealanders in Australia are the most mobile of the overseas born and South Europeans are the least mobile.

The settlement patterns have attracted little interest among economists in Australia and New Zealand. Chapple et al. (1994) note that the significant clustering of migrants in Auckland has benefits and costs. On the benefit side, there is an increased supply of labour, entrepreneurs, new ideas and spending power. On the cost side there is pressure on the infrastructure, certain segments of the labour market and social stability. The impact on individual cities has not yet been researched in New Zealand, but studies of immigration in large cities in Australia are available (e.g. Burnley and Murphy 1994).

It is clear that there are strong economic forces at work which contribute to initial settlement being spatially concentrated. In Australasia, virtually all migrants arrive by aircraft so that the largest cities with international airports are the first places the new migrants encounter. Particularly when relatives or friends live there, there will be an incentive to commence job search in these cities in which there would be potentially a large pool of vacancies to sample. Thus, a perceived higher success rate of labour market search and the accessibility of information flows across the various networks of formal and informal information channels contribute to the attraction of large cities (Poot 1996).

The presence of relatives and friends has a strong impact on locational decisions so that the traditional importance of the family reunification component in the overall immigration flows also contributes to geographic concentration of immigrants. Finally, migrant clusters enable the migrants to maintain their cultural identity and serve as a defence against possible prejudice and discriminatory behaviour among the host population. The presence of urban migrant clusters may enable migrants to avoid being the victims of statistical discrimination in a labour market with asymmetric information. An employer from the same ethnic background as a migrant worker searching for a job, may be able to assess better the likely productivity of the latter than a locally born employer.

It was noted in Section 5.3 that the effects of immigration on economies of scale and technological change are the main factors behind the finding that immigration increases income per head in the long-run. The high degree of urban concentration of migrants plays an important role here as cities provide the 'breeding ground' for the positive externalities. The importance of cities in long-run development has been re-established in the international literature recently (see The Economist 1995, Krugman 1991, but also e.g. Jacobs 1984). Immigrants contribute to an increasing density of economic activity. Ciccone and Hall (1996) show that employment density affects productivity positively through local geographical externalities and the variety of locally available intermediate services. They find that, for the

148

United States at least, such agglomeration advantages more than offset congestion effects.

Given the high degree of labour force participation, high skill levels and entrepreneurial ability, immigrants selected through current policies in Australasia may contribute more to long run urban productivity growth than natural increase or local in-migration would. Little is known about the supply of entrepreneurship by immigrants, but Wooden and Robertson (1989) found no significant difference among migrants and native born in the propensity to be self-employed although there was an increase in the propensity of self-employment among the overseas born with period of residence.[12] Strahan and Williams (1988) found that immigrant-owned businesses in Australia were much more likely than non-immigrant businesses to survive three years. They explain this in terms of migrants' higher personal independence, balanced risk taking and self-motivation. In turn, migrants may have such attributes through the process of self-selection referred to in the previous section. No New Zealand evidence is available.

While the positive externalities associated with immigration may be long run phenomena, there is no doubt that in the short run immigration can put considerable pressure on the urban infrastructure and social services. The main reason is that even when adequate planning procedures are in place, it has proved to be hard to predict population growth in the main cities. Early announcements of immigration targets do not help much because net migration is endogenous. For example, population growth in Sydney is a function of economic conditions in the local urban economy, the remainder of Australia, New Zealand and other countries with which there is a significant population exchange. Given the lags involved in putting new infrastructure in place, inadequate provision during high immigration phases (usually coinciding with peaks in the business cycle) is likely to occur.

In New Zealand, the short-term 'carrying capacity' was exceeded during the early 1970s when net immigration doubled the rate of population growth from a 1 percent annual rate of natural increase. Land prices increased rapidly and there was a shortage of e.g. educational facilities. In contrast, the problems related to the recent increase in New Zealand immigration mentioned in Section 5.2 are somewhat different: government had inadequately provided for post-settlement immigrant services such as extra funding for schools to establish special programs for students with language difficulties. A consequential refusal by school principals to admit new immigrant students with such difficulties got high media exposure and forced the government to provide additional funding.

Immigration has also a significant impact on the housing market. Poot et al. (1988) showed that an increase in net immigration from zero to 15,000 per annum would increase new dwelling construction in New Zealand by 26 percent, compared with an increase in other investment of 9 percent. Increases in the relative price of housing and land would result. As a result of inter-industry linkages, the increase in the demand for housing has also quite noticeable effects on overall resource allocation. This was confirmed by the Australian and New Zealand CGE studies.

Except for the problems associated with peak levels of immigration, the conclusion of Australian research is that immigration had a minor role in infrastructural problems. Murphy et al. (1990) found that even at the time of high immigration levels during the late 1980s, the metropolitan governments of Sydney, Melbourne and Perth did not consider the effects of immigration as a separate issue of significance. Instead, immigration in Australia slowed down depopulation of inner cities through immigrants replacing relocating Australian-born households. The growing internationalization of the urban economies and the associated growth in international short-run business and tourist movements was identified as a more significant issue for future infrastructural planning. The main problems in infrastructural development in Australia appear to be political and relate to defining the responsibilities of federal, state and local government and the associated problem of financing new investments. Limiting immigration would not resolve these problems.

Nonetheless, Burnley and Murphy (1994) did find that immigration during the last two decades increased house prices in Sydney and that it contributed to a shortage of low rent accommodation. The effects on the housing market appear to have been relatively mild such that only if the immigration volume was substantially cut on a sustained basis, house price increases would be significantly lower in Sydney.

In summary, immigration may have reinforced existing infrastructural problems, but it does not seem to have created these on its own. In any case, most literature on this issue in Australia and New Zealand concludes that our knowledge of the external effects of immigration in the urban economy is very limited because substantive research to date has been rather inadequate. The next section outlines some priorities for further research.

5.6   Reflections

Immigration has shaped the societies of Australia and New Zealand throughout their histories, but even in recent decades the impact of international migration on population size and composition in both countries has been large. The impact of immigration on the host society has many dimensions and this review was only able to summarize recent research from the economic perspective. Moreover, only a limited range of topics was covered, namely the impact on wages and employment, the process of migrant adaptation and the impact on urban infrastructure.

The overall conclusion is that, in Australia and New Zealand at least, the policies which encouraged higher levels of skilled and business

150

immigration since the mid 1980s were not misguided because the impact ranged from being rather benign in the short run to having a positive net welfare effect in the long run. The selective nature of immigration policy in Australasia has possibly led to a more positive overall impact there than, for example, in the United States where the apparent decline of the relative skills of immigrant waves in recent decades led Borjas (1994) to a more cautious overall assessment.

While there has never been a full consensus among the population about the desirability of pro-immigration policies and while there has been growing criticism of the high levels of immigration observed in the late 1980s in Australia and more recently in New Zealand, the current policies have not met the fierce resistance yet that can be observed in parts of Europe or the United States. There are several reasons for this. First, being island nations with strict border controls at airports, the number of asylum seekers and illegal immigrants (mainly visa overstayers) has been relatively small. Secondly, as recent as the 1970s in Australia and the early 1980s in New Zealand, immigration policy gave preference to the selection of persons from certain ethnic backgrounds which the governments regarded as being more compatible with the objective of assimilation. Thirdly, as the migration stream became more heterogeneous in Australia, immigrant settlement policy shifted from one of assimilation to integration and, more recently, to multiculturalism. In New Zealand, which has a relatively large indigenous population, multiculturalism is seen as weakening the official policy of biculturalism, which aims to assist in removing the economic and social disadvantage of the Maori population. However, the emphasis on encouraging migration of skilled workers, or of persons with specific occupations, in the latter country would have contributed to the relatively smooth absorption of immigrants. The victims of immigration policy have been the immigrants from Pacific Islands, whose migration was encouraged during labour shortages in the 1960s and 1970s, but who subsequently were most severely affected by the drastic program of micro and macroeconomic reforms which New Zealand embarked upon since 1984. Yet, racial tensions are – by international comparison – not large. They do flare up at times, such as in 1994 and 1995 in Auckland following a large influx of migrants from Asian countries, but the tensions appear to have been fuelled by the visibility of such new immigrants' affluence and by unfounded fear regarding inadequate tax contributions of the new immigrants to public services vis-à-vis their claims on these services.

Although an accumulation of research findings cannot halt political conflict and social tensions, it does provide the basis for developing a better informed immigration policy. In this respect, this chapter showed that policy makers in Australasia now have some robust findings available to them, particularly at the macro level. However, the Australian research has tended to be more extensive, which is partly related to a greater commitment to the public funding of research on immigration in this country. In New Zealand, many ministries and

151

government agencies (national and local) still seem to have to come to terms with the outcomes of the immigration policy adopted in late 1991. A general concern for the post-settlement process is still lacking. Many questions remain (see e.g. Chapple et al. 1994). In both countries, there is a lack of micro level research. An important cause is the lack of micro level data. In New Zealand, for example, a question on years lived in New Zealand was removed from the 1991 census questionnaire, thus making it impossible to generate data on migrant assimilation until the results of the 1996 census, when the question was reintroduced, became available. The Australian government has been more forthcoming in tackling the data problem and the introduction of the Longitudinal Survey of Immigrants in Australia is an encouraging development.

There are four areas which would have priority for further research. The first is a micro level study of labour market outcomes in which the wages, other employment conditions and employment levels of migrants are compared with those of natives over time to focus on substitution or complementarity between the two groups, discrimination, earnings catch up and labour supply behaviour. The second area would be further study of business immigration, that is the immigration of persons who are admitted on grounds of a stated commitment to invest actively or passively in the host economy. The third issue which needs further work is the impact on the public sector in terms of government consumption, investment, taxation and social security. While these issues were studied in detail in the context of the CGE modelling of the late 1980, restructuring of the public sector and changes in the size and composition of the immigration flow suggest that such calculations should be done again. Finally, it is clear that the regional and urban implications, in particular the nature of positive and negative external effects, have not yet been addressed adequately in both countries. Again, micro level work – for example of the role of immigration in innovation and entrepreneurship - would be a first priority.

References

Baker, M. and Wooden, M. (1992), 'Immigration and Its Impact on the Incidence of Training in Australia', *Australian Economic Review*, vol. 98, pp. 39–53.

Beggs, J. and Chapman, B. (1988), 'Immigrant Wage Adjustment in Australia: Cross Section and Time Series Estimates', *Economic Record*, vol. 64, no.186, pp. 161–67.

Beggs, J. and Chapman, B. (1990), 'Search Efficiency, Skill Transferability and Immigrant Relative Unemployment Rates in Australia', *Applied Economics*, vol. 22, pp. 249–60.

Bell, M and Cooper, J. (1995), *Internal Migration in Australia 1986–1991: The Overseas Born*, Australian Government Publishing Service, Canberra.

Bishop, R.V. (1979), 'The Construction and Use of Causality Tests', *Agricultural Economics Research*, vol. 31, pp. 1–6.

Borjas, G. (1989), 'Economic Theory and International Migration', *International Migration Review*, vol. 23, no. 3, pp. 457–85.

Borjas, G. (1994), 'The Economics of Immigration', *Journal of Economic Literature*, vol. 32, no. 4, pp. 1167–217.

Brooks, C. and L.S. Williams (1995), *Immigrants and the Labour Market: The 1990-94 Recession and Recovery in Perspective*, Australian Government Publishing Service, Canberra.

Brosnan, P. and Poot, J. (1987), 'Modelling the Determinants of Trans–Tasman Migration after World War II', *The Economic Record*, vol. 63 (December), pp. 313–29.

Burnley, I. and Murphy, P. (1994), *Immigration, Housing Costs and Population Dynamics in Sydney*, Australian Government Publishing Service, Canberra.

Carmichael, G.A. (ed.) (1993), *Trans-Tasman Migration: Trends, Causes and Consequences*, Australian Government Publishing Service, Canberra.

Chapple, S., Gorbey, S., Yeabsley, J. and Poot, J. (1994), *Literature Review on the Economic Impact of Immigration*, NZ Institute of Economic Research, Wellington.

Chiswick, B. (1978a), 'The Effect of 'Americanisation' on the Earnings of Foreign-Born Men', *Journal of Political Economy*, vol. 86 (October), pp. 897–921.

Chiswick, B. (1978b), 'A Longitudinal Analysis of the Occupational Mobility of Immigrants', in Dennis, B.D. (ed.), *Proceedings of the 30th Annual Winter Meetings*, Industrial Relations Research Association, Maddison, WI.

Ciccone, A. and Hall, R.E. (1996), 'Productivity and the Density of Economic Activity', *American Economic Review*, vol. 86, no. 1, pp. 54–70.

Committee to Advise on Australia's Immigration Policies (CAAIP, Chairman S. FitzGerald) (1988), *Immigration: A Commitment to Australia*, Australian Government Publishing Service, Canberra (three volumes).

Denison, E.F. (1967), *Why Growth Rates Differ: Post-War Experience in Nine Western Countries*, Brookings Institution, Washington DC.

Easton, B (1991), 'Structural Change and Economic Growth in Postwar New Zealand', *Massey Economic Papers*, vol. 9, No. B9103, Department of Economics, Massey University, Palmerston North.

Foster, W. and Baker, L. (1996), *Immigration and the Australian Economy*, 2nd edn. Australian Government Publishing Service, Canberra.

Foster, W. and Withers, G. (1992), 'Macroeconomic Consequences of International Migration', in Freeman, G.P. and J. Jupp (eds), *Nations of Immigrants: Australia, the United States and International Migration*, Oxford University Press, Oxford.

Greenberg, E. and Webster, C.E. (1983), *Advanced Econometrics: A Bridge to the Literature*, John Wiley and Sons, New York.

Greenwood, M.J. and McDowell, J.M. (1994), 'The National Labour Market Consequences of US Immigration' in Giersch, H. (ed.), *Economic Aspects of International Migration*, Springer Verlag, Berlin.

Grimes, S. (1993), 'Residential Segregation in Australian Cities: A Literature Review', *International Migration Review*, vol. 27, no. 1, pp. 103–20.

Gruen, F.H. (1986), 'How Bad is Australia's Economic Performance and Why', *Economic Record*, vol. 62, no. 179, pp. 180–93.

Jacobs, J. (1984), *Cities and the Wealth of Nations*, Random House, New York.

Johansen, L. (1960), *A Multi-Sectoral Model of Economic Growth*, North-Holland, Amsterdam.

Junankar, P.N. and Pope, D. (1990), *Immigration, Wages and Price Stability*, Australian Government Publishing Service, Canberra.

Junankar, P.N., Pope, D., Kapuscinski, C. and Mudd, W. (1993), *Immigration and Australia's External Account Balances*, Australian Government Publishing Service, Canberra.

Kossoudji, S.A. (1989), 'Immigrant Worker Assimilation: Is It a Labor Market Phenomenon?', *Journal of Human Resources*, vol. 24, no. 3, pp. 494–527.

Krugman, P. (1991), *Geography and Trade*, MIT Press, Cambridge, Mass.

Layard, R. and Nickell, S. (1986), 'Unemployment in Britain', *Economica*, vol. 53, pp. S121–S171.

Malakellis, M. 1993, 'Illustrative Results from ORANI-INT: An Intertemporal CGE Model of the Australian Economy', Impact Project Preliminary Working Paper OP-77, Monash University, Melbourne.

McAllister, I. (1995), 'Occupational Mobility among Immigrants: The Impact of Migration on Economic Success in Australia', *International Migration Review*, vol. 24, no. 2, pp. 441–68.

McGill, J.F. (1981), 'Immigration and the New Zealand Economy', Research Paper No. 26, N.Z. Institute of Economic Research, Wellington.

Murphy, P.A. (1995), 'Impacts of Immigration on Sydney', BIMPR Bulletin, vol. 15 (November), pp. 12–14.

Murphy, P.A., Burnley, I.H., Harding, H.R., Wiesner, D. and Young, V. (1990), *Impact of Immigration on Urban Infrastructure*, Australian Government Publishing Service, Canberra.

Nana, G. 1995, 'Developing a Dynamic Multi-Sectoral CGE Model of the New Zealand Economy', Working Paper 12/95, Graduate School of Business and Government Management, Victoria University of Wellington.

Norman, N.R. and Meikle, N.F. (1985), *The Economic Effects of Immigration on Australia*, Committee for Economic Development of Australia (2 volumes), Melbourne.

Page, I. (1991), 'Trends in New Zealand Housing', *New Zealand Real Estate*, vol. 42, no. 2, pp. 11–13.

Peter, M. (1993), 'The Use of ORANI in the Immigration Debate', Centre for Policy Studies General Paper No. G 103, Monash University.

Poot, J. (1986), *Immigration and the Economy: A Review of Recent Australian Findings on the Economic Consequences of Immigration and the Relevance of These Findings for New Zealand,* Institute of Policy Studies; Wellington.

Poot, J. (1993a), 'Trans-Tasman Migration and Economic Growth in Australasia', in Carmichael, G.A. (ed.), *Trans-Tasman Migration: Trends, Causes and Consequences,* Australian Government Publishing Service, Canberra.

Poot, J. (1993b), 'Adaptation of Migrants in the New Zealand Labour Market', *International Migration Review,* vol. 27 no. 1, pp. 121–39.

Poot, J. (1995), 'Do Borders Matter? A Model of Interregional Migration in Australasia', *The Australasian Journal of Regional Studies,* vol. 1, no. 2, pp. 159–82.

Poot, J. (1996), 'Information, Communication and Networks in International Migration Systems', *Annals of Regional Science,* vol. 30, no. 1.

Poot. J., Nana, G. and Philpott, B. (1988), *International Migration and the New Zealand Economy: A Long-Run Perspective,* Institute of Policy Studies, Wellington.

Quirk, B. (1994), 'Immigration Policy', in Multi-Ethnic Aotearoa New Zealand: Challenge of the Future, Proceedings of the 1993 National Conference, New Zealand Federation of Ethnic Councils Inc., Wellington, pp. 23–30.

Rod, T. and Williams, L. (1996), 'Migration Intensification in the Asia–Pacific Region Over the Decade to 1994', in Lloyd, P.J. and L.S. Williams (eds), *International Trade and Migration in the APEC Region,* Oxford University Press; Oxford.

Saunders, P. and King, A. (1994), *Immigration and the Distribution of Income,* Australian Government Publishing Service, Canberra.

Shu, J. (1995), 'Social Network Usage', *BIMPR Bulletin,* vol. 15 (November), pp. 15–17.

Strahan, K. and Williams, A.J. (1988), *Immigrant Entrepreneurs in Australia: a Report to the Office of Multicultural Affairs,* Office of Multicultural Affairs, Canberra.

Swan, N., Auer, L., Chenard, D., de Plaa, A., de Silva, A., Palmer, D. and Serja, J. (1991), *Economic and Social Impacts of Immigration,* Economic Council of Canada, Ottawa.

The Economist (1995), 'Turn Up the Lights: A Survey of Cities', 29 July 1995, 336(7925), supplement.

Tonkin, S. (1993), *Initial Location Decisions of Immigrants,* Australian Government Publishing Service, Canberra.

Trlin, A.D. and Kang, J. (1992), 'The Business Immigration Policy and the Characteristics of Approved Hong Kong and Taiwanese Applicants, 1986-1988', *New Zealand and International Migration: a Digest and Bibliography,* Number 2, Massey University, Palmerston North, pp. 48–64.

Whiteford, P. (1991), *Immigration and the Social Security System,* Australian Government Publishing Service, Canberra.

155

Withers, G. and D. Pope (1985), 'Immigration and Unemployment', *Economic Record*, vol. 61, no. 163, pp. 554–63.

Withers, G. (1987), 'Migration and the Labour Market: Australian Analysis', *The Future of Migration*, OECD, Paris.

Wooden, M. and Robertson, F. (1989), *The Factors Associated With Migrant Labour Market Status*, Australian Government Publishing Service, Canberra.

Zodgekar, A. (1986), 'Immigrants in the 1981 Census', in Trlin, A.D. and P. Spoonley (eds), *New Zealand and International Migration,* Department of Sociology, Massey University, Palmerston North.

Notes

1. The Aborigines of Australia may have lived on the continent as long as 40,000 years and are believed to have migrated there from India. In contrast, New Zealand remained unpopulated until somewhere between 900 and 1300 AD when groups of Maoris arrived in three stages by canoes from Pacific islands in the region of French Polynesia. The indigenous people now account for about 1 percent of the population in the former country and 15 percent in the latter.

2. Previously, applicants for occupational migration to New Zealand had to have an occupation included in an Occupational Priority List which was updated every six months.

3. Some persons approved for permanent residency may postpone actual settlement until a subsequent year, or may not migrate to New Zealand at all. However, the statistics obtained from arrival cards do not report new settler arrivals as a separate category, so that in the New Zealand case the use of statistics on approvals by the New Zealand Immigration Service was preferable.

4. In 1994, 949 'boat people' arrived in Australia (Rod and Williams 1996).

5. This agency was called the Bureau of Immigration, Multicultural and Population Research (BIMPR) and, as its name suggested, fostered also research on other population issues and multicultural issues, which are often intertwined with immigration issues. BIMPR was disestablished in 1996.

6. In addition to Chapple et al. (1994) on international and New Zealand findings, see Foster and Baker (1996) on Australian findings, Borjas (1994) and Greenwood and McDowell (1994) on United States research and Swan et al. (1991) on Canadian Research.

7. The variables enter the equations in a form such that they are statistically stationary.

8. If in addition γ_0 is zero, there is said to be no instantaneous causality.

9. The effect on natives' labour force participation is expected to be small.

10. The latter type of analysis involves a breakdown of the sources of economic growth into components such as the quantity and quality of the labour force and the stock of capital. The part of economic growth which cannot be explained by such factors is referred to as the Denison residual after the extensive work of this nature by E.F. Denison (see e.g. Denison 1967).

11. There has been little migration from the Netherlands to New Zealand in recent years, but large numbers arrived in the 1950s and 1960s. The Dutch community in New Zealand (including the second and third generation and New Zealand born spouses) accounts for about 2 percent of the New Zealand population. Many Dutch immigrants were employed on farms, or became farmers after completing their initial contract. This has contributed to a greater geographical dispersion than for other immigrant groups.

12. It should be noted that self-employment is an inadequate measurement of entrepreneurship, since it includes contract work which is more like wage employment.

Part B
Spatial Clusters: International Patterns and Linkages

6 Differential Urbanization and International Migration: An Urban Systems Approach

MANIE GEYER

6.1 Introduction

Two issues seem to have become increasingly contentious in recent years in international migration studies. One was raised by Clark (1994) in an editorial comment where he came to the conclusion that the work of planners, demographers and social scientists remains marginal to the major debates in international migration because they tend to focus on description and general discussions rather than on predictions and impacts.

Another aspect deserving attention is the fact that most international migration case studies tend to focus on individual countries or parts of countries. Relatively little attention is given to the impact of international migration in a multinational context. However, the international trade agreement in North America and the present momentum towards greater unity in Western Europe make cross country comparative studies of population migration at the multinational level an imperative.

In an attempt to create a conceptual framework in which both these issues can be dealt with, this chapter looks at the potential the concept of differential urbanization holds for the explanation of international migration trends. Scholars who are familiar with the differential urbanization model know it as a model which aims to predict future urban and rural population change, based on past internal migration trends. The concept of differential urbanization, as it was recently introduced (Geyer 1989, 1990, 1996; Geyer and Kontuly 1993, 1996) deals with three issues. First, it conceptually links the processes of urbanization, polarization reversal, and counterurbanization across the development spectrum in the First and Third Worlds. Second, it distinguishes between mainstream and substream migration patterns within countries and indicates how these streams differ over time within a core-peripheral spatial framework. Third, it identifies 'productionism' and 'environmentalism' as potentially powerful concepts explaining mainstream and substream migration within a country.

This chapter first deals with what the differential urbanization concept entails from a national urban systems point of view. Then an attempt will be made to extend the concept by looking at how international migration experience ties in with the fundamentals of the concept from an international urban systems perspective.

6.2 Three Elements of Differential Urbanization

6.2.1 The Development of Urban Systems

In a study of long term population migration trends in the US, Vining and Strauss (1977) predicted a more or less fixed spatial development sequence for developed countries in the future. First urbanization takes place, followed by intraurban diffusion, then by interregional deconcentration from urban to rural regions, eventually ending with deconcentration within rural regions.

Having a narrower focus, that is, on the sequences in the growth patterns of individual 'urban agglomerations' and distinguishing morphologically between the 'core' and the 'ring' of such urban agglomerations, the Klaassen-group (Klaassen et al. 1981a; Klaassen et al. 1981b; van den Berg et al. 1981 and van den Berg et al. 1982) identified various phases through which an urban settlement could go successively: first, is the phase of 'urbanization', i.e. when certain urban settlements grow at the cost of their 'surrounding countryside'. Secondly, the urban settlement enters the phase of 'suburbanization' when the ring starts growing, attracting people from the core. This is followed by a phase of 'disurbanization', when the population loss of the core exceeds the population gain of the ring, resulting in the urban agglomeration loosing population overall. Finally, the urban settlement enters the phase of 'reurbanization', when either the rate of population loss of the core tapers off, or when the core starts regaining population, although the ring might still be loosing population at this stage.

Looking at developing economies, Richardson (1980) sees the spatial dimensions of industrial development almost identical to the Vining group's description of migration processes in the First World. If only the migration element of Richardson's description of the urban development process is highlighted, population accumulates in the primate city at first. This is followed by decentralization within the core initially resulting in a multinodal urban structure, then by interregional deconcentration towards a limited number of nodes within the periphery, and later on, by decentralization within these peripheral regions. The period when agglomeration forces give way to deglomeration forces he calls the polarization reversal phase. The advanced stages of this phase are accompanied by an absolute decrease in the population of the core.

Until now the combination of the process of urbanization and counterurbanization has only been associated with First World migration and those of urbanization and polarization reversal only with advanced developing economies.

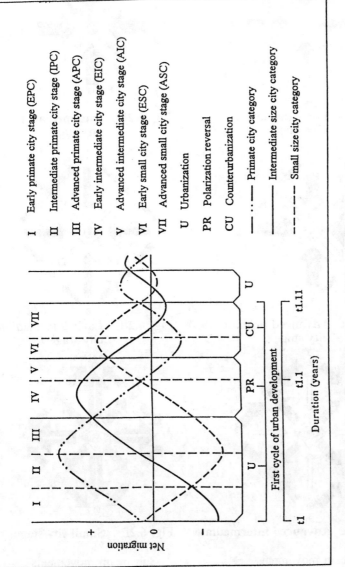

Figure 6.1   Temporal characterization of differential urbanization

Source:Geyer and Kontuly 1993.

I   Early primate city stage (EPC)

II   Intermediate primate city stage (IPC)

III   Advanced primate city stage (APC)

IV   Early intermediate city stage (EIC)

V   Advanced intermediate city stage (AIC)

VI   Early small city stage (ESC)

VII   Advanced small city stage (ASC)

U   Urbanization

PR   Polarization reversal

CU   Counterurbanization

———— Primate city category

————— Intermediate size city category

— — — Small size city category

163

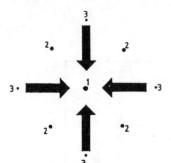

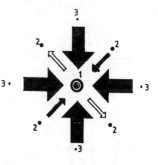

**Fig. 6.2a   Early primate
city stage**

**Fig. 6.2b   Intermediate primate
city stage**

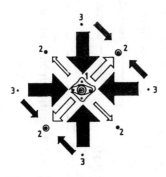

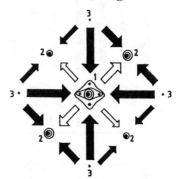

**Fig. 6.2c   Advanced primate
city stage**

**Fig. 6.2d   Early intermediate
city stage**

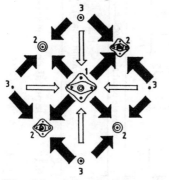

Fig. 6.2e   Advanced intermediate

Fig. 6.2f   Small city stage

Mainstream movements →   Substream movements ⇨

**Figure 6.2   A graphic model of the phases of different urbanization:
main and substream movements**

Chronologically, the graph in Figure 6.1 which depicts how the process of differential urbanization unfolds over time, puts polarization reversal in between the urbanization and counterurbanization phases of development. The reality of the relationship between urbanization, polarization reversal, and counterurbanization and the maturation of urban systems over time is clearly illustrated in the example of migration within France between the 1950s and 1980s. In the French example, a clear distinction can be made between the phases of urbanization, polarization reversal, and counterurbanization (Geyer 1996).

According to the differential urbanization model major cities gain migrants the fastest during the urbanization phase at the expense of small cities, and vice versa during the counterurbanization phase. During polarization reversal, intermediate sized cities grow at the expense of both major and small cities, although major cities may still be gaining population, but at a slower rate than previously.

6.2.2 Main and Substream Migration

The second issue highlighted by the differential urbanization concept is the potential role of main and substream migration in the maturation of urban systems. If one differentiates between the opposing main and substream population migration flows that are evident in developed and less developed countries, differential urbanization can be defined as the sequence of urban development cycles, each cycle consisting of consecutive phases of urbanization, polarization reversal and counterurbanization (Geyer 1996). The phase of urbanization is characterized by main stream migration supporting large city development, followed by main migration streams towards secondary or regional cities during the polarization reversal phase. Finally small city development starts taking place during the counterurbanization phase, while substream migration continues towards intermediate and large cities (Figure 6.2).

6.2.3 Productionism and Environmentalism

Finally the concepts of 'productionism' and 'environmentalism' are highlighted in the explanation of differential urbanization. Productionism refers to the phase in people's lives when improved job opportunities, education, and income are more important in their decision where to stay, than the actual conditions in which they live. During this period people are often willing to bear poor living conditions in order to obtain a job or to earn a better salary. Many clandestine migrants fall in this category.

After having had the opportunity to reap the benefits of productionism, people normally enter the environmentalism phase. This phase is entered into when the need to improve ones actual living environment becomes as important as earning a living. During the environmentalism phase a person would even trade income for pleasant living conditions and in such cases factors associated with productionism become less important. Many of the higher skilled formal migrants fall into this category. Productionism and environmentalism are not entirely mutually exclusive. They go hand in hand, the former enabling a person to achieve the latter. It could, therefore, be argued that productionism and environmentalism are both driven by the same force, that is, the need to improve one's living conditions in all possible respects. But in productionism, improved living conditions can normally not be achieved in the short run, while in environmentalism, improved living and environmental conditions are often an immediate need.

6.3   Differential Urbanization and International Migration

6.3.1   The Historical Development of International Migration Theory

To be able to determine how the differential urbanization concept could be applied in the expansion of international migration theory, it is necessary to look at general conclusions that can be drawn from international migration studies that are relevant to the differential urbanization concept.

First, different migration theories provide different general explanations for international migration. Originally, the emphasis in neoclassical migration theory was placed on economic development differentials between developed and less developed countries and the alleged large scale balancing effect international migration has on labour markets and wage differentials between countries (Moore and Rosenburg 1995).

Subsequently, a theory was developed which emphasizes the role of the multidimentionality of labour markets as a factor influencing international migration. Essentially, it complemented the neoclassical theory of the grand scale balancing of labour and wage disequilibrium between developed and less developed countries by means of international migration. It recognizes the way in which sections of disadvantaged communities exploit labour market segments in developed countries to the benefit of those remaining in the less developed areas. This benefit to the latter communities could take many forms, and could hold direct or indirect advantages. Remittances are one of the important direct benefits.

Later, the global economic theory was developed. According to this theory, market forces extend outwards from global cores and penetrate peripheral economic societies by means of market manipulation practices. This adds to the accumulation of access labour in peripheral communities. Multinational market exploitation leads to the location of labour intensive production in low wage countries and an accumulation of high wage employment opportunities in global cities. The latter process results in global cities having an edge on other large cities in developed and less developed countries in attracting more and more international migrants (Massey et al. 1994).

6.3.2 Specific Lessons from International Migration Studies

A number of specific observations could be made from international migration studies thus far. First, international migrants could be classified on various grounds. These include their permanency (Castles and Miller 1993), legal status, level of development, objectives, or country of origin (Oucho 1995) According to Poot (1996) international migrants may also be classified as permanent settlers, people moving from host countries to a third, people returning to their country of birth, unskilled and semi-skilled contract workers, expatriate professionals, illegal immigrants, asylum seekers, refugees, retired persons, and students. In terms of our typology the first three types of migrants given by Poot (1996) could be further classified in terms of their permanency, the fourth and fifth types in terms of their level of skill, the next three types in terms of their legal status, and the last two in terms of their socioeconomic status. Some of these groups may follow completely different migration patterns which complicate the formulation of theory on this theme. Also, migration patterns during the initial phases of settlement and secondary or relocation phases within the host country may differ (Moore and Rosenberg 1995).

On aggregate, immigrants generally seem to display a dualism in terms of their skills, occupation, and income. There are skilled migrants at the one end and less skilled migrants at the other end of the scale (Champion 1994). Often, the former form part of the more desirable and therefore legal migrants, while the unskilled migrants are normally not allowed to migrate legally, except under special circumstances. Consequently, the latter are often clandestine migrants (Segal 1993). Where less developed countries border onto more developed countries, large numbers of clandestine and refugee migrants normally originate from such countries.

In developed countries with diamond shaped labour forces, bipolar migration does not pose a significant problem, but in less developed countries with pyramidal shaped labour forces, large scale illegal immigration of unskilled people does present a problem at the lower end of the employment sector.

Traditionally, larger metropolitan centres in developed countries, but global centres in particular, serve as the principal magnets for immigrants (Champion 1994). These centres are prominent international destinations because (1) labour market restructuring has been responsible for an expansion of employment opportunities for skilled migrants in world cities, (2) because unskilled migrants are under the impression that proportionally more housing and employment opportunities exist in these centres than elsewhere, and (3) because clandestine migrants can hide more easily in large cities (Massey et al. 1994; Beaverstock 1994).

Immigration figures are fairly insignificant as a percentage of the total population of developed countries generally (Moore and Rosenburg 1995), but due to the concentration of immigrants in certain large cities, a large proportion of the population growth of these centres could be ascribed to the influx of migrants. This leads to many migrant oriented problems in specific areas in these cities.

Initial migration and secondary relocation behaviour of international migrants may differ substantially (see also Chapter 11 of this volume). Substantial differences may also exist between secondary migration patterns of international migrants and internal migration patterns of the local population. However, secondary migration patterns of international migrants who assimilate more easily with the local population may correspond more closely with those of the residential labour force once they have settled down in the host countries.

Other conclusions which can be drawn from international migration studies are that cumulative causation in migration seems to result in a direct relationship between: (a) the degree of communication between migrants and their relatives and friends at home and the propensity of the latter to migrate; (b) the scale of involvement of a community in international migration and the propensity of other members of that community to consider migration; (c) the scale of remittances and the improved economic position of beneficiaries at home relative to other members of that community; (d) international migration and the agglomeration of financial, technical and other professional services in a limited number of global centres throughout the world, and (e) the agglomeration of financial, technical and other professional services in global centres and the creation of employment opportunities for ancillary workers directly as a result of international migration (Massey, et al. 1994). Four factors seem to play an important role in each of the latter conclusions. The volume and direction of international migration between any two countries seem to be determined by the distance between them, their relative levels of development, the cultural-political ties between them historically, and their image as a humanitarian haven and as a financial success.

6.4   Urban Subsystems and International Migration

How can the differential urbanization concept be extended to serve as a conceptual framework for the explanation of international migration trends? Thus far, the concept of differential urbanization has only been associated with internal migration within a national urban framework. Essentially, it provides a graphical framework explaining how different migration trends affect the development of urban systems in countries over time. However, if one looks at population redistribution patterns from an international urban systems perspective, the differential

168

urbanization concept also holds potential for the explanation of certain international migration trends.

This view is based on the fact that, fundamentally, spatial friction should have a similar effect on the development of urban systems at all levels of aggregation. What holds true for the effect of spatial friction on the development of urban systems at the national level should also apply to urban systems at the international level. As in the case of administrative boundaries within countries, national boundaries also tend to distort economic space internationally, but history has taught us that administrative boundaries cannot completely contain functional economic forces in the long run (Perroux 1950). This was effectively demonstrated in South Africa where Bantustan boundaries eventually had to give way to politico-economic pressure. The initial corroding and eventual collapse of the Iron Curtain in Eastern Europe due to similar pressures is another example.

It should immediately be added, of course, that international borders are usually far greater obstacles in the free flow of migrants than administrative boundaries within countries and therefore they also impede labour migration flows much more effectively than the latter. Depending on the personal view of the person who considers the effect of national boundaries, international borders are either regarded as barriers trapping people within pools of political instability and poverty or they are regarded as barriers preserving national interests such as communal values and prosperity.

These factors determine the importance of differential streams of migration at the international level. In terms of the concept of differential urbanization, internal migration is normally either directly or indirectly determined by the spontaneous and deliberate processes of redistribution of wealth in a country. Moral issues such as international redistribution of wealth and the degree of openness of nation states to international labour migration are becoming more and more pressing Also in the international migration debate (Leitner 1995; Helton 1995). As Clark (1994, p.1500) puts it: In the end the problem of immigration will be redressed only when income disparities are redressed at a world scale. In this context the world immigration problem is a problem of resource distribution. This is proven by incidents such as the group of illegal immigrants from former French colonies in Africa who recently resisted deportation from France. The moral question remains whether justice is served when people are deported to areas besieged by low levels of productivity, high rates of population growth, and overwhelming social and political instability, even if they are illegal immigrants.

In the French case, international media attention to the plight of the illegal immigrants forced the French government to declare its willingness to implement a more rigorous development assistance programme in its former colonies than before. In time, this issue could have an effect on the moral imperative for a changed approach to international aid and immigration policy world wide, and eventually, on

169

international migration patterns in general. If this happens the similarities between differential urbanization at the national and international levels could become more evident.

Focusing on the effect spatial friction has on economic forces at the national level, five propositions have been made regarding the development of urban systems (Geyer and Kontuly, 1993). First, many national urban systems initially go through a primate city phase. During this phase a large proportion of economic development and large numbers of migrants are attracted to one or a few primary centres in a country (Richardson 1973).

Second, as the national urban system expands and matures, new urban centres are added to the lower ranks while many of those that already exist develop and move up through the ranks. In this process, economic development gets dispersed, while the urban system becomes spatially more integrated (Friedmann 1966; Richardson 1973).

Third, in such expanding national urban systems, various strata of territorially organized urban subsystems or urban networks develop, from the macro or national level through the regional and subregional levels to the local or micro level (Friedmann 1972; Bourne 1975).

Fourth, the sequence of tendencies observed in the development of urban systems, first towards concentration and then towards dispersion or deconcentration, is not limited to systems at the national level, but can also manifest itself in any of the lower order regional urban networks, because the same spatial forces which operate at the national level, also operate at the subnational levels.

Fifth, in a growing urban environment, the odds normally favour the development of secondary centres closer to primary centres (Richardson 1977, 1980; van den Berg et al. 1982; Gordon 1979; Richter 1985), unless an outlying centre is located in an area with exceptional locational attributes.

Using these five propositions as a premise, the impressionistic illustration showing the functioning of the differential urbanization model was given above (Figure 6.2). As was mentioned before, the same spatial economic principles underlying the evolvement of urban systems at the national level, also seem to apply to urban systems at higher levels of aggregation. As urban networks can be identified at the national, subnational and local levels, so can they be identified at the global, continental, and subcontinental levels.

As part of the world systems theory, an urban network of the highest order has already been identified at the global level (Massey, et al. 1994; Beaverstock 1994). According to this theory, international migration is largely influenced by the globalization of the market economy. As the core nations of the world, Capitalism extends outward form Europe, North America, and the Far East with New York, London, and Tokyo serving as apexes within these cores at the global level (Figure 6.3).

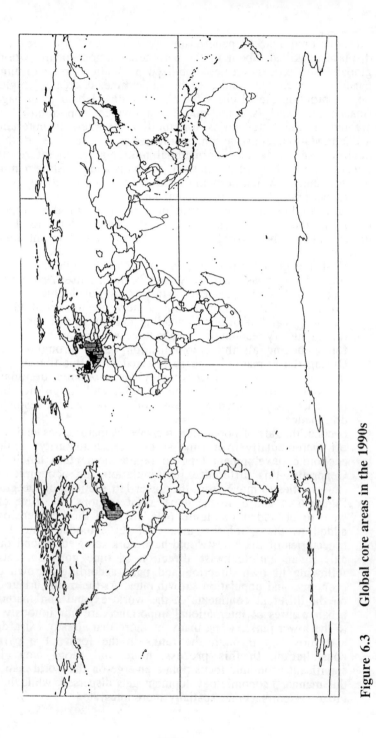

Figure 6.3   Global core areas in the 1990s

International market penetration by developed countries tends to displace unskilled labour in the peripheral regions of the world. This globalization process creates mobilized population prone to migrate in peripheral countries, while, at the same time, it creates employment opportunities in global cities for highly skilled labour in management, finance, and services. As a spinoff, employment opportunities are also created in the latter cities for ancillary workers in entertainment, accommodation, construction, maintenance and services. Both highly qualified and unskilled international migrants are therefore attracted towards the global cities, contrary to main and substream migration inside countries which normally head in opposite directions as a result of productionism and environmentalism.

If one applies the same principles outlined in the propositions regarding the development of national urban systems to the global urban system, the 'world systems' theory could be introduced as follows:

- First, the global urban system has gone through more than one primate city phase in history, and is finding itself, perhaps at the end of yet another cycle of primate city development at present. Economic globalization is not a new phenomenon. Given the technological limitations of leading nations at different points in time in history, economic globalization was one of the main driving forces behind all the colonialization waves throughout history. During the primate city phase referred to in this first proposition, the primate world cities display an economic dominance in particular strategic economic sectors, and large numbers of migrants are attracted to these world centres as a result of this dominance.

- Second, the rate of population increase of major cities tends to taper off incrementally over time as they reach maturity, while their economic development tend to retain momentum much longer. Generally, this difference in population and economic growth causes cities to move from the lower left sections of the graphs in Figure 6.4a and b, to the upper right sections. If a time element were to be added to Figure 6.4a, i.e. if a third dimension were added to the graph by means of an extended time axis, the trajectories of the cities would have cork-screwed around the time axis in an anticlockwise direction as time goes on, each city following its own direction and pace according its own unique economic and population growth rates. As the major urban centres on the different continents of the world expand and mature, new urban centres of international importance are continuously added to the lower ranks, while many of those that already exist, develop and move up through the ranks in the form of a pyramidal constellation. In this process, more and more new globally significant economic focus points emerge on the world map and in this manner economic development gets dispersed, while the world urban system becomes spatially more integrated.

172

- Third, various strata of urban networks develop in this expanding international urban system, from the global through the continental to the subcontinental levels. In most urban networks, whether they are global, continental, or subcontinental, a core apex can normally be identified, surrounded by what could be called an intermediate core zone and a core fringe zone. Geographically isolated cores located in less developed areas normally feature as stand alone cores without extensive surrounding networks of cities.

- Fourth, because exponential advancements in the fields of electronic communication and computer development tend to reduce the friction of distance, more and more former relatively isolated secondary centres offer advantages to international migrants similar to those that are present global cores. Consequently, the former 'secondary' centres tend to become increasingly attractive locations to international investors as well as alternative destinations to prospective international migrants. When the combined migration streams to individual non-global centres equal or exceed the stream towards the global centres, the world urban system could be regarded as proceeding from a primate city growth phase to a secondary city phase. Therefore, the sequence of tendencies observed in the development of urban systems, first towards concentration and then towards dispersion or deconcentration, is not limited to systems at the national level only. It also manifests itself in migration patterns at higher levels of aggregation because the same spatial forces that operate at the national and subnational levels also operate at higher levels of aggregation. Only the timespan of the period in which the international urban system develops should be longer than those of national systems.

- Fifth, as a result of spatial friction, lower order cores closer to primate world centres should have a developmental advantage above those further away and this should lead to higher levels of spatial economic networking and integration between the former centres than between the latter. It is expected that these spatial economies of scale would also be reflected in international migration patterns.

- Finally, ceteris paribus the odds should favour stronger economic ties between developed nations and less developed nations nearer by than between developed nations and less developed nations further away. The existence of globally significant urban focus points in peripheral regions are normally due to the existence of significantly superior locational advantages (Richardson 1973) at those points than elsewhere in such regions.

As a result of the impact of these propositions on the development of the global urban system, several generalizations can be made. First, the world cities and large urbanized regions in their direct vicinity have become spatially integrated to such an extent over the centuries, that, what holds true for individual global cities in terms of capital accumulation and access to markets and resources, also holds true for the urban networks extending over large distances around them. In the United States, New York serves as an apex within the North Eastern Seaboard. Around this inner core area lies an outer core area, stretching roughly from Washington in the south, to Chicago in the west and Montreal in the north. Similarly, London serves as an apex within an inner core area in Western Europe, stretching from Paris in the south to Frankfurt in the East and Amsterdam in the north. This inner core is surrounded by an extensive outer core area, stretching roughly from Lyon and Milan in the south, to Vienna and Berlin in the east, to Stockholm and Oslo in the north, and Manchester and Liverpool in the west. Together these global apexes and their surrounding urban areas constitute urban networks at the highest level of aggregation (Figure 6.3).

As stated in the propositions above, the world core regions are not the only areas advantaged significantly by international economic forces of cumulative causation. Also lesser cores such as Hong Kong, the Johannesburg-Pretoria area, Sao Paulo and Singapore present similar advantages to multinational enterprises, albeit at lower levels of intensity and scale than the global cores. In fact, subcontinental cores in the developing world often provide agglomeration as well as market advantages far outstripping those of other areas in their vicinity and therefore they are becoming choice locations for international investors. The relative locational advantage of these cores cause many influential multinationals, international financial institutions, and international agencies to locate their regional headquarters in these centres. This creates opportunities to prospective skilled and unskilled international migrants which are similar to those offered to them in the world cores.

Table 6.1 Percent population growth per decade for selected cities in the developing and developed world

CITY	1950-1960	1960-1970	1970-1980
DEVELOPING WORLD			
Delhi	65.2	56.2	61.2
Mexico City	71.1	74.7	58.7
Sao Paulo	75.4	69.8	55.9
Singapore	56.8	24.4	52.5
Jakarta	54.4	59.4	48.4
Rio de Janeiro	45.7	41.4	28.4
DEVELOPED WORLD			
London	3.5	-1.3	-2.6
New York	14.7	14.5	-4.2
Paris	30.7	15.4	3.8
Hamburg	16.1	5.2	-0.4

Source: United Nations 1989.

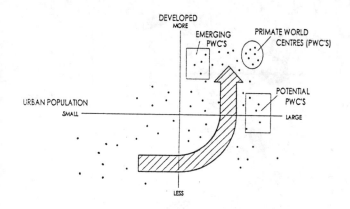

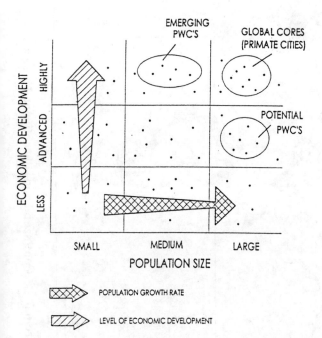

Figure 6.4   A graphic model of the historical relationship between economic and population of urban areas

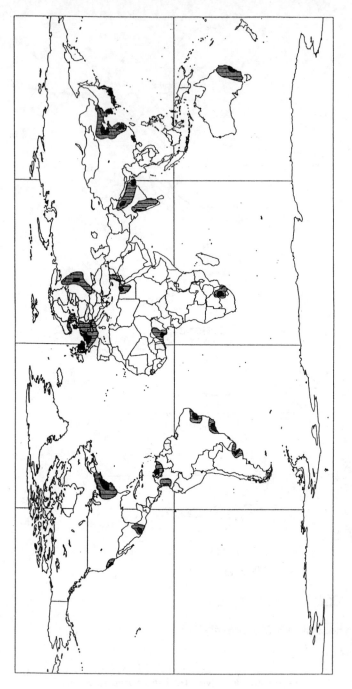

Figure 6.5   Continental and subcontinental core areas

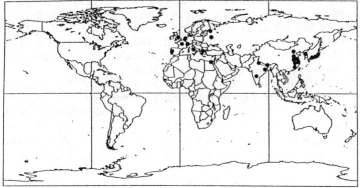

1800

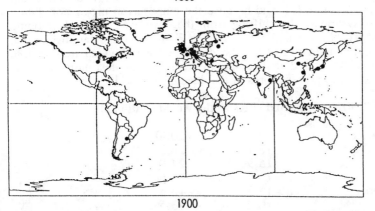

1900

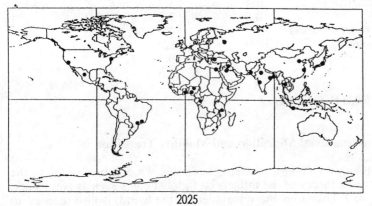

2025

Figure 6.6   The global shift in urban growth since 1800

Examples of subcontinental cores that could be regarded as stand alone intermediate sized cores in a global context, are shown in Figure 6.5. Looking at the urban system of the world as a whole, therefore, urban networks can be identified at the global, continental, subcontinental, national, subnational, and local levels, each level forming a different stratum within the global urban system.

Many subcontinental cores are located in the third world. In terms of human resource potential, Figure 6.6 clearly shows how the focus, at present, is shifting from urban settlements in the developed world towards urban agglomerations in the developing world. Serving as gateways to large tracts of economically less developed territory in the developing world, certain strategically well located Third World cities are already becoming important subcontinental and even continental cores attracting scores of international migrants across the board annually. As a consequence of the process of urban development illustrated in Figure 6.4, and because the emphasis in urban population growth is systematically shifting from the developed to the developing world (see Tables 6.1 and 6.2 as well as Figure 6.6), indications are that the subcontinental cores of the less developed world which are shown in Figure 6.5 are bound to become more important destinations in the future relative to present cores in the developed world.

Table 6.2 Sizes of selected cities in the world (millions)

CITY	1985	2000
Mexico City	18.1	26.3
Sao Paulo	15.9	24.0
Calcutta	11.0	16.6
New York	15.3	15.5
Seoul	10.2	13.5
Rio de Janeiro	10.4	13.3
Cairo	8.5	13.2
Johannesburg-Pretoria	7.0	12.3
Los Angeles	10.0	11.2
London	9.8	9.1
Lagos	3.6	8.3

Source: United Nations 1989.

6.5　International Migration and Mobility Transition

In the previous section it was suggested that what is being said in the world systems theory of the influence of global cores such as New York, London, and Tokyo on the remainder of the world, is also relevant to minor cores such as Rio de Janeiro, Singapore, and Johannesburg at the subcontinental level. The significance of subcontinental cores in international migration, and especially of spatially isolated cores in the developing world at the subcontinental level, can only be fully understood if the concept of differential urbanization is linked with Zelinsky's (1971) concept of mobility transition. If this is done, a number of general statements can be made regarding urban development and population migration in the developed and developing worlds. In the chain of cause and effect a society's spatial mobility is predetermined by its levels of social, educational, occupational, and technological mobility. The higher a society's level of development, the higher its spatial mobility. However, a community's mobility is restricted by spatial friction.

Potential destinations for a large section of prospective international migrants in developing countries are limited to more accessible continental and subcontinental cores closer to home. This is due to a number of positive and negative factors. On the one hand, increasing numbers of people prone to migrate are being created by the process of economic globalization in peripheral countries.

At the same time the mobility of the population in these countries is increased as a result of the associated effects of the world wide process of social transition.

On the other hand, the relative geographical isolation of many developing societies, the limited means of intercontinental travelling available to isolated peripheral societies, and strict international migration control measures limit international migration.

The combined effect of these factors causes continental and subcontinental core regions also to become popular destinations for highly skilled migrants. As in the case of global cities, the availability of high skilled job opportunities in these lower order world cities also create employment opportunities for ancillary workers, although at a smaller scale than in the global cores. South Africa is a case in point. Over the past decade, but especially since the political transition, an estimated 6-8 million clandestine migrants from neighbouring countries have accumulated in the country. Also skilled migrants are migrating to South Africa (Oucho 1995). According to the pattern internationally, it is accepted that a large proportion of these migrants settles in the major metropolitan areas.

These facts make some of the conclusions drawn from studies on low skilled international migrants coming from relatively nearby countries in North America and Europe irrelevant to large sections of migrants originating from more isolated countries in the developing world. A prospective low skilled migrant from Central Africa, for instance, cannot simply cross the border of the United States at night and find him or herself in one of the global cores the following week. Also remittances options and the scale of their effect on local upliftment in countries of origin would greatly differ for countries adjacent to global core nations, from those further removed.

Together, factors such as the levels of development of different communities globally, the distances between countries, and the geographical position of global, continental, and subcontinental core

179

regions relative to one another, determine global patterns of main and substream migration. In contrast to these migration streams which normally head in opposite directions between the same sets of urban areas within countries, it should be expected that smaller volumes of legal international migrants will be migrating to lesser cores than to larger cores globally. In that sense main and substream migration, as a consequence of productionism and environmentalism at the global level, is likely to be more complex than at the national level. Nevertheless, they remain potentially powerful indicators of the relative status of core regions globally, and should be used as a tool to determine how the international urban system evolves over time.

6.6   Conclusions

Many international migration studies do reflect upon the effect factors such as cultural differences between migrants and destination communities, skills and income levels have on international migration. The study of international migration without a more explicit consideration of, firstly, the origin of international migrants, and secondly, the location of one urban network relative to other lower or higher order urban networks in global context, holds certain risks. These risks include erroneous generalizations regarding the ability of migrants to assimilate with resident communities in host countries, remittances relationships, the possible concealment of distinct main and substream redistribution patterns, the obfuscation of underlying continental and subcontinental migration gains and losses, and other aspects of migrant behaviour in destination countries. The differentiation between main and substream international migration could play an important role in unravelling the fundamental forces driving migrants across international borders.

A differential urbanization approach to international migration necessitates the differentiation between main and substream international migration on the one hand and between productionism and environmentalism driven trends on the other hand. To enable one to pick up the subtle spatial intricacies of the concept of differential urbanization at a global scale, international migration will have to be studied in terms of flows between urban settlements within and between urban networks, and to make this possible urban settlements will have to be classified on a global scale in terms of their networking with other centres within particular individual sets of urban networks, as well as in terms of the location of urban networks relative to one another.

If such a differentiation were made, one may have found that mainstream international migration does indeed conform to what is being said in the world system theory. But, at the same time, one might have found that whatever has been said about migration towards world cities also holds true for core cities at the continental and subcontinental urban network levels.

180

Perhaps one would have found that international agglomeration factors such as the globalization of financial and service industries, direct foreign investment, and the location of multinational headquarters not only create a new global division of labour favouring core apexes in developed countries, but they also favour certain core cities in peripheral areas. If this is true, one should expect differences between core cities in the developed world and certain core cities in the less developed world to become less marked over time. These strategically positioned core cities in the developing world will then also start growing faster economically and when that happens, maybe, the world core cities of today will eventually become the Lisbons, the Athenses, and the Romes of tomorrow, while the Hong Kongs, the Singapores, and the Johannesburgs of today might become the New Yorks and the Londons of tomorrow.

Acknowledgement

The author wants to express his gratitude towards Laurette Grobler, Ilse Oliver, Cindy Pretorius, and Laetitia Oosthuizen who assisted with the preparation of the graphics.

References

Beaverstock, J. V. (1994), 'Rethinking Skilled International Labor Migration – World Cities and Banking Organizations', *Geoforum*, vol. 25, pp. 323–38.

Bourne, L. S. (1975), *Urban Systems: Strategies for Regulation – A comparison of policies in Britain, Sweden, Australia, and Canada*, Oxford University Press, London.

Castles, S and Miller, M.J. (1993), *The Age of Migration – International Population Movements in the Modern World*, McMillan, Basingstoke.

Champion, A. G. (1994), 'International Migration and Demographic-change in the Developed World', *Urban Studies*, vol. 31, pp. 653–77.

Clark, W.A.V. (1994), 'International migration and population-policy', *Environment and Planning A*, vol. 26, no. 10, pp.1499–500.

Friedmann, J. (1966), *Regional Development Policy: A Case Study of Venezuela*, MIT, Cambridge, Mass.

Geyer, H. S. (1989), 'Differential Urbanisation in South Africa and its Consequences for Spatial Development Policy', *African Urban Quarterly*, vol. 5, pp. 276–92.

Geyer, H. S. (1990), 'Implications of Differential Urbanization on Deconcentration in the Pretoria-Witwatersrand-Vaal Triangle Metropolitan area', *Geoforum*, vol. 21, South Africa, pp. 385–96.

Geyer, H. S. (1996), 'Extending the Theoretical Foundation of Differential Urbanization. *Tijdschrift voor Sociale en Economische Geografie*', vol. 87, pp. 44–59.

Geyer, H. S. and Kontuly, T. (1993), 'A Theoretical Foundation for the Concept of Differential Urbanization', *International Regional Science Review*, vol. 15, pp. 157–77.

Geyer, H. S. and Kontuly, T. (1996), *Differential Urbanization: Integrating Spatial Models*, Arnold.

Gordon, P. (1979), 'Deconcentration Without A 'Clean Break', *Environment and Planning A*, vol. 11, pp. 281–90.

Helton, A.C. (1995), 'Forced International Migration: A Need for New Approaches by the International Community', *Fordham International Law Journal*, vol. 18, pp. 1623–36.

Klaassen, L.H. (1987), 'The Future of the Larger European Towns', *Urban Studies*, vol. 24, pp.251–57.

Klaassen, L.H., Bourdrez, J.A. and Volmuller, J. (1981a), *Transport and Reurbanization*, Gower, Aldershot, UK.

Klaassen, L.H. and Scimemi , G. (1981b) 'Theoretical Issues in Urban Dynamics', in Klaassen, L.H., Molle, W.T.M. and J.H.P. Paelinck (eds) *Dynamics of Urban Development*, St.Martin's Press, New York, pp. 8–28.

Leitner, H. (1995), 'International Migration and the Politics of Admission and Exclusion in Postwar Europe', *Political Geography*, vol. 14, pp. 259–78.

Massey, D.S., Arango, J., Hugo, G., Kouaouchi, A. Pellegrino, A. and Taylor, J.E. (1994), 'An evaluation of International Migration Theory – the North-American Case', *Population and Development Review*, vol. 20, pp. 699–751.

Moore, E.G. and Rosenberg, M.W. (1995), 'Modeling Migration Flows of Immigrant Groups in Canada', *Environment and Planning A*, vol. 27, pp. 699–714.

Oucho, J. (1995), 'International Migration and Sustainable Human Development in Easten and Southern Africa', *Internationa Migration*, vol. 33, pp. 31–53.

Perroux, F. (1950), 'The Domination Effect and Modern Economic Theory', *Social Research*, vol. 17, pp. 188–206.

Poot, J. (1996), 'Information, Communication and Networks in International Migration Systems', *Annals of Regional Science*, vol. 30, pp. 55–74.

Richardson, H.W. (1973), *Economic Growth Theory. MacMillan*, London.

Richardson, H.W. (1977), 'City Size and National Strategies in Developing Countries', World Bank Staff Working Report, Washington.

Richardson, H.W. (1980) 'Polarization Reversal in Developing Countries', *Papers of the Regional Science Association*, vol. 45, pp. 67–85.

Richter, K. (1985) 'Nonmetropolitan Growth in the Late 1970s: The End of the Turnaround?', *Demography*, vol. 22, pp. 245–63.

Segal, A. (1993), *An Atlas of International Migration*, Hans Zell Publishers, London, UK.

Van den Berg, L., Klaassen, L.H., Molle, W.T.M. and Paelinck, J.H.P. (1981), 'Synthesis and conclusions', in Klaassen, L.H., Molle, W.T.M. and J.H.P. Paelinck (eds), *Dynamics of Urban Development*, St.Martin's Press, New York, pp. 251–67.

Van den Berg, L., Drewett, R., Klaassen, L.H., Rossi, A. and Vijverberg, C.H.T. (1982), *A Study of Growth and Decline*, Pergamon Press, Oxford.

Vining, D.R. Jr. and Strauss, A. (1977), 'A Demonstration that the Current Deconcentration of Population in the United States is a Clean Break with the Past', *Environment and Planning A*, vol. 9, pp. 751–58.

Zelinsky, W. (1971) 'The Hypothesis of the Mobility Transition', *Geographical Review*, vol. 16, pp. 219–49.

7 Immigration: The Spatial Dimension

GABRIEL LIPSHITZ

7.1 Introduction

Immigration is a multidisciplinary research topic. For example, demographers stress the traits of the immigrants; psychologists look at the emotional problems encountered by immigrants when leaving their country of origin and attempting to integrate into the destination country and geographers explore the spatial distribution of immigrants in the destination country on the regional and intra-urban levels. Economists, who regard immigration as movement of labour between countries, stress the macroeconomic effect on the countries of origin and destination (more on the theoretical level than empirically) much more than the regional influence (between regions in the destination country). Finally, jurists look at the legal side and at restrictions on permission for prospective immigrants to enter the destination countries.

The aim of the present study is to look at the spatial aspect of immigration from the perspectives of immigration policy and the spatial distribution of immigrants at the international and national levels. The economic literature (Chiswick 1978, 1986; Borjas 1989; Simon 1992; Fielding 1993a; Greenwood 1994) generally focuses on the national – macro – level rather than the regional level. The present study does not concentrate on regional economics, either. Immigration policy is not directly related to the spatial dimension (except in a few countries whose immigration policy addresses the spatial distribution of the immigrants). Nevertheless, this topic is included in the present study because a country's immigration policy has an indirect effect on the distribution of immigrants on the international and national levels.

7.2 Immigration Policy

Immigration policy is an issue of particular concern to politicians. Immigration policy is a government effort to regulate and control the entry of immigrants into the country, and to establish the terms under which people can settle there permanently, work there temporarily, or obtain political asylum (Cruz 1991). One might ask why immigration policy is needed and why everyone can't be permitted to live wherever he or she wishes. Indeed, in Europe before World War I, there was almost no government intervention in immigration. Such a free

185

immigration policy is supported by economists who advocate a free market of people and goods and by others who regard free migration as a human right (Fielding 1993b). In a study on immigration policy in several countries, Freeman (1992) found that the 1990s are characterized by 'a strong pattern of restrictionism', in view of the mounting pressure of immigration applications.

The problem at present with regard to international migration is thus not the ability to emigrate (after the dissolution of the Communist bloc, very few countries prohibit emigration), but rather permission to immigrate. Improvements in means of transportation and their availability has cut travel costs and consequently increased movement of individuals, including migration. Worldwide economic development has produced cities with cosmopolitan, diverse populations, thereby creating a human infrastructure for immigrant absorption. Moreover, employers in destination countries favour immigration, which supplies them with an unlimited labour force at attractive prices. On the other side are the governments, which oppose uncontrolled immigration, inter alia because of domestic pressures, because they want to preserve the country's cultural and historical hue, and because the immigrants take funds out of the public purse without ever having contributed to it through taxes. The conflict in industrialized countries is between the desire to reduce wage costs and increase labour market flexibility and the desire to preserve the culture and heritage (Fielding 1993b). Widening gaps in standards of living between Western Europe and the Third World has brought about two opposite results: on the one hand the destination countries have tightened restrictions on immigration, and on the other hand the number of illegal immigrants has increased, as has the number of people seeking political asylum as the only possible way of 'migrating' legally.

Countries with long traditions of immigration – such as the United States, Australia, New Zealand and Canada – have recently instituted more stringent policies regarding the admission of immigrants. The main concern of the US immigration policy is countering the massive amount of illegal immigration, chiefly from Mexico (Jones 1995). In this it has failed. NAFTA may reduce immigration pressures by increasing trade and eliminating the need to immigrate, provided that trade and immigration are substitutable (conversely, if they are complementary, then increased trade will boost immigration; see Razin and Sadka 1995). Some sectors in the United States support immigration; among them are farmers and owners of light industry, who need people with little skill to work for minimum wages. The theory that competition in international trade is related to immigration is gaining strength in the United States. The theory maintains that international competition for production and trade increases the desire to take in immigrants as an efficient, production boosting work force; because wages are low, low prices can be set for products, thereby increasing the probability of becoming more competitive in the world marketplace.

In Australia, the general consensus that used to exist with regard to immigration policy is being undermined. Recently the Australian government adopted a series of measures to slow the pace of immigration and tighten control of it. The number of immigrants has indeed declined: from 140,000 in 1989–1990 to about 80,000 in 1992–1993. Interestingly, immigration to Australia increased in the 1970s when there was a recession there. The possible reasons for this are mainly political: pressure from the growth lobby of contractors who own labour-intensive businesses; economists' belief in the favourable effect of immigration on the economy; pressure by ethnic groups; and pressure by liberal intellectual groups that support the admission of immigrants, especially refugees and seekers of political asylum, on humanitarian grounds.

Canada, like Australia, recently considered making its immigration policy more stringent, and the reasoning is mostly economic. Canada's immigration policy is more lenient with regard to skilled workers and academics. In the end, Canada did not curtail the number of immigrants. The official immigration plan set forth in 1990 for 1991–1995 encourages immigration by people with occupations that the country lacks and calls for directing some immigrants to areas where their occupations are needed. The Canadian policy is thus somewhere between the US policy and the Australian one. It does not reduce the number of immigrants as the Australian one does, but it is more careful than the US policy is to link the immigrants' occupation and level of education to market needs and economic development.

In Europe, policy measures are formulated from time to time, chiefly to stem the tide of illegal immigration and the movement of guest workers. Public opinion in host countries – especially in Europe – is becoming more and more opposed to the presence of immigrants, especially non-European ones. The ethnic factor is vital in Western European society. Demands that immigration be reduced or halted are made on ethnic grounds, and ethnicity is a factor in the renewed rise of national identity (White 1993). Various European countries, each in its own way, are trying to cope with refugees, political asylum-seekers, and guest workers, but with little success. In 1989, for example, a law was enacted in Sweden – one of the most liberal countries – restricting the admission of guest workers and asylum-seekers. It was repealed in 1991 due to criticism and pressure from minorities.

Since the 1970s the European migration policy has been based on the premise that immigration can be controlled. After the recession of the 1970s and the oil crisis that followed, all Western European countries declared an 'immigration stop' policy – a meticulous filtering of immigrants and granting of entry permits only to specific categories of people with needed occupations. However, this policy was not successful in most of the countries that tried it. Immigration to Western European countries actually increased during this period (Brochmann 1993). The immigrants found ways of circumventing the entry restrictions. As

Brochmann writes on page 108, 'Control of one gateway may consequently direct the flow on to a new track'.

Another factor that makes control of immigration to Europe difficult is the Maastricht Treaty, which turns Europe into a free trade zone with no passport control at the borders. This makes it difficult to stem the flow of immigrants from one country to another and complicates the stringent policy measures that various countries want to use with regard to immigration.

A country's *immigration policy* encompasses more than just an immigration quota. There are also social, economic, housing, and spatial policies. Few countries have a *spatial immigration policy* for the geographical dispersal of immigrants within the country, as Israel does (Lipshitz 1991). Most countries leave geographic dispersal and employment to market forces. In terms of *sociocultural policies* on immigrant absorption there are two approaches: One is the 'melting pot' approach, under which immigrants from all countries undergo a process of assimilation in the destination country. This concept is based on the argument that social assimilation is important for creating a new social basis for the country, and that this assimilation helps with economic advancement. The second approach is multiculturalism. This policy encourages retention of immigrants' ethnocultural identity and creation of a multicultural nation. The first approach is better suited to the US immigration policy, whereas the second is adopted more by Canada and Australia. In Australia the first strategy was used until the 1960s; since the early 1970s the second has been dominant (Ozdowski 1985; Patterson 1990). In 1947 the Australian population numbered 7.6 million, only 9.8 percent of them foreign-born (and most of these were from the British Empire). Therefore the Anglo-Saxon culture was dominant and the language was uniform. Within 30 years the population doubled and its socioethnic composition changed radically. In 1984 Australia had a population of 15.6 million, 3.2 million of them (21 percent) born in foreign countries, among them Eastern European, Middle Eastern, and South American countries (Patterson 1990). These waves of immigration altered the sociocultural structure in Australia. One manifestation of this change is the multiplicity and diversity of the media. Today there are close to 80 ethnic newspapers and periodicals in 25 languages, in addition to ramified multicultural radio and television broadcasts (Patterson 1990). The radical changes in the ethnic makeup of immigration to Australia forced policy makers to switch from a melting-pot policy to multiculturalism.

There are two main approaches to *housing policy*. Some countries do not intervene at all in the housing of immigrants; they leave the work of housing to the free market. Some Western European countries intervened in the immigrant housing market in the past, building immigrant neighbourhoods for them. This approach increased sociocultural segregation within cities. In several Western European countries – especially West Germany after World War II – immigrants were housed in suburban neighbourhoods near large factories. The homes were provided by the employers (King 1993a; White 1993). Recently several Western European countries and cities have taken steps to prevent immigrants from settling in certain neighbourhoods and in social housing in order to eliminate the segregation, but without success (van Amersfoort and de Klerk 1987; Sporton and White 1989; Arin 1991; White 1993). Since the start of the 1970s and even more so in the 1980s, some public housing has been privatized, and less public housing has been built for immigrants (Krätke 1989). The free housing market in Western Europe (the Netherlands, for example) reduced housing opportunities for immigrants, especially illegal immigrants and refugees of the third, post-industrial, wave. As a result, in some European countries a subsector is emerging in the housing market, based on organization by ethnic communities, in an effort to help immigrants from the same ethnic group find suitable housing (White 1993).

7.3   Spatial Patterns of Immigration: The International Level

The worldwide spatial pattern of international migration in the 1980s and 1990s consists of movement of migrants from the developing countries, where rates of natural increase are high, to the developed, industrialized countries, where rates of natural increase are dropping markedly. For example, the rate of natural increase in the countries of the Common Market/European Community declined from 8.0 per 1,000 population in 1960 to 1.8 per 1,000 population in 1989; in the same period net immigration rose from 0.2 to 3.3 per 1,000 population (Hall 1993). Within this worldwide spatial pattern the regional dimension is of particular importance. Hall argues that much of international migration is 'regional' and geographically short range. For example, most immigrants to Germany are from Eastern Europe; most immigrants to France are from North Africa, especially Algeria; the United States attracts a large number of immigrants from nearby Mexico, though also from the faraway Philippines and South Korea (Hall 1993). Immigration from Asia, as we shall see below, confuses the regional dimension of international migration by increasing its range. Portes and Rumbaut argue that most immigration today is long-range, and that distance is becoming less of a consideration (Portes and Rumbaut 1990). Immigration to Israel from the former Soviet Union is an example of long-range, rather than regional, immigration.

Worldwide political and economic changes have also altered the spatial patterns of international migration (Salt 1989; Castles and Miller 1993; King 1993b; Nijkamp and Spiess 1993, 1994; Gould and Findlay 1994). The *political world order* in the second half of this century has revolved around the Cold War between the United States and the USSR and these two superpowers' control of various parts of the world. When the Communist regime collapsed, bringing down the Iron Curtain between Eastern and Western Europe, Western European and other Western countries experienced new influxes of immigration, requiring special measures by the host countries. Immigration from the former Soviet Union to Israel is one outcome of the recent worldwide political changes.

The *economic world order* in the second half of this century is linked to the growth of multinational corporations and the new geographical division of the worldwide labour force. The multinational corporations transferred their production lines to developing countries, thereby lessening emigration of cheap labour from these countries to the mass production lines of the industrialized countries. Concurrently, however, a 'brain drain' began, as highly skilled workers from Third World countries moved to developed countries. The emigration of young, educated, skilled workers from the developing countries to the developed countries has been one of the most prominent characteristics of international migration in the last several decades. Such migration increases the economic disparity between core and peripheral countries, which in turn induces even more migration.

Significant changes have taken place over time in *spatial patterns (countries of origin and destination)* and in the *profile of the immigrants* (their demographic and economic traits). Western European countries were fed first by Italy, then by Spain, Greece, and Portugal, later by Yugoslavia and Turkey, and eventually by North Africa and the Third World (King 1993c). Salt (1992a, 1992b), in his paper on types of international migration, discusses the changes that have occurred since the middle of this century: In the 1940s migration was mainly related to World War II and the events that followed. The 1950s saw the resumption of permanent international migration, particularly the movement of Europeans to North America, Australia, and New Zealand, and the first trickle of workers migrating to Western Europe. Migration between Eastern and Western Europe was blocked by the Iron Curtain, which separated the countries in the Soviet sphere of influence from the West. The 1960s were marked by migration of workers due to the efforts of Western European countries to develop and rehabilitate their economies and the consequent labour shortage. Migration in the 1970s was characterized mainly by reunification of workers' families, primarily in Europe. During this period other Western countries began to tighten up their immigration policies, including their policies regarding the admission of guest workers, for fear of family reunification and permanent settlement, as was happening in Europe. Because of the intended temporary immigration of guest workers to Europe and the ensuing family reunification, Europe has five million guest workers. In the 1980s the debate over international migration focused on illegal immigrants, political-asylum seekers, and educated, skilled workers. In his analysis of changes in immigration to Europe over time, White states that Western Europe experienced three waves of immigration: a wave of labour immigration; a wave of family reunification; and the post- industrial wave (White 1993).

Whereas in the 1960s and 1970s the main destinations of the migrants were Western Europe, the United States, and Canada, in the 1980s the oil-rich countries of the Middle East took the place of Europe. International migration in the 1980s was made up of a group of *spatial networks* with similarities and differences; for example, migration from North Africa to Europe; from Eastern Europe to Western Europe; from the Caribbean islands and Mexico to the United States; from various African countries to South Africa and some countries on the African coast; and from Southeast Asia to Australia; as well as migration of workers from Southeast Asia to the oil-rich Middle Eastern countries.

Salt's analysis of *international migration networks* demonstrates that there are differences between and within the networks, and that each network changes over time (Salt 1992b). For example, Germany and France have fairly similar numbers of immigrants and rates of immigration, but from different places. Immigrants to England come from still other countries. In the 1960s Italians stopped moving to France and turned to West Germany instead due to wage differentials and the return from Algeria to France of about one million French people.

The Middle Eastern network (migration to the oil-rich countries) differs from the European one not only in the countries of origin but also in immigration policy; most of the migrants are from Arab countries, and family reunification is prevented. In the Arab oil countries – unlike in Western Europe and North America – most immigrants are channelled into limited areas of work, chiefly simple manufacturing and services (Birks, Sinclair, and Seccomb 1988). When oil prices fell in the mid-1980s, the rulers of the countries that employed foreign workers replaced workers from Arab countries with Asians, who are more efficient and cheaper, and thus the composition of migration in the Middle Eastern network changed (Addleton 1991). In 1975, approximately 65 percent of foreign workers in the oil countries were from Arab countries; by 1985 only 30 percent were. In the latter year approximately 63 percent were from southern Asia (Pakistan, Bangladesh, India) and East Asia (the Philippines, Indonesia, Thailand). The Gulf War caused the departure of many Arab workers; their place was taken by workers from southern and eastern Asia.

Until the 1970s the immigration network in Australia was characterized by immigration from Europe; in the 1980s the percentage of immigrants from Southeast Asia increased. Immigration to Canada has undergone a similar trend. In the 1940s and 1950s, 70 percent of immigrants to Canada were from Europe; by the 1980s the figure was down to about 20 percent. The percentage of Asians among the immigrants rose from 10 percent in the 1940s and 1950s to 60 percent in the 1980s. In 1960 about 40 percent of all immigrants to the United States were from Europe; in the 1980s only about 10 percent were. In the United States, too, the Europeans were replaced by southern and eastern Asians: southern and eastern Asians accounted for about 14 percent of all immigrants to the United States in the 1960s, as opposed to 40 percent in the 1980s.

In the 1990s a new region of attraction is emerging: the New Industrialized Countries (NIC) in Southeast Asia. These countries include Thailand, Taiwan, Singapore, and South Korea. Over time these countries have changed their economic structure, and they are now experiencing high rates of growth and attracting people not only from southern and eastern Asia, but from Western Europe and North America as well.

The geography of immigration in the 1990s increasingly reflects the *globalization of the economy* – the structural changes in the world economy (transition from traditional industry to high-tech industry and business services). Consequently, host countries seek professional, managerial, and technical (PMT) workers suited to the changes in their economic structure and their comparative advantage in the world market, and they have reduced their demand for unskilled workers. Demand for workers also depends on unemployment levels: immigration decreases as the unemployment rate rises (King 1993c).

The relationship between immigration and structural changes in the world economy is expressed in the book *Population Migration and the Changing World Order*. The editors, Gould and Findlay (1994), show how multinational corporations caused segmentation of the worldwide labour force, moving work to developing countries, while management and research and development units remained in the West. As expected, this slowed the movement of cheap labour from developing countries to developed countries. Concurrently, however, the 'brain drain' from developing to developed countries increased. This movement of human capital from developing countries harms the regional development potential and facilitates the economic growth of developed countries.

As described above, the global structural changes in the economy alter the pattern of demand for labour. One of the factors determining the spatial pattern of international migration, however, is the extent to which the local market (of each country) can produce workers on a high enough technological and scientific level to meet the demand. (The migration of skilled workers is, of course, also influenced by other factors, such as trade and capital flows and political barriers). The wider the gap is between supply and demand, the more international migration of educated and skilled workers there will be. In Europe, for example, the prevailing view is that skilled workers will have to be imported because of an extremely low rate of natural increase (Coleman 1992). Nevertheless, the increase in the percentage of women in the labour force may well reduce the demand for foreign workers. Coleman estimates the potential of the female labour force in Europe at 33 million workers, and he calls this the 'hidden supply'. Another source of labour within Europe is Eastern Europe, which has a reservoir of skilled workers. The last source of educated and skilled workers in Europe consists of the Western European countries themselves, where the unemployment rate among the university educated is high. There are currently about 15 million unemployed persons in Western Europe, including scientists and skilled workers; as a result international

192

migration in Europe may become predominantly intra-European rather than global (Coleman 1992). Indeed, the new restrictions on immigration, the disintegration of the Soviet regime, the collapse of the Iron Curtain, the reunification of Germany, and the substantial increase in free movement among the EU countries support a new pattern of international migration in Europe – a more European, less international one.

Despite these trends, it can be expected that Europe will also experience immigration of expert workers that the European countries are unable to obtain locally or from elsewhere in Europe. The increase in modern industry and business services requires a high degree of skill that at times can be achieved only by importing workers. Immigration of experts is also a manifestation of the expansion of international trade and the geographical spread of international corporations (Findlay and Garrick 1990).

Jones's study on Australia provides a good example of changes in the spatial patterns of international migration and the creation of a new international-migration network as a result of economic globalization processes (Jones 1994). Australia's close economic ties with Europe, Great Britain, and the United States are weakening, and ties with Asia – especially Southeast Asia – are becoming stronger (Chalkey and Winchester 1991). Between 1970 and 1991, for example, the share of Australian exports to Asia rose from 49 to 67 percent, while the share of exports to Europe fell from 23 to 15 percent. Concurrently, tourism between Australia and eastern and southern Asia increased. The changes in regional economic ties are also manifested in immigration to Australia: 51 percent of immigrants to Australia in 1991–1992 were Asian.

Due to changes in spatial patterns and composition, international migration in the 1990s can be expected to widen worldwide interregional disparities. Most host countries are becoming more selective; they are most interested in educated people with scientific and technological occupations. The era of mass migration of unskilled workers has ended. As Salt writes on page 1081, 'Their need for mass immigration is gone and will not return' (Salt 1992b).

The 1990s also represent the end of a period of fairly easy immigration and the beginning of an era of *strict immigration policies* (Salt 1992a). The popular destination countries are becoming more stringent and selective. This change affects not only the spatial patterns of international migration, but also its composition. People with prestigious occupations in high technology and other fields are permitted to immigrate to attractive destinations. Thus we are likely to see two types of patterns of immigration: legal immigration of young people with higher education and academic and technological occupations and illegal immigration of unskilled labourers.

7.4   Spatial Patterns of Immigration: The National Level

Initially, immigrants tend to settle in the major cities, and within the cities in specific neighbourhoods, usually poor inner-city neighbourhoods (Simon 1992). This tendency was particularly prominent in White's first and second waves of immigration to Europe. In these neighbourhoods the new immigrants find people who arrived in previous waves of immigration from the same countries of origin. The reason for the concentration of immigrants in the big cities has to do with the good job prospects there; sociocultural and economic considerations are behind their concentration in specific neighbourhoods. The spatial patterns set by the first immigrants from a particular ethnic group therefore have a major impact on new immigrants from the same ethnic group. There are even cases in which residents of a town in a certain country of origin settled in a particular town in the destination country and were followed by more migration from the same town of origin to the same destination town (Lipshitz 1992). This has been termed 'chain migration' (King 1993c). Immigrant entrepreneurs who deal in products and services consumed largely by members of their own ethnic group also tend to settle in or near the large ethnic concentration. For them this concentration is an important source of business and a basis for the development of economic ties (Portes and Rumbaut 1990). These spatial patterns hold true more for blue-collar workers and traditional entrepreneurs than for white-collar workers, who tend to spread out even initially.

The spatial distribution of the immigrants' initial place of residence within the cities determines the later spatial distribution of immigrants, too. In London, for example, immigration created geographic concentrations in the heart of the city. About 25 percent of the residents of the inner city of London are minorities (Fielding 1993b). Nevertheless, as immigrants and their children assimilate in the host society, they begin to disperse.

On the national level, too, the spatial distribution of the first immigrants determines the spatial distribution of subsequent immigrants. A good example of this is the spatial distribution of Hispanic immigrants in the United States (Davis, Haub, and Willette 1983). Although there are Hispanics in almost every US state today, most still live in a few states and regions. California, with a population of 6.5 million Hispanics, is the initial place of settlement for one out of every three Hispanic immigrants. Other states with large Hispanic populations are Texas, with 4.1 million Hispanics; New York, with 2.1 million; and Florida, with 1.5 million. This spatial distribution seems to be determined chiefly by the geographical proximity of the countries of origin to US states. Furthermore, 88 percent of the Hispanics in the United States live in metropolitan areas, and more than half of these live in the central cities of those metropolitan areas.

Immigration to specific destinations affects *internal migration* to and from these destinations. The geographic distribution of whites and minorities in the United States in the 1980s was strongly affected by the interplay between immigration and internal migration (Frey 1995a, 1995b). In US states and metropolitan areas that attract immigrants – especially Hispanic and Asian minorities – net internal migration among whites is negative and net internal migration among minorities is positive. These spatial processes function simultaneously in a sort of 'scissor action': large numbers of immigrants move in and large numbers of whites move out. Together they constitute the main factor shaping the spatial distribution of the US population on the national and metropolitan levels. California, New York, and Texas are examples of states whose demographic spatial makeup is determined by international migration (the entry of minorities and the resultant departure of whites), whereas the demography of Arizona, Virginia, and North Carolina is determined mainly by internal migration of whites (positive net migration by the white population).

This dynamic process – which picked up speed in the 1980s and operates in just a few US states – leads to what Frey (1995c) has called a 'racial and ethnic balkanization pattern'. Interestingly, according to Frey the departing whites are those with low levels of income and education. These people are replaceable in the job market by immigrants, who displace the natives. This process occurs with great intensity in US metropolitan areas. The metropolitan areas in which immigrants play an important positive role in population growth and natives play a negative role through internal migration (negative net migration) are the old and long-established ones, such as Los Angeles, Chicago, and New York. In relatively new metropolitan areas, such as Atlanta, Seattle, and Phoenix, the main factor affecting population growth is internal migration.

While the immigrants tend to concentrate in the big cities – and especially in the inner cities – the native-born begin to migrate from the inner cities to the outskirts and the suburbs. In Hall's opinion, one effect of immigration has been a long term decline of the large Western cities (Hall 1993). Hall believes that the stage identified by some researchers as reconcentration of population in the big cities is merely a statistical error or a misinterpretation of spatial processes. The big Western cities are in a stage of super-dispersal or super-deconcentration, accompanied by reconcentration of population in the medium-sized cities in the distant periphery of the big cities and not in the big cities themselves. The bulk of this process is carried out through internal migration by the native-born, whereas the growth of the big cities (the central cities of the metropolitan areas) is accomplished in the West by immigrants (Hall 1993).

The immigrants, Hall says, move to the big cities for the same reasons their relatives and others moved there one hundred years earlier. The reasons for immigration to London, New York, Berlin, and other cities, as in the past, are economic, employment-related (high probability of finding a job of some sort), and sociocultural (proximity to relatives and community services). The big cities in the West are apparently destined

195

to be 'host cities' for the people of the developing world. Immigration is turning the big cities in the West into an economic bridge to the Third World. Vancouver is an interesting example. For many years Vancouver has been a regional economic centre for western Canada, especially for the province of British Columbia. In the past decade it has undergone a significant spatial economic transformation from a regional business centre to an international business centre linking Canada with eastern and southern Asia, including Japan. One of the main factors in this change is immigration to Vancouver, which accelerated greatly in the past decade. The increasingly affluent immigrants in Vancouver are an important human basis for the creation and expansion of economic ties with business centres in their countries of origin.

In some countries the destination regions of immigrants vary over time. Canada is a good example. In the 1940s and 1950s, and even in the 1960s, the main destination regions were the peripheral provinces, especially Manitoba and Saskatchewan. In the 1980s, in contrast, the main destinations were the core provinces: British Columbia and Ontario. In 1911 and 1921 about 40 percent of immigrants to Canada moved to the prairie provinces and 30 percent to Ontario. In 1986 the rates were 15 and 55 percent, respectively. This change reflects the structural changes in the Canadian regional economy: a rapid transition from agriculture to industry and from industry to business services in Ontario and the western provinces (Moore, Ray, and Rosenberg 1990).

The changes over time in immigrants' choice of destination in Canada have also caused a demographic polarization between and within provinces, intensifying the spatial economic polarization. The reason is not only accelerated population growth in a few central provinces due to immigration (which, of course, has an economic impact by raising the threshold and boosting purchasing power) but also – and perhaps primarily – the quality of the immigrants. In 1986 about 12 percent of immigrants to Canada aged 15 and over had university degrees, compared to 9 percent of nonimmigrants. About 16 percent of immigrant men are skilled workers, compared to 12 percent of nonimmigrant men. The longer immigrants have been in Canada, the higher their salaries, and the greater their labour force participation rate. Among some age cohorts it even slightly surpasses the labour-force participation rate of the native population (Meckie and Thompson 1990). In other words, because they are educated, have technological professions, and are highly motivated to integrate economically, the immigrants are an important motivating force in the Canadian economy in general and in the economies of several provinces and cities in particular. Because the immigrants are concentrated in a few regions, they provide impetus to the local economy in these places, while not affecting most other regions. In this way immigration increases interregional and intraregional disparities in Canada. It should be noted that the immigrants respond quickly to changes in the Canadian national and spatial economy. Although in the short term they tend to stay where they initially settled in the country, in the medium term they migrate, especially to those few regions that are experiencing economic growth (Moore, Ray, and Rosenberg 1990).

Changes over time in immigrants' choice of area of residence occur on the intra-urban level, too. In the first wave of migration to Europe (labour immigration; see White 1993), which took place in the 1950s and 1960s, the immigrants – who came mainly for work – settled in the big industrial cities, and particularly in the poor neighbourhoods. Some of these neighbourhoods are located in the inner city, and others in suburbs at a low socioeconomic level. Suburban residential neighbourhoods for immigrants are found most often in countries in which ethnic minorities are eligible for public housing. For example, in Amsterdam and Paris in the 1970s a rapid process of deconcentration of immigrants from the inner city to the suburbs began after public housing was built for them (Sporton and White 1989; Van Amsterfoort 1990). In Britain, the deconcentration of immigrants was not as conspicuous as in the Netherlands and France, because in some British cities public housing was built for immigrants in the inner city. The second wave of the 1970s (family reunification) reinforced the spatial pattern of the 1950s and 1960s. The third (post-industrial) wave in the 1990s, which comprises mainly high-calibre professionals, is concentrated on the national level in cities with high tech industry and business services and in the relatively affluent neighbourhoods of these cities; whereas refugees and illegal immigrants continue to settle in the poor neighbourhoods of the big industrial cities (White 1993).

One of the main reasons for the concentration of the immigrants in specific neighbourhoods is the presence of other immigrants from their countries of origin, including relatives and friends. The relatives and friends give the newcomers psychological, social, and even financial support and guide them through the halls of bureaucracy (Pekin 1989). How long immigrants remain dependent on their relatives is a function of their advancement on the socioeconomic ladder of the host society. The more rapid their advancement, the shorter the period of dependence on relatives. In most cases the desire to live in geographical proximity also lessens (Pekin 1989), and a certain period of time after their initial settlement those who are doing well financially begin to move to other neighbourhoods. They choose their place of residence no longer based on ethnic affiliation, but on socioeconomic status.

This brief survey of the spatial distribution and socioeconomic traits of the immigrants shows that immigrants are increasingly moving to the big cities while natives leave these cities for the metropolitan periphery and medium-sized cities. In addition, migration between Western cities has been dropping, and immigration from developing countries to Western countries has increased markedly. Stringent immigration policies enable Western countries to be selective as to the quality of the immigrants. As a result, in some destination countries the immigrants' socioeconomic and occupational levels are higher than the average in that country. The immigrants tend to move after initially settling somewhere, and a certain percentage of them move to regions based more on their socioeconomic status than on their ethnocultural affiliation. These processes alter the internal sociodemographic and cultural structure of the big cities and reshape the spatial distribution of the population on the national and metropolitan levels.

7.5   Conclusions

The present study surveyed two important aspects of immigration that are closely related indirectly and sometimes directly: the spatial distribution of immigrants at the international and national levels and policy. Government policies governing the admission of immigrants into a country determine not only the number of immigrants each year, but also their quality. In recent years destination countries (Western European and North American countries and Australia) have been very selective regarding applicants for immigration. They prefer young, educated people with academic and scientific occupations. In this way the governments intend to enhance the quality of human capital in their countries, thereby improving their ability to carry out a structural transformation in their economies from traditional industry to high technology (touched upon in Chapter 2).

This policy dictates the changes in economic integration of immigrants in the job market. Whereas in the past most immigrants found jobs as simple production workers in large factories, today more are finding work in high-technology industry, research institutes, and services. The share of immigrants in simple factory jobs is dropping, although in some destination countries it remains significant. Owners of traditional factories want to hire unskilled immigrants because they will work for low wages; as a result, manufacturers can set low prices for their products, thereby boosting their chances of beating the competition. In contrast, Western governments encourage multinational corporations to build factories in Third World countries so as to prevent immigration of unskilled workers to their countries.

Changes in the immigration policies of Western countries and the impact of these policies on the quantity and quality of immigrants also affect the spatial distribution of immigrants in the destination countries. Unskilled and illegal immigrants move to immigrant neighbourhoods with low socioeconomic status, whereas educated and skilled immigrants prefer neighbourhoods with a medium or even high socioeconomic status.

Big cities remain an important destination for immigrants, especially educated and skilled immigrants, because of the high concentration of high-technology businesses. These cities also continue to attract unskilled immigrants counting on finding work there. As a result, the long-time residents of the big cities are moving to small and medium sized cities on the fringes of the big cities.

Immigration is thus a major factor in redesigning the national and metropolitan space in the quantitative, qualitative, demographic, cultural, ethnic, and economic senses. If the planners at all levels – national, regional, and urban – want to have a part in this redesign, they must adopt a multidisciplinary approach. This approach should be based on multidisciplinary research on immigration issues, including the issues that are not covered in this study.

Acknowledgement

This chapter is part of a research project which is fully supported by the German–Israeli Foundation (GIF).

References

Addleton, J. (1991), 'The Impact of the Gulf War on Migration and Remittances in Asia and the Middle East', *International Migration Review*, vol. 29, pp. 509–26.

Arin, C. (1991), 'The Housing Market and Housing Policies for the Migrant Labour Population in West Berlin', in Huttmann, E. et al. (eds), *Urban Housing Segregation of Minorities in Western Europe and the United States,* Duke University Press: London, pp. 199–214.

Birks, J. S., Sinclair, and Seccomb. (1988), 'Labor Migration in the Arab Gulf States: Patterns, Trends and Prospects', *International Migration Review*, vol. 26, pp. 267–86.

Borjas, G. J. (1989), 'Economic Theory and International Migration', *International Migration Review*, vol. 23, pp. 457–85.

Brochmann, G. (1993), 'Control in Immigration Policies: A Close Europe in the Making', in R. King (ed.), *The New Geography of European Migrations*, Belhaven Press, London and New York, pp. 100–15.

Castles, S., and Miller, M.J. (1993), *The Age of Migration – International Population Movements in the Modern World,* Guilford Press, New York.

Castles, B. and Winchester, H. (1991), 'Australia in Transition', *Geography*, vol. 76, pp. 97–108.

Chiswick, B.R. (1978), 'The Effect of Americanization on the Earnings of Foreign–Born Men', *Journal of Political Economy*, vol. 86, pp. 897–921.

Chiswick, B.R. (1986), 'Is the New Immigration as Unskilled as the Old?' *Journal of Labor Economics*, vol. 4, pp. 168–92.

Coleman, D. (1992), 'Does Europe Need Immigrants? Population and Work Force Projections', *International Migration Review*, vol. 26, pp. 413–59.

Cruz, A. (1991), 'Will the European Community Make the 1992 Deadline on the Abolition of Internal Border Controls?', *International Migration*, vol. 24, pp. 477–82.

Davis, C., Haub, C., and Willette, J. (1983), 'U.S. Hispanics: Changing the Fact of America', *Population Bulletin*, vol. 38, pp. 1–43.

Fielding, A.J. (1993a), 'Mass Migration and Economic Restructuring', in King, R. (ed.), *Mass Migrations in Europe: The Legacy and the Future*, Belhaven Press: London, pp. 7–18.

Fielding, A.J. (1993b), 'Migrants, Institutions and Politics: The Evolution of European Migration Policies', in King, R. (ed.), *Mass Migrations in Europe: The Legacy and the Future*, Belhaven Press, London, pp. 40–62.

Findlay, A.M., and Garrick, L. (1990), 'Scottish Emigration in the 1980s: A Migration Channels Approach to Study of Skilled International Migration', *Transactions, Institute of British Geographers*, vol. 13, pp. 177–92.

Freeman, G.P. (1992), 'Migration Policy and Politics in the Receiving States', *International Migration Review*, vol. 26, pp. 1144–167.

Frey, W.H. (1995a), 'Immigration and Internal Migration "Flight": A California Case Study', *Population and Environment*, vol. 16, pp. 353–75.

Frey, W.H. (1995b), 'Immigration and Internal Migration "Flight" from US Metro Areas: Toward a New Demographic Balkanization', *Urban Studies*, vol. 32, pp. .

Frey, W.H. (1995c), 'The New Geography of Population Shifts: Trends Toward Balkanization', in Reynolds Farley (ed.), *State of the Union America in the 1990s, Volume II, Social Trends*, Russell Sage, New York, pp. 271–334.

Gould, W.T.S., and Findlay, A.M. (1994) 'Population Movements from the Third World to Developed World: Recent Trends and Current Issues', in Findlay, A.M. and W.T.S. Gould (eds), *Population Migration and the Changing World Order*, John Wiley and Sons: New York, pp. 115–26.

Greenwood, M.J. (1994), 'Potential Channels of Immigrant Influence on the Economy of Receiving Country', *Papers in Regional Science*, vol. 73, pp. 211–40.

Hall, P. (1993), 'Migration and the Future of Cities', paper presented in *European Migration and Urbanization*, Umea, Sweden, June 1993.

Jones, H.R. (1994), 'Immigration Policy and the New World Order: The Case of Australia', in Gould, W.T.S. and A.M. Findlay (eds), *Population Migration and the Changing World Order*, John Wiley and Sons, New York, pp. 161–72.

Jones, R.C. (1995), 'Immigration Reform and Migrant Flows: Compositional and Spatial Changes in Mexican Migration after the Immigration Reform Act of 1986', *Annals of the Association of American Geographers*, vol. 85, pp. 715–30.

Kemper, F.J. (1993), 'New Trends in Mass Migration in Germany', in King, R. (ed.), *Mass Migrations in Europe: The Legacy and the Future*, Belhaven Press, London, pp. 257–74.

King, R. (1993a), 'European International Migration 1945-1990: A Statistical and Geographical Overview', in R. King, R. (ed.), *Mass Migrations in Europe: The Legacy and the Future*, Belhaven Press, London.

King, R. (ed.), (1993b), *Mass Migrations in Europe: The Legacy and the Future*, Belhaven Press, London.

King, R. (1993c), 'Why do People Migrate? The Geography of Departure', in King, R. (ed.), *The New Geography of European Migrations*, Belhaven Press, London, pp. 17–46.

Krätke, S. (1989), 'The Future of Social Housing: Problems and Prospects of "Social Ownership": The Case of West Germany', *International Journal of Urban and Regional Research*, vol. 13, pp. 282–303.

Lipshitz, G. (1991), 'Immigration and Internal Migration as a Mechanism of Polarization and Dispersion of Population and Development, the Israeli Case', *Economic Development and Cultural Change*, vol. 39, pp. 391–408.

Lipshitz, G. (1992), *Development Towns That Take in Immigrants: Dimona and Qiryat Shemona*, Jerusalem Institute for Israel Studies, Jerusalem.

Meckie, C. and Thompson, K. (1990), *Canadian Social Trends*, Thompson Educational Publishers, Toronto.

Moore, E.G., Ray, B.K. and Rosenberg, M.W. (1990), 'The Redistribution of Immigrants in Canada', Population Working Paper no. 12, *Employment and Immigration Canada*, Ottawa-Hull.

Nijkamp, P. and Spiess, K. (1993), 'International Migration in Western Europe: Macro Trends in the Past, the Present and the Future', *Current Politics and Economics of Europe*, vol. 3, pp. 238–62.

Nijkamp, P. and Spiess, K. (1994), 'International Migration in Europe: Critical Success Absorption Factors', *Journal of Regional Studies*, vol. 12, pp. 331–35.

Ozdowski, S.A. (1985), 'The Law, Immigration and Human Rights: Changing the Australian Control System', *International Migration Review*, vol. 29.

Patterson, R. (1990), 'Development of Ethnic Multicultural Media in Australia', *International Migration Review*, vol. 28.

Pekin, H. (1989), 'Effect of Migration in Family Structure', *International Migration Review*, vol. 27, pp. 281–93.

Portes, A., and Rumbaut R.G. (1990), *Immigrant America*, University of California Press, Berkeley.

Razin, A. and Sadka, E. (1995), *Population Economics*, MIT Press, Cambridge, Mass.

Salt, J. (1989), 'A Comparative Overview of International Trends and Types, 1950-1980', *International Migration Review*, vol. 23, pp. 431–56.

Salt, J. (1992a), 'Migration Processes Among the Highly Skilled in Europe', *International Migration Review*, vol. 26, pp. 484–505.

Salt, J. (1992b), 'The Future of International Labor Migration', *International Migration Review*, vol. 26, pp. 1077–143.

Simon, J.L. (1992), *The Economic Consequences of Immigration*, Routledge, London.

Sporton, D., and White, P.E. (1989), 'Immigrants in Social Housing: Integration or Segregation in France?', *The Planner*, vol. 75, no. 4, pp. 2–31.

Van Amersfoort, H., and de Klerk, L. (1987), 'Dynamics of Immigrant Settlement: Surinamese, Turks and Moroccans in Amsterdam, 1973–1983', in Glebe, G. and J. O'Loughlin (eds), *Foreign Minorities in Continental European Cities*, Steiner, Wiesbaden, pp. 199–222.

201

White, P. (1993), 'The Social Geography of Immigrants in European Cities: the Geography of Arrival', in King, R. (ed.), *The New Geography of European Migrations*, Belhaven Press, London, pp. 47–65.

8 Contemporary Patterns of Labour Based Migration to The Netherlands

AREND ODÉ AND BERT VAN DER KNAAP

8.1 Contemporary Labour Market Conditions

Modern employment opportunities for migrants strongly differ from those circumstances which played a role during the period of mass labour migration about three decades ago. Most importantly, recent substantial levels of unemployment in Western Europe no longer allow for large numbers of immigrants. During the post-war decades until the energy crisis of the 1970s the fast growth of employment – both in manufacturing and service activities – served as a crucial explanatory factor for the presence of guest workers (King 1990). Nowadays, highly developed economies are no longer facing shortages of a quantitative nature. Due to both a severe industrial restructuring and new groups of participants entering the national labour markets, Western economies are confronted with enduring surpluses of labour. Nonetheless, labour migration to these countries has continued to exist. These mobility patterns must be explained by labour market imbalances of a strictly qualitative nature. In fact, contemporary immigrants mainly serve as 'gap fillers' on national labour markets of the most industrialized countries (Böhning 1991). As explained in detail by Piore (1979), the particular function of migrant workers is often closely associated with motivational problems among the national labour force to carry out activities at the very bottom of the social hierarchy. Moreover, since educational achievements among the national labour force have changed much more progressively as compared to the quality of employment, the willingness of the former to participate in standardized and menial activities has further declined during the last three decades. Particularly in domestic and various commercial services, migrant workers are filling shortages of unqualified employment (Sassen 1991). These services are predominantly concentrated in large urban areas (see, e.g. Daniels 1993; Marshall and Wood 1995). As a consequence, mobility patterns of less skilled migrants are mainly oriented to these urbanized regions as well (Odé 1996).

However, unlike previous decades a large proportion of migrant workers is also employed in more qualified or even specialized occupational categories. In fact, this upward mobility pattern arises from two major labour market developments. Firstly, rapidly changing patterns of demand for skilled labour may have caused short term imbalances. This process of employment restructuring has been most outstanding in expanding urbanized or industrialized regional labour markets. In such regional economies, including most large metropolitan areas of Western Europe, a rapid growth of advanced business services and often high tech industries has induced acute shortages of technical engineers, researchers and other specialists, such as marketing or legal advisers (CEC 1994). However, as stressed by Martin et al. (1990), so far only small scale mobility patterns may be associated with these upper level labour market imbalances. Regional recruitment efforts or local training programmes, rather than the recruitment of foreign workers are still conceived of as efficient solutions to solve temporary shortages of labour. Accordingly, within the European Union we notice only a limited exchange of (highly) qualified labour, despite many political efforts to encourage such mobility patterns (Odé et al. 1993). Secondly, along with the increasing importance of multinational private and public organizations, cross-border internal labour markets have become more prominent in Western Europe (Amin et al. 1992). Closely related to both personnel strategies carried out by these large firms and corresponding career paths of individual staff members, intra-firm mobility patterns have strongly augmented as well (Salt and Findlay 1989). Technical specialists and managers constitute the most important occupational categories in this area. Again, large agglomeration economies and modern industrialized areas are likely to attract a considerable share of these intra-firm movements.

In short, there is no evidence to show large scale labour migration to the most industrialized countries. Some qualitative imbalances at the lower and very upper levels of the labour market, together with the increasing importance of cross-border internal labour markets are recognized as the most relevant explanations for migration. As such, the nature of migration is likely to be rather dualistic with high shares of migrants being employed in low qualified functions as well as in specialized activities.

8.2 New Political Responses to Labour Immigration

Undoubtedly, legal possibilities of labour based immigration to Western Europe have always been closely associated with afore mentioned labour market changes. Since the early 1970s, all Western European countries have been executing rather restrictive policies with regard to possible inflows of migrant workers from abroad (King 1990; Penninx 1986). However, these policy measures strongly differ with respect to various groups of nationalities and countries of origin. Briefly summarized, a distinction can be made between migrants originating from the European Union (EU) and those from countries which are not members of the EU.

Within the EU, an integral part of the creation of a common labour market is the right to take up gainful employment in another member state. As stated by EEC Treaty Art. 48 (2): 'Such freedom of movement entail the abolition of any discrimination based on nationality between workers of the Member-States as regards employment, remuneration and other conditions of work and employment'. During the course of time, Community legislation has extended this right of free movement to family members of EEC nationals and some categories of persons who do not take up gainful activities in another member-state, including students, pensioners and other nonsalaried persons (Callovi 1993; Niessen 1994).

In addition, 1985 the European Commission presented its White Paper on the completion of the Single Market. These proposals have resulted in the Single European Act (1987), on the basis of which several inter - governmental agreements have been concluded. Of most importance in this respect is the so-called Convention applying the Schengen Agreement of 1990, signed by all EU member-states, except for the United Kingdom, Ireland and Denmark. This agreement covers both the abolition of checks at internal borders and necessary compensatory measures, i.e. strict controls, at the external borders of the Schengen area (Niessen 1994; OECD 1993).

These and other initiatives all intend to encourage intra-EU labour mobility. Policy measures with regard to immigration from countries outside the EU have been hardly harmonized between the individual member-states. Efforts in this field have been undertaken at the Maastricht Conference in December 1991. However, due a lack of unanimity among the individual countries to bring immigration policy under the control of the EU, so far merely a few initiatives have been undertaken by the member-states to accomplish joint actions in migration issues (O'Keefe 1995). Nonetheless, national policy measures with respect to these so called 'third country' citizens are not very different from each other. Particularly with regard to unskilled and semi-skilled labour based migrants, Western European governments attempt to limit such inflows as much as possible. In fact, most countries have established a legal act which allows such workers on the base of only one central criterium, namely the absence of a suitable (unemployed) labour force (Groenendijk and Hampsink 1995). Indeed, as highest unemployment figures in Western Europe are applicable for low skilled labour this criterium may serve as a clear selective mechanism in favour of better skilled labour immigrants. In addition, staff members of large multinational enterprises are allowed to migrate to the European Union without any serious legal obstacle. These movements form part of world wide investment strategies, executed by both Western European and other large companies. However, in case national labour markets are facing persistent shortages at the lower levels of demand, for instance in horticulture, construction or standardized services, countries may decide on more liberal migration policies (Groenendijk and Hampsink 1995). A striking example in this respect is the very presence of many thousands of Central-Eastern European manual workers in the German labour market, particularly in construction activities in the city of Berlin (Werner 1995).

In more detail for the Netherlands, the Employment of Foreigners Act (*Wav*) of 1995 allows foreign workers from non-EU countries to be employed in the Dutch labour market only if no so-called 'priority' labour force is available. Workers enjoying priority status include unemployed persons in the Netherlands as well as in other EU member states. In practice, this criterium implies that employers must fulfil a minimal number of conditions before the Dutch Employment Board is likely to issue an employment document to a migrant worker. These conditions refer to recruitment efforts and vacancy registration. In addition, however, a request for employment permits may be refused if the employment conditions in a firm are considered as not conforming Dutch standards in this field. Such conditions may refer to the level of payments, the terms of employment or the duration of contract. Conversely, migrant workers within the framework of intra-firm movements are not submitted to any labour market test.

Undoubtedly, this legal act has resulted in different rates of refusal according to occupational category and, consequently, country of origin of the migrant worker involved. Nowadays, (highly) skilled migrant workers with the nationality of a Western industrialized country may rather easily obtain an employment permit in the Netherlands. In contrast, between 1979 and 1993 almost half of all low skilled foreign workers originating from the less developed world were not accepted in the Dutch labour market (Odé and Van der Knaap 1995).

8.3 The Occupational Structure of Migrant Workers in The Netherlands

Between 1979 and 1993 more than 150,000 employment permits were issued by the Dutch Central Employment Board. Indeed, an average yearly number of about 12,000 documents does not indicate a strong dependence on migrant workers like being true for the 1960s and early 1970s. Less than one percent of all employed persons in the Netherlands falls under the scope of the *Wav*. However, a large share of those guest workers of the 1960s and 1970s still participate in the Dutch labour market. Since most of these minority groups have a residence permit or a permit to stay for an unlimited period of time, they are free to be employed in the Netherlands without the obligation of an employment document. In 1991, 5.6 percent of all employed persons in the Netherlands was either born in a foreign country or had no Dutch nationality (Martens et al. 1994). Obviously, this share is considerably higher in comparison with the group of migrant workers as defined by the *Wav*.

Table 8.1 Issued employment permits and total numbers employed in the Netherlands by occupational category, (in %) 1985–1992

occupational category	share of employment permits	share of total employed	index of concentration[1]
agriculture, manual labour	8.8	4.9	180.0
manufacturing & construction, manual labour	9.2	30.1	30.0
cleaning & domestic services	4.9	3.9	130.0
administration	2.3	19.9	10.0
hotel and catering services	9.9	3.1	320.0
other low qualified services	3.0	4.8	60.0
qualified public services	6.6	12.7	50.0
qualified business services	4.3	2.5	170.0
specialized technical activities	10.5	7.1	150.0
other specialized services	5.6	4.5	120.0
management	14.3	4.6	310.0
entertainment and sports	20.6	1.8	1140.0
total	100.0	100.0	100.0

[1]If_s/In_s * 100, with If_s=share of migrant workers in category s and In_s=share of the national work force in category s.

Source: Central Employment Board (1993) unpublished data; The Statistics Netherlands (1993) Enquete Beroepsbevolking 1993.

Despite the existence of large numerical differences in the size of issued employment documents between the 1960s and 1970s on the one hand and recent years on the other, some important structural differences may be distinguished. Unlike the first three post-war decades, contemporary migrant workers are employed in a broad range of activities in the Dutch labour market. During the early 1970s, manufacturing industries attracted almost 75 percent of the total foreign workforce (The Statistics Netherlands 1971). Nowadays, migrant workers are largely concentrated into agriculture and some service activities, including trade, the hotel and catering industry, and business services. Less than one out of every six migrant workers is still employed in the manufacturing sector, particularly in metal manufacturing and electronics.[1]

207

In addition to the sectoral structure, the composition according to occupation demonstrates the actual position of migrant workers in the Dutch labour market (see Table 8.1). Production-oriented activities in agriculture and manufacturing, together with low qualified services amount to about 40 percent of all issued permits between 1985 and 1992. Together with high numbers of activities in entertainment and sports (which are to a considerable extent of a low qualified nature), we may conclude that a majority of permits has been issued for the purpose of rather unsophisticated activities. This result is very much in accordance with most studies on labour migration to the Netherlands, which draw attention to a structural dependence of western economies on migrants who are willing to fill shortages of low qualified labour (see, e.g. Van Amersfoort and Penninx 1993; Groenendijk and Hampsink 1994; Muus 1993). In comparison with the occupational distribution of the national labour force in the Netherlands, as expressed by the index of concentration, migrant workers appear to be largely concentrated in agriculture, cleaning and domestic services, as well as several hotel and catering activities. Nonetheless, with regard to manual labour in manufacturing and administrative services, the relative number of migrant workers is much less than the figure for the national labour force. It should be emphasized, however, that these activities are not one-sidedly of a low qualified nature. Manual labour in Dutch industries increasingly requires specialized skills and often involve on-the-job training programmes. With regard to administrative activities, the introduction of information technology has 'upgraded' many of such jobs as well (Kloosterman and Elfring 1991).

In addition, the occupational composition of employment permits contains a considerable share of more qualified employment. Particularly, with respect to technical and other specialized services as well as management activities the relative number of employment permits largely exceeds proportions of the national employed labour force. This orientation towards highly qualified activities certainly contrasts with the presence of overall unskilled or semi-skilled immigrants during only a few decades ago. Moreover, as of the late 1970s the relative importance of (highly) qualified jobs among labour immigrants has further increased, particularly with regard to managerial activities, as well as qualified and specialized services (see Figure 8.1). In addition, the relative importance of training activities among migrant workers has increased significantly. Particularly large firms in the Netherlands make use of such constructions in order to offer short term educational programmes to persons already employed in an establishment of the same firm abroad. Instead, the contribution of low qualified jobs in manufacturing and service activities has diminished significantly, i.e. from about 60 percent in the early 1980s to less than 30 percent during the early 1990s. Only for low qualified and seasonal activities in agriculture a notable increase in the number of requested permits has become apparent during the period under study. Thus, from a dynamic perspective the dependence on foreign workers becomes

increasingly manifest at the very upper levels of the Dutch labour
market.

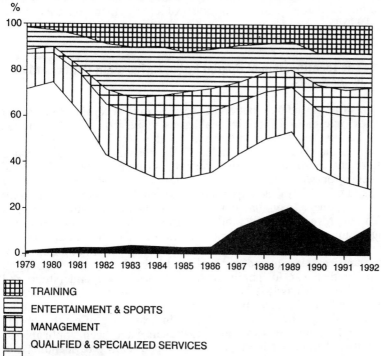

%

TRAINING
ENTERTAINMENT & SPORTS
MANAGEMENT
QUALIFIED & SPECIALIZED SERVICES
MANUFACTURING & LOW QUALIFIED SERVICES
AGRICULTURE

**Figure 8.1   Yearly distribution of employment permits according to
economic activity, 1979-1992**

Source: Central Employment Board (1993) unpublished data.

The above developments somehow reflect the overall patterns of
growth and decline of jobs in the Netherlands. Highest increases count
for employment in services, particularly business and other commercial
services (The Statistics Netherlands 1993). Only with respect to
agriculture, a rather divergent development may be indicated. The ratio
of employment in agriculture to the total number of jobs in the
Netherlands has strongly decreased during the 1980s and early 1990s.
In contrast, the number of permits yearly issued in agriculture as
compared to the total number of permits granted has certainly increased
during the last decade or so. As such, this evidence does not allow for

209

any conclusions which may indicate a systematic substitution of foreign workers by the national labour force or vice versa. Most occupational categories show a more or less complementary development of total employment change and the number of employment permits issued (Odé 1996).

8.4 The Identification of Spatial Labour Migration Patterns to the Netherlands

At a global level, the distribution of work permits according to different countries or regions of origin enables us to identify a more detailed spatial context of labour migration to the Netherlands. Table 8.2 illustrates some main features, including the absolute numbers of issued employment permits and the varying growth patterns of these documents for some geographical clusters of nationalities. As clearly demonstrated, the most important traditional suppliers of migrant workers, i.e. the ex-colonial country Surinam, the Maghreb countries and Turkey, reveal a considerable reduction in their contribution to the whole number of migrants oriented to the Dutch labour market. Between the late 1970s and early 1990s, the majority of migrants from these countries have entered the Netherlands by family (re-)unification programs rather than for purely economic reasons (van Amersfoort and Penninx 1993; Muus 1993). In contrast, the relative importance of nationalities which may be associated with the group of most industrialized countries in the world has increased significantly. In this respect, highest increases of migrant workers have been applicable to nationalities from Northern America, Japan and the Scandinavian countries. In addition, migrant workers from the group of East-Central European countries have increasingly made their way in the Dutch labour market. Indeed, this tendency is not only related to the demand for labour migrants from this region; also increased legal possibilities to emigrate from these countries must be taken into account (Fassmann and Münz 1994). All other mentioned regions of nationalities present a slight increase in their shares of issued permits. In absolute numbers, however, nationalities from Latin America and most Asian and African countries have been only of minor importance in the ethnic composition of migrant workers in the Netherlands.

In addition to these differences in absolute and relative numbers, different nationalities of migrant workers in the Netherlands also have produced distinct labour market profiles (see Figure 8.2). Migrant workers from the ex-colony Surinam as well as the Mediterranean region appear to be largely concentrated in low qualified production and service activities. Also migrant workers originating from East-Central Europe and the former Soviet Union have been largely concentrated in low qualified activities, particular in agriculture, manufacturing and the entertainment sector.[2] Conversely, labour migrants originating from the group of most industrialized countries in the world appear to be much more oriented towards (highly) skilled activities – including qualified and specialized services, as well as management functions. In fact, we may conclude a clearcut distinction between labour migrants from the more developed countries with high socioeconomic positions in the Dutch labour market and those workers from the less developed world who have been predominantly employed in a broad variety of low status jobs.

Table 8.2 Distribution and change in employment permits issued according to nationality, 1979–1992

region of nationality	number of issued permits	share in 1980/81 (%)	share in 1991/92 (%)	change 1980/81 –1990/91
ex-colonies[1]	23478	37.6 (1)	7.3 (5)	-30.3
Turkey & Maghreb[2]	23730	24.4 (2)	4.4 (8)	-20.0
OECD-countries[3]	26869	11.1 (3)	34.1 (1)	22.4
other Asia[4]	12639	6.2 (4)	9.4 (3)	3.2
South-Eastern Asia[5]	11584	5.8 (5)	7.9 (4)	2.1
Southern Europe[6]	8618	5.1 (6)	5.7 (6)	0.6
Latin America	4089	3.2 (7)	4.6 (7)	1.4
Eastern Europe[7]	17780	2.9 (8)	21.7 (2)	18.8
other Africa[8]	5179	2.4 (9)	3.3 (9)	0.9

1=Surinam, Republic of Indonesia, 2=Turkey, Algeria, Tunisia and Morocco, 3=all (former) EFTA-countries, the United States, Canada, Japan, Australia and New Zealand, 4=all Asian countries, except for South-Eastern Asia, Japan and the Republic of Indonesia, 5=Philippines, Republic of Korea, Thailand, (British) Hong Kong, Singapore, Taiwan and Malaysia, 6=Spain, Portugal and Yugoslavia, 7=Hungary, (former) USSR, Czechoslovakia, Rumania and Poland, 8=all African countries, except for the Maghreb-region.

Source: Central Employment Board (1992) *Statistisch overzicht Wabw 1979-1992.*

8.5   Migrant Workers in Dutch Agriculture

Descending from general to more specific levels of analysis, the presence of migrant workers in Dutch agriculture will be shortly discussed. Unlike most other production oriented activities in the Netherlands, migrant workers are still highly represented in the primary sector. At this level of analysis, the nature of labour market developments and sector-specific policy measures will be discussed in more detail. In addition, a few elements with regard to the possible impact of personal networks will be explained.

211

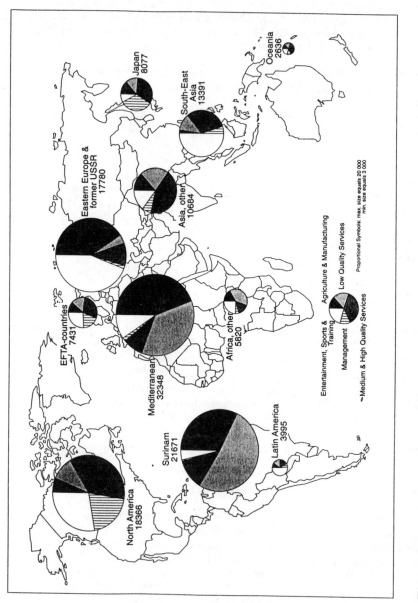

Figure 8.2   The occupational structure of migrant workers according to nationality, 1979–1992

8.5.1 The Economic Background

For about two decades, a tendency towards increasing economies of scale and the introduction of commercial labour contracts – instead of family employment – strongly increased the need for labour in the primary sector. These developments have been particularly true for Dutch horticulture; employment in farming and cattle breeding has strongly declined since the 1970s (Spierings and Van den Hoek 1989). However, due to poor employment conditions, comparatively low payments and very short-term labour contracts, Dutch horticulture has been facing large scale shortages of labour for many years. Despite the availability of large numbers of unemployed low skilled labour, this subsector exerts only a low attraction on the national labour force. Moreover, these imbalances have been aggravated by the existence of strong seasonal differences in production: only for limited periods of about two months many employees are needed. The North-West and South-East of the Netherlands especially have been facing acute seasonal shortages for many years. The former region has an extensive bulb-culture, in the latter outdoor mushroom and vegetable production is concentrated (Overbeek and Hillebrand 1993). In the past, large numbers of occasional workers, consisting of teenagers, students and housewives, were attracted during these periods of peak production. However, due to increasing possibilities of – often better paid – alternative employment, these workers are less liable to participate in horticulture (Van der Burgh and Van Santen 1991). In the South-East of the Netherlands in particular, with harvest periods of only six weeks and comparatively bad employment conditions, employers largely appeal to the Dutch Employment Board to issue employment permits. These requests have been largely motivated by the unwillingness among the national labour force to participate in such activities.[3] Conversely, in the North-West, the introduction of new machines has somewhat decreased the demand for labour. Besides, we may notice an increasing tendency of temporary production replacement abroad, especially to Poland.[4] In this respect, a first move of production relocation to countries with low labour costs, as happened in several manufacturing branches a few decades ago, has been made in the primary sector as well. Nonetheless, as most types of production are not easy to replace, problems of acute shortages are not likely to be solved in the coming years.

8.5.2 The Political Framework

During the 1980s, about 30,000 foreign workers were every year employed in Dutch agriculture. This group was largely composed of Polish citizens who entered the Netherlands with a tourist visa. In order to reduce the number of undocumented workers, since 1989 annual agreements are concluded between the Dutch government, employment authorities and employers in horticulture. These agreements aim at increasing levels of labour participation among the national (unemployed) labour force, together with a declining dependence on foreign workers. Only when registered vacancies were not filled up by the Dutch labour force, the Central Employment Board could decide to allow employment of migrant workers in this sector. In addition, strict controls were carried out to reduce the number of illegal foreign workers.

The results of these measures were, however, rather ambiguous. In the North-West of the Netherlands, as of the early 1990s public initiatives have resulted in project-based employment of several hundreds of low skilled unemployed, particularly originating from the large cities surrounding these rural areas. Moreover, the number of requests for employment permits considerably declined during the early 1990s.[5] However, as has been estimated, illegal workers still added to a share of 20 percent of the total workforce in horticulture (Van der Burgh and Van Santen 1991). In addition, Dutch employers also resorted to various improper constructions in order to employ foreign workers from the European Union, especially the United Kingdom and the Irish Republic.[6] Eventually, after many debates in Dutch parliament, in April 1993 the employer organisations, trade unions, and various public authorities resorted to concluding a general covenant, the so-called *Landelijk Tuinbouw Akkoord*. In this covenant the parties stressed their willingness to cooperate and find solutions in order to improve the functioning of the labour market in Dutch horticulture. The most important measures in this agreement refer to the abolition of illegal employment, special labour market initiatives, proper terms of employment and possible exemptions from social security contributions in special cases (Central Employment Board 1994). At this stage, concrete results from the covenant cannot be confirmed. Indeed, increased cooperation among the various labour authorities has resulted in a greater number of workers available. So far, however, these additional labour reservoirs appeared to be willing to accept employment in agriculture only to a minor extent. Nonetheless, a continuous restrictive policy with regard to the issuing of employment permits has certainly reduced the dependence on migrant workers as compared to only one decade ago.

The South-East of the Netherlands, another important area of outdoors horticulture, has been less successful in decreasing its reliance on migrant workers. Despite several regional initiatives to attract more national labour, acute shortages of labour still occur. In 1993 and 1994 numerous farmers, especially producers of asparagus, even went to court to challenge the decision not to issue employment permits. The court ruled that under circumstances of an unavailable (priority) labour force, employment permits could not be refused (Groenendijk and Hampsink 1995). As a consequence, the Central Employment Board was obliged to issue several hundreds of employment documents to employers in this region. In 1995, however, the continuous unwillingness of the farmers to adjust their terms of employment to common Dutch

214

standards enforced the court to decide not to issue employment permits any longer. For the first time since several years, employers in horticulture had to find different ways to attract sufficient labour. Nonetheless, since problems of labour shortages are limited to only very short term periods and no serious attempts are made to increase the attractiveness of employment in this subsector, no lasting solutions may be expected.

8.5.3 Personal Networks

Migrant workers in Dutch horticulture largely originate from the Polish countryside. The very selective nature in the ethnic composition of labour immigrants must be understood by a long term tradition of such workers coming every year to the Netherlands. In more detail, the possible existence of a close relationship between the Dutch employer and the Polish migrant worker has been investigated among some 50 employers in the North-West of the Netherlands. A vast majority of these employers responded to have made use of Polish employees during the 1980s until the early 1990s (when the legal possibilities for labour immigration strongly reduced in this region). In addition, two third of these employers indicated that Polish migrants came every year to the Netherlands without having arranged an employment contract in advance. As such, these spontaneously arriving Polish workers presented themselves many years to the same firm. The other one third of employers responded to have frequently got in contact with Polish families several months before the harvest started, for instance through telephone calls or postcards. In Figure 8.3 the likelihood of such social networks is further demonstrated.[7] Between 1990 and 1992 all employment permits granted to Polish workers in Dutch agriculture are illustrated according to the region of destination and origin of the migrants involved. Polish migrant workers originate from only a relatively small number of regions. These locations mainly include a number of more urbanized areas, such as Warsaw, Gdansk and Lodz. In addition, only a few municipalities in the Netherlands have attracted a large majority of all Polish migrant workers. Thus, the mobility of migrant workers from Poland to the Netherlands may be further specified as the migration of persons between only a few Polish cities and some Dutch villages.

Another important feature with regard to the nature of migration patterns oriented to Dutch horticulture is the overall high educational achievement among the migrants involved. As may be concluded from the registered documents, Polish migrant workers in Dutch horticulture are relatively well educated, broadly ranging from medium vocational training to university degrees. Strikingly enough, about one out of every four migrants has finished or still participates in higher vocational or academic training. These figures certainly surpass the average educational achievement among Dutch employees in agriculture.[8]

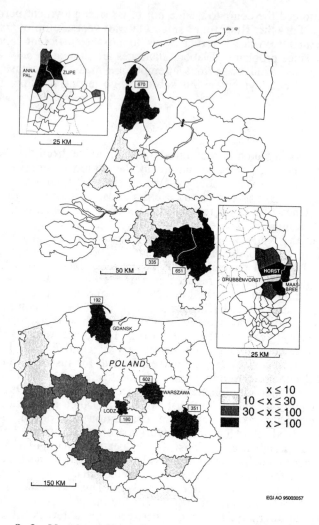

Figure 8. 3 **Number of issued employment permits to Polish workers in Dutch horticulture according to region of destination in the Netherlands and region of origin in Poland, 1990-1992**

Source: Central Employment Board (1993) unpublished data.

Moreover, it appears that a vast majority of migrant workers has been trained in skills which are not related to the agricultural sector. Administrative, commercial and technical careers have been mostly indicated on the application documents. Obviously, the high education and service oriented skills of migrant workers in agriculture contrasts with the rather low qualified and production oriented activities which are carried out in the Netherlands. More in general, the picture of poorly educated migrants from the rural (and mostly backward) regions of the Mediterranean and working in the Dutch industrialized areas, as was very much the case during the 1960s and 1970s, certainly contrasts with the nature of contemporary migrants in Dutch agriculture. Relatively well educated Polish migrants, originating from large cities have proved to be very willing to carry out low qualified activities in the rural areas of the Netherlands.

8.6   Concluding Remarks

The Dutch labour market is all but dependent on large numbers of labour immigrants. Nonetheless, at the level of distinct subsectors or occupational categories substantial numbers of migrant workers are still present in the Netherlands. Such patterns of concentration have been closely connected with qualitative imbalances at the lower or very upper levels of the Dutch labour market. In addition, intra-firm movements have become increasingly important in the composition of labour immigration. With respect the most important tendencies of labour migration to the Netherlands during the 1980s and early 1990s, highly qualified and managerial activities show the highest increases. Instead, with respect to low qualified employment, the importance of migrant workers has become less important, except for activities in agriculture. Nonetheless, when compared with the national labour force migrant workers are still highly oriented towards various low qualified activities, including manual labour in agriculture, hotel and catering services as well as domestic and cleaning activities.

The concentration of migrant workers in these menial activities has been further investigated for the sector of horticulture. As it appeared, the low attractiveness of such seasonal activities, rather than absolute shortages are responsible for a high pressure of employers on the permit system. However, public initiatives – both with regard to an increasingly restrictive policy and other measures to solve the labour market problems in this sector – have somehow influenced this need. Particularly in the North-West of the Netherlands, the need for migrant workers has strongly decreased. However, the size of illegally employed has been estimated as considerable. Besides, the South-East of the Netherlands has proved how difficult successful public intervention may be. Particularly with regard to this region, one may argue that when even some minimal employment conditions are no longer offered, the recruitment of foreign workers seems an unavoidable option. Both in

217

terms of payment and duration of contract, the bulb-culture in the North-West of the Netherlands may be considered as more attractive as compared with the production of asparagus in the South-East (Odé 1996). Along this line, the Netherlands Court of Audit concluded recently that the recruitment of unemployed workers in the production of asparagus may be politically desirable, but in practice not realistic.[9] This conclusion illustrates that labour immigration is inextricably related to the nature of the specific labour market conditions of the sector involved. It can even be questioned that when such conditions are dramatically unfavourable compared to the national standards, the sector has any chances of survival at all without labour immigration.

References

Amersfoort, H. van and Penninx, R. (1993), 'Migratieontwikkeling en Migratie-beheersing', *Migratie, Bevolking en Politiek*, Van Amersfoort (eds), Instituut voor Sociale Geografie, Universiteit van Amsterdam.

Amin, A., Charles, D.R. and Howells, J. (1992), 'Corporate Restructuring and Cohesion in the New Europe', *Regional Studies*, vol. 26, no. 4, pp. 319–31.

Böhning, W.R. (1991), 'Integration and Immigration Pressures in Western Europe', *International Labour Review*, vol. 13a, no.4, pp. 445–58.

van der Burgh, Y and van Santen, P. (1991), *Personeelsvoorziening in de Bloembollenteelt,* Research voor Beleid bv, Leiden.

Callovi, G. (1994), 'Regulation of Immigration in 1993: Pieces of the European Jig-Saw Puzzle', *International Migration Review*, vol. xxvi, no. 2, pp. 353–72.

CEC (1994), *Europa 2000+, Samenwerking voor de ruimtelijke ordening van Europa*, Commission of the European Communities: Brussel and Luxembourg.

Central Employment Board (1991), *Evaluatie Regeling Personeelsvoorziening Agrarische Sector 1990,* Arbeidsvoorziening, Rijswijk.

Central Employment Board (1992), *Statistisch Overzicht Wabw 1979–1992.* Arbeidsvoorziening, Rijswijk.

Central Employment Board (1993), *Jaarverslag uitvoering Wet Arbeid Buitenlandse Werknemers,* Arbeidsvoorziening, Rijswijk.

Central Employment Board (1994), *Evaluatie-onderzoek 1994 Landelijk Tuinbouwakkoord,* O&A Werkdocument 94–18, Arbeidsvoorziening, Rijswijk.

Daniels, P.W. (1993), *Service Industries in the World Economy*, Blackwell Publishers, Oxford.

Fassmann, H. and Münz, R. (1994), *European Migration in the Late Twentieth Century.* IIASA, Laxenburg.

Groenendijk, K. and Hampsink, R. (1995), 'Temporary Employment of Migrants in Europe', *Reeks Recht & Samenleving No. 10*, Katholieke Universiteit, Nijmegen.

King, R. (1990), 'The Social and Economic Geography of Labour Migration: From Guest Workers to Immigrants', *Western Europe, Challenge and Change*, Pinder (ed.), Belhaven Press, London.

Kloosterman, R.C. and Elfring, T. (1991), *Werken in Nederland*, Academic Service, Schoonhoven.

Marshall, J.N. and Wood, P. (1995), *Services & Space, Key aspects of urban and regional development*, Longman Scientific & Technical, Essex.

Martens, E.P. Roijen, J.H.M. and Veenman, J. (1994), *Minderheden in Nederland, Statistisch Vademecum 1993/1994*, ISEO/CBS, Voorburg/Rotterdam.

Martin, P.L.; Hönekopp, E. and Ullmann, H. (1990), Europe 1992: Effects on Labor Migration', *International Migration Review*, vol. xxiv, no. 3, pp. 591–603.

Muus, P. (1993), *Internationale migratie naar Europa*, SUA, Nijmegen.

Niessen, J. (1994), 'European Community Legislation and Intergovernmental Cooperation on Migration', *International Migration Review*, vol. xxvi, no. 3, pp. 676–84.

Odé, A.W.M.; Van der Knaap, G.A. and Nijsse, P. (1993), 'International Migratie en Arbeidsmarkt in de Europese Gemeenschap en Nederland', *EGI Onderzoekspublicatie 10*, Economic Geography Institute, Erasmus University Rotterdam.

Odé, A.W.M. and Van der Knaap, G.A. (1995), 'Migrant Workers in the Netherlands', *EGI-Onderzoekspublicatie 29*, Economic Geography Institute, Erasmus University Rotterdam.

Odé, A.W.M. (1996), 'Migrant Workers in the Dutch Labour Market Today', *Dissertation, Tinbergen Institute Research Series 126*, Thesis Publishers, Amsterdam.

OECD (1993), *Free Movement of People in the European Communities, 1993 outlook*, Working Party on Migration; DEELSA/ELSA, Paris.

O'Keefe, D. (1995), 'The Emergence of a European Immigration Policy', *European Law Review*, vol. 20, no. 1, pp. 20–36.

Overbeek, M.M.M. and Hillebrand, J.H.A. (1993), *De Agrarische Arbeidsmarkt een Apart Verhaal?*, Landbouw-Economisch Instituut (LEI-DLO) Afdeling Structuuronderzoek, Den Haag.

Penninx, R. (1986), 'International Migration in Western Europe since 1973: Developments, Mechanisms and Controls', *International Migration Review*, Volume XX, no. 4, pp. 951–73.

Piore, M. (1979), *Birds of Passage, Migrant Labor and Industrial Societies*, Cambridge, University Press.

Salt, J. and Findlay, A. (1989), 'International Migration of Highly–Skilled Manpower: Theoretical and Developmental Issues', Appleyard, R. (ed.) *The Impact of International Migration on Developing Countries*, OECD, Paris.

Sassen, S. (1991), *The Global City: New York, London, Tokyo*, Princeton University Press, Princeton, New Jersey.

219

Spierings, C.J.M. and Van den Hoek, J.M. (1989), *Ontwikkelingen in het personeelsbestand op agrarische bedrijven*. Landbouw-Economisch Instituut, Den Haag.

The Statistics Netherlands (1971), *Population and Medical Statistics*, CBS, Voorburg.

The Statistics Netherlands (1993), *Enquête Beroepsbevolking 1992*, CBS, Voorburg.

Werner, H. (1995), 'Economic Integration and Migration – The European Case', *Labour Market Research Topics*, Institute for Employment Research, Nürnberg.

Werner, H. (1996), 'Temporary Migration of Foreign Workers', *Labour Market Research Topics*, Institute for Employment Research, Nürnberg.

Notes

1. Almost 40 percent of all migrant workers in manufacturing between 1979 and 1993 has been employed in metal manufacturing and electronics. Apart from skilled manual labour, also a considerable share (of about 30 percent) was attracted as technical specialists or managers to establishments of large firms in this subsector.

2. A large proportion of migrant workers in entertainment consist of persons participating in classical or folkloristic music and dance societies. However, increasing numbers of migrant workers have come to the Netherlands to work as dancers or bunny-girls in nightclubs. Permit requests for prostitution activities are not approved (*Wav*, Art. 8).

3. Within the framework of the *Project Uitvoering Bemiddeling Seizoenswerk 1993*, 1202 unemployed persons were approached to work in horticulture. Of this number 133 persons declared to be willing to accept temporary employment, of which only 39 matched to potential employers. Eventually only 22 persons were actually employed. For 1994, 3,421 persons were summoned to participate in the project *Seizoensbemiddeling Agrarische Sector*, resulting in a number of 188 (or about six percent) who actually got a temporary job in this sector.

4. The introduction of new machineries and the relocation of some production was indicated in a telephone survey among 50 employers in horticulture in the region Noord-Holland Noord. About one third of the approached employers declared to have become less dependent on occasional workers, due to the above developments. This survey forms part of a dissertation study on migration to the Netherlands (Odé 1996).

5. In the region Noord-Holland Noord, i.e. the North-West of the Netherlands, the number of requested employment permits decreased from more than 1200 during the period 1988–1990 to merely 50 between 1991 and 1993 (CBA 1993).

6. Many of these immigrants were employed by so-called E-101 forms. This legal construction provides a possibility to avoid paying taxes and social security premiums according to the standards of the country of employment. Actually, this procedure is meant for short term activities of self-employed persons and those in secondment constructions, and not for regular employees in agriculture.

7. The information is derived from about 1200 employment documents, granted between 1990 and 1992 to Dutch employers in horticulture to employ Polish migrant workers. These documents, containing information about the place of residence and employment of the migrant worker involved, are registered at the Central Employment Board in Rijswijk.

8. Of all temporary workers in agriculture, as registered by the Statistics Netherlands, one out of every five has achieved more than lower vocational training. The educational skills of fixed personnel are a little higher with about one out of every three employees having achieved more than some secondary or lower vocational training (Overbeek and Hillebrand 1993).

9. The Netherlands Court of Audit (April 1996) *Aspergesteken: seizoenarbeid in de tuinbouw*.

Part C
Spatial Clusters: Regional and Urban Patterns and Assimilation

9 Segregation, Polarization and Urban Policies in Amsterdam: An International Perspective

SAKO MUSTERD, WIM OSTENDORF AND
MATTHIJS BREEBAART

9.1 Introduction

In many countries in the Western world residential patterns in cities change due to international migration and urban clustering. These changes cause significant reactions and public debates. Not seldom the processes are associated with increasing segregation of the population and with social polarization. In this context, concepts such as 'dualization' or the 'rising ghetto-underclass' are easily applied. In social science literature too these issues are frequently addressed, generally in relation to the economic restructuring and welfare state transformations countries have to cope with.

Until now, neither in society nor in research, has concensus been reached about the processes themselves, their causes, and the local and national policy responses. In other words, there is insufficient insight in this matter. In this contribution we make an effort to expand the knowledge in the field looking at the Amsterdam experience with segregation, polarization and policy responses. We will focus attention on the ethnic dimension in particular (ethnic segregation, social polarization of ethnic groups, and so on). As far as the ethnic *segregation* and policy responses are concerned we are able to do that in an international comparative framework. The basis for that is an extensive comparative research project of which the results have recently been published (Breebaart et al. 1996). For this moment an empirical comparative framework in the field of socio-ethnic *polarization* is still lacking. Therefore, the discussion of social polarization will be focused upon Amsterdam only.

The outline of this chapter is as follows. After a discussion of some of the potential backgrounds of spatial and social divisions of ethnic groups and after having formulated the questions explicitly (Section 9.2), we will present the spatial outcomes of the immigration and ethnic clustering processes in Amsterdam and compare these with data from three other European cities: Frankfurt, Brussels and London (Section 9.3). In Section 9.4 we turn the attention to the socio-ethnic polarization process in Amsterdam. In Section 9.5 the policy responses to these processes will be dealt with. Here again the Amsterdam experience will be compared with the experiences in the other cities mentioned. Finally, in Section 9.6 some conclusions will be presented.

9.2 The Triggers of Ethnic Spatial Segregation and Social Polarization: The Debate in The Literature

Some authors believe that social polarization, social exclusion and underclass formation are first of all related to the global *economic restructuring processes* (e.g. Sassen 1991; Fainstein et al. 1992). In virtually all European and North American cities manufacturing has declined and/or is becoming increasingly capital and information intensive. Also the sector is decentralizing spatially. The services sector has counterbalanced this process in terms of job creation, but not so much in spatial terms. Most firms that are characterized by non-control types of employment (those which are not involved in the top management decision making process) tend to locate decentrally.

The restructuring brought about a new demand for high skilled labour capable to operate with varied bundles of international information and communication. Sassen (1991) and others (e.g. Warf 1990) argue that at the same time also huge numbers of new jobs were created at the bottom end of the market (in the consumer services sector in particular). Many low skilled immigrants could and still can enter the labour market here. Despite the fact that low skilled people are not entirely excluded from the labour market, frequently the jobs turn out to be dead-end jobs not offering any perspective to put another step on the social ladder. Together these changes would result in increasing social polarization. Because of the differences in skills between different ethnic groups, also socio-ethnic polarization could be discerned.

Surprisingly, however, Hamnett (1994) found out that such a process of polarization was not occurring in London, while London was also one of the cases of Sassen's research. He stated that the most important process was that of professionalization: all labour proved to be able to improve its skills and to move into higher professional classes between 1960 and 1990. At the same time he underlined that the gap between the rich and the poor in London was large and widening during the 1980s.

One influence should not be forgotten in this debate, since that seems crucial to understand the European situation. That is the *organization and restructuring of the welfare state* in a broader sense. In fact this is the second major explanation of the social and ethnic division of the urban population. The welfare state models have important implications in many respects. European models differ from each other, but also from the US model in terms of the attention given to (access to) social benefit systems, income redistribution systems, health care programmes, housing subsidies and housing allocation systems. These differences will translate in socioeconomic differences between households, and because of that to an increase or decrease of the spatial separation. As far as the

226

attitude towards the functioning of the labour market is concerned, several European countries rely on a corporatist (regulated) model in which specific rights for those who are employed exist (Esping Andersen 1990). Among these rights are the existence of minimum wage levels and the fact that employees appear to have relatively solid labour market positions once they succeed in getting a job. It is evident that these specific characteristics also prevent labour market entry at the bottom end of the market. Somewhat euphemistically, the outcome of the application of such welfare state models as far as the labour market is concerned, is labelled a 'mismatch' between the demand for and the supply of labour. This does not mean that no new jobs are created. In fact in several European countries, among them The Netherlands, very high figures of newly created jobs can be shown. The majority of these jobs, however, is to be found in part time and temporary contracts. The corporatist character of many European welfare states, such as The Netherlands, Belgium and Germany, although successful in avoiding poverty, clearly have negative implications for employment. This is particularly true for immigrant or newly settled households, because their level of education is generally low and because of that their orientation to the lower ends of the market is high.

A third factor, which is particularly relevant to the understanding of spatial segregation patterns in cities, is the *urban history* itself. Recent research findings show that international migration is increasingly urban in its orientation (Champion 1994). The suggestion is that ethnic segregation (immigrants in the city, others outside) has only just begun. But of course these processes are as old as cities are. So, an understanding of the history of a city may help to understand segregation patterns. In this respect also the major restructuring processes and urban renewal activities should be taken into account, since these may have serious implications for the change of social patterns in the city. Paris, unlike Amsterdam and London, for example, had its (then poor) inner city completely reconstructed by Baron le Haussmann some 150 years ago. The socio-spatial effects of that physical restructuring process are well-known: the rich took over the centre and the poor were pushed into the direction of the banlieu (Wagenaar 1993). History is also important to understand ethnic segregation since the moment at which specific immigrant categories enter the country and city is extremely important in understanding the further development of the population pattern (King 1993).

A fourth major impact on urban social issues is assumed to be related to the *spatial segregation* itself. A spatial concentration of poor (immigrant) people may have extra negative effects on an individual's opportunities to escape from poverty. In the end, the spatial concentration may result in even sharper segregation and increased social polarization (e.g. Wilson 1987; De Lannoy and Kesteloot 1990).

All in all, however, there are good reasons to refrain from uncritically supporting the predominantly American experiences and social polarization theory in which the global economic restructuring and ghetto neighbourhood-effects are the most prominent features. In Europe, the effects of the global economic restructuring process may well have been mitigated by the functioning of the welfare states. In general it may be argued and shown that segregation and social polarization will be more extensive in liberal than in corporatist welfare states. As a result ethnic spatial segregation and socio-ethnic polarization may have developed in a much more moderate way in most of the European countries and cities (White 1993), including Amsterdam. Consequently, an independent negative effect of the spatial concentration of poor people or ethnic minorities may also not have occurred.

One counter-argument should receive attention here (Musterd 1994). Esping Andersen's classification of welfare states pays almost no attention to the differentiation between countries with regard to the provision of social housing. Clear differences appear to exist between countries and these do not seem to parallel the classification of welfare states on the basis of social security and labour market characteristics only. Social housing, to give an example, was much more prevalent in Great Britain even in 1990 when Britain already was labelled 'liberal' in labour market terms. On the other hand, social housing in Belgium appears to be a small sector. The Brussels housing market is almost entirely privatized. Again in contrast, the Amsterdam housing stock consists of over 50 percent of social housing, and almost 80 percent of the stock is subject to housing allocation rules set by the municipality and the housing associations. So, housing market differences do not parallel the welfare state classification based on the functioning of the labour market. Still, the functioning of the housing market may be extremely important, again in terms of the (unequal) *spatial* distribution of the population according to their social position. Cities with a large social housing stock are expected to have better opportunities to realize socio-spatial mixes of the population compared to cities in which the private stock is dominating the picture, assuming that the social stock is more than sufficient to meet the needs of lower class households. For that reason, socio-spatial segregation will, ceteris paribus, be more prominent in cities such as Brussels than in cities such as Amsterdam or London.

So far we have not shown much evidence to support our view. Therefore it makes sense to present some new empirical data that may be relevant to the discussion. To be more specific in the sections to come we will try to answer the following questions:

- Is the spatial pattern of ethnic segregation in Amsterdam really moderate and how does it compare to patterns in other European cities (Section 9.3)?
- How does the process of social polarization develop in Amsterdam, again focusing upon immigrant or ethnic categories (Section 9.4)?
- How are the ethnic segregation patterns and the social polarization process in Amsterdam related to the policy responses at the local

and national level and how do these responses compare to policies in other European countries (Sections 9.5 and 9.6)?

9.3 Segregation in Amsterdam, Compared with Brussels, Frankfurt and London

As in many other cities the share of the population of non-Dutch origin living in Dutch cities rose rapidly starting from the sixties, when guest workers were hired to meet the need of a booming economy. In 1975 a still moderate 6.2 percent of the Amsterdam population was of non - Dutch origin. In 1990 the percentage was as high as 21.4 (SCP 1994). In 1993 the definition changed. The percentage of non-Dutch was since then measured on the basis of the country of origin of the person him/herself or of one of the parents. In 1995 those who came from Turkey, Morocco, Surinam, The Dutch Antilles, Southern Europe or another non-industrialized country amounted to 32.2 percent (Breebaart et al. 1996). This rapid increase of the share of non-Dutch did not result in a parallel sharpening of the segregation pattern. The Index of Segregation[1] appeared to increase only slightly (Table 9.1). The index refers to the percentage of the population category that has to move to another neighbourhood or area in order to achieve a distribution in proportion to the size of the category.

In Rotterdam and The Hague, two Dutch cities next in size to Amsterdam, the indexes slightly decreased. The only marginal increase in Amsterdam appears to be related to the dynamics of the pattern (Musterd and Ostendorf 1996). Most immigrant households were able to shift from lodging housing in the private sector to family housing in the social sector. As a result an ethnic ghetto did not develop. The large stock of social housing and the allocation of rental housing in a tight housing market situation, as well as moderate differences between households in terms of spending power are amongst the most likely to explain factors of the only moderate differences.

Table 9.1 Index of segregation in Amsterdam, for major immigrant categories, 1980–1990

	1980	1986/87	early 90s
Turks	37.3	38.8	41.1
Moroccans	38.6	36.9	39.0
South-Europeans	27.7	24.1	18.7
Surinamese	27.8	33.7	35.9

Source: SCP, Rapportage Minderheden, Tables 3.4 and 3.5.

But how does Amsterdam compare to the other cities? As mentioned, we compared Amsterdam with Frankfurt, Brussels and London. The

229

decision to select these cities is based on several arguments. Of course, the availability of data on a detailed level was an important consideration, but also we looked for similarities and dissimilarities in several respects. One of these was the welfare state model of the states involved. Britain seems to be the most liberal of the four. The others represent variants of corporatist states. Furthermore, London and Amsterdam are relatively comparable in terms of their urban history. Brussels and Frankfurt resemble Amsterdam in size. And finally, Amsterdam, Brussels and Frankfurt are fairly similar in terms of the percentages of 'immigrants'.

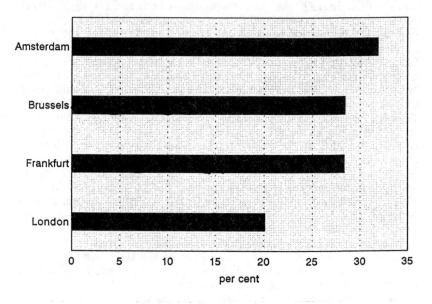

Figure 9.1   The proportion of 'immigrants' in four cities

Note: Amsterdam (1995): minorities; Brussels (1991), Frankfurt (1993): foreign nationality; London (1991): non-white.

At this point we should briefly draw attention to the problems of comparative research. Among the biggest problems we had to deal with were the spatial levels and the definition of 'immigrant' (in some cases 'foreigner', or 'minority' or 'ethnic group'). As far as the problem of the spatial level was concerned we tried as much as possible to use data which were available at an areal level of approximately 10,000 inhabitants per area. Regarding the definitions we should notice that in Germany and Belgium the population categories are distinguished from each other on the basis of nationality. In The Netherlands and the United Kingdom the definition is based on ethnic groups; in addition,

230

the UK registers according to self-identification, whereas the other countries register the data according to the information given in the passport. These differences should be kept in mind when comparing the figures.

As is shown in Figure 9.1, the percentages of 'immigrants' in Amsterdam, Brussels and Frankfurt are nearly the same. The comparable figure of non-Whites in London is somewhat smaller.

However, the share of 'immigrants' is probably less important than the (un)equal spatial distribution across the urban area. Two instruments were used as means to describe the spatial patterns: segregation indices and maps. In Figure 9.2 segregation indices (IS-values) are shown with regard to Amsterdam and the other cities. Whereas Amsterdam and London take the intermediate position, Brussels shows the highest values, and Frankfurt the lowest, the latter indicating a relative mix of the category concerned in comparison with the rest of the population.

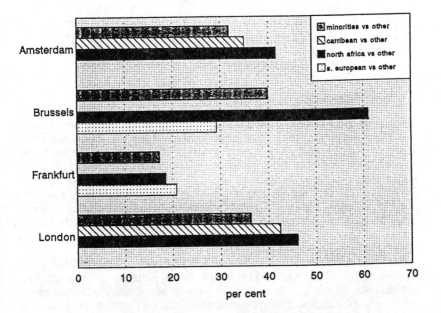

Figure 9.2   The index of segregation of 'immigrants' in four cities

Note: London: North Africa should be read as Indian Continent.

The conclusions drawn from the indices of segregation are in a way confirmed with information on the indices of dissimilarity (ID-values) for specific – broad – categories. In Table 9.2 we have presented a selection of ID-values. Here too, Brussels shows the highest ID-values, although London would score higher if more detailed population

231

categories could have been distinguished. Again the ID-values in Frankfurt are relatively low. Even more remarkable is that in most cities the 'immigrant' versus 'immigrant' indices are relatively high too, indicating separation of different 'immigrant' categories within the cities involved. This is not true for Frankfurt however. An example is the mix between people from southern and northern Mediterranean countries. In Frankfurt an ID-value of 14 was reached, in Brussels the figure is 42.

Table 9.2 Selected index of dissimilarity values of European cities; two highest scores per metropolitan area (immigrants from rich countries excluded: significant categories only)

Amsterdam	Surinamese/Antillean vs Turks/Moroccans	43
Amsterdam	Turks/Moroccans vs autochthone Dutch	42
Brussels	South Mediterranean vs Belgian	65
Brussels	Moroccan vs Turks	53
Frankfurt	Turks vs Germans	27
Frankfurt	(former) Yugoslavs vs Germans	26
London	Blacks vs Indian Continent	49
London	White vs Indian Continent	48

Source: Breebaart et al. (1996).

The IS and ID-values show the degree to which the spatial distributions are even. However, they give little indication of the exact and main locations of population categories within the metropolitan area, and neither about whether neighbourhoods with an overrepresentation of a population category are located adjacent to other neighbourhoods with overrepresentation or not. The best way to solve this problem is to show a series of maps. Figure 9.3 shows patterns of the most general category of 'immigrants' (or ethnic groups) in each of the four metropolitan areas and patterns of one specific, most significant or most segregated – generally low income – 'immigrant' category.

The patterns reveal a wide variety of settlement histories and opportunities. The Amsterdam maps show patterns of decentralized settlement, outside of the inner city. There are some concentrations in 19th century neighbourhoods surrounding the city centre. However, the centre of gravity clearly can be found in 20th century neighbourhoods, where social rental housing is predominant. A comparison of the map of Amsterdam showing the pattern for Turks and Moroccans with the general map of all 'minorities' implicitly reveals the pattern of the Surinamese in Amsterdam. They tend to be clustered in the South Eastern part of the city, clearly – though not absolutely – segregated from the Turks and Moroccans (see also Table 9.2).

232

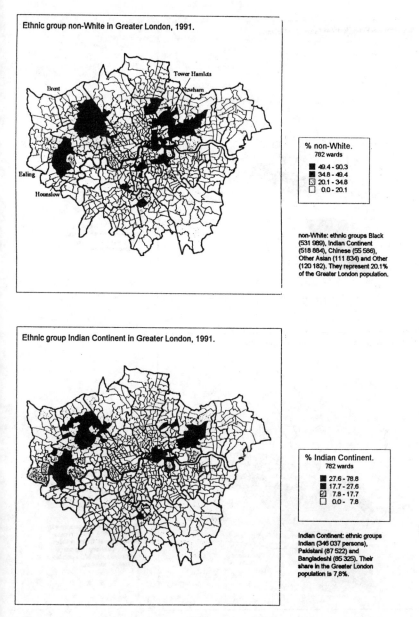

Ethnic group non-White in Greater London, 1991.

Tower Hamlets
Brent
Newham
Ealing
Hounslow

% non-White.
782 wards

■ 49.4 - 90.3
■ 34.8 - 49.4
▨ 20.1 - 34.8
□ 0.0 - 20.1

non-White: ethnic groups Black
(531 989), Indian Continent
(518 884), Chinese (55 586),
Other Asian (111 834) and Other
(120 182). They represent 20.1%
of the Greater London population.

Ethnic group Indian Continent in Greater London, 1991.

% Indian Continent.
782 wards

■ 27.6 - 78.8
■ 17.7 - 27.6
▨ 7.8 - 17.7
□ 0.0 - 7.8

Indian Continent: ethnic groups
Indian (346 037 persons),
Pakistani (87 522) and
Bangladeshi (85 325). Their
share in the Greater London
population is 7,8%.

Figure 9.3   Segregation patterns of 'immigrants' in four cities

Source: OPCS census, MCC & UK borders.

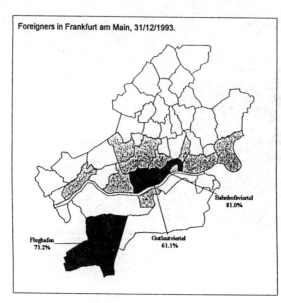

Foreigners in Frankfurt am Main, 31/12/1993.

% foreigners.
45 Ortsteile.

■ 57.0 - 81.0
■ 42.7 - 57.0
▨ 28.3 - 42.7
☐ 0.0 - 28.3

Foreigners: 28.3% of the
population of Frankfurt am
Main does not have the
German nationality.

Bahnhofsviertel
81.0%

Flughafen
73.2%

Gutleutviertel
61.1%

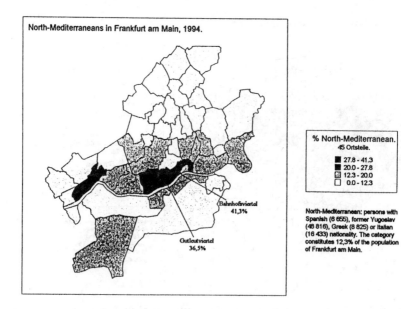

North-Mediterraneans in Frankfurt am Main, 1994.

% North-Mediterranean.
45 Ortsteile.

■ 27.8 - 41.3
■ 20.0 - 27.8
▨ 12.3 - 20.0
☐ 0.0 - 12.3

North-Mediterranean: persons with
Spanish (6 655), former Yugoslav
(48 816), Greek (8 825) or Italian
(16 433) nationality. The category
constitutes 12.3% of the population
of Frankfurt am Main.

Bahnhofsviertel
41.3%

Gutleutviertel
36.5%

Figure 9.3 (continued)

Source: Amt für Statistik, Wahlen en Einwohnerwesen, Stadt Frankfurt.

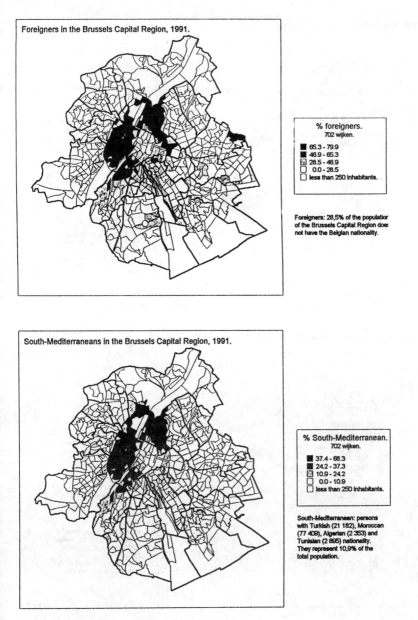

Foreigners in the Brussels Capital Region, 1991.

% foreigners.
702 wijken.

■ 65.3 - 79.9
■ 46.9 - 65.3
▨ 28.5 - 46.9
□ 0.0 - 28.5
□ less than 250 inhabitants.

Foreigners: 28,5% of the population of the Brussels Capital Region does not have the Belgian nationality.

South-Mediterraneans in the Brussels Capital Region, 1991.

% South-Mediterranean.
702 wijken.

■ 37.4 - 68.3
■ 24.2 - 37.3
▨ 10.9 - 24.2
□ 0.0 - 10.9
□ less than 250 inhabitants.

South-Mediterranean: persons with Turkish (21 182), Moroccan (77 409), Algerian (2 353) and Tunisian (2 895) nationality. They represent 10,9% of the total population.

Figure 9.3   (continued)

Source: N.I.S. volkstelling 1991, KU Leuven kaartmateriaal.

235

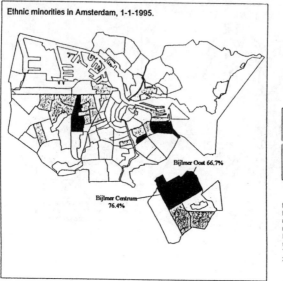

Ethnic minorities in Amsterdam, 1-1-1995.

Bijlmer Oost 66.7%

Bijlmer Centrum
76.4%

% ethnic minorities.
93 buurtcombinaties.

■ 63.3 - 76.4
■ 47.7 - 63.3
▨ 32.2 - 47.7
☐ 0.0 - 32.2
☐ less than 250 inhabitants

Ethnic minorities: ethnic groups
Black Caribbean (Surinamers
and Antillianen), South Mediterranean (Turken, Marokkanen),
North Mediterranean and
non-industrialised countries.
Their share of population is
32.2%.

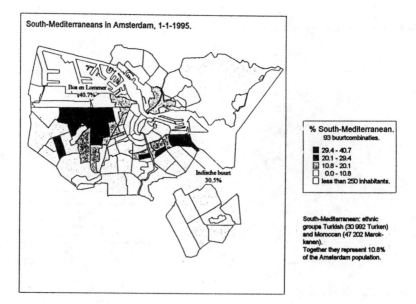

South-Mediterraneans in Amsterdam, 1-1-1995.

Bos en Lommer
40.7%

Indische buurt
30.5%

% South-Mediterranean.
93 buurtcombinaties.

■ 29.4 - 40.7
■ 20.1 - 29.4
▨ 10.8 - 20.1
☐ 0.0 - 10.8
☐ less than 250 inhabitants.

South-Mediterranean: ethnic
groups Turkish (30 992 Turken)
and Moroccan (47 202 Marokkanen).
Together they represent 10.8%
of the Amsterdam population.

Figure 9.3   (continued)

Source: O+S, Het Amsterdamse Bureau voor Onderzoek en Statistiek.

236

The contrast between Amsterdam and Brussels is evident at a glance. Although 'foreigners' can be found all over the Brussels metropolitan area, the highest concentrations are *in* the centre of the area, in a much more concentrated pattern than in Amsterdam. This is especially true for low income 'foreigners', such as the South Mediterranean. Two interrelated factors are important here. Firstly, Brussels' low income immigrants have to rely on the residualized and cheaper parts of the private sector of the housing market and that sector is clearly concentrated in some 19th century neighbourhoods. Secondly, the quantitative housing shortage in that sector is moderate, which stimulates spatial segregation (Kesteloot 1994).

The maps of Frankfurt also suggest a fairly centralized pattern of immigrant settlement. A closer inspection, however, reveals that there are many more neighbourhoods with a relatively high share of 'foreigners'. In fact, there is no 'Ortsteil' (neighbourhood) with less than ten per cent of its population belonging to the 'foreigners'. So, in general the pattern appears to be of a much less concentrated type, albeit that some concentration occurred in the inner city.[2] The relatively high percentage of 'foreigners' in the two centrally located neighbourhoods, Gutleutviertel and Bahnhofsviertel, is related to the low level of segregation between immigrant groups in Frankfurt.

Again another type of pattern exists in London. The non-White population (predominantly Blacks (8 percent) and people from the Indian Continent (7.8 percent) can be found in central London as well as in outer boroughs. As shown, the general pattern is closely associated with the pattern of immigrants from the Indian Continent. This ethnic group, however, is far from homogeneous. The early settled Indians and Pakistani were successful in finding a dwelling in the outer districts of London. The recently immigrated Bangladeshi however, are settled in boroughs of inner London. In the ward Spitalfields in the borough of Tower Hamlets, no less than 63.8 percent of the population appeared to be Bangladeshi, living in relatively poor conditions. The spatial pattern of Blacks (not shown here) appears to be more centralized, but not in the sense that high local concentrations can be found, as in the United States. In none of the 782 wards of London Blacks are a majority. The highest figure is 46.7 percent in Liddle (a ward in Southwark) (Breebaart et al. 1996). In the USA ID-values for blacks versus whites usually vary between 80 and 90 on a scale ranging from 0 to 100.

The spatial patterns and the evidence on the segregation of 'immigrants' or ethnic groups in Amsterdam, Brussels, Frankfurt and London allow for several (preliminary) conclusions. Firstly, the levels of segregation of these European cities tend to be much lower than the levels in most American cities. The metaphor of the ghetto neighbourhood is still not applicable in the cities we looked at. Secondly, there is a wide variety of patterns of segregation within Europe, illustrating the variety of situations (urban and migration histories) within Europe. Thirdly, Amsterdam showed segregation at an intermediate level, compared with Brussels, Frankfurt and London. That means that also the relationship between the share of social housing on the one hand and spatial segregation on the other hand, is not a proportional one. Amsterdam, with its extremely high share of social housing shows sharper segregation than Frankfurt and seems almost comparable to London. Fourthly, there is no clear relationship between the share of 'immigrants' in the urban population and the level of segregation.

9.4   Increasing Polarization in Amsterdam?

The level of segregation of the immigrant population in Amsterdam can be labelled 'moderate'. And although the spatial pattern is not stable at all, the indexes of segregation and dissimilarity do not reveal the development of ghetto-like neighbourhoods. However, the relative stability of the separation of different population categories does not necessarily imply that there is also in socioeconomic terms no increase of the gap between population categories. In other words, the socioeconomic polarization between immigrant or ethnic groups may increase even if the spatial segregation between these groups does not increase. According to some, this situation should certainly be expected in a city like Amsterdam, since the spatial distribution of the population is assumed to be associated (be it unproportionately) to the housing allocation process and to its relatively homogeneous and social housing market. It is assumed that there is a higher probability of realizing a socioeconomically mixed population in a housing market that is predominantly social compared to one predominantly privatized. Yet, a stable socio-spatial mix does not have to imply a stable social mix. So we must look at the dynamics of the social structure too.

There are several approaches to discuss the phenomenon of social polarization. One approach looks at intergenerational differences between the 'success-rates' (social positions) of people and their children. Another approach follows individuals during their professional life. A third approach compares averages of a group at fixed times. The first two approaches are clearly preferable, but because of data problems they are rarely applied. We have managed to get some data with regard to Amsterdam, to follow the third approach, looking for evidence to support the hypothesis that distinct ethnic groups have recently grown apart in socioeconomic terms. We will focus on the gap between those who are of Dutch origin and the so-called non-Dutch, or people labelled 'ethnic minority' in terms of income, education and employment, and particularly on the dynamics with regard to those gaps.

From statistics on unemployment we know there is a wide gap between the Dutch population and the non-Dutch. The unemployment rate of the non-Dutch labour force is three times higher than the rate of the Dutch. In 1994, six percent of the Dutch were unemployed, against 19 percent of the non-Dutch. The unemployment rate appeared to be

238

highest among Turks (36 percent) and Moroccans (31 percent), and somewhat lower among Surinamese (18 percent). However, the gap between the groups distinguished has neither increased nor decreased over the past seven years (Kwartaalbericht Arbeidsmarkt 1996).

However, these general figures may not be applicable to the situation in the cities. What can we say about the dynamics in Amsterdam? In Table 9.3 we have shown some data on income, education, unemployment and those receiving disability benefits in 1987, 1990 and 1994. Data are derived from large random, representative samples of the registered population of 18 years and older (over 4,000 responses each, face-to-face interviews). Although the exactness of the figures may be disputed, analysis revealed that the *changes* noticed are unrelated to non-response or serious data-quality factors. The instrument applied was identical in each of the measurements.

Table 9.3 Differences between the Dutch population and ethnic 'minorities' in Amsterdam, 1987–1994

	1987 Dutch	E.M.	1990 Dutch	E.M.	1994 Dutch	E.M.
% income < f2,500,=	51.6	86.6	57.0	77.7	46.2	67.9
% low education	19.5	38.8	17.0	36.5	11.8	29.6
% unemployed/disabled	12.5	36.7	8.4	20.5	9.6	23.2
% < f1,500 low edu	27.4	42.6	40.7	33.3	33.7	27.9
% f1.500-2.500 low edu	53.2	53.9	43.4	55.6	40.0	59.6
% unemployed low educ	15.0	44.5	11.6	24.5	10.1	25.8

Source: Surveys AME, University of Amsterdam.

The first three items are based on the total survey; the last three items only relate to people with a low level of education. Ethnic minorities comprise Turks, Moroccans, Surinamese and Antilleans.

The evidence of an increase of the social polarization between ethnic groups is neither clear nor convincing. Generally, the gap between the Dutch and the so called 'ethnic minorities' is large, but not systematically growing. A tendency of a decreasing social gap can be shown in the late eighties, but a somewhat widening gap shows up in the early nineties. The most alarming development is the difference between the Dutch and ethnic minorities with regard to the speed of the reduction of the share of people with only lower education. Both categories show a decrease of the percentage of people with only low educational achievements, but ethnic minorities seem to lag behind in this process. However, not all indicators of the social position point in the same direction, even during the early nineties. The share of people with a very low income is decreasing faster for ethnic minorities, and also the gap between the Dutch and the non-Dutch with respect to the unemployment rate does not seem to increase further, apart from the low-skilled unemployed. In conclusion, we have to state that the picture is unclear.

9.5   Policy Responses in Amsterdam, Compared with Brussels, Frankfurt and London

All countries in our research project show a certain degree of policy attention to ethnic segregation and ethnic social polarization issues. They all try to mitigate the problems that are assumed, rightly or wrongly, to be associated with the ethnic immigrants and with their spatial position in the metropolitan areas under investigation.

In our policy analysis we focused upon state level and local level policies and made a distinction between general policy, with measures accessible for everyone, irrespective of nationality or ethnic origin, and specific policy, accessible for specific national or ethnic categories. Within each of these 'mega' types of policy – general and specific – we distinguished between other types of variation. General as well as specific policy may be of an integrative area based character or of a sectoral type (housing policy, labour market policy etc. separately). Special attention was given to two types of specific policy. The first relates to spatial dispersion of ethnic categories or specific nationalities. The second relates to efforts to compensate for those who lag behind in these categories in order to reduce social differences.

As a rule, in all countries we have studied, forms of specific policy were applied, directly aimed at the immigrant categories, at least alongside general policy.[3] Here we will focus the attention upon the two forms of specific policy: aimed at spatial dispersion and aimed at compensation.

9.5.1 Spatial Dispersion Policy

In Amsterdam, as in other cities under investigation, efforts were made to implement a spatial dispersion policy. The idea was that a dispersed (mixed) immigrant population would help to integrate immigrants or ethnic groups in society and to avoid the development of ethnic ghetto's. However, the proposals in Amsterdam failed, predominantly because more or less identical efforts in Rotterdam were declared illegal by the national government. Spatial dispersion policy was regarded as unconstitutional. Amsterdam shares its experience with London, where spatial dispersion policy also did not pass the discussion stage. In Brussels and Frankfurt, however, spatial dispersion policy was or still is part of official policy. In Belgium a nationwide spatial dispersion policy was operating until 1995. Municipalities were allowed to refuse settlement of non EU citizens on the basis of section 18bis, once they received permission from the federal government. However, according to insiders section 18bis was merely meant as a signal to the indigenous

240

population rather than an effective instrument. Most municipalities that were applying section 18bis did allow immigrants to settle on an informal basis. In Frankfurt dispersal policy is formal and laid down in a Treaty, the *Frankfurter Vertrag*, signed by the municipality, the housing authority and private developers. The core of the Treaty is a fixation of the shares of several population categories in each neighbourhood in order to prevent the rise of ghetto's. However, some old neighbourhoods already house 60 percent or more immigrants and could house more because of the type of dwellings available. Under the treaty, further growth is impossible and this even leads to vacancies because few indigenous German households want to live in a 'foreign' area. On the other hand, some high rent areas have serious problems to find sufficient immigrant households to settle there. Here too the higher income German households try to stop the (moderate) invasion of immigrant households. Furthermore the rental sector is not large enough to house all immigrants.

At this stage it is interesting to notice that in Belgium and Germany local governments have a much stronger position, compared with Britain and the Netherlands, where the position of central government is much stronger. This may have been relevant to develop and really implement spatial dispersion policies. We think it is also important that in Frankfurt the awareness of the permanency of the presence of immigrants has only recently become clear. Only a few years ago they were still referred to as 'guest-workers'.

9.5.2 Compensating Policy

Over the past decades specific compensating policy was well developed in Amsterdam. Table 9.4 provides some summary information with regard to Amsterdam, Brussels, Frankfurt and London. The relatively high score of Amsterdam in the policy field of education is related to the fact that schools receive more money if they have a higher number of immigrant children. In the sphere of the labour market, specific policy was developed to stimulate proportional employment opportunities for ethnic immigrants. There appeared to be only few compensatory measures in Brussels and Frankfurt.

Table 9.4 Specific compensating policy

	Field of policy			
	General	Education	Housing	Labour
Amsterdam	xx	xx	-	xx
Brussels	x	x	-	x
Frankfurt	x	-	-	-
London	xx	x	x	x

x   specific attention was given to ethnic immigrants.
xx   relatively much attention was given to ethnic immigrants.

241

In London and in many other British cities, as in Amsterdam, many specific initiatives aimed at improving the integration of immigrants can be shown. Linkworkers, who try to help immigrants who need to contact the municipality; ethnic monitoring to provide signals of unequal labour market participation in certain segments of the labour market; equality targets to the year 2000, etc., are among the initiatives. Specific compensating policy, however, appears to have passed its peak in British cities. Compensating policy instruments are redirected from specific immigrant targeting to general policy. Former section 11 funds in the UK, for example, meant to stimulate integration of immigrant households, are now becoming unearmarked part of the Single Regeneration Budget.

The tendency of a shift from specific to general policy is also noticed with regard to Amsterdam. The only things left are – at best – specific language courses, meant to facilitate integration processes, and general information to specific categories.

Budgetary problems, the fear for positive discrimination, and the political response in that respect, seem to be the most important factors triggering the change of the policy direction.

9.6 Conclusions

In this contribution we provided evidence that Amsterdam experiences only relatively moderate – though not really low – levels of ethnic segregation of the population. The city is also not showing an indisputable increase of the social polarization between Dutch and non-Dutch. If we look at the policy instruments applied to mitigate problems and to reduce social polarization, we can point at a relatively high level of attention to these issues in the city of Amsterdam. But how do segregation and polarization relate to the policy applied?

If we try to link the levels of ethnic segregation with the levels of policy intervention, we must conclude they do not coincide. Two cities under investigation have shown relatively high levels of segregation (but still much lower than US cities) and are also well known because of their urban problems, especially problems with an ethnic dimension. These are London (riots in Brixton 1981, 1985) and Brussels (riots in 1991). Contrary to this, and as stated before, Amsterdam and Frankfurt show more moderate and even low levels of segregation, and are both characterized by relatively quiet urban scenes. In addition, Amsterdam does not show clear signs of increasing social polarization among ethnic groups. Remarkably, the policy attention seems to be inversely proportional to the situations described. Amsterdam and Frankfurt are cities which appear to have been most active in the field of specific policy aimed at reducing segregation and/or deprivation of ethnic immigrants. Unfortunately, our analysis does not allow us to say much about the causality of the relation at this point in time. It is likely that the organization of the welfare state in a broader sense is relevant here, as we already hypothesized in Section 9.2. It may be important to relate the outcomes to the state's attitude towards the social rights of the unemployed or, in other words, to those who are *outside* the system. The position of outsiders seems to differ from one country to another.

Studies of segregation in general, and of ethnic segregation in particular are frequently carried out under the assumption that a concentration of deprived people is a factor on its own which further reduces the already modest perspectives of the people involved, and is also a factor prohibiting integration and assimilation. We would like to stress that these assumptions are not based on systematic research carried out in Europe. This does not mean that these assumptions are irrelevant or unrealistic. On the contrary, they are extremely important, since they form the legitimization for study and policy aimed at 'concentrated' neighbourhoods. They could be realistic, and they have already coloured the perception of people. But the assumptions should be the focus of research first. Therefore, we would like to stress that more systematic research needs to be undertaken that is focused on the neighbourhood effect, or the concentration effect on an individual's perspective. The need to carry out such research is becoming even more important since the transformations going on in society might result in higher levels of segregation rather than in lower levels. This hypothesis is based on the direction of change many states show us today: high levels of state involvement are replaced by more market-led philosophies. Embracing free market principles will result in larger socioeconomic differences, more competition, growing income inequalities, less redistribution, fewer subsidies, and in general in more differentiation between households in terms of income, access to good quality housing, access to health care and access to education. This will result in sharper segregation patterns in which those who can express some choice will become separated from those who are left with a 'constrained choice'. The 'liberalization' trend will also bear the risk of increasing the social polarization in general, although – that is the other side of the coin - entry to the labour market will be stimulated as well. However, it remains to be seen whether such a model really helps to create the conditions for real upward social mobility.

References

Breebaart, M., Musterd S. and Ostendorf, W. (1996), *Etnische segregatie en beleid; een internationale vergelijking*, AME, Universiteit van Amsterdam, Amsterdam.

Champion, A.G. (1994), 'International Migration and Demographic Change in the Developed World', *Urban Studies*, vol. 31, nos. 4/5, pp. 653–77.

De Lannoy, W. and Kesteloot, C. (1990), *Het scheppen van sociaal-ruimtelijke ongelijkheden in de stad*, Werkgroep Mort-Subite, Barsten in België, EPO, Berchem.

Esping-Andersen, G. (1990), *The three worlds of welfare capitalism*, Polity Press, Cambridge.

Fainstein, S.S., Gordon, I. and Harloe, M. (eds) (1992), *Divided Cities, New York and London in the Contemporary World*, Blackwell, Cambridge, UK, Cambridge, US.

Hamnett, C. (1994), 'Social Polarisation in Global Cities: Theory and Evidence', *Urban Studies*, vol. 31, no. 3, pp 401–24.

Kesteloot, C. (1994), 'Three Levels of Socio-Spatial Polarization in Brussels', *Built Environment*, vol. 20, no. 3, pp. 204–17.

King, R. (ed.) (1993), Mass Migrations in Europe. The Legacy and the Future., Belhaven, London.

Kwartaalbericht Arbeidsmarkt (1996), Ministerie van Sociale Zaken en Werkgelegenheid, The Hague.

Musterd, S. (1994), 'A Rising European Underclass?', *Built Environment*, vol. 20, no. 3, pp. 185–91.

Musterd, S and Ostendorf, W. (1996), 'Ethnicity and the Dutch Welfare State; The Case of Amsterdam', in Roseman, C., Laux, D. and G. Thieme (eds), *EthniCity*, Rowman & Littlefield Publishers Inc., Maryland, pp. 121–40.

Sassen, S. (1991), *The Global City*, Princeton University Press, Princeton, New Jersey.

SCP (1994) *Sociaal en Cultureel Rapport* 1994, Sociaal en Cultureel Planbureau, Rijswijk.

Wagenaar, M. (1993), 'Monumental Metropolis, Airy Suburbs. Two Spatial Strategies to Solve Europe's Urban Crisis, 1850–1914, in Wagenaar, M., Cortie, C. and G. Dijkink (eds), *Capital Cities in Europe. Vistas, Worries and Interrogations*, Centre for Metropolitan Research, Amsterdam.

Warf, B. (1990), 'Deindustrialization, Service Sector Growth, and the Underclass in the New York Metropolitan Region', *Tijdschrift voor Economische en Sociale Geografie*, vol. 81, no. 5, pp. 332–47.

White, P. (1993), 'Immigrants and the social geography of European cities', in King, R. (ed.), Mass Migrations in Europe. The Legacy and the Future, Belhaven, London pp.65–82.

Wilson, W.J. (1987), *The Truly Disadvantaged, The Innercity, The Underclass and Public Policy*, University of Chicago Press, Chicago.

Notes

1. The Index of Segregation is a special case of the Index of Dissimilarity, which is defined as:

$$ID = 0.5 * \sum_{i=1}^{i \to n} \left| \frac{x_i}{x} - \frac{Y_i}{Y} \right| * 100$$

X = the number of cases of the first population category

$x_i=$ the number of cases of the first population category in area i

Y =the number of cases of the second population category

$y_i=$ the number of cases of the second population category in area i

i =   one of the n areas (neighbourhoods)

n =   number of areas

If both categories together comprise the entire population the index is referred to as the Index of Segregation.

2. The high percentage of foreigners in Flughafen is of only marginal importance, since only 380 residents are living there.

3. In fact, France, not dealt with here, was the only exception. France continues its focus on general policy measures only. Also the recently introduced type of Marshall plan, focusing upon the banlieux of the large cities, should be considered as a form of general, area-based policy aiming at everyone living there.

10 Socioeconomic Implications of the Changing Spatial Distribution and Labour Market Experience of Ethnic Minorities in Britain

ANNE GREEN

10.1 Introduction

In Europe there is a tendency to equate 'immigrants' with 'ethnic minorities'. Here reference is made to both ethnic minority groups in Britain and to residents of Britain born elsewhere, but the main emphasis is on the former rather than the latter group.

As in some other western European countries, members of ethnic minority groups have been present in Britain for many years – particularly in port cities and in London – but it was following World War II that their numbers increased dramatically. However, there are difficulties in estimating the numbers of people from ethnic minorities over the period since World War II due to a lack of time series data. The population of England and Wales from ethnic minority groups was estimated to be only 103 thousand in 1951, rising to 415 thousand in 1961 (although this latter figure from the Census of Population is generally considered to be an underestimate). Between 1966 and 1980 the ethnic minority population more than doubled in size – from 886 thousand to 2.1 million, and increased by a quarter between 1981 and 1991: according to the 1991 Census of Population (the first UK Census to include a question on ethnic origin) ethnic minority groups accounted for over 3 million people (5.5 percent of the population of Britain).

The highest levels of immigration to Britain from the New Commonwealth were experienced from the late 1950s to the early 1970s. As in other European former colonial powers, these flows were linked to the decolonization process. It is possible to trace the trend of immigration over time by ethnic group using data on the 'dates of arrival' from the Labour Force Survey (see Figure 10.1). 'Mass migration' started in the late 1950s. The peak of immigration occurred in the early 1970s; at the time East African and Asians were expelled from Kenya and Uganda. After a downturn in the early 1980s, immigration rose again later in the decade. The earliest arrivals were the

West Indians and Indians - with a peak in immigration occurring in the early 1960s, and a decline from the mid 1960s. The number of arrivals from these two groups decreased in the 1980s. In contrast, the arrivals from smaller ethnic minority groups increased throughout the period.

People have been asked to state their country of birth in every British Census since 1841, but the 1991 Census of Population was the first in Britain to include a question on ethnic group, after plans to introduce such a question in 1981 were abandoned. The categories used were a mixture of racial, ethnic and national classifications, and proved reasonably successful in delivering data on the key commonly recognized ethnic groups. Of the 3 million residents in Great Britain belonging to ethnic minority groups in 1991, the largest groups were the Indians, the Black Caribbean group and the Pakistanis (see Table 10.1).

Table 10.1   Ethnic group composition of the population of Great Britain, 1991

Ethnic group	population (thousands)	% of GB total population	% of GB ethnic minority population
White	51,843.0	94.5	n/a
Ethnic minorities	3,006.5	5.5	100.0
Black	*885.4*	*1.6*	*29.4*
Black Caribbean	499.1	0.9	16.6
Black African	207.5	0.4	6.9
Black Other	178.8	0.3	5.9
Southern Asian	*1,476.9*	*2.7*	*49.1*
Indian	840.8	1.5	28.0
Pakistani	475.8	0.9	15.8
Bangladeshi	160.3	0.3	5.3
Chinese & Others	*644.3*	*1.2*	*21.4*
Chinese	157.5	0.3	5.2
Other Asian	196.7	0.4	6.5
Other Other	290.1	0.5	9.6

Source: 1991 Census of Population.

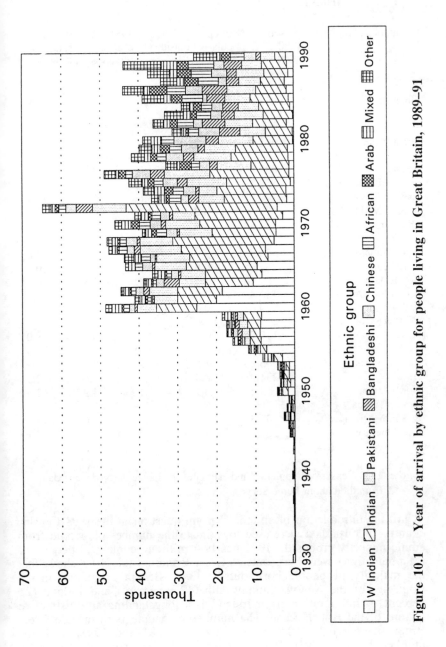

Figure 10.1 Year of arrival by ethnic group for people living in Great Britain, 1989–91

Table 10.2   Geographical regions of birth of residents of Great Britain

Geographical region of birth	persons (000s) 1991	% of GB population 1991	% born outside GB 1991	1981–91 change (000s)	1981–91 change (%)
Great Britain	50,897.8	92.7	n/a	943.7	1.9
Born outside Great Britain	3,991.0	7.3	100.0	388.2	10.8
Ireland	837.5	1.5	21.0	-12.9	-1.5
Other EU and EFTA	552.2	1.0	1.5	63.7	13.0
Eastern Europe &CIS	142.9	0.3	3.6	-29.4	-17.1
Near & Middle East	128.3	0.2	3.2	44.4	53.0
Old Commonwealth	177.4	0.3	4.4	24.6	16.1
New Commonwealth	*1,688.4*	*3.1*	*42.3*	*175.0*	*11.6*
Caribbean	264.6	0.5	6.6	-30.6	-10.4
South Asia	787.5	1.4	19.7	132.8	20.3
South East Asia	150.4	0.3	3.8	13.6	10.0
East Africa	220.6	0.4	5.5	23.4	11.9
West & southern Africa	110.7	0.2	2.8	40.7	58.0
Rest of world	*566.2*	*1.0*	*14.2*	*152.2*	*36.9*
Asia	231.0	0.4	5.8	79.6	52.5
North Africa	44.6	0.1	1.1	4.9	12.3
Rest of Africa & South Africa	102.3	0.2	2.6	31.0	43.5
The Americas	185.0	0.3	4.6	34.8	23.1

Source: 1991 Census of Population and estimates of change derived using data from the Labour Force Survey.

Until the introduction of an ethnic group question in the 1991 Census, country of birth data were used to estimate the number of people from ethnic minority groups. In 1991 nearly 4 million people (7.3 percent of the population) were born outside Great Britain. Table 10.2 shows that the majority of people born outside Great Britain originated in the Countries of the New Commonwealth (42.3 percent) and Ireland (21 percent) – immigration from Ireland is a longstanding and distinctive feature of the British scene. The number of people born outside Great Britain increased by 10.8 percent between 1981 and 1991, while the number born in Great Britain increased by 1.9 percent. The main countries of origin of those born outside Great Britain are the Irish Republic, India, Northern Ireland, Pakistan and Germany (some of these will be the children of parents in the Armed Services stationed in Germany). There was a geographical shift in the origins of the population during the decade, with a decline in the number of people born in Ireland, eastern Europe and the Caribbean, and rapid growth in the numbers born in Bangladesh, Pakistan, Germany, the United States, parts of Africa and Turkey.

By 1991 nearly half (47 percent) of people from ethnic minority groups were born in Britain, illustrating the inadequacy of a 'country of birth' indicator for estimating ethnic minority groups. In the Black Other group the proportion increases to 84 percent (many of these are the children of persons of 'Black Caribbean' origin, who chose to classify themselves as 'Black British' in the Census ethnic origin question), whereas in the Other Asian and Chinese groups the proportion is less than 30 percent. Sixty-one percent of the population born outside Great Britain are white. In countries outside the New Commonwealth this proportion rises to 89 percent. A fifth of the New Commonwealth born population is white – these are British colonists, colonial officers and their families.

10.2   Settlement Patterns

With ethnic minority groups accounting for over 3 million people (5.5 per cent of the population of Britain) in 1991, a quantitative perspective on ethnic minority groups is clearly important. Similarly, there is an interest in the settlement patterns of the population born outside Great Britain (Green and Owen 1995). From a regional and local perspective, the spatially uneven distribution of such groups is of key significance. 'Segregation' tends to reflect the degree of assimilation of a group, but the patterns are also powerfully influenced by economic and social factors acting to channel particular ethnic groups into a given type of economic activity, housing or residential environment.

There are particular concentrations of ethnic minority groups in Greater London and other metropolitan areas – such as the West Midlands metropolitan boroughs (Owen 1992) (see Table 10.3). As in other west European countries, the largest single concentration of ethnic minority groups is found in the largest cities, notably the capital. Over 20 percent of the population of Greater London is from ethnic minority groups (accounting for 44.6 percent of the ethnic minority population of Great Britain), but in the boroughs of Brent and Newham the proportion exceeds 40 percent (and is projected to exceed 50 percent by 2011), while in Tower Hamlets, Hackney, Ealing and Lambeth the share is greater than 30 percent.

Table 10.3 Regional distribution of population by ethnic group and country of birth

Region and metropolitan country	White % of region	White % of GB	Ethnic minorities % of region	Ethnic minorities % of GB	Born outside GB % of region	Born outside GB % OF GB
South East	90.1	29.9	9.9	56.2	12.9	55.7
Greater London	*79.8*	*10.3*	*20.2*	*44.6*	*22.3*	*37.3*
East Anglia	97.9	3.8	2.1	1.4	6.1	3.1
South West	98.6	8.8	1.4	2.1	4.6	5.3
West Midlands	91.8	9.1	8.2	14.1	7.0	9.1
West Midlands MC	*85.4*	*4.2*	*14.6*	*12.4*	*10.4*	*6.7*
East Midlands	95.2	7.3	4.8	6.2	5.5	5.5
Yorks & Humberside	95.6	8.9	4.4	7.1	4.6	5.5
South Yorkshire	*97.1*	*2.4*	*2.9*	*1.2*	*3.1*	*1.0*
West Yorkshire	*91.8*	*3.6*	*8.2*	*5.4*	*6.6*	*3.3*
North West	96.1	11.6	3.9	8.1	4.9	7.6
Greater Manchester	*94.1*	*4.5*	*5.9*	*4.9*	*6.5*	*4.1*
Merseyside	*98.2*	*2.7*	*1.8*	*0.9*	*3.1*	*1.1*
North	98.7	5.8	1.3	1.3	2.4	1.8
Tyne & Wear	*98.2*	*2.1*	*1.8*	*0.7*	*2.5*	*0.7*
Wales	98.5	5.4	1.5	1.4	2.9	2.1
Scotland	98.7	9.5	1.3	2.1	3.5	4.4
GreatBritain	94.5	100.0	5.5	100.0	7.2	100.0

Source: 1991 Census of Population.

At more disaggregated spatial scales even more marked concentrations of ethnic minority groups are evident, such that it is no longer 'accurate' to consider such groups as 'minorities' within some neighbourhoods. At the opposite end of the spectrum, in the South West, Northern region, Wales and Scotland less than 2 percent of the population is from ethnic minority groups, and there are large swathes of Great Britain – particularly some rural areas – where (from a local perspective) notions of a 'multiracial, multicultural society' may seem irrelevant, since ethnic minority groups account for only a tiny proportion of the total population.

Those born outside Great Britain are also disproportionately concentrated in the South East: while this region contains only 31.4 per cent of the total population of Great Britain, it contains 55.7 percent of

252

those born outside Great Britain (Owen 1993a). Greater London contains 37.3 percent of those born outside Great Britain, with such residents accounting for over a fifth of London's population. The ten local authority districts with the largest shares of their population born outside Great Britain are all located in Greater London: in Kensington and Chelsea, Westminster and Brent more than a third of the population were born outside Great Britain.

Clearly the bulk of the ethnic minority population and of those born outside Great Britain live in the South East – more particularly in Greater London. However, there are some important variations in the settlement patterns of the different ethnic minority/national groups. The Black ethnic groups are most heavily concentrated in London: more than 60 percent live in London alone. South Asians display a contrasting pattern, with only just over a third living in London, but nearly a fifth resident in the West Midlands. The share accounted for by the East Midlands, Yorkshire and Humberside and the North West in the Great Britain total is also much higher than the ethnic minority average. The Chinese and other ethnic groups have the most dispersed patterns of settlement. This regional level pattern conceals an even stronger tendency for ethnic minority groups to concentrate in particular localities – notably Inner London Boroughs, Birmingham, Leicester and the 'mill towns' of Lancashire, Greater Manchester and Yorkshire. Similarly, there are regional and local variations in the settlement patterns of the various groups born outside Great Britain. For example, those from Ireland and the Indian subcontinent are more likely to live in the conurbations of the Midlands and northern England than other non-British born people. Smaller national groups – such as the Turks and the Cypriots – are concentrated into a few London boroughs. Again, this general picture of distinctive local concentrations of particular groups is replicated in other western European countries.

10.3 Socioeconomic Characteristics of Local Areas with Concentrations of Ethnic Minority Groups

So, what are the main socioeconomic features of local areas characterised by high proportions of residents from ethnic minority groups? Table 10.4 lists the characteristics of eight groups of areas identified in a cluster analysis of local authority districts using demographic, social structure, prosperity, housing structure and economic structure indicators as the classificatory indicators (Owen 1995). For presentational purposes, the district types are ranked on 1991 unemployment rates, with Central London and Declining Industrial Areas displaying the highest incidence of unemployment, and High tech Britain and the Affluent commuter towns the lowest unemployment.

Table 10.4 Types of area identified in a cluster analysis

Central London: characterised by high population density, high proportion of population living in flats and low rates of owner occupation, high proportion of population born outside UK, low rates of car ownership, high proportion with higher qualifications and working in service sector, slow population growth and marked employment loss;

Declining industrial centres: major cities of northern Britain and the Midlands suffering high rates of employment and population loss, high unemployment rates, an older housing stock (with high proportions of terraced housing);

Stagnating urban areas: mainly smaller urban centres, relatively low rates of owner occupation, low proportion of population born outside Britain, old housing stock, relatively high proportion of children in population, low employment growth, manufacturing more significant than in other area types;

Retirement resorts: coastal (mostly resort) areas, characterised by elderly populations, high rates of owner-occupation, low economic activity rates, and relatively high population and employment growth;

Rural periphery: lowest population density, relative deficit of young adults, much lower than average proportions of population born outside Great Britain, relatively high rates of population and employment growth;

Rural heartland: mainly concentrated in the southern half of England, low population density, relatively old population, high rates of owner occupation, low unemployment rates, relatively rapid employment and population growth;

Affluent commuter towns: mainly located in outer London and Home Counties, characterised by moderately high economic activity rates, relatively high proportion of population of prime working age, high percentages of highly qualified people in 'white collar' jobs and the service sector;

High-tech Britain: characterised by employment growth, low unemployment rates, relatively youthful populations living at low densities, with high rates of home and car ownership.

Table 10.5 shows the relative concentration of ethnic groups by district type. The bottom line shows the proportion of the entire population living in each cluster, while the figures in the body of the table show the differences from this average for each ethnic group: a positive value indicating overrepresentation relative to the total population in that cluster and a negative value indicating underrepresentation. (The clusters vary in size – the Stagnating urban areas and the Declining industrial centres each accounting for approximately a fifth of the population, and the Central London and Retirement resorts clusters being much smaller.)

Relative to the population as a whole, ethnic minority groups are overrepresented in Central London, Affluent commuter towns and Declining industrial centres. They are underrepresented in the Rural heartland, the Rural periphery, Retirement resorts, High tech Britain and Stagnating urban areas. This distribution highlights the relative exclusion of ethnic minority groups from the most successful parts of the British space economy, and concentration in areas of economic decline. However, not all ethnic minority groups live in disadvantaged areas – for example, they are overrepresented in the Affluent commuter

254

towns (mainly located around London) and are underrepresented (albeit to a lesser extent) in Stagnating urban areas. The aggregate picture disguises considerable differences in the distribution of individual ethnic minority groups. For example, the Black groups are more concentrated in Central London than the other main ethnic minority groups, Pakistanis are more concentrated in Declining industrial centres and Stagnating urban areas than the other ethnic minority groups, and of all the ethnic minority groups the Indians and Other Asian group are most concentrated in Affluent commuter towns.

Table 10.5   The relative concentration of the ethnic groups in the eight cluster types

Percent of ethnic group population minus
percent of Great Britain population in each cluster

Ethnic group	Central London	Declining industrial centres	Stagnating urban areas	Retirement resorts	Rural periphery	Rural heartland	Affluent commuter towns	High tech Britain
White	-1.4	-0.2	0.2	0.3	0.5	0.6	-0.3	0.3
Ethnic Minority Groups	*23.8*	*2.9*	*-3.9*	*-5.0*	*-8.0*	*-10.2*	*4.7*	*-4.3*
Black	*41.3*	*-1.3*	*-11.5*	*-5.3*	*-8.2*	*-10.9*	*0.6*	*-4.6*
Black Caribbean	40.0	1.5	-10.9	-5.7	-8.8	-11.1	0.0	-5.1
Black African	55.0	-9.9	-17.0	-5.1	-8.2	-11.7	2.7	-5.7
Black other	28.4	1.1	-6.8	-4.6	-6.6	-9.4	-0.2	-2.0
South Asian	*14.3*	*8.1*	*2.8*	*-5.5*	*-8.8*	*-10.6*	*4.6*	*-5.0*
Indian	14.0	8.0	-4.3	-5.4	-8.6	-9.4	10.7	-5.0
Pakistani	6.1	11.9	17.2	-5.8	-9.0	-12.3	-3.5	-4.7
Bangladeshi	39.8	-2.4	-3.1	-4.9	-8.3	-11.5	-3.4	-6.2
Chinese & Other	*21.3*	*-3.2*	*-8.8*	*-3.3*	*-6.3*	*-8.2*	*10.6*	*-2.1*
Chinese	16.2	-0.3	-7.1	-2.8	-5.5	-6.3	7.9	-2.1
Other Asian	26.9	-7.5	-11.8	-4.1	-7.4	-10.0	16.6	-2.8
OtherOther	20.3	-1.8	-7.7	-3.1	-5.9	-8.0	7.9	-1.7
Entire population	5.9	19.9	23.0	6.1	9.3	13.5	14.3	8.1

Source: Adapted from Owen 1995.

Across all districts in Great Britain, 72 percent of white people in the economically active age groups are in employment, compared with only 55 percent of those from ethnic minority groups. However, these 'averages' mask considerable differences in the labour market experience of different ethnic minority groups across all district types. In general, those in high tech Britain and the Affluent commuter towns tend to fare better than those in Central London and the Declining industrial centres. In aggregate, ethnic minority groups tend to fare as badly or worse than the white ethnic group in the most deprived clusters, but members of ethnic minority groups living outside these clusters fare considerable better than average (and better in relative terms than the white ethnic group).

Table 10.6   The proportion of the economically active age groups in employment by broad ethnic group in the eight cluster types

Relative to ethnic group mean (=100)

Ethnic group	Central London	Declining industrial centres	Stagnating urban areas	Retirement resorts	Rural periphery	Rural heartland	Affluent commuter towns	High tech Britain
White	98.3	88.4	99.0	100.8	101.5	104.4	106.6	109.0
Ethnic minority groups	96.0	89.0	92.0	114.9	115.4	119.3	115.5	121.6
Black	93.5	94.6	106.9	101.8	108.4	114.7	113.0	123.2
South Asian	96.2	90.6	87.8	127.6	126.1	128.0	121.4	120.2
Chinese & Other	93.2	82.6	100.3	109.5	108.5	110.0	109.4	118.1
Entire Population	95.5	88.3	99.1	102.1	102.8	105.7	106.6	110.1

Source: Adapted from Owen (1995).

This pattern is highlighted by the figures presented in Table 10.6, showing for each of the broad ethnic groups the percentage of persons in the economically active age groups who are in employment. Relative to the mean, ethnic minority groups display the lowest employment rates in the Declining industrial centres and the Stagnating urban areas. There are also some variations in experience between the broad ethnic groups, with the Chinese and other group faring particularly poorly relative to the group mean in the former cluster, while the South Asian group fare worst in the latter. Given the concentration of ethnic minority groups in the largest cities, it is worthy of note that like other world cities, Central London is distinguished by coexistence of very favourable and disadvantageous characteristics, and the implication is that the unfavourable characteristics apply particularly to people from ethnic minority groups – suggesting that London's economic decline has affected people from ethnic minority groups particularly badly. Turning from the district to the neighbourhood scale, some insights into the concentration of ethnic minority groups into neighbourhoods (i.e. wards) characterized by high unemployment rates may be gained by ranking all wards in Great Britain on the unemployment rate, and then dividing the distribution into decile groups (with decile group 10 experiencing the highest unemployment rates). A greater proportion of all ethnic minority groups reside in neighbourhoods falling in the higher decile groups on the unemployment rate indicator than the white population (Green 1994). Approximately four-fifths of the Bangladeshi, Pakistani and Black populations reside in wards in the eighth, ninth and tenth decile groups. Hence, not only are these most disadvantaged groups concentrated in the most disadvantaged area types at local authority district level, they also tend to be concentrated in the most disadvantaged neighbourhoods within those districts.

Recent research for the Department for Education and Employment has been concerned with the development of a classification of wards in Great Britain suffering the most severe labour market disadvantage (Green and Owen 1996). The wards identified as suffering severe labour market disadvantage cover 11 percent of the total population, and nearly one in four of the ethnic minority group population of Great Britain, compared with one in ten of the white population. For those ethnic minority groups identified in other studies as suffering the most pronounced degree of labour market disadvantage the proportions exceed one in four: Bangladeshi population (43 percent), Pakistani population (39 percent) and Black Caribbean (26 percent).

Recent qualitative research (Wrench and Qureshi 1996) suggests that many young people from ethnic minorities feel that their employment opportunities are adversely affected by their residential location – as the following two quotes from young Bangladeshi men in London and Birmingham indicate:

> ... I sometimes don't bother putting down my postcode when I apply for jobs. I used to, and then I thought of all the times that the people I applied to just put the application straight into the bin when they saw I was from East London. ...

> ... Where I live is one of the ghettos of Birmingham, everybody knows that. ... I really want to move away from this area, and I think I will have to in the future if I'm going to get a good job. ...

Although blatant exclusion from employment on the grounds of racism is no longer common, 'racialization' of areas into Black/Asian spaces and white spaces has undesirable effects on employment patterns of different communities:

257

... I would work anywhere in London except the Isle of Dogs, ... simply because I wouldn't feel safe travelling in that part of East London. It is a racist area, you only have to go there and the white people give you funny looks. ...

... I don't mind getting a job locally (East London) as long as it isn't too far ... the Isle of Dogs is definitely a no-go area for Bangladeshis. The place is full of racist whites, no way would I go there for a job. The developments with Docklands isn't really for us, it is for people from the City. ...

In the absence of quantitative estimates to 'back up' this qualitative research, it is difficult to assess the extent to which the types of problems/perceptions identified above are a feature of racism, rather than other features of the operation of urban labour markets. As highlighted in a review of social exclusion and economic reintegration (McGregor and McConnachie 1995), stigmatisation by employers of residents of disadvantaged areas due to the negative image many of these areas have acquired through time, is only one of a number of factors (along with localized job losses, poor transport access to employment opportunities in the wider labour market, lack of educational qualifications and vocational skills, etc.) which act to create barriers to effective participation in the labour market.

10.4 Employment Patterns in the Context of Industrial and Occupational Growth and Decline

The labour market experience of ethnic minority groups and foreign workers has been the focus of academic and policy attention for some time (Jones 1993; Mason 1995; Sly 1995; Salt 1995). Table 10.7 outlines some of the key features of economic position by ethnic group. White people have economic activity rates around ten percentage points higher than for ethnic minority groups as a whole (Owen 1993b). However, there are substantial variations in economic activity rates between ethnic minority groups: for the Black Caribbean group economic activity rates for males and females are similar to those for white people, while for Pakistani and Bangladeshi groups economic activity rates are much lower. Unemployment rates are higher for both men and women amongst ethnic minorities than for white people. Male Bangladeshis have the highest unemployment rates, followed by Black ethnic groups and Pakistanis, while the Chinese experience the lowest unemployment rates.

At the regional level, ILO unemployment rates for non-white ethnic groups in Spring 1994 ranged from 14 percent in the Rest of the South East (i.e. the South East region excluding London) to 24 percent in Greater London and over 26 percent in Yorkshire and Humberside; (the respective proportions for the white group were 8 percent, 9 percent and

258

11 percent) (Sly 1994). In Greater London, the unemployment rate is particularly high amongst the Black ethnic group, whereas in Yorkshire and Humberside the incidence of unemployment is particularly high amongst the South Asian group.

Table 10.7   Population and economic activity by activity group in Great Britain, 1991

Ethnic group	Male				Female			
	Econ. activity rate	% in work	% unemployed	% inactive	Econ. activity rate	% in work	% unemployed	% inactive
White	87.0	77.5	9.4	13.9	68.3	63.8	4.5	31.7
Ethnic minority groups	*79.6*	*63.4*	*16.2*	*20.4*	*56.6*	*47.7*	*8.8*	*43.4*
Black	*81.9*	*61.2*	*20.7*	*18.1*	*69.2*	*57.6*	*11.6*	*30.8*
Black Caribbean	86.4	65.7	20.7	13.6	73.3	63.2	10.1	26.7
Black African	70.4	50.0	20.4	29.6	61.4	46.2	15.2	38.6
Black Other	83.7	62.3	21.4	16.3	64.8	52.9	12.0	35.2
South Asian	*78.3*	*64.3*	*15.3*	*20.4*	*47.6*	*39.8*	*7.8*	*52.4*
Indian	82.3	71.2	11.0	17.7	60.4	52.8	7.6	39.6
Pakistani	71.3	54.1	21.6	24.3	28.3	19.9	8.3	71.7
Bangladeshi	74.3	51.4	22.9	25.7	22.2	14.5	7.7	77.8
Chinese & Others	*76.7*	*64.8*	*11.9*	*23.4*	*57.0*	*50.1*	*6.9*	*43.0*
Chinese	72.4	64.8	7.6	27.6	56.7	52.1	4.7	43.3
Other Asian	78.2	67.1	11.1	22.1	56.2	49.2	6.9	43.8
OtherOther	78.5	63.0	15.5	21.5	58.2	49.5	8.7	41.8
Entire Population	86.6	76.8	9.8	13.4	67.6	62.9	4.7	32.4

Source: 1991 Census of Population.

At a more detailed level of spatial disaggregation, Table 10.8 lists those districts with unemployment rates in excess of 25 percent for each of the broad ethnic minority groups. Tower Hamlets has the highest incidence of unemployment amongst all ethnic minority groups (36 percent); (for the South Asian group the unemployment rate rises to 44 percent). Other major urban centres – notably Manchester, Birmingham and Bradford – are represented amongst those districts with unemployment rates in excess of 25 percent for ethnic minority groups. Of the twelve districts recording unemployment rates in excess of 25 per cent amongst the Black ethnic group, ten are in London. By contrast, only three of the seventeen districts appearing in the list of unemployment rates in excess of 25 percent for the South Asian group are in London. Tower Hamlets and Hackney – both amongst the most deprived Inner London boroughs – display extreme unemployment rates for all ethnic groups.

Table 10.8 **Extreme unemployment rates (>25 percent) at the local authority district level for broad ethnic minority groups, 1991**

All ethnic minority groups	Black	South Asian	Chinese & other
Tower Hamlets*	Manchester	Tower Hamlets*	Hackney*
Calderdale	Hackney*	Calderdale	Tower Hamlets*
Hackney*	Kensington/-Chelsea*	Oldham	Southwark*
Blackburn	Wolver-hampton	Blackburn	Greenwich*
Oldham	Haringey*	Burnley	
Bradford	Lambeth*	Hyndburn	
Manchester	Tower Hamlets*	Bradford	
Hyndburn	Southwark*	Hackney*	
Southwark*	Newham*	Peterborough	
Lambeth*	Camden*	Birmingham	
Birmingham	Islington*	Manchester	
Newham*	Westminster*	East Staffs.	
		Wycombe	
		Rochdale	
		Bolton	
		Newham*	
		Kirklees	

Note: *represents a London borough.

Source: 1991 Census of Population.

There are longstanding concerns that certain ethnic minority groups may be discriminated against by some employers, and hence that they may experience difficulty in achieving equal access to labour market opportunities (Brown, 1984; Phizacklea 1988). A number of studies have indicated that direct and apparently intentional discrimination remains a feature in employment selection decisions (Daniel 1968; National Association of Citizens Advice Bureaux 1984; Brown and Gay

260

1985). Table 10.9 presents statistics from the Brown and Gay (1985) study, in which employers were offered artificial job applications from candidates who were similar in every way except ethnic origin (West Indian, Asian and white 'applicants' were included in the experiment). Just under half of employers treated all candidates equally (responding positively to all three). However, while overall only 9 percent of White candidates were rejected, the proportions for Asian and West Indian candidates were 63 percent and 62 percent, respectively. A more recent study (Noon 1993), involving matched letters of inquiry from two similar fictitious candidates (named 'Evans' and 'Patel') to personnel officers at top UK companies, also revealed that just under half of the companies did not treat the two 'candidates' equally, and that overall responses were more helpful and encouraging to 'Evans' (the 'white' candidate) than to 'Patel' (the 'Asian' candidate). Such experiments would appear to uncover direct discrimination. However, in addition it is necessary to be aware of processes of indirect discrimination, where selection criteria are applied equally to everyone, but where they disproportionately affect members of particular groups. A number of studies (for example, Jenkins 1986 and Jewson et al. 1990) have revealed that negative stereotypes of ethnic minority groups are widespread amongst managers responsible for recruitment decisions.

Table 10.9   Results of 'test' applications – white, Asian and West Indian applicants

Patterns of responses	All (column %)	Male applicants (column %)	Femane applicants (column %)
All positive	46	47	44
white applicant rejected	4	4	4
Asian applicant rejected	10	12	8
West Indian applicant rejected	10	10	10
white and Asian applicant rejected	2	2	2
white and West Indian applicant rejected	3	3	3
Asian and West Indian applicant rejected	25	22	28

Source: Adapted from Brown and Gay (1985).

Moreover, stereotypes operating at various institutional levels can influence the labour market choices of particular groups. If such questions of discrimination and disadvantage are to be addressed, it is important to ascertain the extent to which ethnic minority groups may

261

be concentrated ('segregated') in particular industries and occupations, and to assess the likely implications of such 'segregation'.

The main features of recent and forecast employment change by industry over the period to 2001 include a continuation of long term shifts from primary and manufacturing industries to the service sector, and substantial employment growth in the service sector – particularly in other/miscellaneous services, hotels and catering, and health and education. Industrial change also has implications for occupational change. In general, changes in industrial structure have tended to favour white collar jobs in the service sector at the expense of manual jobs in primary and manufacturing sectors. Technological and organizational changes within industries have also tended to favour higher skilled white collar non-manual jobs at the expense of low skilled manual jobs. Key features of recent and forecast employment change include a general increase in highly skilled white collar employment at the expense of low skilled manual occupations; a substantial increase in managerial and professional and associate professional jobs, along with growth in personal and protective service occupations; and a decline in employment opportunities for those with craft skills, plant and machine operatives, and the unskilled (Institute for Employment Research 1995).

On the basis of the employment trends outlined above, it is possible to classify industries and occupations into a number of different categories of 'growth' and 'decline' (see Green (1997) for further details), and to examine the distribution of ethnic minority groups across growing and declining industries and occupations. It is apparent that relative to their White counterparts, men from ethnic minority groups are relatively less concentrated in declining industries; but, this is entirely a function of the underrepresentation of men from the Chinese and Other group in such industries. Men from South Asian (notably the Pakistani group) and Black groups (notably those of Black Caribbean origin) exhibit a slightly greater concentration in declining industries than White men. Overall women from ethnic minority groups are relatively more concentrated in declining industries than White women, and so, holding other influences constant, would be expected to suffer disproportionately from employment decline and not benefit to the same extent as White women from employment growth. However, this is a function of the overrepresentation of women from the South Asian group in such industries, while Chinese and Other and Black women are less concentrated in declining industries than are White women. Black Caribbean and Pakistani men are particularly concentrated in declining occupations, while a greater share of Indian and Chinese men than of white men are employed in growing occupations. Black women and white women are employed in declining occupations in similar proportions; while South Asian women are disproportionately concentrated in declining occupations and Chinese women in growing occupations.

The differences in the industrial occupational profiles of specific ethnic minority groups are such that it is a gross over-simplification to make general statements regarding labour market 'disadvantage' suffered by ethnic minority workers: rather the patterns of industrial and occupational concentration are complex, and vary by ethnic minority group. In regions with smaller than average ethnic minority populations, workers from ethnic minority groups tend to be more concentrated in high skilled white collar occupations than in regions with larger than average ethnic minority populations; suggesting that labour market disadvantage and segregation of ethnic minority groups – perhaps as a result of more entrenched 'stereotyping' – is most prevalent in areas with a relatively large number of ethnic minority workers.

In summary, no straightforward picture emerges: ethnic minority groups are unlikely to fare universally well/badly in the face of forecast labour market change, although some particular groups are more vulnerable than others. Using this data it is not possible to identify (often very crucial) differences within occupations and industries, and between types of employer. Moreover, there is no information on the processes leading to patterns of industrial and occupational segregation; for example, why are certain occupations options for young people from ethnic minority groups, while other industries and occupations are characterised by a low take-up?

10.5 Implications for Labour Market Policy

In the British context, many training programmes and other labour market initiatives are delivered through a network of Training and Enterprise Councils (TECs) in England and Wales; (Local Enterprise Companies in Scotland). The principle underlying such a local network is that labour market policy and programme provision should be made more locally responsive. Under their operating agreements all TECs are obliged to make provision for people with special training needs – including needs for people with literacy/numeracy support, people with special language needs (notably English for speakers of other languages), etc.; and equal opportunities groups who may face disadvantage in the labour market as a result of prejudice/discrimination – including ethnic minorities (for further background on the role of TECs in multiethnic areas see Pitcher 1994).

'Performance indicators' are central to the monitoring and assessment of the performance of TECs. Many of these performance indicators relate to people participating in training programmes and the 'outcomes' they experience. In a recent review Boddy (1995) indicated that TECs should be able to establish baseline information on the proportion of ethnic minorities in the potential client population for particular programmes, participation in and outcomes from particular programmes by ethnic origin, training needs particular to ethnic minorities and pointers to appropriate forms of action to remedy. Since some sub-groups of training programme participants face greater

263

difficulties in achieving job outcomes than others, it may be assumed that inter-TEC variations in the characteristics of participants will have implications for the costs and outcomes of training provision, and consequently impact upon TEC performance. Management information from 1993/94 indicated that the 'success rates' in obtaining employment for programme participants on the major adult employment training programme in operation at the time was 35 percent for all participants, but only 26 percent for those from ethnic minority groups and for those with disabilities, 21 percent for those with English as a second language and 20 percent for those with literacy/numeracy difficulties. The proportion of programme participants from each of these groups varies widely between TECs: for example, in TECs in London the proportion of participants from non-white ethnic groups exceeds 40 percent, compared with less than 1 percent in some other TECs; and in East London 13 percent of participants are identified as having language needs, compared with only 3 percent at the national level. Research has been undertaken to examine the ways in which performance indicators can be adjusted to take into account such inter-TEC variations in participant profiles and base populations (Winnett and Green 1994), such that TEC performance may be assessed across a 'level playing field'. This research highlighted considerable variations in the rates of participation of ethnic minority groups in government training programmes, and in the 'penetration' of such training programmes amongst special training needs and equal opportunities groups.

More recently, there has been a growing emphasis on inter-agency coordination in policy delivery, with labour market and other agencies coming together in preparing bids for Single Regeneration Budget funding to finance programmes of support to enhance the competitiveness of deprived individuals and communities. Similarly, there has been increasing attention paid to formulating bespoke mixes of policy instruments to meet local needs. 'Best practice' approaches for those suffering 'exclusion' often include one or more of the following interlinked elements: compacts and education-business partnerships, home-school support schemes, raising the quality of vocational guidance to school leavers, counselling the long term unemployed, personal development programmes, vocational training programmes, directly accessing jobs, accessing the intermediate labour market, enabling the unemployed to take advantage of employment/training opportunities, and after care – to facilitate successful reintegration into the labour market (McGregor and McConnachie 1995). Such policies may be particularly successful in meeting addressing the problems faced by local concentrations of ethnic minority/refugee groups.

10.6 Conclusion

The number of people from ethnic minority groups in Britain continues to grow, although the peak of immigration has passed. Traditionally 'immigrants' have been equated with ethnic minorities, but the fact that 47 percent of people from ethnic minorities were born in Britain, and 61 percent of people born outside Great Britain were of white ethnic origin, indicates that it is becoming less appropriate to treat 'ethnic group' and 'country of origin' as surrogates one for the other.

As in other countries, ethnic minority groups and the population born outside Great Britain display uneven geographical distributions at regional and local scales. Both groups are concentrated in Greater London and the South East, although settlement patterns for different ethnic groups vary in detail. Whereas 45 percent of the ethnic minority population of Great Britain reside in London (making up a fifth of London's population), in large swathes of Britain – especially the more rural areas – only a very small proportion of the population is from ethnic minority groups. However, in these latter areas press coverage points to a growing problem of rural racism, and the difficulties of meeting the needs of small/isolated minorities (Steele 1995):

Question: Who is visible and invisible at the same time?

Answer: Black people living in England's villages and country towns. They are highly visible in that they stand out from the crowds and people in rural areas are not used to thinking of England as a multi-ethnic community. They are invisible in terms of provision because they are a small minority.

It has been shown that ethnic minority groups tend to be excluded from the more successful parts of the British space economy, and concentrated in areas of economic decline – although not exclusively so. They are overrepresented relative to the population as a whole in Central London, declining industrial centres and affluent commuter towns. Hence they do not all live in disadvantaged areas; rather individual ethnic groups display different distributions. In general, ethnic minority groups tend to fare as badly or worse than white people in the most deprived district types, but better than average elsewhere. Within local authority districts, ethnic minorities tend to be concentrated in neighbourhoods characterised by high unemployment rates – this is particularly the case for the Black group and Pakistani and Bangladeshi populations. Moreover, at the neighbourhood scale ethnic minorities are particularly concentrated in certain types of neighbourhoods suffering severe labour market disadvantage. However, differences in industrial and occupational profiles of specific ethnic minority groups are such that it is an oversimplification to make general statements about the concentration of ethnic minority groups in declining/growing industries and occupations. Nevertheless, a continuing challenge remains to counter disadvantage and (increasingly sophisticated) discrimination faced by ethnic minorities – the so called 'ethnic penalty' in the labour market – whereby ethnic minority groups (including members of the second generation born in Great Britain) are less successful than native born whites in converting their qualifications into salaried jobs and in avoiding unemployment (Karn 1997).

References

Boddy, M. (1995), *TECs and Racial Equality*, SAUS, Bristol.

Brown, C. (1984), *Black and White Britain: The Third PSI Survey*, PSI, London.

Brown, C. and Gay, P. (1985), *Racial Discrimination: 17 Years after the Act*, PSI, London.

Daniel, W.W. (1968), *Racial Discrimination in England*, Penguin, Harmondsworth.

Green, A.E. (1994), *The Geography of Poverty and Wealth*, IER, University of Warwick, Coventry.

Green, A.E. (1997), 'Patterns of Ethnic Minority Employment in the Context of Industrial and Occupational Growth and Decline', in Karn, V. (ed.) *Employment, Education and Housing Among The Ethnic Minority Populations of Britain*, ONS, London, pp. 67–90.

Green, A.E. and Owen, D.W. (1995), 'Ethnic Minority Groups in Regional and Local Labour Markets in Britain: A Review of Data Sources and Associated Issues', *Regional Studies*, vol. 29 no. 8, pp. 729–35.

Green, A.E. and Owen, D.W. (1996), 'A Labour Market Definition of Disadvantage: Towards an Enhanced Local Classification', Department for Education and Employment Research Series 11. HMSO, London.

Institute for Employment Research (1995), *Review of the Economy and Employment: Occupational Assessment*, IER, University of Warwick, Coventry.

Jenkins, R. (1986), *Racism and Recruitment*, Cambridge University Press, Cambridge.

Jewson, N., Mason, D. Waters, S. and Harvey J. (1990), 'Ethnic Minorities and Employment Practice: A Study of Six Employers', Department of Employment Research Paper 76, Employment Department, London.

Jones, T. (1993), *Britain's Ethnic Minorities*, PSI, London.

Karn, V. (1996), '"Ethnic penalties" and Racial Discrimination in Education, Employment and Housing: Conclusions and Policy Implications', in Karn, V. (ed.), *Employment, Education and Housing Among Ethnic Minority Populations of Britain*, ONS, London, pp. 265–90

Mason, D. (1995) *Race and Ethnicity in Modern Britain*, Oxford University Press, Oxford.

McGregor, A. and McConnachie, M. (1995), 'Social Exclusion, Urban Regeneration and Economic Reintegration', *Urban Studies*, vol. 32 no. 10, pp. 1587–600.

National Association of Citizen's Advice Bureaux (1984), *Unequal Opportunities: CAB Evidence on Racial Discrimination*, NACAB, London.

Noon, M. (1993), 'Racial Discrimination in Speculative Applications: Evidence from the UK's Top One Hundred Firms', *Human Resource Management Journal*, vol. 3 no.4, 35–47.

Owen, D.W. (1992), 'Ethnic Minorities in Great Britain: Settlement Patterns', 1991 Census Statistical Paper 1, NEMDA, CRER, University of Warwick, Coventry.

Owen, D.W. (1993a), 'Country of Birth:Ssettlement Patterns,' 1991 Census Statistical Paper 5, NEMDA, CRER, University of Warwick, Coventry.

Owen, D.W. (1993b), 'Ethnic Minorities in Great Britain: Economic Characteristics', 1991 Census Statistical Paper 3, NEMDA, CRER, University of Warwick, Coventry.

Owen, D.W. (1995), 'The Spatial and Socio-Economic Patterns of Minority Ethnic Groups in Great Britain: Settlement patterns', Scottish *Geographical Magazine*, vol. 111, pp. 27–35.

Phizacklea, A. (1988), 'Gender, Racism and Occupational Segregation', in Walby, S. (ed.), *Gender Segregation at Work*, Open University Press, Milton Keynes.

Pitcher, J. (1994), 'TECs and Local Communities: The Role of Research in a Multi-Ethnic District', *Local Economy*, vol. 9, 62–72.

Salt, J. (1995), 'Foreign Workers in The United Kingdom: Evidence from the Labour Force Survey', *Employment Gazette*, vol. 103, 1–19.

Sly, F. (1995), 'Ethnic Groups and The Labour Market: Analyses from The Spring 1994 Labour Force Survey', *Employment Gazette*, vol. 103, pp. 251–62.

Steele, J. (1995), 'The Hate behind Country Hedges', The Guardian 2 December, pp. 25.

Winnett, C. and A.E. Green, (1994) *Analysis of Participation in ED Programmes and the Impact of Variations in Participant Profiles at the TEC Area Level*, IER, University of Warwick, Coventry.

Wrench, J. and T. Qureshi (1996), 'Higher Horizons: A Qualitative Study of Young Men of Bangladeshi Origin', Department for Education and Employment Research Series 30, Stationary Office, London.

11 Integration of Immigrants from the Former Soviet Union in the Israeli Housing and Job Markets: Regional Perspectives

GABRIEL LIPSHITZ

11.1 Introduction

The geography of the worldwide movement of migrants in the 1990s reflects the *globalization of the economy* (King 1993; Gould and Findlay 1994; Nijkamp and Spiess 1993, 1994). Host countries seek skilled workers who are suited to the changes in the structure of their economy and their relative advantage in the world market, and they have less demand for unskilled workers.

This chapter is concerned with one specific migration flow – that from the former Soviet Union to Israel in the 1990s – and considers this flow with reference to the housing and labour markets. This immigration is not primarily driven by migration networks phenomena or the globalization of the economy. It is chiefly the result of a political and economic push and a national-religious and economic pull. Israel has a stringent immigrant-admission policy for non-Jews. For Jews, however, not only is immigration not restricted, but it is strongly encouraged under the Law of Return.

In most countries integration of immigrants in the housing market and their spatial distribution are handled by market forces, with virtually no intervention from above in steering the immigrants to specific geographical locations. Under the influence of market forces, the immigrants' initial place of settlement within the cities – especially in poor neighbourhoods – determines the spatial distribution of future immigrants, as the places they live become marked as destinations for immigrants. Along with the geographic dispersion and social assimilation, there is also a 'pushing' process at work: the newcomers are pushed into segregated ethnic neighbourhoods and they push out the previous round of immigrants or their children (Portes and Rumbaut 1990). At the *national level*, also, the spatial distribution of the first immigrants determines the spatial distribution of subsequent immigrants. Israel is one of the few countries which, due to geopolitical and security considerations, intervene directly and indirectly to direct the immigrants geographically. This intervention was much more widespread in the 1950s and the 1960s than it is in the 1990s.

An examination of the degree of integration of the immigrants in the job market should consider two questions: How do the immigrants adjust to and assimilate into the economic system of the host country? And what effect does international migration have on the economies – production, employment, and wages – of the countries of origin and destination? Although no single theory can answer these questions, the *human capital theory* is one of the more important in the field, and therefore many researchers use elements of it to examine the integration of the immigrants in the economy of the destination country (Chiswick 1978; Borjas 1989).

It should be noted that most studies of the integration of immigrants in the job market of the destination country *do not* examine this process on the geographical level. They do not consider whether there are geographical differences in the quality of the immigrants' human capital or whether there are regional differences within the destination country in terms of the level of unemployment following immigration. The present study discusses geoeconomics, inter alia, and looks at various economic aspects of the immigration wave from the former Soviet Union in the 1990s, with emphasis on the regional dimension.

This study has two objectives: *The first objective* is to examine the geographic distribution of the immigrants from the former Soviet Union in Israel, which reflects the *geographic distribution of demand,* for housing, which is manifested in the immigrants' initial place of settlement and their redistribution by means of internal migration. In other words, the first objective is to examine the integration of the immigrants from the former Soviet Union in the Israeli housing market from a regional perspective. *The second objective* is to examine the national and spatial economic aspects of the immigration wave from the former Soviet Union, with emphasis on two parameters: characteristics of human capital and the degree of integration in the job market, particularly the regional dimension. The conclusion of the paper will present an approach for a differential policy that links regional economic integration and regional integration in the field of housing and spatial distribution of the population.

11.2 The Israeli Context

From the establishment of the State of Israel in 1948 until 1995, approximately 2,450,000 immigrants arrived in Israel, including 700,000 – most of them from the former Soviet Union – between 1990 and 1995. Approximately 24 percent of the recent immigrants settled in the Israeli national periphery: the Northern and Southern districts. About 63 percent settled in the core districts (Tel Aviv, Central, and

270

Haifa districts); 10 percent in the Jerusalem District; and 2 percent in
Judea and Samaria (see Figure 11.3).

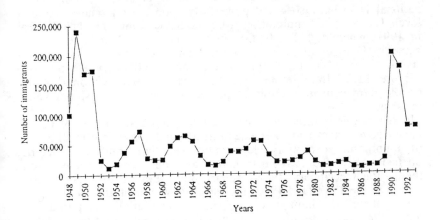

Figure 11.1 Immigration to Israel, 1948–1995

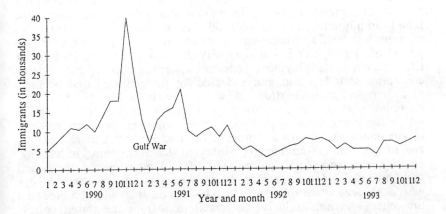

Figure 11.2 Immigrants from the former Soviet Union by month of immigration, 1990–1995

Source: Central Bureau of Statistics, *Immigration to Israel 1993*, special
publication no. 973.

271

Immigration to Israel has not been steady quantitatively. Generally, very large numbers of immigrants arrive in short periods of time, known as 'waves of immigration' (see Figure 11.1). The waves of immigration to Israel produce a 'shock of change', and they affect the economic, social, settlement, and cultural structures of the country, not only on the national level but also – and powerfully – on the regional-geographic level. The wave of immigration from the Soviet Union reached its peak in 1991, when roughly 200,000 immigrants arrived in Israel; 40,000 came in October alone (see Figure 11.2). After 1991, immigration stabilized at 5,000–6,000 per month, and 60,000–70,000 per year (Figure 11.2). Immigrants from the former Soviet Union (700,000 people) now constitute about 15 percent of the total Jewish population in Israel.

In the previous three decades, and even more so in the 1950s, the Israeli government had intervened directly and vigorously in all aspects of immigrant absorption. New towns were built and new factories opened to give the newcomers homes and jobs; most of these were in the national periphery: the Northern and Southern districts. In other words, in the 1950s and 1960s the Israeli government did not let *market forces* absorb the immigrants, disperse them spatially, and find them jobs. '*Planning from above*' dominated immigrant absorption, as it did other aspects of Israeli economic life (Shachar 1971).

The absorption of the immigrants from the former Soviet Union in the past five years is marked by a completely new policy conception, known in Israel as '*direct absorption*'. This policy constitutes a reversal in the manner of thinking regarding immigrant absorption. Upon landing in Israel, immigrants now receive an 'absorption basket' from the government, with a certain sum of money meant to last for a limited period of time. With this sum they may do as they see fit in all areas of life: housing, employment, education, consumption, etc. Direct absorption thus lets immigrants decide for themselves, based on their own personal considerations, how they wish to be absorbed. The declared goal of the government's direct-absorption policy was to lessen the immigrants' dependence on national and local government; to streamline the absorption process itself and make it more flexible; and to speed up the immigrants' ability to start functioning in housing, employment, and social and cultural life. In other words, the Israeli government decided *to replace its strategy of intervention from above with a strategy of absorption by market forces*. It should be noted that this change is not exclusive to Israeli immigrant-absorption policy; similar changes have been taking place in the economic policy of the Israeli government for close to twenty years, as the country moves gradually from a (relatively) centralized economic regime to a free market regime. As immigration from the former Soviet Union increased (far beyond the forecasts), the Israeli government decided to abandon the idea of absorption exclusively by market forces and started to intervene somewhat, chiefly in housing. The government built thousands of dwelling units, most of them in the national periphery, where there were large reserves of public land; the private sector built mainly in central Israel. The geographic research units in this study are the six districts of Israel (see Figure 11.3).

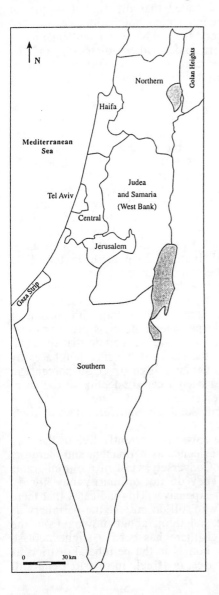

Figure 11.3 The geographical division of Israel into districts

11.3 The Spatial Pattern of Demand for Housing among Immigrants

At the end of Section 11.2 it was stated that the spatial supply of housing for immigrants and the general Israeli population was divided between the public and private sectors: the public sector built mainly in the peripheral districts (the Northern and Southern districts), and the private sector built mainly in the core (the Tel Aviv and Central districts). *What is the spatial manifestation of demand for housing by immigrants? Where do the immigrants choose to purchase houses?* It turns out that the immigrants' spatial behaviour in purchasing homes reinforces the spatial behaviour of the private market. They tend to prefer central Israel, where most building has been done by the private sector, over the national periphery, where most building was done by the government because there were large reserves of state-owned land in the periphery. Further evidence of this is presented in Table 11.1, which shows the geographic distribution of housing purchases by immigrants. The table shows clearly that the core districts have the highest percentage of purchases; Haifa is in second place; Jerusalem and the south alternate in third place; and the north is last. Between 1989 and 1994, for example, immigrants bought 91,000 apartments, 40 percent of them in the Tel Aviv and Central districts, 20 percent in the Haifa District, and 20 percent in the Northern and Southern districts.

These findings show that a large percentage of new immigrants in the core districts see these districts as their permanent place of residence and therefore make the effort to buy an apartment. A large proportion of the new immigrants who live in the peripheral districts prefer to rent (rather than buy) apartments, because they are not certain that they will remain in those areas. Interestingly, the share of housing purchases by immigrants in central Israel was particularly high (over 50 percent) in 1989 and 1990; since then there has been a certain decline in the share of purchases in this district as a percentage of all home purchases in Israel, and the share in the Northern, Southern, and Jerusalem districts increased.

What this means is that the immigrants who currently live in the core regions of Israel see their place of residence as permanent and therefore buy apartments whenever they can. Conversely, most of the immigrants in the periphery are fence-sitters. They do not ordinarily buy homes, even though homes are relatively inexpensive. This indicates that there is a floating reserve of immigrants who still do not see the periphery as their permanent place of residence and think about moving from the periphery to central Israel. Although there has been a slight increase over time in the share who purchase homes in the peripheral districts as a percentage of all housing purchases in Israel, the basic trend still prevails.

Table 11.1   Immigrants from the former Soviet Union who purchased homes with housing loans, by district of the Ministry of Construction and Housing (Pct.)

Minister district	Total (absolute numbers)	Total	1989	1990	1991	1992	1993	1994
Galilee (North)	8,969	9.8	1.7	5.8	7.7	10.4	11.8	8.9
Haifa	21,5689	23.5	15.1	28.3	24.2	25.5	23.0	20.9
Centre	35,362	38.6	54.9	50.9	39.5	35.6	34.7	43.4
Jerusalem	11,368	12.4	3.7	4.5	15.4	9.9	13.2	13.3
Negev (South)	12,953	14.1	24.0	9.9	12.2	16.2	15.6	12.1
Rural areas	1,222	1.3	0.5	0.3	0.7	2.1	1.4	1.2
Not classified	222	0.2	0.2	0.3	0.3	0.3	0.2	0.2
Total	91,685	100.0	100.0	100.0	100.0	100.0	100.0	100.0

* The districts follow the division of the Ministry of Construction and Housing. The Central District of the Housing Ministry includes the Tel Aviv and Central districts as presented in Figure 11.3.

Another manifestation of the immigrants' preference for the centre over the periphery can be seen in Table 11.2, which shows the geographic distribution of the immigrants as compared with that of Jewish nonimmigrants in 1990, 1991, 1992, and 1993.

Table 11.2 shows that approximately 65 percent of the immigrants chose the core districts – Tel Aviv, Central, and Haifa – and only 25 percent chose the peripheral districts – the Northern and the Southern. In fact, *the new immigrants adapted themselves to the spatial - distribution pattern of the nonimmigrant population*: they, like the nonimmigrants, prefer the core districts. In each year, the disparity between the share of nonimmigrant Jews in each district as a percentage of the total Jewish population of Israel and the share of immigrants in each district as a percentage of the total immigrant population is fairly low (Table 11.2). In 1990, for example, 27.4 percent of the total Jewish population of Israel lived in the Tel Aviv District, whereas 25.6 percent of immigrants lived there. In 1993, 10.2 percent of the total Jewish population in Israel lived in the Northern District, while 10.0 of the total immigrant population lived there. Twenty-four percent of the total Jewish population lived in the Central District, while 20.6 percent of immigrants did so. There was a fairly large disparity between immigrants and nonimmigrants in the Haifa District in 1990, but it decreased over time.

Table 11.2 Immigrants and nonimmigrants by district, 1990–1993

District	1990		1991		1992		1993		1994	
	No.	Pct.	No.	Pct.	No.	Pct.	No.	Pct.	No.	Pct.
Jerusalem										
Nonimm.	427,100	10.8	444,300	10.7	455,100	10.7	464,000	10.7	473,200	11.0
Imm.	13,963	7.1	14,955	8.5	7,676	10.0	6,128	8.0	5,965	7.5
Northern										
Nonimm.	394,000	10.0	430,500	10.4	437,700	10.3	447,000	10.3	458,700	9.8
Imm.	20,839	10.5	28,041	15.9	7,879	10.2	7,777	10.2	9,201	11.6
Haifa										
Nonimm.	518,100	13.1	537,300	13.0	542,500	12.8	550,900	12.7	562,600	12.9
Imm.	42,966	21.7	29,454	16.7	12,179	15.8	12,566	16.4	13,743	17.6
Central										
Nonimm.	947,300	24.0	989,240	23.9	1,018,800	24.0	1,041,300	24.0	1,071,800	23.9
Imm.	45,857	23.2	36,697	20.9	15,861	20.6	15,007	19.6	14,826	18.7
Tel Aviv										
Nonimm.	1,078,700	27.4	1,112,300	26.7	1,119,300	26.4	1,115,800	25.8	1,115,400	27.7
Imm.	50,731	25.6	38,189	21.7	19,859	25.9	20,443	26.7	18,287	23.0

Table 11.2 (continued)

District	1990 No.	1990 Pct.	1991 No.	1991 Pct.	1992 No.	1992 Pct.	1993 No.	1993 Pct.	1994 No.	1994 Pct.
Southern										
Nonimm.	499,900	12.7	537,200	12.9	564,400	13.3	600,200	13.8	632,600	12.7
Imm.	22,189	11.2	27,097	15.4	12,626	16.4	13,795	18.0	16,416	20.7
Judea-Samaria										
Nonimm.	81,600	2.0	93,600	2.2	104,800	2.5	115,600	2.7	121,800	2.0
Imm.	1,462	0.9	1,594	0.9	861	1.1	862	1.1	946	1.2
Total										
Nonimm.	3,946,700	100.0	4,414,600	100.0	4,242,500	100.0	4,335,200	100.0	4,441,100	100.0
Imm.	198,007	100.0	176,027	100.0	79,941	100.0	76,578	100.0	79,384	100.0

277

Table 11.2 also shows a very small gap in the Southern District in 1990 and 1991 between nonimmigrants and immigrants; in 1992 and 1993 the gap was up to 3–4 percent in favour of the immigrants. It turns out that the massive government building that began in 1990 in the peripheral districts – and especially in the Southern District – produced notable spatial results that are manifested in internal migration by new immigrants who settled in the core districts and moved to the periphery, especially to the Southern District.

However, the overall spatial result of the government's housing policy – ultimately – is a preference by immigrants for the core districts. Employment considerations and a sociocultural desire to live in or near the metropolitan areas outweighed housing considerations (cheap, subsidized prices in the periphery). Evidently, the immigrants are willing to live in less comfortable conditions – sometimes with several families in an apartment – in order to have access to jobs that suit their skills and to social and cultural centres (Hasson 1993; Lipshitz 1992). Surveys conducted in the development towns in the Israeli periphery indicate that most of the immigrants are satisfied with housing conditions in the development towns and are willing to remain in these towns provided that they find suitable jobs in these towns or within a one-hour commute. As long as such jobs are not available, they consider moving to central Israel (Lipshitz 1992).

11.4   The Redistribution of the Immigrants

Does the spatial pattern of the geographic distribution of immigrants' initial place of settlement remain constant over time? What is the spatial pattern of the later internal migration of the immigrants? Internal migration by the immigrants from their initial place of settlement is a further manifestation of the spatial pattern of housing demand among the immigrants. It expresses the immigrants' spatial preferences after they have become familiar with the economic-cultural spatial structure of their new country. Table 11.3 shows the spatial trends of internal migration among immigrants following their initial settlement. It turns out that internal migration changes the spatial distribution of the immigrants slightly in favour of the peripheral districts, especially the Southern District. The number of immigrants who leave the Tel Aviv, Jerusalem, and Haifa districts after initially settling there is greater than the number of immigrants who move to these districts, and in the Tel Aviv and Jerusalem districts the gap between the number of immigrant out-migrants and the number of immigrant in-migrants increases over time (Table 11.3 and Figure 11.4). In the Northern and Southern peripheral districts the picture is different. In the Southern District the number of immigrant in-migrants from other districts exceeds the number of immigrants who move to these districts from the Southern District, and this gap increases over time. In the Northern District the trend resembles that in the Southern District until 1991; then the trend

278

reverses, as more immigrants leave the Northern District for other Israeli districts than move to it from them.

Table 11.3 depicts the migration of thousands of immigrants from the Tel Aviv, Central, and Haifa districts to the Northern and Southern peripheral districts. This phenomenon is unexpected and even opposed to the general migration trend of immigrants in Israel, which is primarily from the periphery to the centre (Lipshitz 1986). In 1991, for example, net internal migration by immigrants was 4,800 in the Northern District, 6,100 in the Southern District, – 4,900 in the Tel Aviv and Central districts, and – 6,000 in the Haifa District. A similar pattern prevailed in 1990, too; internal migration by nonimmigrants increased population concentration, whereas that by immigrants tended to increase population dispersion.

The phenomenon ended in 1992, when net internal migration of immigrants remained positive in the Southern District but was already negative in the Northern District. Thus in 1992 internal migration added immigrants to the peripheral districts but did not substantially change the spatial distribution of the immigrants, which shows a clear trend toward the metropolitan districts of Tel Aviv and Haifa.

There is evidence to support the hypothesis that migrants from the centre to the periphery are mainly 'weak' – the elderly, the unemployed, and those in need of welfare services. These people prefer comfortable housing in the periphery to high rent in the centre. The migrants also assume that welfare services for immigrants in the development towns of the Galilee and Negev are well developed. At the same time, a 'strong population' leaves the periphery in the hope of obtaining jobs in the centre that suit their technological skills (Lipshitz 1992).

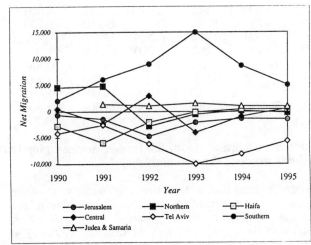

Figure 11.4 Net internal migration of the immigrants by districts, 1990–1995

279

Thus, internal migration by immigrants, which modifies the spatial distribution of the immigrants slightly by increasing their share in the Northern and Southern districts at the expense of the core, simultaneously increases the percentage of 'weak' immigrants in these regions somewhat.

Table 11.3 Internal migration: in-migrants and out-migrants of immigrants and nonimmigrants by district

In-migrants	1990		1992		1994	
District	Total	Thereof: immi- grated since 1990	Total	Thereof: immi- grated since 1990	Total	Thereof: immi- grated since 1990
Jerusalem	12,700	1,200	13,200	3,200	13,600	3,000
Northern	22,900	6,900	25,200	10,400	23,000	9,400
Haifa	24,300	6,200	27,000	10,600	28,700	11,700
Central	46,000	7,700	54,900	18,300	62,600	16,300
Tel Aviv	54,800	10,200	51,400	12,900	48,900	12,200
Southern	23,500	4,000	37,200	16,700	41,000	19,500
Judea-Samaria	9,800	600	14,000	2,200	13,500	2,500
National total	194,100	36,900	222,900	74,300	74,500	231,500

Out-migrants	1990		1992		1994	
District	Total	Thereof: immi- grated since 1990	Total	Thereof: immi- grated since 1990	Total	Thereof: immi- grated since 1990
Jerusalem	15,400	1,800	17,900	5,300	17,900	4,300
Northern	18,200	2,300	28,300	13,300	23,400	9,200
Haifa	28,900	9,000	31,400	12,500	29,600	11,200
Central	41,300	7,200	47,000	15,300	53,600	17,200
Tel Aviv	60,600	14,400	64,200	19,000	69,000	20,300
Southern	24,900	1,900	27,700	7,700	31,500	10,800
Judea-Samaria	4,800	300	6,400	1,100	6,600	1,400
National total	194,100	36,900	222,900	74,300	74,500	231,500

11.5 The absorption of immigrants from the former Soviet Union in the Israeli labour market: the national level

The Bank of Israel report states that at the end of the fourth year of the large wave of immigration, the extent of the economic absorption of the immigrants in Israel can be summed up as a partial success (Bank of Israel 1994, p. 3; see also Beenstock and Ben-Menachem 1995). The rate of immigrant participation in the labour market is high, and the unemployment rate among the immigrants declined from 40 percent to 20 percent. The unemployment rate was 8.2 percent in the first quarter

280

of 1989, but it had risen to 9.2 percent by the last quarter of the year. In 1990 unemployment was up to 9.7 percent, and it rose to 11 percent in 1991 and 11.3 percent in 1992, before dropping to 9.0 percent by the fourth quarter of 1993. During this period, too, real wages among wage earners in the business sector dropped by 6 percent in total. The decline in hourly wages was greater. The drop in real wages primarily reflects the effect of the increase in unemployment. Real wages in the public sector continued to rise during this period, but at a moderate pace. Because a very high percentage of the immigrants from the former Soviet Union are between the ages of 30 and 65, a large number of immigrants joined the labour force within a short period of time. The main dilemma that confronted and still confronts policy makers in this field is how to create jobs, especially jobs that suit the skills and occupations of the immigrants.

Ofer et al. (1991), in a study that looks at the macroeconomic significance of the entry of Soviet immigrants into the job market, stress that the present wave of immigration is marked by high calibre human capital, as manifested in a very high rate of university graduates with technical and medical professions compared to the Israeli labour force. In their opinion, 'their integration in Israel will make the country's labour force the most educated in the world' (p. 135). The problem, however, is that the economic structure of the Israeli economy is not prepared in the short term to take in such highly developed human capital. Due to the disparity between supply of and demand for a labour force with a relatively high percentage of university graduates, the researchers foresee a high rate of change and downward adjustment of the immigrants' occupations (Ofer et al. 1991).

In a later study, the researchers show substantial difficulties in absorbing the immigrants in accordance with their academic and technological qualifications. They point out that the economic growth was in a direction that is not desirable in the long run (Plug and Kasir 1994). In the amount of time that it took earlier immigrants to find work in their original fields, only a small portion of the recent immigrants had done so, especially in fields that call for high-calibre human capital. Quite likely, this situation is one of the reasons for the decline in the rate of immigration of people with scientific professions and higher education since 1990.

Table 11.4 describes the high quality of human capital that reached Israel during the wave of immigration from the former Soviet Union. It shows that 50–60 percent of the immigrants aged 15 and over have had at least 13 years of education, whereas the Israeli average is 30 percent; 35–40 percent of the immigrants in the labour force have academic or scientific occupations, compared to the Israeli average of 12 percent; 30–35 percent have technical occupations, compared to an Israeli average of 14 percent. The percentage of immigrants from the former Soviet Union with higher education and scientific or academic professions drops from 39 percent in 1990 to 27 percent in 1993 Table 11.4).

281

Table 11.4 **Distribution of occupations and education of immigrants, 1990–1993**

Occupation	1990 immi-grants	1991 immi-grants	1992 immi-grants	1993 immi-grants	1990–93 immi-grants
Scientific professions	39.0	35.5	32.6	27.1	35.3
Thereof: Doctors	6.2	4.3	3.8	3.4	4.8
Engineers	25.4	22.3	19.9	15.9	22.3
Other professional, technical and re-lated workers	34.3	32.4	32.7	33.3	33.3
Industrial workers (skilled and unskilled)	15.7	19.1	23.2	26.4	19.3
Total employed in USSR (in 1000s)	96.1	79.7	33.8	33.2	242.8
Total (percent)	100.0	100.0	100.0	100.0	100.0
Education of those aged 15 and over					
9–12 years	31.9	35.0	39.0	43.1	35.4
13 or more	57.3	52.7	48.8	43.1	52.7

Source: Bank of Israel report, 1993 (based on data from the Central Bureau of Statistics). Occupation as declared by the immigrant.

Even if we take into account the fact that some of the reports regarding the immigrants' education and occupations are untrue, there is no doubt that *the immigration from the Soviet Union is an import of high-calibre human capital.* Under normal conditions a country would have to invest extensive resources to attain such a level of human capital. In an era in which high-tech industry and computer and information services are important elements in economic growth, this immigration wave brought great potential for the growth of the Israeli economy. So far, however, it is the scientific and technological professionals who have had the hardest time finding appropriate work.

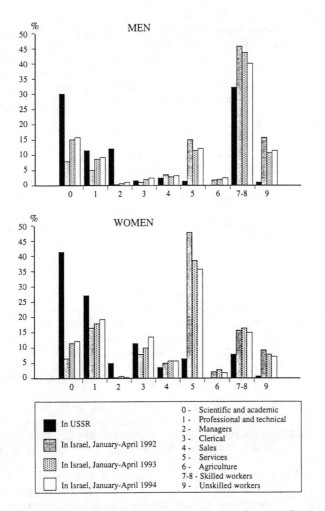

Figure 11.5 Immigrants' occupations in the former Soviet Union and Israel

Source: Central Bureau of Statistics, *Supplement to the Monthly Bulletin of Statistics*, no. 4, 1993.

Figure 11.5 clearly shows the *gap between the distribution of the immigrants from the former Soviet Union by their occupations in their country of origin and in Israel*. As it turns out, many of the immigrants found work in the services and as production workers in traditional industry; only a few jobs that suit their academic and scientific skills. About 33 percent of the men who moved to Israel have academic and

283

scientific occupations, and in 1991 only 7 percent of them worked in this occupation; among women the gap is 35 percent. In the services, figure 5 shows that in the Soviet Union 3 percent of the men and 5 percent of the women worked in services, whereas in Israel 15 percent and 45 percent, respectively, do so. Failure to take advantage of the human capital of the immigrants who had arrived by the end of 1993 produced a loss of $2 billion to the national economy (Eckstein 1994).

11.5.1 Employment Characteristics of the Immigrants over Time

Does the gap between immigrants' occupations in the USSR and in Israel narrow over time? Do the unemployment rate and income level of the immigrants improve? The following findings, which are based on data from the Central Bureau of Statistics (*Monthly Bulletin of Statistics*, April 1992) and on a survey of the employment and economic status of the immigrants who came from the Soviet Union in the latest wave of immigration – from October 1989 until the beginning of 1992 – provide clear answers to these questions (Naveh, Noam, and Benita 1993).

- *The similarity between the employment rate of the immigrants and that of the general Jewish population is greater among the younger age cohorts.* Among 25–34-year-olds there is hardly any disparity in the employment rate between the immigrants and the population at large (63 and 66 percent, respectively). Among those aged 55–64, the gap is wider: 27 percent of the immigrants are employed, as opposed to 48 percent of the general Jewish population.
- The rate of employment among the Jewish population in age groups that correspond to the immigrants included in the survey (25–64) was 66 percent in 1991: 78 percent among men and 55 percent among women. Among Soviet immigrants who have lived in Israel for two years or more, 62 percent were employed. Seventy-eight percent of men were employed, a rate similar to that of the Jewish population at large; 51 percent of women were employed. *The employment rate among the immigrants improves with time*: after two years in Israel, the percentage of men employed has risen from 57 percent to 78 percent, and that of women from 22 percent to 49 percent.
- The highest percentage of immigrants employed in an occupation similar to their occupation in the Soviet Union is found among skilled workers in industry (75 percent). The largest gap is in academic and scientific professions: *only 25 percent of immigrants with professions requiring a university education work in these professions in Israel. It is important to note, however, that the percentage of immigrants who work in the professions in which they worked in the Soviet Union, including scientific and academic professions, increases the longer they remain in Israel. The*

284

percentage employed in scientific and academic professions increases from 4 percent among immigrants who have been in Israel for half a year to a year to 17 percent among those in the country for two years or more. The percentage employed as other professional, technical, and related workers increases from 1 percent among those who have been in Israel for one year to 17 percent for those who have been in Israel for two years or more.

• The improvement in the correlation of occupations in the Soviet Union and in Israel – particularly among immigrants with scientific, academic, and technical professions – is also manifested in improved income levels. *Immigrants' incomes increase the longer they are in Israel:* average net monthly income from all sources (including government financial support and support by parents who receive old-age pensions and live with their children) was NIS 1,640 among immigrants who have been in Israel for six months to a year, and NIS 2,710 among immigrants who have been in Israel for two years or more. The average net income of immigrant families headed by wage earners was NIS 2,770 a month; it rose to NIS 3,030 a month among those who have been in Israel for two years or more.

The findings presented above indicate that the main dilemma *on the national level* was and remains how to create jobs that suit the academic, scientific, and technical occupations of the immigrants. What are the spatial-economic trends regarding the absorption of immigrants from the former Soviet Union in Israel? This is discussed in the next section.

11.6 Economic Aspects of the Absorption of Immigrants from the Former Soviet Union in Israel: The Regional Level

11.6.1 Human Capital

The differences between the immigrant and nonimmigrant populations in terms of the rates of higher education and academic and scientific professions are particularly prominent in the peripheral districts of Israel (see Table 11.5). In the Southern District, for example, approximately 65 percent of the immigrants in the labour force have scientific, academic, or technical professions, as opposed to only 30 percent of the nonimmigrants. The data show clearly that in all districts the ratio of the percentage of immigrants with academic and scientific professions to the percentage of nonimmigrants with such professions is above 1, as is the ratio with respect to higher education. These ratios are particularly high in the Southern and Northern districts. In other words, the immigrants' socioeconomic level in every district is higher than that of the nonimmigrant population, and the differences are greatest in the periphery.

Table 11.5 Employment, education, and age of immigrants and nonimmigrants, by district

District	Scientific, academic and technological occupations		13 or more years of education		Age cohorts Immigrants			Age cohorts Nonimmigrants		
	Imm.	Nonimm.	Imm.	Nonimm.	0–14	15–64	65+	0–14	15–64	65+
Northern	58.6	29.6	48.5	25.0	24.1	60.0	15.5	33.8	58.6	7.6
Southern	65.2	30.9	50.2	24.3	22.3	65.4	12.3	33.2	60.6	6.2
Tel Aviv and Central	60.2	35.1	56.5	30.1	23.3	65.0	11.2	28.1	60.7	11.2
Haifa	67.2	43.0	55.7	39.8	21.4	65.9	12.7	32.5	59.4	8.1
Jerusalem	60.4	35.2	53.1	29.9	22.6	65.0	12.4	29.7	60.2	10.1
National average	60.4	35.2	53.1	29.9	22.6	65.0	12.4	29.7	60.2	10.1

* The figures for the nonimmigrant population are an estimate based on the 1983 census. The figures for the immigrants are based on data from the Ministry of Immigrant Absorption.

What this means is that the high-quality human capital has good potential for structural change in the regional economy as well as the national economy. An important factor that determines the location of high tech industry is human capital. The level of human capital in the Israeli core was high even before the immigrants arrived, and therefore high tech industrial parks opened there. The Israeli periphery has suffered for three decades from the departure of the young and educated (Lipshitz 1990). This migration perpetuated the traditional job structure and the lack of variety in industry for many years. The 'import' of such highly developed human capital to the periphery produced a rare opportunity to change the structure of the regional economy – from a traditional structure to a modern technological structure. Although the national government and local governments in the periphery initiated several projects to take advantage of the human capital, they were on a relatively small scale. As we shall see, most of the immigrants found jobs in the large traditional factories, and the opportunity for change in the regional economic structure – especially that of the peripheral regions – was lost.

11.6.2 Trends in Unemployment Rates over Time: The National and Regional Levels

Unemployment rates in Israel, which increased steadily beginning in 1988 to a peak of 11.2 percent in 1992, dropped in 1993 to an average of 10 percent (Table 11.6). The increase in unemployment was substantial between 1988 and 1989 (from 6.4 percent to 8.9 percent). From 1988 to 1992 the unemployment rate in Israel rose more than 4 percentage points (Table 11.6). The number of unemployed persons in Israel doubled between 1988 and 1992, from 99,900 to 207,600; in 1993 it fell to 195,000 (Table 11.7). The increase in the unemployment rate at the start of 1989 was caused by the slump in economic activity, which was due in part to the dramatic increase in wages in the wake of the stabilization plan (Bank of Israel report, 1993). After 1989 the continued increase in unemployment was chiefly due to a large increase in the supply of labour, as the immigrants joined the labour force. Although the immigration also boosted demand and created jobs, the net result was an increase in the unemployment rate.

An additional 100,000 people were employed in 1993, and this produced a sharp decline in the unemployment rate. According to the Bank of Israel report, the increased employment was influenced by expectations of accelerated growth in the next few years and the quarantine of the territories, because of which workers from the territories were replaced with Israelis. Other factors included several policy measures designed to reduce unemployment, including subsidization of the increased employment under the Business Sector Encouragement Law, which made it possible for employers to afford the adaptation and training costs involved in a substantial increase in employment; public-works projects; and a toughening of the criteria for

287

obtaining unemployment compensation. Another factor had to do with the immigrants themselves. Many of them were determined to find work, and they began to seek jobs very soon after immigrating to Israel (Lipshitz 1992).

Table 11.6   Unemployment rates, 1988–1993, by district (percent)

District	Unemployment rates					
	1988	1989	1990	1991	1992	1993
Jerusalem	7.3	8.5	9.4	10.9	10.8	8.7
Northern	6.6	9.1	9.0	9.9	10.4	10.6
Haifa	7.0	9.5	10.7	13.0	13.5	12.0
Central	5.6	8.4	9.5	10.4	10.4	10.1
Tel Aviv	5.5	8.3	8.8	9.4	10.4	8.3
Southern	8.5	11.4	11.8	12.2	13.8	12.2
Total	6.4	8.9	9.6	10.6	11.2	10.0

Table 11.7   Number of unemployed persons, 1986–1993 (in thousands) (aged 15 and over)

District	Number of unemployed persons							
	1986	1987	1988	1989	1990	1991	1992	1993
Jerusalem	12.1	10.9	12.4	15.0	17.0	19.9	20.6	16.7
Northern	19.8	14.2	15.0	21.7	21.9	26.0	30.1	32.5
Haifa	16.0	14.9	15.4	20.7	24.0	32.9	35.2	32.0
Central	19.5	17.8	19.9	30.1	35.7	42.8	44.0	44.3
Tel Aviv	22.6	18.9	21.9	33.7	36.8	41.2	47.7	39.2
Southern	13.5	12.7	14.0	19.7	20.5	23.0	28.0	27.7
Total	104.0	90.4	99.9	142.5	158.0	187.2	207.6	195.0

Source: Central Bureau of Statistics, *Labour Force Surveys, 1993*, special publication no. 998.

A look at the integration of the immigrants into the job market shows a mixed picture. Employment among immigrants increased substantially, and their unemployment rate dropped significantly; however, a large portion of the immigrants were forced to work in occupations that do not make use of their skills (Bank of Israel report, 1993). A survey conducted in May 1992 among a representative sample of 1,530 immigrants found that 42 percent of the employed immigrants were working in their original occupation or in a related occupation. Most of the immigrants suffered a decline in their professional status upon moving to Israel: 62 percent worked in lower-prestige fields, and 59 percent worked in jobs that did not require their levels of education (Bar–Tzur and Hendels 1993)

In 1993, unemployment rates in Israel fell for the first time since the start of the wave of immigration (Table 11.6). The unemployment rate decreased in all sectors – among nonimmigrants and immigrants and among men and women. Among the hard core of the unemployed, however – those who had been out of work for more than a year – the rate increased. Many of these people are immigrants, especially older ones whose chances of finding work are slim. People in the 45+ age group, including a high proportion of women and people with a relatively low level of education, have had the hardest time finding jobs. Many of them (about 70 percent) have given up looking for work, because they do not believe they have a chance of finding any in Israel (Bar–Tzur and Hendels 1993).

It should be noted that the gaps between unemployment rates among men and women increased during the wave of immigration to Israel, from about 1.5 percent in 1988 to 5 percent in 1992. This is one of the results of the high unemployment rate among immigrant women (Bank of Israel report 1993).

The increase in unemployment is not uniform geographically. Unemployment rates continue to be high in the Northern and Southern peripheral districts, as well as in the Haifa District, where there is a particularly high concentration of immigrants (Table 11.6). For example, in 1988 – just before the immigrants began to arrive – the national unemployment rate was 6.4 percent, while the unemployment rate in the Southern District was 8.5 percent and in the northern districts it was 6.6 percent. In 1992 the national unemployment rate was 11.2 percent, and the unemployment rates in the Northern, Haifa, and Southern districts were 10.4 percent, 13.5 percent, and 13.8 percent, respectively. It should be noted that the unemployment rates in the Tel Aviv, Jerusalem, and Central districts were below the national average. This spatial pattern changed slightly in the years following the start of the wave of immigration (from 1990 on). Beginning in 1990, the unemployment rates rose in the Central District, presumably because of the many immigrants who chose to settle there.

289

11.7 Conclusion

An examination of immigrants' spatial behaviour in the housing market shows that the geographic distribution of immigrants from the former Soviet Union closely resembles the geographic distribution of nonimmigrants, with a slight preference for the Southern District. This distribution has done very little to change the geographic distribution of the Israeli population.

The macro-level analysis indicates that when immigrants' selection of a place of residence is influenced chiefly by market forces (direct absorption) rather than government intervention (spatial policy), they decide the same way immigrants to Western Europe and North America do. The immigrants to Israel – like immigrants to other countries – favour the core regions, where job prospects are good.

The spatial preferences of demand for housing by the immigrants correspond to the spatial supply of apartments in the private market. The private market clearly preferred residential building in the core regions. Conversely, the spatial supply of the public market was more prominent in the peripheral regions, where substantial reserves of public land were available.

Government residential building in the peripheral districts, and especially in the Southern District, at fairly low prices and with substantial subsidies, prompted immigrants to move to the peripheral districts. Many immigrants who initially settled in the Tel Aviv, Central, and Haifa districts moved to the peripheral districts, and they were joined by immigrants who chose these districts as their initial place of settlement. It is important to point out, however, that the rate of housing purchases by immigrants is high in the Tel Aviv, Central, and Haifa districts and low in the peripheral districts. In other words, while immigrants show signs of residential permanence in the core districts, in the peripheral districts a temporary feeling is dominant.

A closer look at the data (Lipshitz 1992) shows that the preferred regions and towns in the peripheral districts are those located on the seam between the periphery of the core and the national periphery (the peripheral districts), such as Ashdod, Ashqelon, Qiryat Gat, Migdal Ha'emeq, and Karmiel. With improvements to the transportation infrastructure, some of these towns have become part of the distant periphery of the Tel Aviv and Haifa metropolitan areas. Immigrants and nonimmigrants alike in these towns enjoy two advantages of location: relatively low housing prices and reasonable access to metropolitan job centres. The remote towns in the national periphery do not attract immigrants who previously lived in the centre, and those who do move to them tend to be socioeconomically weak. This trend harms the economic growth potential and the quality of welfare services.

From an *economic standpoint*, the wave of immigration from the former Soviet Union to Israel is a success story: the unemployment rate among the immigrants improves over time, and after two years it approaches that of the nonimmigrant population, especially among the young. Thus, within a relatively short period of time the unemployment rate among the immigrants declined considerably. The longer the immigrants have been in Israel, the higher the percentage of immigrants employed in the occupations in which they worked in the USSR, including scientific and academic professions. These favourable changes also improve their income levels considerably within a relatively short time. The integration of the immigrants in the job market is a well known process in international migration, and – as was described in the introduction of the present study – it depends on several variables. It seems, however, that the immigrants from the former Soviet Union integrated into the Israeli job market more quickly than expected, and on the national level this is a success story. The main problem that remains at the national level is insufficient utilization of such high-calibre human capital to produce a structural change in the Israeli national economy. A relatively high percentage of immigrants who have higher education and scientific or academic occupations have still not found work that suits their level of education and occupations. This has caused the national economy a considerable loss of production.

At the spatial level there has been less economic success. The unemployment rate among immigrants is higher in the periphery than in the core. It is especially high among people with higher education and scientific or academic professions, because the quality of the immigrants' human capital in the peripheral districts is lower than that of the immigrants in the central districts, but much higher than that of the nonimmigrant population. When they settled in the peripheral regions, they brought with them great potential for the economic development of these regions. This potential was not utilized, however, and many of the 'strong' immigrants (the young, the educated, and so on) are migrating from the periphery to the core. The main reason for their migration is dissatisfaction with their occupations in Israel. Satisfaction among immigrant workers (and their employers) is found mainly among those who were industrial production workers in the former Soviet Union (Lipshitz 1992). They integrated well into the traditional factories in the peripheral regions. People with academic and scientific occupations and higher education, however, are extremely dissatisfied and consequently tend to migrate to central Israel (Lipshitz 1992).

The extent to which the immigrants integrate into the regional job market will thus determine not only the spatial distribution of the immigrants (and consequently the spatial housing market), but also the spatial distribution of socioeconomic traits. This will, of course, have an impact on all aspects of regional planning in Israel: housing, employment, welfare, and public services.

The findings of the present study indirectly suggest recommendations for spatial policy. In an age of rapid development spurred by immigration, it is worth assigning different levels of housing and job development to different regions or towns. These development levels should be adapted for each region or town based on its economic, social, and geographic characteristics. For example, in towns located between metropolitan areas and the national periphery but within commuting distance of jobs in the major cities, rapid development of housing and moderate development of jobs may be encouraged (at least in the short and medium terms). These towns should be considered 'open geopolitical economies', in which jobs are not located next to the residential area. More remote regions and towns should be treated as 'closed geoeconomic economies'; these require rapid development of local or regional employment sources and slow development of housing. In the metropolitan areas intervention from above is unnecessary, both in the job market and in the housing market; alternatively, weak government intervention might be considered in both issues.

Acknowledgement

This chapter is part of a research project which is fully supported by the Germany-Israeli Foundation (GIF).

References

Bank of Israel (1993), *Bank of Israel Report, 1992*, Bank of Israel, Jerusalem (Hebrew).

Bar-Tzur, R. and Hendles, S. (1993), *Needs and Preferences of Immigrants from the Former Soviet Union in the Areas of Health and Employment*. Tel Aviv, Institute for Economic and Social Research, General Federation of Labour in Israel, (Hebrew).

Beenstock, M. and Ben-Menachem, Y. (1995), *The Labour Market Absorption of CIS Immigrants to Israel: 1989–1994*, Falk Institute for Economic Research (draft).

Borjas, G.J. (1989), 'Economic Theory and International Migration', *International Migration Review*, vol. 23, pp. 457–85.

Central Bureau of Statistics (1993), *Immigration to Israel 1992*, Special publication series no. 944, Central Bureau of Statistics, Jerusalem.

Chiswick, B.R. (1978), 'The Effect of Americanization on the Earnings of Foreign-Born Men', *Journal of Political Economy*, vol. 86, pp. 897–921.

Eckstein, Z. (chair) (1994), Final report of the committee appointed to examine plans for promoting the employment of immigrant engineers and other immigrant experts and for utilizing the human capital of the present wave of immigration (first draft), presented to the Minister of Immigrant Absorption (Hebrew).

Gould, W.T.S. and Findlay, A.M. (1994), 'Population Movements from the Third World to Developed World: Recent Trends and Current Issues', Gould, W.T.S.

and A.M. Findlay (eds), *Population Migration and the Changing World Order*, New York, John Wiley and Sons, pp. 115–26..

Hasson, S. (1993), *From Immigration to Internal Migration: Choice of Place of Residence by Immigrants from the Former Soviet Union*, Jerusalem, Jerusalem Institute for Israel Studies and Ministry of Construction and Housing (Hebrew).

Lipshitz, G. (1986), 'Migration to, from and within Galilee 1961–1983', *The Economic Quarterly*, vol. 130, pp. 738–56 (in Hebrew).

Lipshitz, G. (1990), *Development Towns – a New Basis for Policy Planning*. Jerusalem: Jerusalem Institute for Israel Studies (Hebrew).

Lipshitz, G. (1992), *Development Towns That Take in Immigrants: Dimona and Qiryat Shemona*, Jerusalem Institute for Israel Studies, publication no. 47 (Hebrew).

Naveh, G., Noam, M. and Benita, E. (1993), *The Employment and Economic Status of the Immigrants: Selected Findings from a Countrywide Employment Survey of Soviet Immigrants*, JDC–Brookdale Institute (Hebrew).

Nijkamp, P. and Spiess, K. (1993), 'International Migration in Western Europe: Macro Trends in the Past, the Present and the Future', *Current Politics and Economics of Europe*, vol. 3, pp. 238–62.

Nijkamp, P. and Spiess, K. (1994), 'International Migration in Europe: Critical Success Absorption Factors', *Journal of Regional Studies*, vol. 12, pp. 331–35.

Ofer, G., Plug, K. and Kasir, N. (1991), 'Employment of Soviet Immigrants in 1990 and Later: Occupational Stability and Switching', *Economic Quarterly*, vol. 148, pp. 135–79 (Hebrew).

Plug, K. and Kasir, N. (1993), *Employment of Immigrants from the CIS: The Short Term*, Jerusalem, Bank of Israel Research Department (Hebrew).

Portes, A. and Rumbaut, R.G. (1990), *Immigrant America*, Berkeley, University of California Press.

Shachar, A. (1971), 'Israel's Development Towns: Evaluation of National Urbanization Policy', *Journal of the American Institute of Planners*, vol. 17, pp. 271–91.

Simon, J.L. (1992), *The Economic Consequences of Immigration*, London, Routledge.

293

12 Employment and Structural Change: Economic Integration of Immigrants in the Swedish and Malmö Labour Markets 1970–1990[1]

PIETER BEVELANDER

12.1 Introduction

Sweden developed during the first two decades of the post-war period into one of the wealthiest countries in the world. This change in the wealth of the country was accompanied by immigration on a previously unknown scale. Sweden's remarkable economic growth has been facilitated by this immigrant flow, which consisted almost entirely of European labour migrants during the period up to the early 1970s. Over the past twenty years this symbiotic relationship has changed drastically, however. The Swedish economy has suffered from a relatively low growth rate, while undergoing a transformation towards increased service sector employment and decreased industrial employment. Simultaneous with the economic changes, the composition of immigration to Sweden has also changed significantly, shifting from European labour migrants to non-European refugees and tied movers.[2]

The economic development of the region of Malmö can be seen as a reflection of the national economic development in a magnified form in the last twenty years. The Malmö economy has to a larger degree than the national one been characterized by economic activity that was negatively influenced by the 1970 crisis. The immigrant influx to the Malmö region coincides with the shift in national immigration. Political refugees and tied movers settled in the region, diminishing the earlier strong connection of immigration and economic development.

Sweden has experienced therefore a changing immigrant labour market from both a demand as well as a supply perspective. It is this combination of factors which is believed to lie behind the decreasing labour market attachment of migrants, specifically the lower employment rates that have been noticeable over the past decades.

The purpose of this chapter is to give an overview of this decreasing labour market attachment among immigrants to Sweden in the period 1970 to 1990, and discuss the forces behind it. Points of special interest here are the employment rates of various immigrant nationalities at the national level compared to the regional level. In this case the region of Malmö will be studied in greater depth.

In this chapter, cross-optimal data on the entire immigrant population at the individual level is utilized. The chapter also combines a structural-analytical approach with human capital theory in an attempt to account for both demand and supply forces on the immigrant labour market. Earlier research has concentrated upon human capital composition of migrants, with only minor attention given to economic structure. We propose here a new view to the problem which also incorporates structural change in the economy as an important factor in the economic assimilation process of immigrants.

12.2 Earlier Research and Hypotheses

Earlier research regarding the economic integration of immigrants into the Swedish society has pointed to the very high labour market attachment during the 1950s and 1960s. These studies refer to high employment rates, low unemployment rates and relatively high incomes compared to natives among both male and female citizens born in foreign countries (Wadensjö 1973; Ohlsson 1975; Ekberg 1983). Current research into the situation of the 1970s and 1980s shows a different picture evolving, characterized by extremely low immigrant employment rates (Ekberg 1991a, b; Bevelander 1995 and Scott 1995).

This trend has also been noted in international immigration research. Studies of immigrant cohorts in the USA during the 1960s show a positive relationship between labour market assimilation, primarily in the form of income, and increasing time in the country (Chiswick 1978). Later investigations using data in which income was recorded at more than one point in time and examining cohorts entering the United States and Canada during the 1980s tells a different tale, being much less positive concerning the income catch-up process of immigrants (see e.g. Borjas 1985, 1987 and 1989; LaLonde and Topel 1992; Wright and Maxim 1993 and Baker and Benjamin 1994).

In the debate, various explanations have been brought forward dealing with the weak labour market attachment of the more recently immigrated cohorts. The main explanations that are referred to in this chapter are related to both supply and demand sides of the labour market.

The majority of research states that the decline in economic status of later cohorts is highly correlated with changes in the 'quality' of the immigrants. More immigrants come from developing countries rather than industrialized countries and are generally less skilled and less successful in host countries. The increase in the share of family and refugee immigration, with a decrease in the share of independent immigrants, has changed the average level of positive self-selection of the total and newly arrived immigrant population. The new immigrant groups are no longer supposed to be selected on human

296

capital/employability criteria and might be expected to do less well on average in the labour market compared to independent immigrants (Wright and Maxim 1993). This can even be reinforced by income support for refugees after arrival lowering incentives for job search (Broomé et al. 1996).

One of the key determinants of labour force activity, earnings and occupational status is education. It is expected that immigrants with a higher educational level would have less problems finding employment in a new country (Chiswick 1978). Other human capital characteristics also play a major role in the determination of socioeconomic outcomes, however. Lower levels of human capital among immigrants could explain the disadvantages that immigrants experience in economic assimilation. Examples here are found in lower status family backgrounds, less experience within the host country, poor language skills and other cultural disadvantages (see for example Borjas 1994; Chiswick and Miller 1993; Dustmann 1993 and Broomé et al. 1995). Cultural disadvantage is in this case the effect of characteristics of country of origin, in other words, a collection of sociocultural resources that can promote or hinder labour market assimilation

Other hypotheses which could have influenced the employment assimilation of immigrants draw more attention to the labour market demand side. An important factor for labour demand is the business cycle. The usual explanation for the lower labour market attachment of immigrants is the cyclical downturn of the economy of the 1990s. Especially during cyclical downturns is this expected to affect immigrants. Without denying that the crises of the 1990s aggravated the situation, there is no doubt that the labour market attachment of immigrants weakened during the last 20 years with a culmination during the crisis of the 1990. Not even during the cyclical upturn of the 1980s, with very low unemployment rates for natives and high labour demand, did the situation improve for immigrants.

The hypothesis concerning the development of the Swedish economy as one of the major factors causing the deterioration of labour force attachment of the immigrant population is basically of structural nature. The hypothesis described here can be seen in a long term cyclical development of the Swedish economy in the international environment.

Basically, it is assumed in this chapter that the structural change of the economy, with a relatively decreasing industrial and increasing service sector during the last decades, implied a long term change towards more information and communication-intense working processes. The development during the late 1970s and 1980s involved increasing demand for employees with a proportionately higher general competence, while unskilled labour was made redundant through efficiency improvements. Serial production, automation and specialization was increasingly replaced by teamwork, influence on working processes and job rotation. Without reducing the importance of formal education and skill, the importance of informal competence increased. This informal competence includes, for instance, culture

297

specific proficiency, language skills and the understanding of different patterns of behaviour in teamwork and in relations with authorities and labour market organizations (Broomé et al. 1996).[3] In other words, without ignoring other contributing processes, the fundamental hypothesis is that the problematic situation of immigrants in the labour market is primarily a result of a growing gap between immigrants' skills and qualifications and those demanded in the market.

This growing gap could have led to different types of discrimination by authorities and employers. Especially employers 'discriminating under uncertainty' want to minimize the risk of hiring someone with low productivity. Immigrant groups are here seen as proxies for the individual. Actual or expected higher turnover of an immigrant group leads to well educated members of this group being discriminated against when they seek employment in higher professions (Schierup and Paulson 1994 and Brune 1993).

12.3   Data and Method

Problems with the Swedish and international research to date is that it has often been at a highly aggregated level, with immigrant groups consisting of various nationalities with different cultural characteristics. This complicates identification of differences between the various nationalities. Another great problem is that these studies are often based upon samples, which involves a certain reduction in reliability based on sample selection methods and biases.

At the national level, this chapter analyses *employment rates* of different immigrant groups over the period in question (Bevelander 1995; Bevelander and Scott 1996). The statistics are based on the five most recent Swedish censuses (1970, 75, 80, 85, 90), from which data can be obtained at the individual level regarding age, sex, education, civil status, country of origin, employment status and year of immigration. The basic definition of employment rate in this investigation is the quotient between those who are *registered as employed* and the *registered total population* in the *ages 16–65*, at the time of data collection.

The various censuses have different degrees of margin of error regarding employment data. The omissions for the censuses of 1970, 1975 and 1980 are minimized by only calculating the employment rates of those persons with certain information. Persons with 'no employment information' are excluded in the numerator and denominator when calculating the employment rates. The omissions in the 1985 and 1990 censuses are minimized by calculating the employment rates of those persons who actually answered the census. In this way a group with 'no employment information' is eliminated. The same calculation procedure as in the earlier three censuses is used and gives the upper limit of the immigrants' employment rate and the possibility to compare the different censuses over time. To be registered as employed a person has to be employed *one* hour or more per week during the month of census data collection. An account of further aspects of the calculation procedure of the employment rates is given in Appendix 12.1.

At the regional level basically the same source is used. Employment data at this level is obtained from the national employment registers.[4] The data presented in the paper contains the employment rates of various immigrant groups distributed by sex, age and immigration year.

Because of the large number of different immigrant countries represented in the immigrant population a reduction to fewer country groups has been necessary. The formation of the various immigrant groups is mainly based on size and geographical/cultural nearness of the particular immigrant group in Sweden during the period and is accounted for in Appendix 12.2.

Table 12.1   Foreign born population in Sweden for selected countries

Country / Year	1970	1975	1980	1985	1990
Swedish born	7539318	7658093	7690282	7702491	7800185
Foreign born	537585	550451	626953	655649	790445
Nordic born	320913	315775	341253	315184	319082
European born	176463	181488	190990	200215	220806
African born	4149	5849	10025	13919	27343
North American born	15629	14575	14484	15660	19087
South American born	2300	5290	17206	26247	44230
Asian born	9841	19605	45112	76529	150487
Danish born	39152	48302	43501	41159	43931
Finnish born	235453	222147	251342	228050	220497
Norwegian born	44681	43842	42863	42856	52744
West German born	41793	39543	38696	37458	36558
Greek born	11835	14676	15153	13632	13171
Yugoslavian born	33779	36956	37982	38380	43346
Italian born	7268	6222	6062	5868	5989
Polish born	10851	14461	19967	28658	35631
Czechoslovakian born	7392	7228	7529	7830	8432
Ethiopian born	346	902	1797	3204	10027
Turkish born	3768	6143	14357	19264	25528
Iranian born	411	998	3348	8900	40084
Lebanese born	240	486	2170	4709	15986

Source: Statistics, Sweden Population Statistics.

This study deals with first generation immigrants, or foreign born as was registered during the censuses of 1970-1990. Children born in

Sweden to immigrant parents are not part of the examination. The statistical material examined at the national level consists of the *total population in working age 16–65*, taken from the Swedish censuses which are carried out every five years. The lower age limitation, 16 years of age, is explained by the fact that school attendance is compulsory until the age of 16, while the upper age limitation, 65 years of age, is legal retirement age in Sweden.

12.4 Immigration and Structural Change

A simplified view of immigration to Sweden would divide the post-war period into two eras, with the first being characterized by primarily labour force immigration, while the second saw a shift towards refugee and tied immigration. This first period can be said to have existed from 1945 up to the years around 1970. During this time, Sweden's economy expanded rapidly, not hampered by the destruction experienced by her European neighbours. This rapid expansion could not be met by an appropriate increase in the Swedish labour force, and the introduction of foreign workers was necessary in order to avoid bottle-necks in production. The problem was solved in the 1950s through the import of skilled labour, which served as a complement to the native labour force. This skilled labour was mainly recruited in northwestern Europe with the majority coming from Western Germany, Italy, and the Nordic countries (see Table 12.1)

For the region of Malmö the immediate post-war period also had positive effects on the development of the engineering and shipbuilding industries, resulting in a substantial expansion of employment in these sectors in the 1940s. The shortage of skilled labour was, however, a bottleneck. The consumer goods industry also expanded and the textile industry in particular generated a large demand for unskilled labour. War refugees and women relieved this shortage. In the 1950s the consumer goods industry started to decline but the industrial sector continued its expansion with a demand for skilled labour, raising the general employment in the city somewhat above the national level in this period. The demand for skilled industrial labour was mainly relieved by active recruiting of companies in cooperation with the Swedish and Foreign labour market organizations. The larger part of this skilled labour came from West Germany, Denmark and Italy in this period (Ohlsson 1978 and 1995).

In the 1960s, the industrial sector in the region of Malmö, as in Sweden as a whole, showed the characteristics of structural change: an intensive rationalization process and declining industry. Automation, division of labour, specialization and large scale production in industry made it possible to use employees without any special skills. Women and foreign labour filled the vacancies at the assembly lines whereas native workers started to work in the expanding service sector. In other words, were these workers, in contrast to their counterparts of a decade

300

earlier, used more as substitutes for the native work force than as complements? While earlier immigrants allowed the economy to grow in size, the immigrants of the 1960s facilitated a widening of the economy. The fact that these newly vacated jobs could be filled by unskilled workers is a result of industrial investment aimed at increasing international competitiveness and reducing costs (Ohlsson 1975 and Lundh and Ohlsson 1994a and b). In the region of Malmö, again the shipbuilding and engineering industries dominated this development. Labour force immigrants during this decade came largely from Nordic countries but also from Mediterranean countries like Greece, Yugoslavia and Turkey.

Table 12.2   Share Swedish and foreign born working in industry and service sector 1960, 1970, 1975, 1980, 1985 and 1990

Group	1960	1970	1975	1980	1985	1990
Male						
Swedish born						
Industry	39.4	35.9	36.1	33.7	31.6	29.4
Service	28.4	38	41.4	45.3	49.1	51.3
Foreign born *Industry*						
immigrated before 1975	57.6	58.5	56	50	45.8	42
immigrated after 1975	*	*	*	40.8	36.2	36
Foreign born *Service*						
immigrated before 1975	25.8	28.2	33.1	39.1	43.8	64.3
immigrated after 1975	*	*	*	50.4	57.4	66.9
Female						
Swedish born						
Industry	24.8	17.6	16	13.5	12.1	11.4
Service	69.3	76.1	78.1	80.7	83.2	84.7
Foreign born *Industry*						
immigrated before 1975	37.2	36.4	32.2	26	21.9	20
immigrated after 1975	*	*	*	20.5	19.5	18
Foreign born Service						
immigrated before 1975	59.4	60.8	65.1	71.3	76.1	79.5
immigrated after 1975	*	*	*	78	79.3	79.3

Source: Statistics Sweden Population Statistics and Scott (1995).[5]

By the end of the 1960s, however, the situation began to change for the immigrants. The trade unions saw immigration as producing a number of negative side effects. One such side effect was the delaying of industrial transformation through the steady supply of workers to replace Swedes who moved into the service sector. This supply of labour also served to depress wage increases in industry, which could otherwise have occurred due to scarcity of labour. In this way, immigration was seen as preserving the traditional industrial structure in a time when it would otherwise have been forced to undergo large changes. The government responded to these criticisms through a change in the rules governing entrance to Sweden. The new rules were enforced in 1968, and meant that future applicants for work and residence permits from non-Nordic countries must apply before they enter the country, and at that time have arranged for both a job and a place to live. This dramatically cut down the labour immigration of non-Nordic countries during the next decades.

As stated earlier, Swedish economic growth dropped to a lower level, from 4 percent to less than 2 percent, following the oil crisis of the early 1970s. At the same time the economy passed through a period of transformation with a decreasing industrial sector and an increasing service sector (see Table 12.2).

As for the country as a whole, the region of Malmö showed a stagnating industrial sector after 1975. The structure of the region's industry meant that companies faced great difficulties in changing their production. Management and the strongly specialized labour were suited to a specific productive apparatus which was highly inflexible. At the same time, an employment increase in the public sector, already started in the late 1960s, was taking place. The economic growth of the 1960s gave rise to a demand for public services like child care, education, old age care, medical care, etc. The large increase of the public sector, also during the 1970s, and a stagnating industrial sector led to structural problems in the economy, with low growth and high unemployment especially among low skilled workers. It was only during the late 1980s that a transformation of the economy took place. Decentralization of production processes entailed an increasing demand for employees with proportionately higher general competence. As mentioned before, there occurred a shift in production techniques from a more traditional basis in 1970 to more group-oriented procedures in the late 1970s and 1980s. The common base of jobs in the service- and industrial sector are to a large extent culture specific knowledge or social competence, in which language, communication ability and familiarity with the functioning of the Swedish society is crucial. This so called 're-industrialization' was for a large part in the industry-based service sectors such as transportation, wholesale and retail trade and trade supplying (Bengtsson and Johansson 1994).

The construction of a *GRP* (Gross Regional Product) for the years *1970–1993* and divided by different sectors and branches for the Malmö region confirms this analysis (Schön 1996). The general GRP per employee compared to GDP per employee for Sweden, although fluctuating with the business cycle, decreased until 1989 whereafter it strongly increased until 1994. The GRP per employee in the industrial sector of the region of Malmö follows this pattern and consequently dominates the development of the region. Further, is it confirmed that the share of white colour workers increases during the whole period, especially in the knowledge-intensive and labour-intensive industry branches. The increase in GRP per employee in the late 1980s would mark the end of a period of structural transformation with negative economic activity in the region, and the start of a new period based on high skilled employment.

During this period the Nordic labour migration, especially Finnish, gradually declines. This is largely because of a diminishing gap in the standard of living between Sweden and Finland and an increasing demand for labour in Finland. While labour migration dwindled, other types of migration, mainly tied movers and different categories of refugees, increased substantially during the 1970s and 1980s. This also led to a major shift in the country of origin mix of the immigrant population, with a greater share of non-European immigrants having non-economic motives behind their migration. The major contributors to the immigrant population in Malmö during this period were Chileans, Iranians and immigrants from Asian countries (see Table 12.3). In 1990 16.4 percent of the population of Malmö were foreign born.

Table 12.3 Foreign born population in Malmö for selected groups 1984 and 1990

	1984	1990	% of Pop in in Malmö 1990	% of foreign Pop in Sweden 1990
Total population	229582	233887		
Foreign born	37422	38260		4.8
Nordic born	9646	7050	18.4	2.2
European born	22173	20232	52.9	9.2
African born	479	987	2.6	3.6
North American born	552	593	1.6	3.1
South American born	1566	2325	6.1	5.3
Asian born	2647	6556	17.1	4.4
Danish born	5478	3920	10.2	8.9
Finnish born	2920	2015	5.3	0.9
Norwegian born	995	809	2.1	1.5
West German born	2548	1811	4.7	5
Greek born	772	557	1.5	4.2
Yugoslavian born	7706	6536	17.1	15.1
Italian born	533	348	0.9	5.8
Polish born	4362	4891	12.8	13.7
Chilean born	697	1237	3.2	4.5
Iranian born	87	1556	4.1	3.9
Turkish born	815	619	1.6	2.4

Source: Statistics Sweden, Population Statistics.

Table 12.4 Age standardized employment rate, Swedes and selected immigrant groups, in Sweden 1970–1990 (16–65)

Year	Male					Female				
	1970	1975	1980	1985	1990	1970	1975	1980	1985	1990
Swedish born	84.3	83.9	82.8	82.7	83.5	52.1	62.4	69.2	76.2	80.1
Foreign born	86.8	81.8	76.8	72.7	71.0	56.3	63.0	65.3	67.7	66.7
- Nordic born	87.8	82.2	78.1	75.9	76.4	56.3	63.0	67.2	72.4	75.0
West European born	86.6	85.5	81.7	77.9	79.2	52.7	60.7	65.5	68.9	72.1
South European born	86.4	79.3	73.0	69.0	67.4	58.3	66.7	63.3	61.1	57.6
East European born	80.4	79.9	75.7	72.1	72.5	55.0	61.3	61.9	63.8	66.0
African born	73.5	74.0	70.6	68.1	63.6	48.8	50.1	53.8	57.5	41.4
North American born	73.4	75.5	76.6	71.6	73.3	41.6	54.6	63.6	65.4	69.4
Latin American born	73.6	64.5	64.4	68.1	74.7	46.6	46.8	50.1	59.1	63.8
East Asian born	73.7	80.3	74.7	67.0	68.8	44.1	54.5	52.4	53.2	60.9
South Asian born	74.9	76.6	75.9	70.5	72.8	46.5	53.7	51.2	52.6	53.9
Middle Eastern born	77.1	72.9	62.7	53.9	50.4	45.2	49.4	38	38.5	34.7
Danish born	87.8	86.8	82.8	78.7	79.8	51.5	58.4	65.7	69.8	74.5
Finnish born	87.6	80.0	75.6	74.8	74.7	58.2	64.3	67.6	73.1	75.6
Norwegian born	84.7	82.9	79.0	72.3	77.9	49.0	58	63.7	68.1	73.3
West German born	87.7	86.6	82.4	78.4	79.8	53.7	61.6	66.0	71.3	73.7
Greek born	84.1	77.1	67.0	63.2	62.0	53.7	66.8	61.1	54.4	48.6
Yugoslavian born	86.6	79.2	72.7	68.2	66.8	58.5	67.1	62.6	61.4	57.9
Polish born	73.5	78.0	74.1	67.5	69.6	47.8	57.8	58.7	59.9	63.7
Czechoslovakian born	83.6	72.0	75.7	74.3	73.9	53.1	58.7	63.0	66.6	69.4
Ethiopian born	NA	NA	56.4	69.2	70.7	NA	NA	54.8	63.2	50.1
Turkish born	80.3	76.0	66.5	61.9	54.5	47.9	59.2	39.2	41.6	40.8
Iranian born	NA	57.5	56.4	41.8	45.8	NA	33.6	37.3	42.2	32.3
Lebanese born	NA	NA	67.5	50.6	46.1	NA	NA	38.5	36.0	25.4
Italian born	86.7	81.5	79.4	73.1	71.8	59.4	60.7	61.2	61.8	64.2

Source: Statistics Sweden, 1970, 1975, 1980, 1985, & 1990 Censuses of the Population.

12.5 Employment Assimilation, Sweden and Malmö

In Tables 12.4 and 12.5 the development of the employment rates[6] between 1970 and 1990 of different immigrant groups is presented for Sweden and the region of Malmö. In general, Table 12.4 shows that foreign born men in Sweden have a decline of more than 15 percentage points in the employment rate during this period. Nordic, West European, East European, Latin and North American as well as South Asian born immigrants are somewhat above this level in the 1990 census, while south Europeans, Africans, east Asians and Middle East born men are beneath this level. An important feature for most of the groups is the gradually decreasing employment rate after the 1970 census, especially for the large labour migration groups which came mainly during the 1950s and 1960s. Other groups show this decrease first after the 1975 census. Also, many groups show a small increase between the censuses of 1985 and 1990 which could be caused by the very favourable Swedish labour market at the end of the 1980s.

The main feature of the female employment rate in Sweden during this period is the increase in participation of nearly all groups. Foreign women as a whole increase their employment rate by 10 percentage points between 1970 and 1990. Yet, compared to Swedish women, who show an exceptional increase in employment rate during this period, female immigrant groups show a slower increase in employment rate (or no increase at all).

Labour migration groups (Nordic, west, south and east European and north American) immigrating during the 1950s and 1960s show the largest increase, except for south European women. Of the immigrant groups mainly arriving during the 1970s and 1980s, Latin Americans and east and south Asians show increasing employment rates during the period. Middle Eastern women show a decline in employment after 1975. African women, who came in larger numbers during the late 1980s, show a heavy decline in employment between the censuses of 1985 and 1990.

Although not available for the whole period the employment rates for the various immigrant groups in the region of Malmö presented in Table 12.5, show basically the same pattern indicated for the national level in Table 12.4, but on a generally lower level. The generally lower level of employment rate is in line with the hypothesis that the Malmö region had more difficulties readjusting its economy compared to the national level during this period. The drop to far lower levels in 1993 was caused by the economic recession that struck the Swedish economy at the beginning of the 1990s.

The problem with the employment rates of the different groups in the different censuses shown in Tables 12.4 and 12.5 is that they account for the stock of every immigrant group in the respective census year, irrespective of the fact why and when immigrants came into the country.

In line with earlier investigations of the income catch-up process and time spent in the new country, the employment rate by years in Sweden for different groups based on the censuses of 1970 and 1990 is presented.[7]

Table 12.5 Age standardized employment rate of Swedes and selected immigrant groups in the region of Malmö, 1986, 1990 and 1993 (16–65)

	men			women		
	1986	1990	1993	1986	1990	1993
Swedish born	79.5	82.6	68.9	77.3	82.4	71.0
Foreign born	61.4	65.3	41	59.5	61.1	41.6
Nordic born	67.0	72.4	49.9	69.2	76.6	59.1
West Europe	72.0	79.5	59.9	62.9	70.2	59.7
South Europe	64.0	65.8	47	62.7	60.9	42
East Europe	55.9	63.1	42.3	52.8	57.3	41.5
North America	57.3	64.7	37.4	44.5	54.5	32.8
Latin America	56.8	69.2	46.8	47.6	61.7	40.2
Africa	55.3	57.3	30.2	47.0	54.9	22.2
Asia	45.1	57.4	34	40.6	47.3	25
Middle East	44.7	43.9	38.9	32.8	27.3	13.7
Finland	66.5	69.3	49	72.9	72.9	61.2
Norway	60.3	78.7	64.8	70.0	90.8	67.1
Denmark	67.3	74.4	47.5	66.6	75.2	55.9
Germany	73.7	81.1	66.8	66.4	69.8	60.3
USA	62.1	70.1	42.2	42.9	53.9	39.3
Chile	59.5	69	48	48.6	62.1	40.2
Yugoslavia	64.3	64.2	45.6	63.3	59.8	40.7
Poland	54.1	65.7	44.4	52.9	59.3	41.3
Greece	55.9	55.8	37.1	48.5	50.4	37.8
Turkey	59.5	59.5	39.2	42.0	45.7	24.9
Iran	28.2	36.8	19.1	11.0	23.2	15

Source: Statistics Sweden, Årssys (Yearly employment data).

Figure 12.1 presents immigrant groups who immigrated during the post war period up to the 1970 census, mainly labour immigrants. Figures 12.2 and 12.3 present immigrant groups with the larger part immigrating during the 1970s and 1980s, primarily refugees and tied movers. In the figures we go back in time by five year periods and present employment rates for every cohort. In this way a proxy for the adaptation time of different immigrant groups in Sweden is shown

306

during different periods. Care must be taken however, since the diagrams do not represent one single cohort over time.

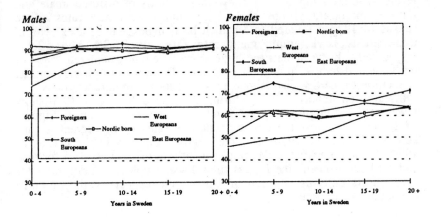

Figure 12.1 Employment rate of different immigrant groups in Sweden, 1970 Census, Swedish males = 84.3, females = 52.1

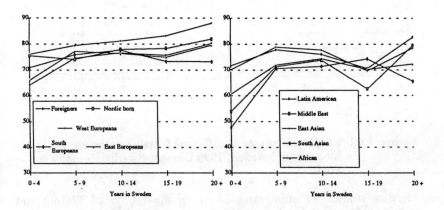

Figure 12.2 Employment rate of different male immigrant groups by years in Sweden, 1990 Census, Swedish males = 83.5

307

Earlier human capital based research on incomes of immigrants argues for a rapid income catch-up process of immigrants arriving prior to 1970. The employment rate of immigrants arriving during this period equal the rates of natives and for some groups even exceed Swedish levels. A look at Figure 12.1 shows that cohorts of different male and female immigrant groups show high employment rate rates in the census of 1970 compared to Swedish born males and females, who in this census have employment rate rates of 84.3% and 52.1% respectively. In particular, the high on-entry employment rate rates of the male and female immigrant groups could be seen as proxies for fast adaptation to the Swedish labour market of these immigrant groups.

Research on cohorts coming during the period following 1970 show lower rates of employment rate and income for immigrants. Figures 12.2 and 12.3 show the employment rate rates of immigrant groups coming during the 1970s and the 1980s registered in the census of 1990. When compared to the employment rate of natives (83,5 for men and 80,1 for women), the figures show lower employment rate rates for the cohorts entering Sweden in this period, especially the on-entry employment rate rates.

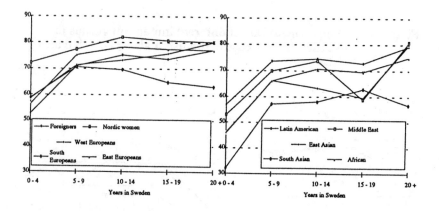

Figure 12.3 Employment rate of different female immigrant groups by years in Sweden, 1990 Census, Swedish females = 80.1

Earlier studies on immigrants living in the region of Malmö and immigrated to Sweden before 1970 presented high employment rates for the various immigrant groups. Table 12.6 shows the employment rates for the various immigrant groups by years in Sweden for the Malmö region in 1990. Here again a general lower employment rate is registered for immigrant groups arriving during the 1970s and 1980s. Comparing the rates of the national level with the rates for the Malmö

308

region, again the Malmö region shows lower levels, supporting the poorer labour market assimilation of immigrants in the region.

Comparing the immigrants coming during the 1950s and 1960s to the immigrants coming during the 1970s and 1980s, the differences are obvious. More recently immigrated groups show higher on-entry differentials and slower adaptation to native rates of employment rate. Further, the splitting of the immigrant groups in a group of mainly tied movers (except the Nordic countries) and a group which consists for the most part of refugees (Figures 12.2 and 12.3) is in line with the concept that later immigrant groups can take advantage of countrymen already established in the new country. On the other hand, these figures cannot tell us if this is the main reason for lower employment rates of the refugee and tied mover immigrant groups in comparison to labour market immigrants. Another reason, that could be the problem is cohort quality. Differences in educational levels between those immigrants that came during the 1950s and 1960s and those who came during the 1970s and 1980s, as well as differences between the groups in the same period could explain the differences in employment rates.

In Table 12.7, the education level is charted for different immigrant groups from the 1970 and 1990 censuses. The table presents a changing educational level, moving towards a higher general level for all groups including natives. More precisely, age standardized relative educational levels for the foreign born population shifted from being slightly above native figures to being only slightly below. If it is assumed that education has an impact on labour market assimilation, in this case employment rate, the first suggestion would be that the declining employment rates of the various immigrant groups is due to the lower general educational level compared to natives.

Table 12.8, however, shows another picture. Here the probability for immigrants from certain countries having employment relative to Swedes of the same sex, educational level, and civil status is charted. Results similar to those in Figures 12.1, 12.2 and 12.3 were obtained through the use of a simple logistic regression.[8] With this increased specificity, the main result is that the large difference between rates obtained by cohorts arriving before 1970 and those coming after 1970 remains. In other words, in spite of controlling for sex, educational level, civil status and by immigration year cohort, immigrants do worse during the 1970s and 1980s than their counterparts during the 1950s and 1960s. Immigrants who came to Sweden prior to 1970 had fewer problems gaining employment than did their later counterparts. The table also indicates that there does seem to occur a lowering of the chance of having work as cultural distance between the home and destination country increases. This difficulty seems to be fairly short lived, however, with a closing of the gap between foreigners occurring with increased time in country, but it nonetheless gives us reason to believe that different culture-specific human capital demanded in the labour market could complicate a smooth labour market assimilation of immigrants.

Table 12.6 Employment rate of different immigrant groups by years in Sweden, living in the region of Malmö 1990

	men						women					
Years in Sweden	0-1 years	2-4 years	5-9 years	10-14 years	15-18 years	19- years	0-1 years	2-4 years	5-9 years	10-14 years	15-18 years	19- years
Foreign born	45.9	53.9	59	68.3	63.6	58	28.4	43.4	54.2	54.8	61.7	49.6
Nordic born	66.9	55.6	47.6	77.8	63.3	55.8	59.7	65.5	60.2	64	68.8	48.6
West Europe	59.6	61.2	62.4	62	68.3	63	41.7	35.8	47.5	54.5	49.4	44.3
South Europe	52.8	59.3	62.7	74	65.2	61.5	31.8	52.8	54.3	49.5	58.2	56.6
East Europe	40.2	54.6	62.5	69.1	58.4	50.1	25.7	45.6	56.2	59.9	61.6	44
North America	51	58.9	48.4	61.3	58.8	47.2	30.6	35.7	40.5	37.4	66.7	26.5
Latin America	53.3	62.7	69.7	61.5	69.1	66.7	35.9	52.8	57.8	47.7	70	68.4
Africa	51.9	67.1	65.2	80.9	64.2	72.6	31.5	56.3	67.9	79	72.7	56
Asia	25.6	45.3	54.4	62.4	60.7	62.8	19.2	30.4	48	47.1	56.3	71.7
Middle East	23.6	47.7	50.6	58.4	72.5	60	7.5	29	43	41.2	44.4	44.4
Finland	58.1	36	59.5	74.4	61.3	65	47.6	66.7	60	66.3	71.2	62.3
Norway	74.6	64	47.1	71.7	59.3	40.2	84.4	66.7	79.2	84.7	64.3	42.2
Denmark	65.1	55.5	41.5	77.6	64.7	53	59.8	60.3	55.2	58.2	68.4	40.1
Germany	64.3	65	54.5	62.3	75.6	61.7	25	35	44.8	42.3	41.5	42
USA	57.1	61.5	45	54.6	58.3	47.4	28.6	50	33.3	32.3	66.7	20.2
Chile	60	68.2	75.3	66.9	59.4	71.4	40	59.1	60	47.6	63.3	33.3
Yugoslavia	54.2	63.6	64.6	78.1	66.7	61.1	31.9	56.3	56.3	49.9	61.3	57.2
Poland	48.5	56.7	65	71.6	62.1	42.7	30.3	45.2	55.5	62.1	64.1	40.1
Greece	38.5	29.4	46.2	62.8	58.3	52.1	50	23.1	25	49.1	45.5	36.5
Turkey	47.8	59.4	65.2	59.1	78.8	62.1	18.2	26.7	50.9	35.2	52.4	54.3
Iran	18.5	49.8	58	53.1	50	47.1	7.2	37.1	57.1	57	na	na

Source: Statistics Sweden, Årssys, (Yearly employment data).

Table 12.7   Age standardized education distribution by selected countries, 1970 and 1990

1970 Education level	Men Prim	Sec	Uni	Women Prim	Sec	Uni
Swedish born	62	32	7	67	26	7
Foreign born	57	36	7	66	28	6
Norwegian born	51	39	10	69	28	3
Danish born	56	38	26	66	28	6
Finnish born	72	25	3	74	22	4
German born	26	61	13	46	46	8
USA born	44	35	21	50	32	18
Greek born	76	21	3	91	7	2
Italian born	55	41	4	72	25	3
Turkish born	62	28	10	81	16	3
Yugoslavian born	59	37	4	75	22	3
Polish born	37	45	18	50	37	13

Source: Census of Population 1970 and 1990.

This together supports the hypothesis that not only the supply side, but also the demand side of the labour market had a great deal of impact on the lower employment rate levels of old and new immigrants. From a macro level perspective, the generally lower level and slower adaptation of the employment rate of the immigrants arriving during the 1970s and 1980s can probably be partially explained by the transformation of the economy in the 1970s and 1980s. The sector segregation with relatively more immigrants employed in the industrial sector is one reason for lower employment rate rates of immigrants, with employment in this sector declining relative to the service sector during the 1970s and 1980s. Besides, during this period demand for labour was changing in pace with this new transformation of economic life. Labour demand became, to a great extent, based on labour with specialist knowledge in the new, expanding sectors of the economy. Culture specific knowledge, social competence, good knowledge of the Swedish language, social communication and knowledge of the functioning of the Swedish society became more important prerequisites for finding employment. In other words, despite the educational levels only slightly lower than Swedes, the requirements and competence demanded in the labour market did not match the competence of these new immigrants. Immigrant cohorts who arrived before the change and had skills suitable for this earlier period were equally estranged by this new development.

311

Table 12.8 Relative probability of employment for selected nationalities, in Sweden, 1970 and 1990: controlling for educational level and civil status, Sweden = 100

Years in Sweden	Male					Female				
	1 - 4 Years	5 - 9 Years	10 - 14 Years	15 -19 Years	20 + Years	1 - 4 Years	5 - 9 Years	10 - 14 Years	15 -19 Years	20 + Years
Norwegian born 70	101	88	86	100	103	116	88	110	97	96
Norwegian born 90	83	67	86	90	96	75	68	84	91	97
Danish born 70	91	90	89	92	100	110	90	97	92	91
Danish born 90	87	80	84	91	96	71	73	87	92	95
Finnish born 70	78	92	96	99	96	90	92	91	86	97
Finnish born 90	73	78	85	85	98	78	88	96	96	100
German born 70	100	92	92	96	94	109	92	103	91	96
German born 90	71	68	88	89	98	49	64	82	86	92
USA born 70	111	97	90	108	95	120	97	101	114	95
USA born 90	58	74	79	80	101	42	51	62	74	86
Greek born 70	101	93	110	103	89	58	93	70	NA	NA
Greek born 90	57	69	72	71	94	60	60	64	60	59
Italian born 70	99	90	88	89	74	87	90	82	76	96
Italian born 90	58	71	75	74	100	39	62	76	79	86
Turkish born 70	105	97	72	89	92	81	97	91	NA	NA
Turkish born 90	47	61	61	62	105	33	52	56	63	60
Yugoslavian born 70	87	90	98	102	67	60	90	53	NA	NA
Yugoslavian born 90	69	71	74	75	98	61	80	80	77	80
Polish born70	111	100	107	96	80	106	100	86	82	94
Polish born 90	65	74	73	70	104	47	72	80	77	82
Czech'an born 70	102	90	94	97	77	96	90	87	84	91
Czech'an born 90	62	76	71	80	98	43	66	77	85	83
Chilean born 90	81	89	88	67	83	58	88	91	81	81
Iraqian born 90	43	66	81	99	73	22	58	70	95	39
Iranian born 90	47	63	76	78	59	29	48	65	81	31
Ethiopian born 90	74	90	96	86	54	49	99	90	96	74
Vietnamese born 90	56	80	92	54	85	39	70	83	57	96

Source: Statistics Sweden, 1970 and 1990 Censuses of Population.

A strengthening of this hypothesis can be seen in the economic development of the Malmö region during the same period. The Malmö region experienced a labour market with a declining industrial sector and a slow-growing private service sector in the 1970s and 1980s. Only in the late 1980s could an increase in the industrial and industry-based service sectors be observed. In relation to other metropolitan areas in Sweden, the situation was worse in the region of Malmö.

If it is assumed that the human capital characteristics and motivation for immigration to the region of Malmö are the same as for Sweden, the tables of immigrant performance in the Malmö region in the early 1990s show that the various immigrant groups have experienced grave difficulties in dealing with this situation. The immigrant population in the region of Malmö, compared to the national level, showed worse labour market performance.

The prolonged structural transformation of the regional economy of Malmö and the increase in demand for cultural-specific labour made it more difficult for both old and new immigrants to obtain employment.

12.5 Conclusions

This chapter has attempted to briefly summarize selected findings of a study on the employment rate of immigrants in Sweden. The employment rate is seen as an important part of the economic and social assimilation of immigrants in a new country. Without employment, no regular income can be obtained, and this influences the present as well the future living standard of the person in question.

The main purpose of the chapter was to analyse labour market assimilation of selected immigrant groups defined as employment rate convergence and the structural change of the Swedish and regional economy of Malmö between 1970 and 1990.

The majority of research on economic assimilation of immigrants has stressed 'human capital' characteristics as being the key to successful labour market assimilation. These characteristics are naturally important in this respect, and in empirical studies human capital they have been used to explain labour market performance of immigrants. The analysis in this chapter also had its origins in questions of how human capital characteristics like formal education and civil status could explain the employment assimilation of immigrants in the Swedish labour market. In summary, we controlled for formal human capital, education and civil status as well as time in the country. First, immigrants who came during the 1970s and 1980s have generally lower employment rates than those who came during the 1950s and 1960s. Second, this difference is noticed irrespective of the motivation for immigration. Third, men and women of the various immigrant groups show the same development between the different time periods. Fourth, large differences in employment assimilation appear between the various immigrant groups who have settled in Sweden during the 1970s and

1980s, indicating increased difficulty in obtaining employment with increased cultural distance.

All in all, formal human capital characteristics of immigrants cannot explain alone the differences in labour market performance between the two periods.

The answer to the question lies, in our opinion, more in changes in the demand for labour during the last few decades. As stated earlier, it is postulated here that the structural change which the Swedish economy passed through between 1970 and 1990 made it more difficult for immigrants with the same general human capital as Swedes to obtain employment. The number of monotonous jobs demanding low and unskilled labour in the industry and service sector decreased and were replaced by jobs which were organized in work teams and demanded labour with higher communication and social skills. The new growing sectors of the economy shifted labour demand towards labour with higher informal competence including, for instance, culture-specific proficiency, language skills and the understanding of formal and informal codes in the labour market. This change, together with a shift in immigrant groups with little proximity to the Swedish culture and society, could explain a great deal of the deteriorating labour market attachment of immigrants during this period. Especially 'discrimination under uncertainty' by employers could contribute to explaining the low labour market attachment of immigrants during this period.

The economic development and employment assimilation of the various immigrant groups in the region of Malmö strengthens the idea that the dynamic functioning of the economy must be taken into account for a more complete understanding of the economic assimilation process of immigrants.

Appendix   12.I

The employment rate in the different censuses is calculated by taking the quotient between those who are *registered as employed* and the *registered total population* in the *ages 16–65,* at the time of data collection. The difficulty with the computation of this rate is that there are different degrees of margins of error according to employment data and the registered population. In all the censuses, employment information is not available for a part of the population and in the census is registered as a group under 'no employment information.'[9] Not filling in the census, 'not known at address', illegible entries and being out of the country without registering with the local authorities are some of the reasons for this group. In this group 'no employment information', immigrants were over-represented. Employment rate calculations by the national census bureau were made by taking the quotient of the registered population and the population with employment information, which led to an underestimation of employment for foreigners.

Data on the number for whom employment information is not available in every age group and by nationality makes it possible to revise the employment information in the censuses of 1960, 1970, 1975 and 1980. Persons with 'no employment information' are, in the new calculations, not included in the numerator and denominator. The new calculation is then based on those we have 'certain' information about, divided by the nationally registered population, minus those not available in every age group.

or: $C_t = E_t / (P_t - M_t)$ C = revised employment rate in age group t
E = number of 'certain' employed in age group t
P = population in census in age group t
M = not available employment information in age group t

By not including the persons with no employment information the employment rate of the 'known' population is calculated. It could be that the rate for the population with no employment information is lower than for the known population. Persons with low society attachment probably also have low labour market attachment. The new calculated employment rate is in this way the upper level in every age group.[10]

In the censuses of 1985 and 1990 the national census bureau changed the method of gathering employment data. In these censuses employment information was gathered from a yearly register called 'Årsys' and based on employers' control reports on wages and employment. This new method increased the security of employment data but not the employment rate. The denominator in their calculations was still the nationally registered population and led again to low employment rates for immigrants.

To minimize the omissions in these two censuses and be able to compare the different censuses, a similar procedure as in the earlier censuses was necessary. Unfortunately, owing to the change in gathering information, the group with 'no employment information' was not available in these censuses. On the other hand, these censuses had variables which in case of irregularities, such as mentioned earlier, led to a group under 'no information'. This group with 'no information' is assumed to be the same as the 'no employment information' group of earlier censuses.

or: $C_t = E_t / (P_t - M_t)$ C = revised employment rate in age group t
E = number of 'certain' employed in age group t
P = population in census in age group t
M = unavailable information in age group t

315

This new computation of the employment rates of the different groups in the censuses of 1985 and 1990 can be seen, as in the earlier censuses, to be the upper level of the different groups.

The age standardized labour employment rates in this investigation are obtained by calculating the employment rate for 5-year age groups.

Appendix   12.2

The immigrant population examined in this investigation consists of those Swedish residents who were *born abroad* in;
A, one of the following geographical areas and B, specific countries.

1 **Nordic countries**
   Norway, Denmark, Finland and Iceland
2 **West European countries**
   Germany, France, The Netherlands, Belgium, Great Britain, Ireland, Austria, Switzerland, Luxembourg and Liechtenstein
3 **South European countries**
   Spain, Portugal, Italy, Greece, Malta, Andorra, Cyprus, San Marino, former Yugoslavia
4 **East European countries**
   Albania, Bulgaria, Hungary, former East Germany, Estonia, Lithuania, Latvia, Czechoslovakia, Poland, the Soviet Union, and Rumania
5 **American countries**
   (**North America**) USA and Canada
   (**Latin America**) Argentina, Bolivia, Brazil, Columbia, Ecuador, Guyana, Paraguay, Peru, Surinam, Uruguay, Venezuela, Chile, The Caribbean Isles, Mexico, Costa Rica, El Salvador, Guatemala, Honduras, Nicaragua, Panama
6 **African countries**
   Algeria, Angola, Egypt, Benin, Botswana, Burkina Faso, Burundi, Central African Republic, Comorerna, Djibouti, Equatorial Guinea, the Ivory Coast, Morocco, Gabon, Gambia, Ghana, Guinea, Guinea Bissau, Cameroon, Cape Verde Islands, Kenya, Congo, Lesotho, Liberia, Libya, Madagascar, Malawi, Mali, Mauritania, Mauritius, Mozambique, Namibia, Nigeria, Rwanda, Senegal, Sierra Leone, Somalia, Sudan, South Africa, Tanzania, Chad, Togo, Tunisia, Uganda, Ethiopia, Zaire, Zambia, Zanzibar and Zimbabwe
7 **Asian countries**
   (**East Asia**) Brunei, the Philippines, Hong Kong, Indonesia, Japan, Kampuchea, Taiwan, China, Korea, Laos, Malaysia, Mongolia, Vietnam and Singapore,
   (**South Asia**) Afghanistan, Bangladesh, Bhutan, Burma, India, Pakistan and Sri Lanka,
   (**Middle East**) Turkey, Lebanon, Iraq, Iran, Israel, Yemen, Jordan, Kuwait, Saudi Arabia, South Yemen, Syria, Bahrain and Oman.

References

Baker, M. and Benjamin, D. (1994), 'The Performance of Immigrants in the Canadian Labour Market', *Journal of Labour Economics*, vol. no. 3.

Bengtsson, T and Johansson, M, (1994), *Förnyelse, Utbildning och Flyttningar Exemplet Malmöhus Län* (Renewal, Education and Movements – the example of Malmöhus Län), Rapport 11, Malmö.

Bevelander, P. (1995), *Labor Force Participation of Immigrants in Sweden 1960-1990*, Fil. Lic-dissertation Economic history, Lund.

Bevelander, P and Scott, K, (1996), 'Labor Force Participation and Income Performance of Immigrants in Sweden, 1970–1990', *Yearbook of Population Research in Finland*, XXXIII.

Borjas, G. (1985), 'Assimilation, Changes in Cohort Quality, and the Earnings of Immigrants', *Journal of Labor Economics*, vol. 3, no. 4.

Borjas, G. (1987), 'Self Selection and the Earnings of Immigrants', *American Economic Review*, vol. 77.

Borjas, G. (1989), 'The Self-Employment Experience of Immigrants', *Journal of Human Resources*, vol. 21.

Borjas, G. (1994), 'Immigrant Skills and Ethnic Spillover', *Journal of Population Economics*, vol. 7, no. 2.

Brune Y, (1993), *Invandrare i svenskt arbetsliv* (Immigrants in Swedish working life), Tranås.

Broomé. P., Bäcklund, K., Lundh, C. and Ohlsson, R. (1995), *Invandrarna, kompetensen och den svenska arbetsmarknaden* (Immigrants, Competence and the Swedish Labor Market), Rapport till Invandrar- och flykting kommitén.

Broomé, P., Bäcklund, K., Lundh, C. and Ohlsson, R. (1996), *Varför sitter "brassen" på bänken? eller Varför har invandrare så svårt att få jobb?* (Why do immigrants experience difficulties in finding employment?), Stockholm.

Chiswick, B. (1978), 'The Effects of Americanization on the Earnings of Foreign born Men', *Journal of Political Economy*, vol. 86.

Chiswick, B.R.and Miller, P.W. (1993), 'The Endogeneity Between Language and Earnings: An International Analysis', Paper presented at the conference, Economics of International Migration: Econometric Evidence, Konstanz, Germany, 26–27 February.

Dustmann, C. (1993), 'Speaking Fluency, Writing Fluency and the Earnings of Migrants', paper presented at the conference Economics of International Migration: Economic Evidence, Konstanz, Germany, 26–27 February.

Ekberg, J. (1983), *Inkomsteffekter av invandring* (Income Effects of Immigration), Växjö.

Ekberg, J. (1991a), 'Försämrad sysselsättning för invandrarna under 1980-talet' (Decreasing Employment of Immigrants during the 1980s), *Ekonomisk Debatt*, vol. 2.

Ekberg, J. (1991b), *Vad hände sedan? En studie av utrikes födda på arbetsmarknaden* (What Happened Next? A Study of Foreign Born in the Labor Market), Växjö.

LaLonde, R.J. and Topel, R.H. (1992), 'The Assimilation of Immigrants in the US Labor Market', in Borjas, G.J. and F.B. Freeman (eds), *Immigration and the Work Force; Economic Consequences for the United States and Source Areas*, Chicago.

Lundh, C. and Ohlsson, R. (1994a), *Från arbetskraftimport till flyktinginvandring* (From Labor Import to Refugee Immigration), Stockholm.

Lundh, C. and Ohlsson, R. (1994b), 'Immigration and Economic Change', in Bengtsson, T. (ed.), *Population, Economy and Welfare in Sweden*, Berlin.

Ohlsson, R. (1975), *Invandrarna på Arbetsmarknaden* (Immigrants in the Labour Market), Lund.

Ohlsson, R. (1978), *Ekonomisk strukturförändring och invandring* (Economic Structural Change and Immigration), Lund.

Ohlsson, R (1995), *Malmö Stadshistoria del 7* (Malmö City history part 7), Bjurling, O. (ed.).

Poot, J. (1993), 'Adaptation of Migrants in the New Zealand Labour Market', *International Migration Review*, vol. 27 no. 1, pp. 121–39.

Schierup, C.U. and Paulson S. (eds) (1994), *Arbetets etniska delning* (Ethnic segregation of Employment).

Schön, L. (1996), *Malmö, Från kris till tillväxt, Ett långsiktigt perspektiv på strukturomvandlingen och en konstruktion av BRP 1970–1994.* (Malmö, From Crisis to Growth, A Long Term Perspective on Structural Change and the Construction of GRP 1970–1994), Malmö.

Scott, K. (1995), *Migrants in the Labor Market. Employment Patterns and Income Development of Immigrants to Sweden 1970–1990*, Fil. Lic dissertation Economic History, Lund.

Wadensjö, E, (1973), *Immigration och Samhällsekonomi* (Immigration and Social Economy), Lund.

Wright, R.E. and Maxim, P.S. (1993), 'Immigration Policy and Immigrant Quality', *Journal of Population Studies*, vol. 6 no. 4, pp. 337–52.

Notes

1. This chapter is part of two larger research projects entitled 'Migrants in the Post-Industrial Age: Immigration and Structural Change in the Swedish Economy, 1968-1993', supported by the Swedish Council for Social Research and 'Immigrants in Stockholm, Gothenburg and Malmö, supported by the Education association for Industry and Society. The projects are being carried out by members of the Research Group in Population Economics, Department of Economic History, Lund University.

2. Tied movers refer here to those immigrants entering Sweden for non-economic, non-refugee reasons. This generally means relatives of earlier migrants or those with connections to Swedish citizens.

3. This is the basic hypothesis in the research project 'Migrants in the Post-Industrial Age: Immigration and Structural Change in the Swedish Economy 1970-1990'.

4. 'Årssysselsättning' (yearly employment) is a yearly register on employment starting in 1985 and based on the employment information from employers. This information is also used to define employment in the national censuses of 1985 and 1990.

5. 'The industrial sector' in this investigation refers to the industrial manufacturing sector. For further division into sub-sectors and other references, see Scott (1995).

6. Employment rate, unemployment rate and labour force participation rate are complementary in the Swedish labour market statistics. For the period in question though, the employment intensity rate and the unemployment rate (Labour Force Investigations AKU) show the same pattern for the larger immigrant groups.

7. Although empirically used to predict earnings differentials, it is here assumed that it can also be used to predict variations in employment rates between native and immigrant groups. (See also, e.g. Poot 1993.)

8. Prob (Y = 1) = $e^{\beta'x}/(1+e^{\beta'x})$
   Y = indicator of having employment, β = coefficient and x = independent variables
   Sweden = 0, all other countries = 1.

9. Especially the 1970 census lacks employment information for the registered population (SOU 1974:69 (Swedish Official Report)). Other studies, Ekberg.(1983) concerning the census of 1975 show that there is no information for 4.5% of foreign citizens. For total population and Foreign born naturalized population this share is only 1 percent. In the census of 1985 and 1990 the employment information is taken from a yearly employment register in order to minimize the margins of error in earlier censuses. This new procedure for collecting employment data for these censuses has minimized the number of population with missing employment information in the 1985 and 1990 census.

10. The described procedure is based on Ekberg (1983).

Part D
Migration Models

13 A Network-Based Model of International Migration

BRIGITTE WALDORF

13.1 Conceptual Background

The proposed model of the international-interregional movements of immigrants is based on a network-theoretical view that emphasizes the behavioural interdependencies between immigrant stocks and flows as salient factors creating the internal dynamic of an international migration system. More specifically, the conceptual model posits that a network of social ties links the immigrant stock residing abroad with immigration and return migration flows (Massey et al. 1993; Waldorf 1996). These ties are manifested in migrants serving as a source of information, aiding in the assimilation of other migrants, and attempting to reunite their families abroad (Waldorf et al. 1990). The network induced interdependencies between immigrant stocks and flows lead to the attraction of additional immigrants. Since these social ties require the existence of an immigrant community abroad, network effects play a role in the *perpetuation* of international migration flows, as opposed to their initiation (Massey et al. 1993, Martin and Widgren 1996). Social networks thus become the catalyst for the internal dynamic of international migration systems. Moreover, as a corollary, the conceptual framework also suggests that international migration may continue even if economic incentives of migration diminish.

While theoretical and empirical studies have long recognized the importance of network effects on the movement from origin to destination countries, network effects have not received adequate attention in the study of international return migration. Instead, the literature by large ignored the return of migrants and often erroneously assumed that the return is motivated by economic factors similar to those motivating immigration. An example of this line of reasoning is expressed by Blejer and Goldberg (1980) who, in human capital parlance, describe return migration as a correction of an initial investment decision. However, several studies find that economic considerations such as the economic well-being of the origin country does not affect immigrants' return migration propensities (King et al. 1985; Waldorf and Esparza 1991). Waldorf and Esparza (1991) particularly stress the importance of immigrants' assimilation in accounting for variations in return migration propensities, and the assimilation ability is strongly influenced by the social network provided through the immigrant community. Thus, networks of social ties also affect the retention of immigrants already living abroad and thus serve to promote immigrants' permanency abroad. In particular, recent immigrants rely on the adaptive functions of the network (Gurak and Caces 1992) that deal with short term assistance in housing and employment search provided through the already established immigrant community. At the same time, recent immigrants are less capable of contributing to the adaptive functions of the social network, thereby diminishing the network effectiveness. A large proportion of returnees can thus be interpreted as a failure of the social network in providing these adaptive functions. A return migration may be a deliberate step in a lifetime savings-consumption plan. These linkages between the immigrant community and the flow of returnees have substantial impacts on the self-perpetuating dynamic of the international migration system. Return migration has an influence on the size and composition of the immigrant stock, and thus affects its attraction potential for future immigration flows. At the same time, the stock characteristics also influence the effectiveness of the network in promoting immigrants' permanence abroad.

The influence of the social network on attracting and retaining immigrants clearly has a regional dimension. It results from the fact that the immigrant stock is not uniformly distributed throughout the destination country. Instead, the regional distribution of immigrants is characterized by migrant clusters, leading to regional disparities in the network's effectiveness, the attraction of future immigrants and the return of immigrants. Moreover, the regional unevenness of the network not only influences and is affected by movements across international boundaries, but also affects and is influenced by immigrants' interregional relocations within the destination country.

Empirical studies of the interrregional redistribution of immigrants within the destination country show that there are distinct differences between immigrants' redistribution and that of the native born population. Compared to the native born population recent immigrants not only have a greater propensity to move (Travato 1988) but also a greater propensity to move over longer distances (Belanger and Rogers 1991). Moreover, the literature also suggests that these differences may be the result of network effects that govern not only who moves but also where immigrants will relocate within the destination country. For example, immigrants' propensity to make an interregional move is influenced by the extent of social ties within the region. In particular, it has been shown that the probability of not making an interregional move and instead staying in a particular region, depends on the size of the immigrant stock in that region (Kritz and Nogle 1994). For foreign born persons in the United States, Kritz and Nogle's research shows that nativity concentration deters interstate migration and they suggest that social capital that is derived from the proximity to the immigrant community is more influential than human capital variables or economic conditions.

For immigrants who do migrate to another region, the existence of a sizable immigrant community in the destination region becomes an important pull factor (Walker and Hannan 1989). The immigrant community within a particular region not only provides important social ties and network functions, but also represents the economic opportunities available to the immigrant population. For example, if immigrants are constrained to certain sectors of the labour market --for example, the secondary sector in a dual labour market system-- then the size of the immigrant population in the destination region is a proxy for the magnitude of this sector.

It is argued that immigrants' regional distribution and redistribution is the important yet frequently neglected component of the international migration system. It is at the regional (or subregional) level that the economic implications of large scale immigration are felt even if the locational choice is primarily influenced by social network factors rather than economic factors. For example, ethnic concentrations that emerge and persist through the distribution and redistribution of immigrants are crucial to the discussion of the effects of immigrant concentrations on income and employment opportunities of native born (Walker 1992; Frey 1995a, 1995b). The basic argument of this discussion states that immigrants may act as substitutes or complements of the native born labour force. If immigrants act as substitutes, then they diminish employment opportunities for native born and suppress wages because of increased labour supply. One possible behavioral response of the native born labour force is to leave the region and find employment elsewhere. Alternatively, if immigrants act as complements then the increased labour supply will affect neither employment opportunities nor wages of the native born labour force. In this case, the availability of the immigrant labour force may actually enhance employment opportunities for native born and thus lead to additional (internal) inmigration.

The model presented in the following section therefore integrates the regional distribution and redistribution of immigrants with the international movements and focuses on the network effects that lead to the internal self-perpetuating dynamic of the system and foster the emergence and persistence of regional immigrant clusters. From a modelling point of view, the network perspective of the perpetuation of international migration draws attention to the internal dynamic resulting from the complex relationships between immigrant stock and immigrant flows. This internal dynamic is overlooked in the more traditional neoclassical modelling approaches which focus exclusively on external factors, mostly economic push and pull factors, and their impact on the temporal variations in the magnitude and composition of international migration flows.

13.2 The Model

Past research has, by and large, focused separately on the different components in the international-interregional migration system. For example, there are countless studies of the flows from origin to destination countries. However, these studies tend to ignore variations in the initial locational choices of immigrants. The destination is specified either as the entire country or as a specific region within the destination country. More recently, there has also been an intensification in the study of international return migration (King et al. 1985; Petras and Kousis 1988; Bailey and Ellis 1993; Waldorf 1995). But again, variations in return migration typically are not linked to the regions within the destination country from which migrants return home. Finally, the interregional migration component of international migration has also received some attention in the literature. For example, Newbold (1996) analyses the interregional redistribution of immigrants in Canada but without explicitly addressing the immigration and return migration components. There are also a number of studies on the regional distribution of immigrants in destination countries which are the composite outcomes of immigration, return and regional redistribution (e.g., O'Loughlin 1985; Giese 1978).

The mixed international-interregional migration model presented in this chapter simultaneously links these different components of the migration system. First, the emigration component captures the movements from an origin country into a destination country. Second, the interregional migration component focuses on immigrants' regional redistributions within the destination country. The third component consists of immigrants' return into the origin country. The model is cognizant of network effects and their influence on the size and composition of migration flows in and out of the destination country as well as the emergence and perpetuation of migrant clusters at regional levels. Viewed from a micro-level perspective, the model links sequential moves of immigrants' migration histories including emigration, interregional moves and repatriation. Viewed from a macro level perspective, the model captures the regional distribution and redistribution of the foreign-born population and thereby allows to evaluate the economic, social and political consequences of aggregate outcomes of individual decisions.

Each component of the system is captured in a transition probability that is responsive to the underlying component-specific behavioural mechanisms. The transition probabilities are integrated in a stochastic matrix that allows to evaluate the redistribution potential of the international-interregional migration system. In the presence of network effects, the redistribution potential will not lead to a neutral migration process as defined by Liaw (1990), and thus will affect regional economic disparities within the destination country. The presentation of the model will begin by introducing the stochastic transition matrix that links the three components of the international-interregional migration system, and then proceed by specifying the transition probabilities for each component.

13.2.1 The Transition Matrix

Assuming an origin country, 0, and a destination country divided into k=1,...,n regions, a stochastic matrix T of transition probabilities[1] t_{kj} (k, j = 0,1,...,n) summarizes the migration propensity of an individual at risk of migrating from location k to j during a fixed period of time.

Destination Regions

	Origin 0	**1**	**2**	**.....**	**j**	**...**	**n**
Origin 0	t_{00}	t_{01}	t_{02}		t_{0j}		t_{0b}
1	t_{10}	t_{11}	t_{12}		t_{1j}		t_{1n}
2	t_{20}	t_{21}	t_{22}		t_{2j}		t_{2n}
.							
.							
k	t_{k0}	t_{k0}	t_{k2}		t_{kj}		t_{kn}
.							
.							
n	t_{n0}	t_{n1}	t_{n2}		t_{nj}		t_{nn}

The transition probabilities in the diagonal denote the probabilities of staying in the current location: t_{00} indicates the probability that a person living in the origin country will not emigrate during the time interval while t_{kk}, k=1,..., n are the probabilities that an immigrant living in region k will remain in region k. The emigration probabilities t_{0j} (j=1,...,k) are located in the first row. The return migration probabilities from region k back to the origin, t_{k0} (k=1,...,n), are in the first column. All other entries t_{kj} (k,j = 1,...,n) describe the probability of moving from region k to region j.

The specification of transition probabilities is at the very core of the model. Since the migration system consists of three different types of migration (i.e., emigration, interregional migration and return migration), the transition probabilities of each component need to be responsive to the respective underlying behavioural mechanisms. This precludes the use of a generic formula for the transition probabilities. Moreover, the network theoretical perspective further precludes the use of time-invariant or fixed transition probabilities (Rogers 1990). Fixed transition rates are irresponsive to the network-induced connections between immigrant stock and immigrant flow because they ignore the influence of changing population sizes in the destinations on people's migration propensity (Plane 1993; Rogerson 1984).

13.2.2 The Emigration Component

One of the dominant factors influencing emigration from an origin country to a destination country are network effects. The network refers to the social linkages among the immigrants abroad and the pool of potential migrants in the origin country. Its role is to attract additional migrants and to facilitate their assimilation in the destination society. In its most simple specification, the network effects may be portrayed by specifying the number of migrants as a function of the size of the immigrant stock abroad (Diamantides and Constantinou 1989, Massey et al. 1993; Waldorf et al. 1990; Waldorf 1996). That is:

$$M_0^{(t)}. = f(P^{(t)}), \tag{13.1}$$

where $M_0^{(t)}$ is the number of emigrants from origin 0 into the destination at time t, and $P^{(t)}$ is the size of the immigrant stock already living abroad at time t. Disaggregating the destination into separate regions k=1,...,n yields:

$$M_{0k}^{(t)} = f(P_k^{(t)}) \tag{13.2}$$

where $M_{0k}^{(t)}$ is the number of emigrants into region k of the destination country, and $P_k^{(t)}$ is the size of the immigrant stock already living in region k at time t. Consequently, the transition probabilities for the emigration component should not be fixed transition probabilities (Rogers 1990) but at the very least incorporate a destination-population weighted component as suggested by Plane (1993). Thus:

$$t_{ij}^{(t)} = \frac{t_{ij}^{(0)})P_j^{(t)}/P_j^{(0)}}{\sum_{k=0}^{n} t_{ik}^{(0)}P_k^{(t)}/P_k^{(0)}} \tag{13.3}$$

In this specification, the transition probabilities at time t are a function of the transition probabilities at time t=0, weighted by the ratio of destination populations at time t and t=0. The denominator ensures that the marginal row sums equal 1 as is required for a stochastic matrix. Note that the relevant population component is not the entire population of region k but only the immigrant population living in region k.

A second key element in the network theoretically founded definition of the emigration probabilities is length of the stay of the immigrant stock abroad. The length of stay has been identified as a key attribute in determining the strength of network linkages and thus the emigration propensities (Waldorf 1996). In particular, recent immigrants tend to have strong attachments to their home country and thus are expected to be particularly influential in attracting additional migrants through their reunification and information transfer potential (Waldorf et al. 1990, Waldorf 1996). This influence of newcomers can be incorporated via:

$$
t_{ij}^{(t)} = \frac{t_{ij}^{(0)} M_{0j}^{(t-1)} P_j^{(t)} / P_j^{(0)}}{\displaystyle\sum_{k=0}^{n} t_{ik}^{(0)} M_{0k}^{(t-1)} P_k^{(t)} / P_k^{(0)}}
$$

(13.4)

where $M_{0j}^{(t-1)}$ is the number of immigrants to region j during the previous time period t−1.

In a similar fashion, employment opportunities and other external factors can be incorporated into the specification of emigration probabilities. However, as the international migration system matures, these external factors lose their influence on emigration propensities and their role diminishes in light of the increasing strength of network effects (Waldorf 1996).

13.2.3 The Return Migration Component

International return migration is a poorly understood process that only recently received more attention in the literature (Zlotnik 1992; Waldorf and Esparza 1991; Waldorf 1995). Empirical studies indicate that return migration is not influenced by changing characteristics of the origin country (which becomes the destination of a returnee). In particular, the population size of the origin country, which is often seen as a proxy for the magnitude of opportunities, does not seem to be influential either in accounting for temporal variations in return migration propensities[2]. Consequently, a destination population weighted model seems to be inappropriate for the return migration component of the transition matrix.

Yet return migration rates are not constant over time (Glavac 1995) and these temporal variations are most likely the result of heterogeneities in the population at risk of returning (Waldorf 1996). Of pivotal importance are heterogeneities with respect to the duration of stay abroad. For example, Waldorf and Esparza (1991) have shown that return hazards of foreign workers in Germany tend to decrease as foreigners extend their sojourn abroad. Thus, the specification of transition probability for the return migration component must necessarily take into account the distribution of foreigners with respect to their length of stay abroad. As a general trend, we expect the transition probability for the return migration component to rise as the proportion of recent immigrants in the immigrant stock rises. From a network theoretical perspective this expectation is explained by the increased demand for support by newcomers who strongly rely on the adaptive functions of the network (Gurak and Caces 1992). To capture these compositional effects with respect to the duration of stay, the transition probabilities for the return migration component are specified as:[3]

$$
t_{k0}^{(t)} = q^{(t-1)} \frac{M_{0k}^{(t-1)}}{P_k^{(t)}} + q^{(t-2)} \frac{M_{0k}^{(t-2)}}{P_k^{(t)}} + \ldots + q^{(0)} \frac{M_{0k}^{(0)}}{P_k^{(t)}}
\tag{13.5}
$$

where $q^{(t-s)} \in (0,1)$ is a factor indicating the return migration propensity at time t of immigrants who arrived $t-s$ time periods ago. For $s > 1$, the factor $q^{(t-s)}$ rapidly converges to zero. Using this convergence to simplify $t_{k0}^{(t)}$ yields a formulation which also avoids accounting problems in the presence of interregional migration:

$$
t_0^{(t)} = q_r \frac{M_{0k}^{(t-1)}}{P_k^{(t)}} + q_1 \frac{P_k^{(t)} - M_{0k}^{(t-1)}}{P_k^{(t)}}
\tag{13.6}
$$

where q_r is the return migration propensity of recent immigrants and q_1 is the return migration propensity of long term immigrants, and $q_r > q_1$.

13.2.4 The Interregional Migration Component

Once immigrants have chosen their initial location, they are not only at risk of returning to one of the regions in their home country, but can also migrate to another region within the destination country, thereby affecting the regional distribution of the foreign-born population. The immigrants' propensity to make such an interregional move is influenced by the extent of social ties within the region. In particular, it has been shown that the probability, t_{jj}, of staying in region j, depends on the size of the immigrant stock in j (Kritz and Nogle 1994). For immigrants who do migrate to another region, the immigrant community in the destination region becomes important in that it not only provides important social ties and network functions, but also represent the economic opportunities available to the immigrant population. In addition, I suggest that the transition probabilities include a factor that relates the immigrant population to the native-born population. This factor allows us to assess the degree to which additional immigrants can be absorbed into the destination region. For example, if the proportion of the immigrant population increases beyond a threshold, then the degree to which additional immigrants are welcome or can be absorbed will decline. This specification is consistent with spillover effects and diffusion that have been established in the context of foreign-born persons in Germany (Giese 1978; O'Loughlin 1985).

Mathematically, the conceptualization is akin to the density dampened destination-population weighted model suggested by Plane (1993). However, density is defined as the 'density' or ratio of the immigrant population relative to the native population. This adds a new dimension to the migration dynamics because the denominator of the 'density' is no longer constant but depends on the interregional migration behaviour of the native population. Thus, for the interregional migration probabilities we obtain:

$$
t_{ij}^{(t)} = \frac{t_{ij}^{(0)} Q_{ij}^{(t)} P_j^{(t)} / P_j^{(0)}}{\sum_{k-0}^{n} t_{ik}^{(0)} Q_{ik}^{(t)} P_k^{(t)} / P_k^{(0)}}
$$

(13.7)

where $Q_{ij}^{(t)}$ is defined via the ratios of immigrant to native population in the respective regions $D_i^{(t)}$ and $D_j^{(t)}$:

$$
Q_{ij}^{(t)} = \begin{cases} q D_j^{(t)} / D_i^{(t)} & \text{if } D_i^{(t)} / D_j^{(t)} > q \\ 1 & \text{if } D_i^{(t)} / D_j^{(t)} \in [1/q, q] \\ D_j^{(t)} / q D_i^{(t)} & \text{if } D_i^{(t)} / D_j^{(t)} < 1/q, \end{cases}
$$

(13.8)

where $D_j^{(t)} = P_j^{(t)} / N_j^{(t)}$, P and N represent the immigrant and native population respectively, and q is a threshold factor.

If the transition probabilities are defined as in Equation (13.7), then the sum of the interregional transition probabilities from region j to all destination regions k (k=1,...,n) will sum to 1. However, in order to ensure that the transition matrix T is a stochastic matrix, the sum must equal the return migration probability t_{j0} as defined in Section 13.2.1. Thus, each t_{jk} must be multiplied by a factor of $(1 - t_{j0})$.

Equation (13.7) implicitly assumes that changes in the regional distribution of the native population are exogenous. However, recent research has found evidence that the migration behaviour of the native population may be strongly influenced by the distribution of the immigrant population (White and Imai 1994, Walker, Ellis and Barff 1992). In the extreme case, this dependence takes the form of internal migration flight due to the presence of immigrants (Frey 1995a, 1995b).

Incorporating such interdependencies into the model requires a specification of transition probabilities for the native population which are dependent on the distribution of the immigrant population. Let S =

331

$\{s_{kj}, k,j=1,...,n\}$ define the transition probability matrix that characterizes the interregional migration process of the native-born population. Then s_{kj} may be defined in a similar fashion as t_{kj} except that the destination population weight is defined by the total population (as a proxy for economic opportunities) and the threshold factor q is likely to be different for the native-born than the immigrant population. Thus, in the case of interregional migrations, the process pattern inter-dependencies gain in complexity as the process characterizing the immigrant redistributions are not only affected by the locational pattern of immigrants abroad but also by the simultaneously changing pattern of native-born population.

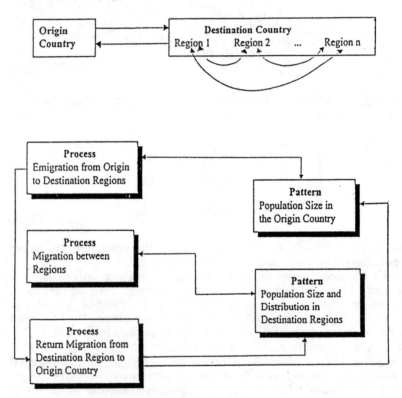

Figure 13.1 Pattern-process relationships in an international-interregional migration system

13.3 Summary and Conclusion

International migration is a complex phenomenon that not only has global but also smaller scale regional implications. This chapter alludes to the importance of analytically integrating the various components of the international migration system, i.e. the initial movement from the origin country to a region within the destination country, the interregional redistribution, and the ultimate return to the home country.[4] It also emphasizes the need to look at the internal, self-perpetuating dynamic of the system that is created by the network effects influencing immigrants' movements in space. Figure 13.1 summarizes the network induced complex relationships between the immigrant stock abroad, unevenly distributed over the regions of the destination country, and immigrants' migration flows across international boundaries and within the destination country. It is important to note that these relationships suggest that the redistribution potential of the international-interregional migration system is not a neutral migration process (Liaw 1990) but has a substantial impact on the relative population distributions, both at the international and interregional scales. Furthermore, the model also suggests that although non-economic factors, in particular social ties, drive the internal dynamic of the system, the resulting patterns of migrant clusters, potentially have strong economic implications such as the employment impact for the native born population in the receiving country.

References

Bailey, A. and Ellis, M. (1993), 'Going Home: The Migration of Puerto Rican-born Women from the United States to Puerto Rico', *The Professional Geographer*, Vol. 45, pp. 148–58.

Belanger, A. and Rogers, A. (1991), 'The Internal Migration and Spatial Redistribution of the Foreign Born Population in the United States: 1965-70 and 1975-80', *International Migration Review*, vol. 26, pp. 1342–69.

Blejer, M.I. and Goldberg, I. (1980), 'Return Migration – Expectations versus Reality: A Case Study of Western Immigrants to Israel', *Research in Population Economics*, vol. 2, pp. 433–49.

Castles, S. and Miller, M.J. (1993), *The Age of Migration: International Population Movements in the Modern World*, Guilford Press, New York.

Diamantides, N.D. and Constantinou, S.T. (1989), 'Modeling the Macrodynamics of International Migration: Determinants of Emigration from Cyprus, 1946–85', *Environment and Planning A*, vol. 21, pp. 927–50.

Frey, W. (1995a), 'Immigration and Internal "Flight" from U.S. Metropolitan Areas: Toward a New Demographic Balkanization', *Urban Studies*, vol. 32, pp. 733–57.

Frey, W. (1995b), 'Immigration and Internal Migration "Flight": A California Case Study', *Population and Environment*, vol. 16, pp. 353–75.

Giese, E. (1978), 'Räumliche Diffusion ausländischer Arbeitnehmer in der Bundesrepublik Deutschland', *Die Erde*, vol. 109, pp. 92–100.

Glavac, S. (1995), *Return Migration from Australia*, MA Thesis, University of Queensland, Australia.

Gurac, D.T. and Caces, F. (1992), 'Migration Networks and the Shaping of Migration Systems', in Kritz, M.M., Lim, L.L. and H. Zlotnik (eds), *International Migration Systems*, Oxford University Press, Oxford, pp. 150–76.

King, R., Strachan, A. and Martimer, J. (1985), 'The Urban Dimension of European Return Migration: The Case of Bari, Southern Italy', *Urban Studies*, vol. 22, pp. 214–35.

Kritz, M.M. and Nogle, J.M. (1994), 'Nativity Concentration and Internal Migration among the Foreign-Born', *Demography*, vol. 31, No. 3, pp. 509–24.

Liaw, K.-L. (1990), 'Neutral Migration Process and its Application to an Analysis of Canadian Migration Data', *Environment and Planning A*, vol. 22, pp. 333–43.

Martin, P. and Widgren, J. (1996), 'International Migration: A Global Challenge', *Population Bulletin*, vol. 51, no. 1, Population Reference Bureau, Inc., Washington, DC.

Massey, D. Arango, J. Hugo, G., Kouaouci, A., Pellegrino, A. and Taylor, J.E. (1993), 'Theories of International Migration: A Review and Appraisal', *Population and Development Review*, vol. 19, pp. 431–66.

O'Loughlin, J. (1985), 'The Geographic Distribution of Foreigners in West Germany', *Regional Studies*, vol. 19, pp. 365–77.

Petras, E. and Kousis, M. (1988), 'Returning Migrant Characteristics and Labor Market Demand in Greece', *International Migration Review*, vol. 22, pp. 586–608.

Plane, D.A. (1993), 'Requiem for the Fixed-Transition-Probability Migrant', *Geographical Analysis*, vol. 25, pp. 211–23.

Rogers, A. (1990), 'Requiem for the Net Migrant', *Geographical Analysis*, vol. 22, pp. 283–300.

Rogerson, P. (1984), 'New Directions in the Modelling of Interregional Migration', *Economic Geography*, vol. 60, pp. 111–21.

Schaeffer, P. (1991), 'Guests who Stay', *Geographical Analysis*, vol. 23, pp. 247–60.

Travato, F. (1988), 'The Interurban Mobility of the Foreign Born in Canada', *International Migration Review*, vol. 22, pp. 59–86.

Waldorf, B. (1995), 'Determinants of International Return Migration Intentions', *The Professional Geographer*, vol. 47, pp. 125–36.

Waldorf, B. (1996), 'The Internal Dynamic of International Migration Systems', *Environment and Planning A*, vol. 28, pp. 631–50.

Waldorf, B., Esparza, A. and Huff, J. (1990), 'A Behavioral Model of International Labor and Nonlabor Migration: The Case of Turkish Movements to West Germany, 1960-1986', *Environment and Planning A*, vol. 22, pp. 961–73.

Waldorf, B. and Esparza, A. (1991), 'A Parametric Failure Model of International Return Migration', *Papers in Regional Science*, vol. 70, pp. 419–38.

Walker, R. and Hannan, M. (1989), 'Dynamic Settlement Processes: The Case of U.S. Immigration' *The Professional Geographer*, vol. 41, pp. 172–82.

Walker, R., Ellis, M. and Barff, R. (1992.), 'Linked Migration Systems: Immigration and Internal Labor Flows in the United States', *Economic Geography,* vol. 68, pp. 234–48.

White, M.J. and Imai, Y. (1994), 'The Impact of U.S. Immigration upon Internal Migration', *Population and Environment,* vol. 15, pp. 189–210.

Zlotnik, H. (1992), 'Empirical Identification of International Migration Systems', in Kritz, M.M., Lim, L.L. and H. Zlotnik (eds), *International Migration Systems,* Oxford University Press, Oxford, pp. 19–40.

Notes

1. Similar model formulations have also been used to link international migration with mobility between labour markets rather than regions (see Schaeffer 1991).

2. This seems to hold true at least at the national scale where the number of returnees relative to the population size in the origin will always be very small independently of how many emigrants decide to return home. There may be such an effect on a smaller scale, say e.g. at the village/town or county level but this has not been established empirically.

3. This formulation is acceptable as long as interregional migration is nonexistent. If we allow interregional migration then the immigrant stock of duration t-s residing in region k at time t includes persons who originally emigrated to other regions at time t-s but are in region k at time t due to interregional migration (this may include one or more moves).

4. This does not need to be the last move in the entire migration path of an individual.

14 An Explanatory Analysis of International Migration Flows Within the European Economic Area

LEO VAN WISSEN AND HARRIE VISSER

14.1 Introduction

In many European countries international migration is now the most important component of population change; in a large number of countries within the European Economic Area[1] net migration accounts for more than 50 percent of total population increase in recent years (Salt and Singleton, 1995). In the period from 1985 to 1993 the total number of immigrants into the EEA countries increased from 0.9 million to 2.6 million persons (ICMPD, 1994). These people are not only registered immigrants; the number of asylum seekers, displaced persons from former Yugoslavia and illegal immigrants constituted in 1993 almost 50 percent of the total inflow into the EEA.

Although the causes of international migration in general are well studied and there is agreement with regard to the most important factors determining the migration flows between countries, until now there has been hardly any attempt to link these theoretical considerations with empirical data on international migration flows. The limited use of migration flow data is partly due to the problem of measuring international migration. The measurement of international migration is problematic for various reasons. First, data are not consistent between countries. Flows between countries are usually recorded both by the sending and the receiving country, but these figures are often inconsistent. Second, there is no agreement among countries over the proper definition of a migrant. Third, not all immigration is registered. Especially illegal immigration is hard to measure. Consequently, a consistent system of international migration statistics has been lacking until now. Only recently, attempts are being made in this direction; a process that involves both methodological (Poulain 1991; Willekens 1994) and technical (Rierink 1995) inputs.

Traditionally, demographers study net migration of countries. However, this view of the process is too limited and denies the inherent dynamic nature of migration, whereby different causes may be responsible for migration flows in opposite directions between any pair of countries. An explanatory analysis of migration should focus on the

337

level of migration flow, since at this level the amount of information contained in the covarying variables is maximized. Therefore, at the level of the migration flows between countries the factors influencing the size and direction of the migration flows can be studied adequately. In this chapter we will use migration flow data in combination with macro data on the national level to test some of the common assumptions regarding the causes of international migration.

Explanatory analysis is a useful step towards better projection models of migration. In principle knowledge of covarying exogenous variables may be used in conditional forecasting and scenarios of migration. Up to now, international migration projections are largely based on implicit or qualitative assumptions, or simply trend extrapolation. A second goal of this chapter is therefore to assess the predictive value of a migration model that is based on exogenous variables.

For this test we use a statistical model of migration flow data and a set of explanatory key variables derived from an overview of the main determinants of international migration, as described in Section 14.2, 14.3 and 14.4. Section 14.2 provides a general background to international migration theories, whereas Section 14.3 describes the main determining factors itself. Section 14.4 gives an overview of the data that are used for the model. The model itself is a spatial interaction model derived from the Poisson distribution. Although it is well known that the Poisson distribution is not appropriate for flow data of this type, a statistical model may be formulated that retains many attractive features of the Poisson model. This is described in Section 14.5. The empirical results are discussed in Section 14.6. Finally, Section 14.7 presents the main conclusions.

14.2   Determinants of Migration

Migration flows, or more generally spatial interaction phenomena may be decomposed into three types of factors, viz. (1) push factors that generate a flow of interaction out of the origin regions; (2) pull factors, that attract interaction into the destination region, and (3) interaction factors, that cause certain destinations to be more attractive than others, starting from certain origins, but not from others. To explain the origin of migration and its continuation over time, several theories have been developed. For a more detailed overview see Massey et al. (1993). From these theories it can be deduced that disparities between locations, information flows between locations, networks in and distance between locations are important factors at play. The push factors disperse migrants without a specific direction and are responsible for the so called migration pressure from within an area. Pull factors work in the area of destination and give a direction to the migration movement. Pull factors can be defined as those factors that migrants perceive to be better in the receiving area than in the area of origin.

338

Push and pull factors are related. Emigration is always defined with reference to the boundary of the region. The larger the region, the smaller the emigration rate, simply because the probability of finding a destination within the same region increases with size. Therefore, if the pull factors of the region become more important, more moves originating in the region will again be attracted to the same region. Thus, increasing pull factors may be associated with decreasing push factors.

Distance, in terms of financial, physical and psychological costs, is a factor which is the link between push and pull forces. The greater the distance, the less likely migration is to take place, and the more likely migration flows will be directed towards less 'costly' destinations where benefits are expected. Distance can be bridged by access to transport, communication and networks.

Information is necessary to base the migration decision on. Information is received through media and networks. With the globalization of the information channels and the expansion of networks, migrants can be well informed about countries of destination.

People tend to make decisions which contribute to their well-being. Since security is one of the basic needs to be fulfilled, any move which might increase insecurity will be avoided. However the insecurity of migration can be reduced by the existence of friends and/or family members at the place of destination, and by moving to those places where the (need for) adaption to languages and customs will be minimal.

Alternatively, the factors explaining international migration flows may be divided in three categories, viz. (1) economic factors, (2) social networks of migrants, and (3) political factors. Economic factors and social networks are the main determinants of migration within the EEA. Political and environmental events are hardly a motivation for people to move from one EEA member country to the other. Indirectly though, political factors may have an impact on international migration within the EEA. Treaties like the European Convention for the protection of Human Rights and Fundamental Freedoms, the Treaty of free movement for EU nationals, and more recently the Schengen Agreement, make it possible for EEA nationals to move relatively freely between countries. Therefore it can be concluded that EEA nationals are able to migrate to those destinations where they expect the maximum advantage of their migration move. In addition, the structural funds of the Economic Union are aimed at increasing the economic development of poorer regions within the Community. If economic differences are important, as will be hypothesized below, then political factors should have a decreasing effect on international migration. However, testing this hypothesis is outside the scope of this chapter. Instead, attention will be focused on economic and network explanations of international migration within the EEA.

14.3   Factors Explaining Recent Migration Patterns within the European Economic Area

Push and pull factors generate different types of migrants. Political turmoil for example can generate refugees, while poverty and unemployment can generate labour migrants. Within the European Economic Area (EEA) mainly labour migration and migration related to family formation/reunification can be distinguished. They will be discussed briefly below.

14.3.1 Economic Circumstances

Relative poverty induces economically motivated migration. The size of the flow of economically motivated migration is amongst others a function of the difference in wealth (wage and employment) between countries. The greater this difference the greater the relative attractiveness, the greater the motivation for people to migrate. Within the EEA the existence of large emigrant groups (Greeks and Italians in Germany, Spaniards and Portuguese in France, and Irish in the UK for example), can be explained by economic differences between countries.

Employment opportunities and wage levels are important factors which play a role in the migration decision process, and explain migration patterns between the more advanced economies in the north (which experience a positive net migration) and the less advanced economies in the south (which experience a negative net migration).

Although the OECD foresees a moderate economic growth in the years to come, this does not necessarily mean that employment will rise. In Germany, France and the United Kingdom for example, GDP doubled since 1960, while employment decreased. The cause of high unemployment in Europe can be attributed to the lack of incentives for employers to offer employment and the insufficient incentives for employees to accept jobs that are offered. Heavy taxation make it attractive for employers to substitute capital for labour, while post-income transfers cause the differences between workers and non-workers salaries to be too small (OECD 1994). Depending on government policies, economic growth can therefore result in an increase or decrease of employment.

Economic changes in the 1980s seem to have coincided with changes in mobility within the EEA. In the first half of the 1980s, economic stagnation and increasing unemployment could be observed in conjunction with a decrease in immigration from other EEA members in most countries in North-West Europe (Belgium, Denmark, Germany, Luxembourg, the Netherlands, the United Kingdom, Finland, Iceland, Norway and Sweden) . During the second half of the 1980s, a period in which in general the economy recovered, the same countries experienced an increasing immigration (see Figure 14.1). For Germany similar developments could also be observed during and after the oil crisis at the beginning of the 1970s.

340

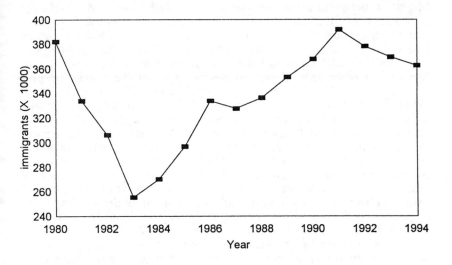

Figure 14.1 Total immigration from EEA countries into North-West Europe in 1992 (B, D, DK, L, NL, UK, FIN, IS, N, S)

Source: Eurostat. 1994b.

Visser (1995) analysed the relation between international migration and unemployment using Dutch data. He found that the unemployment rate in The Netherlands in the period 1980-1994 was negatively correlated with the level of immigration to The Netherlands from various countries in North West Europe. However, economic variables of the country of origin were not taken into account in this analysis. Therefore, differences in economic opportunities were not tested for significance. Heijke (1986) on the other hand, studied the size of different mediterranean populations in northwestern European countries and found significant effects of wage differentials, employment size in the destination country and the size of the potential labour supply in the origin country, using simple regression.

Although the increase in mobility can be explained by the creation of employment – the unemployment rates decreased in most of the EEA countries during the second half of the 1980s – also the general improvement of incomes and better access to information and easier (or even the abolishment of) entry regulations are some additional explanations for the increasing mobility within the EEA.

341

14.3.2 Networks

Migration networks consist of spatially dispersed persons who exchange information or funds (remittances). Networks provide potential migrants with the necessary information on which the migration decision can be based. The existence of networks furthermore reduces the psychological costs, the financial costs and the risks to migrate, since some mental, financial or other form of support can be expected. Networks also play a role in family formation and reunification. The availability of networks therefore makes it easier to decide to migrate, thereby reducing the importance of economic advantages of a country. Networks grow as each new immigrant will have relations with persons in the country of origin and therefore networks can contribute to the continuation and increase of migration flows. Through networks, potential migrants get informed about the situation in the place of destination. Networks are important because they fulfil to a certain extent cultural and societal needs, like mutual understanding with respect to customs, values, norms, religion and language. Also the availability of shops with special (culture based) products, and cultural activities organised by the local community are for many a reason to stay in the proximity of the 'own group'. Networks furthermore assist in the search for jobs and housing.

Some of these hypotheses may be tested using data on migration flows between countries within the EEA. More specifically, we may expect the following relations to hold in empirical research of international migration flows:

Economic hypotheses:
- migration flows increase the larger the difference in real wage level is between country of destination and country of origin
- migration flows increase the larger the difference in unemployment rates is between country of origin and country of destination

Social network hypotheses:
- migration flows increase with the size of the migrant population related to the country of origin who live in the country of destination
- migration flows increase with the size of the migrant population related to the country of destination who live in the country of origin
- migration flows decrease with increasing distance between the country of origin and country of destination
- migration flows are larger between countries that share a common language

These hypotheses will be tested using an explanatory model of international migration. First, the data will be presented. Next, the statistical model is described in some detail.

14.4 Data on International Migration

Theoretically, for each pair of countries, the sum of the total net migration between both countries should equal zero. In practice however, despite international attempts to harmonize the registration and definitions of migrants (Eurostat, 1994a) definitions and observations with respect to migration differ between the EEA countries, and consequently consistency in international migration statistics is often not achieved. Moreover, many countries do not register migration of EEA nationals. Therefore, not all international migration flows between all countries within the EEA are taken into account, but only those flows where definition and measurement problems are minimal.

Basically, the input for the migration model are the known immigration figures (by country of previous residence) for the countries Denmark, Germany, Ireland, the Netherlands, the United Kingdom, Finland, Iceland, Norway and Sweden (Eurostat, 1994 b). For the United Kingdom immigration from Ireland was not available, therefore emigration from Ireland to the UK was taken instead. Immigration data for Greece, Spain and Portugal were available, but not used because they were much lower than the corresponding emigration data of Denmark, Germany, Ireland, the Netherlands, the United Kingdom, Finland, Iceland, Norway and Sweden to Greece, Spain and Portugal suggested. Immigration data for Greece, Spain and Portugal as well as for the countries Belgium, France, Italy, Luxembourg and Austria were therefore derived from the emigration data of the countries Denmark, Germany, Ireland, the Netherlands, the United Kingdom, Finland, Norway and Sweden. This yielded a data set of 165 observations. Lichtenstein was left out because of lack of data. Iceland was also not included due to its isolated location and the resulting problems of measuring the distance friction. It should be noted that the observed immigration into the United Kingdom from Germany could be too high because returning military could in the UK be registered as immigrants, while in Germany they are not counted as emigrants. It should also be noted that migration within the EEA area not only consists of EEA nationals. Also non-EEA nationals will constitute a part of the migration stock, though data is scarce. It can be assumed that non-EEA members will not as easily migrate within the area as EEA members, since for non-EEA nationals the immigration policies are more strict. Their share in the total migration within the EEA most probably will be small.

The explanatory variables used in the model are listed below and summarized in Table 14.1:
- population size of the receiving country
- population size of the sending country
- the number of foreigners (of the nationality of the sending country) in the receiving country
- the number of foreigners (of nationality of receiving country) in the sending country

- distance between sending and receiving country
- difference in GDP between receiving and sending country
- differences in unemployment percentages
- difference in language, defined in four large language groups, between receiving and sending country

Population size of the country of origin gives an indication of potential movers, while population size of the country of destination is an indicator of available opportunities. The size of foreign groups is supposed to be a measure for networks, but it is known that it also reflects the impact of past socioeconomic developments on migration, which are fairly constant over time (Jones 1990).

Distance is an indication for the costs involved (financially) and for the familiarity one has with other countries and cultures. It may be measured in different ways, each with its special merits and drawbacks. In order to test for the possible limitations of one measure, two alternative scales were used here. Primarily, distance is measured along a straight line between the capital cities, in millimeters on a map, scale 1:15 million. Alternatively a dummy variable was defined with values 1 if the two countries share a common border, and 0 if not. Both variables were tried separately and in combination.

Differences in GDP per capita are an indication for the extra economic benefits which can be obtained in the place of destination, while unemployment percentages in the place of origin and destination form an indication for the possibilities to obtain these extra benefits.

Difference in language gives an indication to what extent a destination differs in culture, and to what extent efforts to adapt oneself are necessary. The variable language was introduced as a dummy variable. For each pair of countries the value is 0 if both countries fall within the same language group and 1 otherwise. Four language groups were used: Roman, German, Finnish and Celtic.

14.5 The Statistical Model

The analysis of spatial interaction flows has a long tradition that goes back to Ravenstein's (1885) attempt to model the interaction between cities as a gravity model. The gravity model was reformulated as an entropy maximizing model by Wilson (1970). Willekens (1980, 1983) and Baxter (1984) showed that the estimates of the entropy maximizing model and the Poisson model for the analysis of contingency tables are equivalent. The Poisson model has some clear advantages since it is based on standard statistical theory and allows explicit hypothesis testing. However, the distribution of (international) migration flows is in general not Poisson. More specifically, the assumption that the mean and the variance of the distribution are equal, conditional on the density parameter of the process, is a very strong assumption which in general is not met by migration flow data. Typically the variance is much larger than the mean; this phenomenon is known as overdispersion.

There are various reasons for overdispersion in migration data. First, households, not individuals make migration decisions. De Jong (1985) estimated that this dependence among migrants increases the variance in migration flow data in The Netherlands with a factor between 2 and 3. Second, there is temporal and spatial dependence in migration decisions that should be taken into account (e.g. duration effects). Thirdly, migrants are a heterogeneous population. In principle many, but not all of these factors can be taken into account in a migration model. However, if they are not taken into account, in general spurious correlation will be present in the data, and the constancy of variance and mean is violated (see also Congdon 1993).

Fortunately, it turns out that the Poisson model provides consistent parameter estimates, even if the Poisson assumption is violated. There is one serious consequence of overdispersion when using the Poisson model. The standard errors of the estimated coefficients of the model are too small and statistical tests of the significance of specific variables are therefore not valid. In order to correct these standard errors of the estimates, two methods have been proposed (Davies and Guy 1987). The first model is called the overdispersion model, and introduces a mean/variance ratio other than 1; the second model does not require any assumption about the variance and is therefore called the generalized model. More details may be found in Davies and Guy (1987).

One may conjecture that the data used here are population data and that hence no statistical inference is necessary. However, we think there are sound reasons for using these data as one possible outcome of an underlying but unobserved population model. First, these data refer to one year. Sampling in a different year will yield other data that are another realization of the same population model. Second, migration flow data are subject to measurement error.

14.5.1 The Standard Poisson Model

The standard Poisson model is easy to use and has a number of attractive computational features not shared by other models. The Poisson model for spatial interaction flows may be written as:

$$\Pr(F_{ij} = k) = \frac{\lambda_{ij}^{k} \exp(-\lambda_{ij})}{k!}$$

(14.1)

and

$$\lambda_{ij} = \exp(x_{ij}^{T} \beta)$$

(14.2)

The variable F_{ij} is the migration flow of country i to country j, λ_{ij} is the intensity of the process, which may be expressed as a linear function of independent variables x_{ij} and parameters ß.

345

The essential feature of the Poisson model is that the mean and the variance of the function are identical:

$$E(F_{ij}) = \lambda_{ij} = var(F_{ij}) = \exp(x_{ij}^T \beta)$$ (14.3)

14.5.2 Relaxing the Mean/Variance Ratio Introducing a Dispersion Parameter

The simplest way to relax this assumption is to introduce a dispersion parameter θ^2 for the variance. Hence, in the so called overdispersion model the mean and variance are related through:

$$E(F_{ij}) = \lambda_{ij} = \exp(x_{ij}^T \beta) = var(F_{ij})/\theta^2$$ (14.4)

It turns out that the parameters of this model may be estimated consistently by standard Poisson regression, but that the standard errors from the Poisson regression model in this case are incorrect. Fortunately, these standard errors υ^* of the parameter estimates of this formulation are related to the Poisson standard errors υ as $\upsilon^* = \theta\upsilon$. The dispersion parameter θ may be estimated as:

$$\theta = \frac{1}{IJ-p} \sum_{i=1}^{I} \sum_{j=1}^{J} \frac{[F_{ij} - \text{estimate } F_{ij}]^2}{\text{estimate var } (F_{ij})}$$ (14.5)

where p is the number of parameters in the regression equation.

14.5.3 A More General Model without any Variance Assumption

The dispersion parameter introduces a relaxation of the stringent Poisson assumption, but may still be questioned on theoretical grounds. Specifically, it is assumed that the mean/variance ratio is independent of the explanatory variables. A more general approach is possible and based on the Poisson model with even less stringent assumptions. It may be shown, using pseudo-likelihood theory, that the Poisson regression model may be used for the estimation of the parameters ß under the single assumption that the mean of the process is correctly specified: $E(F_{ij}) = \exp(x^T_{ij} ß)$. No assumptions regarding the variance of the process are required. This more general model is very appropriate for modelling international migration flows. It is reasonable to assume that the log of the migration flows may be explained using a linear function. However, it is very difficult to make assumptions about the variance of the flows. Therefore, the pseudo-likelihood model is the preferred approach. The standard errors of the Poisson regression for this

346

pseudo-likelihood model are again not correct. In this case the relation with the Poisson standard errors does not reduce to a simple scale parameter θ, but is more complicated. Nevertheless, the computation can be done using simple matrix algebra. The standard errors of the parameters are estimated by the square root of the diagonal elements of the matrix $C=H^{-1}GH^{-1}$, where H is equal to $H=X^TXA$, the matrix A being diagonal with elements $a_{ii} = exp(x^T_{ii}\text{ ß})$ and G is equal to $G=X^T$ XB. B is also diagonal with elements $b_{ii} = \{F_{ii}- exp(x^T_{ii}\text{ ß})\}^2$. Additional details may be found in Davies and Guy (1987).

In the next section we will present results of the three models discussed here: the Poisson model, the overdispersion model and the generalized model.

14.6   Model Results

14.6.1 Model Specification

In Table 14.1 the variables used in the model estimation and described in Section 14.4 are listed and some summary descriptive statistics are given. The model is expressed in the form: $E(F_{ij}) = exp(x^T_{ij}\text{ ß})$. For all population variables and the number of foreigners as well as distance, a linear as well as a loglinear relationship was estimated. For all these variables except distance the logarithmic form performed superior. The other variables were expressed in their original form, which means that the migration flow F is related to these variables in an exponential relationship. The final specification of the model is therefore:

$$F_{ij} = \beta_0(POPD)^{\beta_1}(POPO)^{\beta_2}(FORD)^{\beta_3}(FORO)^{\beta_4}.$$

$$exp(\beta_5DIST+\beta_6UNEM+\beta_7GDP+\beta_8LANG) \qquad (14.6)$$

347

Table 14.1   Definition of explanatory variables

Mnemonic	Description	Mean	S.dev.
POPD	Population size of destination country (in 10^6 units)	22.79	25.08
POPO	Population size of origin country (in 10^6 units)	23.72	25.16
FORD	Number of foreigners of origin country in destination country (in 10^6 units)	0.02	0.08
FORO	Number of foreigners of destination country in origin country (in 10^6 units)	0.02	0.08
DIST	version 1: Straight line distance between countries (in 10^6 km units)	86.37	49.37
	version 2: Dummy variable denoting whether origin and destination country share a common border (1) or not (2)	0.13	0.34
UNEM	Difference in unemployment rate between destination and origin country: UNEMD - UNEMO	1.03	5.95
GDP	Difference in GDP per capita between destination and origin country: GDPD - GDPO	−0.92	8.49
LANG	Dummy variable denoting whether origin and destination country belong to the same language group (1) or not (0)	0.51	0.50

14.6.2 Estimation Results

Table 14.2 presents the estimation results of the three models. As described in the previous section, the Poisson regression gives consistent parameter estimates for all three models. The only difference is the estimation of the standard errors. When looking at these standard errors, the estimates for the overdispersion are much larger than for the standard Poisson model, and the results for the generalized model are equal to or up to a factor 2 as large as the results of the overdispersion model. For a number of variables, the results of the overdispersion model are quite close to the values found in the more difficult to calculate generalized model. For practical purposes, the simpler to calculate overdispersion model gives a reasonable estimate of the value of the standard error. In any case, the standard errors of the Poisson model should not be used. For interpretation of the significance we use the standard errors of the generalized model.

Turning first to the mass terms of the population size of the origin and the destination countries, we find that the parameter values are significant and that the population of the sending country is more important in determining the size of the flow than that of the receiving country. Note that the parameter values of the population variables POPO and POPD as well as those of the number of foreign people in

348

sending and receiving countries FORO and FORD may be interpreted as elasticities. The elasticity of POPO is 0.1952, which means that an increase of the size of the population of the sending country with one percent has the effect of increasing the size of the outflow with almost 0.20 percent. Similarly, an increase in the population size of the receiving country with one percent increases the size of the inflow with almost 0.16 percent.

In comparison with the population mass terms we find that the effect of the number of foreigners in sending and receiving countries is much stronger. In terms of elasticities the effect on the outflow of the size of the migrant population resident in the sending country (FORO) is 0.4461, and the corresponding result for the size of the migrant population living in the receiving country on the inflow is 0.4290. In other words, migration between pairs of countries is much more influenced by the composition of the population in terms of nationality than by the size of the population as such. The impact of nationality is more than twice as much as the impact of population size.

The distance effect, measured as straight line distance between capital cities is not significant and of the wrong sign, i.e. positive. Further investigation reveals that if the variables FORO or FORD are specified without logarithmic transformation the distance effect becomes significant and negative. The overall fit of the model reduces dramatically however. It appears that the effect of distance is eliminated when taking into account the composition of the population in terms of nationality. For instance, it is likely that neighbouring countries have a high percentage of each other's population, and therefore distance is redundant. As an alternative, the variable BORDER was used, but with similar results: it has a negative sign and is not significant.

Table 14.2 Estimation results for the three models

Variable	estimate	poisson s.e.	t-value	overdispersion s.e.	t-value	generalized s.e.	t-value
Popd	0.1583	0.0015	100.20	0.0392	4.03	0.0405	3.9086
Popo	0.1952	0.0016	119.81	0.0405	4.82	0.0383	5.0966
Ford	0.4290	0.0014	297.42	0.0358	11.97	0.0516	8.3140
Foro	0.4461	0.0014	308.46	0.0359	12.41	0.0403	11.0695
Dist	3.1660	0.4461	7.09	11.0800	0.29	18.000	0.1759
UNem	0.0088	0.0003	26.75	0.0082	1.08	0.0129	0.6822
Gdp	0.01098	0.0003	39.23	0.0069	1.58	0.0122	0.900
Lang	−0.0290	0.0037	−8.46	0.0853	−0.34	0.1549	−0.1872

Dispersion parameter	1			607			
Pearson χ^2	97531						
d.f.	158						

The economic variables are not significant at all: the difference in unemployment between receiving and sending country (UNEM) is even of the wrong sign. The difference in GDP is positive, as it should be, but insignificant. Apparently, the differences in these economic indicators between countries within the EEA countries do not trigger migration movements between countries. This contradicts the findings of Visser (1995), mentioned earlier, where the unemployment level of the receiving country proved significant as a regressor for migration flows into and out of The Netherlands. The results of the more elaborate model shows that when taking into account other variables as well and using an appropriate statistical model, this relationship vanishes. Investigation of these results show that there is some multicollinearity between the number of foreigners in sending and receiving country and unemployment differences. In order to assess the effect of this multicollinearity the variables FORO and FORD were removed from the regression. The coefficient of unemployment differences remains positive and insignificant, whereas the coefficient of the difference in GDP increases only little and remains insignificant.

Finally, the effect of language differences is insignificant and of the wrong sign. This result may be attributed to the same relationship; the effect could also be captured by the variables indicating past migration patterns.

14.6.3 Model Fit

Overall model fit (based on the estimates shown in Table 14.2) may be assessed in a number of ways. First, the difference between observed and predicted flows may be evaluated using the Pearson R^2 value. Another measure that is used frequently for interaction flow data is the root mean square error (RMSE), which is equal to

$$
RMSE = \sqrt{\frac{\sum_{i=1}^{I} \sum_{j=1}^{J} (O_{ij} - E_{ij})^2}{I \times J}} \tag{14.7}
$$

where O_{ij} is the observed flow between country i and j and E_{ij} is the estimated flow given the model. For interpretation purposes the relative measure $RMSE/\bar{O}$ is useful: the relative size of the RMSE value compared to the mean of the flows $\bar{O}$. These measures may be calculated for all flows (all valid pairs (i,j)), or for the total immigration or emigration separately, i.e. the marginal totals of the interaction matrix. In Table 14.3 the resulting fit values are given. The predictive value of the model with respect to migration flows between countries is 0.886. Although the R^2 value for the Poisson model has only a heuristic value, since the model is not linear and the R^2 is not used as the

350

optimization statistic, for practical purposes it can be said that 88 percent of the variance in the flows is 'explained' by the model. The RMSE of the predicted flows is 1790, which is 88 percent of the average migration flow. This indicates the order of magnitude of the relative error. Thus, at the level of the flows the average prediction error is in the order of magnitude of the mean flow level.

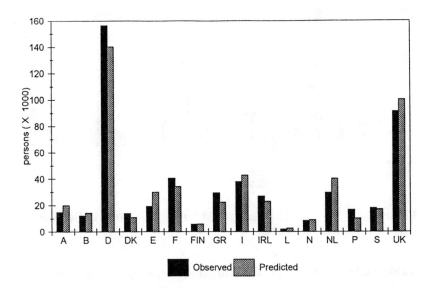

Figure 14.2 Observed and predicted outmigration from individual EEA countries

The results of the marginal totals of the migration matrix are better, however. Naturally individual errors at the flow level cancel out when aggregated over all destinations or all origins. The R^2 values are 0.968 and 0.986 for out- and immigration respectively, while the RMSE values are 6987 and 5062, or 21 and 15 percent of the average gross out- and inflow. Clearly, this indicates a reasonable fit. Total inflow is somewhat better predicted than total outflow. Finally, the predictive value of this approach for net migration, the difference between in- and outmigration, is very small: the R^2 value is only 0.112, and the relative error is 1.22. In other words, the predictive power of the chosen variables for net population change due to migration is not very high. It appears that the difference between the gross in- and outflow is not predictable in terms of size of the (foreign) population.

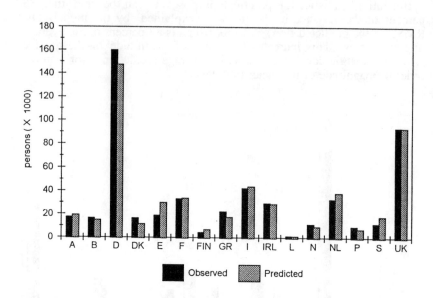

Figure 14.3 **Observed and predicted immigration into individual EEA countries**

Table 14.3 **Fit values for the estimated migration flow matrix**

Subtable:	R^2	RMSE	Mean Value	RMSE/$\overline{O}$
All flows	0.886	1790	2043	0.88
Emigration	0.968	1747	32691	0.21
Immigration	0.986	1266	32691	0.15
Net Migration	0.112	4408	3628*	1.22*

*Since the mean value of net migration is 0, here the mean absolute value of net migration was taken.

Table 14.4 Observed Origin-Destination matrix of international migration between EEA countries

Origin \ Destination	A	BK	D	DK	E	F	FIN	GR	I	IRL	L	N	NL	P	S	UK	Total
A			13975	145			19					64	347		155	250	14955
B			4445	484			41			250		152	4463		247	2000	12082
D	15692	4494		2741	10201	17214	242	17102	35405	1900	1074	730	10112	5655	901	33000	156463
DK	134	566	4104		797	1335	192	243	611	250	191	2289	423	135	1803	1000	14073
E			8952	1017			175			1300		484	1754		593	5000	19275
F			18715	1268			59			1700		618	2678		556	15000	40594
FIN	26	40	368	340	210	86		38	49		10	259	218	37	3073	1000	5754
GR			24599	243			58			250		52	837		391	3000	29430
I			32801	675			99			600		130	1253		265	2000	37823
IRL			6389	159									901			19400	26849
L			1132	151			18		250			35	172		55		1813
N	84	163	660	2343	414	451	201	84	104		16		296	54	2643	1000	8513
NL	343	6939	10444	606	1834	2321	50	417	922	250	231	385		549	257	4000	29548
P			10825	138			38			250		48	1258		101	4000	16658
S	219	363	1352	2499	572	655	3309	441	308		81	4554	478	138		3000	17969
UK	1000	4000	21110	3695	5000	11000	193	4000	5000	22700		1782	7635	3000	1146		91261
Total	17498	16565	159871	16504	19028	33062	4694	22325	42399	29700	1603	11582	32825	9568	12186	93650	523060

Source: EUROSTAT, 1991.

Table 14.5 Estimated Origin-Destination matrix of international migration between EEA countries

Origin \ Destination	A	B	D	DK	E	F	FIN	GR	I	IRL	L	N	NL	P	S	UK	Total
A			17987	99			71					89	553		409	968	20176
B			5190	191			56			227		117	5696		243	2699	14419
D	17039	5228		2610	14854	16585	1124	11716	29777	1419	1033	1224	13855	3973	3126	16767	140330
DK	99	179	2353		387	594	173	184	407	86	21	1631	360	82	2041	2321	10917
E			14878	444			223			352		347	2688		971	9933	29837
F			16903	659					181	613		457	2853		994	11349	34056
FIN	55	46	914	170	177	154		93	190		6	194	113		3173	610	5909
GR			15050	199					153	111		121	993	24	862	4989	22479
I			29186							404		176	2231		759	9495	42890
IRL			1419										391			21040	22936
L			956	20		7				1533		8	129		17		2672
N	77	108	1128	1616	308	411	221	81	160		8		335	62	2650	1770	8935
NL	563	6189	14913		2883	2999		805	2412	426	147	335		703	508	6693	40155
P			5539	87		43				63		97	919		279	3120	10147
S	349	215	2834	2080	849	870	3597	586	676			2640	424	175		1799	17110
UK	1001	2962	18313	2584	10644	12205	822	4086	10428	23658	16	2101	6722	2386	2182		100094
Total	19182	14926	147561	11668	30101	33846	7057	17551	44012	28893	1231	9594	38263	7406	18214	93554	523060

Tables 14.4 and 14.5 present the observed and estimated migration flows between the countries of the EEA, while Figures 14.2 and 14.3 give both observed and predicted levels of total outmigration and immigration for each of the 16 EEA countries. The difference between observed and predicted migration may be assessed both in terms of absolute and relative numbers. With respect to outmigration, large relative overprediction occurs in Austria, Spain, Luxembourg and The Netherlands. In absolute numbers outmigration from Spain, The Netherlands and the United Kingdom is considerably overpredicted. Substantial relative underprediction occurs for Portugal, Greece and Denmark, but the largest underprediction error gives Germany (16 thousand), although this is only 10 percent of the total outmigration flow. The immigration results are slightly better. Spain, Finland and Sweden show the largest relative overprediction, whereas in an absolute sense the Dutch numbers are large. German immigration gives the largest absolute error; again this error is small in relation to the total German inflow.

The results for emigration and immigration are highly related. This is not surprising, for two reasons. First, the model is almost symmetrical with respect to origins and destinations. Second, total observed emigration and immigration per country are highly correlated. From these findings we may conclude that the migration system within the EEA is largely in equilibrium. Migration processes within the EEA are triggered by population size and composition according to nationality at both the sending and receiving end of the migration movement. Moreover, the effect of origin and destination factors is almost equal, implying small net redistibution of population due to intra-EEA migration. Current economic differences within the EEA are not important for explaining migration flows.

14.7 Conclusions

In this chapter we have tested a number of variables that indicate theoretically important concepts for the explanation of international migration flows between countries of the European Economic Area. In particular we were interested in two types of factors that, according to migration theory may be important in directing international migration *within* the EEA area, viz. economic factors, and networks of migrants. The results show that the indicator variables for the existence of networks of migrants are the most important variables for predicting migration flows. The size of the foreign population resident in the country of origin (originating from the destination country) as well as the foreign population resident in the destination country (originating from the origin country) are the two most important influencing variables in this respect. They indicate past migratory movements. The results also show that economic factors are insignificant. Both the difference in GDP and the difference in unemployment rates between countries have no influence in determining the size of the migrant flows. These results indicate that economic differences within the EEA region have no impact on population redistribution processes.

Apart from the search for explanations for migration flows one other aspect of the gravity model exercise was to assess the predictive power of the explanatory variables. The explanatory variables population size and size of the migrant population are able to predict gross out- and inflow of each country (the marginal totals of the migration matrix) fairly accurate. At the level of the migrant flows (the cells of the migration matrix) the results are somewhat less accurate. Since gross flows almost balance in most cases within the EEA, the difference, net migration, is not well captured by the explanatory variables used for modelling the migration flows.

The negative results for the economic variables (unemployment rate and GDP per capita) could be caused in part by the fact that the observed differences in economic indicators within the EEA at the national level are not very large. Differences in economic development between the EEA and other regions in the world are generally much larger, and migration processes at this scale may be triggered to some extent by these economic factors. Empirical research should validate this hypothesis.

References

Baxter, M.J. (1984), 'A Note on the Estimation of a Nonlinear Migration Model using GLIM', *Geographical Analysis*, vol. 16, pp. 282–86.

Congdon, P. (1993), 'Approaches to Modelling Overdispersion in the Analysis of Migration', *Environment and Planning A*, vol. 25, pp. 1481–510

Davies, R.B. and Guy, C.M. (1987), 'The Statistical Modeling of Flow Data When The Poisson Assumption is Violated', *Geographical Analysis*, vol. 19, no. 4, pp. 300–14.

De Jong, P. (1985), *Prediction Intervals for Missing Figures in Migration Tables*, PhD thesis, University of Groningen.

Eurostat (1991), 'Migration Statistics 1991', Yearbook on Population and Social Conditions, European Commission, Luxembourg.

Eurostat (1994a), 'Improvement of the Historical Series of Statistics on International Migration in Europe', Paper prepared on behalf of Eurostat by John Salt and Ann Singleton, Migration Research Unit, Dept. of Geography, London.

Eurostat (1994b), Migration Statistics, 1994. Yearbook on Population and Social Conditions, European Commission', Luxembourg.

Heijke, J.A.M. (1986), *Migratie van Mediterranen: Economie en Arbeidsmarkt* (Migration of Mediterraneans: Economy and Labour Market), Stenfert Kroese, Leiden

Jones H.R. (1990), *Population Geography*, Paul Chapman Publishing Ltd., London, UK.

Massey D.S. et al., (1993), 'Theories of International Migration: A Review and Appraisal', *Population and Development Review,* vol. 19, no. 3, p 431–66.

OECD (1994), 'Societies in Transition; The Future of Work and Leisure, Organisation for Economic Cooperation and Development.

Salt, J. and Singleton, A. (1995), 'Analysis and Forecasting of International Migration by Major Groups', paper presented at the International Seminar, New Long Term Population Scenarios for the European economic Area, Luxembourg.

International Centre for Migration Policy Development, ICMPD (1994), The Key to Europe- a comparative analysis of entry and asylum policies in Western Countries, Vienna.

Poulain, M. (1991), 'Un Projet d'Harmonisation des Statistiques de Migration Internationales au Sein de la Communauté Européenne', *Revue Européenne des Migrations Internationales,* vol. 7, no. 2, pp. 115–38.

Ravenstein, E.G. (1885), 'The Laws of migration, *J. Royal Statistical Society.*

Rierink, B. (1995), 'Database Internationale Migratie', manuscript, NIDI, The Hague and Technical University, Delft.

Visser, H. (1995), 'Long-term International Migration Scenarios for the Countries of the European Aconomic Area', paper presented at the international seminar 'New Long-Term Population Scenarios for the European Economic Area, *Eurostat,* Luxembourg.

Willekens, F. (1980), 'Entropy, Multiproportional Adjustment and Analysis of Contingency Tables, *Sistemi Urbani,* vol. 2, no. 3, pp. 171–201.

Willekens, F. (1983), 'Specification and Calibration of Spatial Interaction Models: A Contingency Table Perspective and An Application to Intra-Urban Migration in Rotterdam', *Tijdschrift voor Economische en Sociale Geografie,* vol. 74, no. 4, pp. 239–52.

Willekens, F. (1994), 'Monitoring International Migration Flows in Europe: Towards a Statistical Data Base Combining Data from Different Sources', *European Journal of Population,* vol. 10: pp. 1–42.

Wilson, A.G. (1970), *Entropy in Urban and Regional Modelling,* Pion, London.

Note

1. The European Economic Area consists of all countries of the Economic Union plus Iceland, Liechtenstein and Norway.

15 Migration and Earnings Attainment: A Comparison Between the United States and The Netherlands

JOUKE VAN DIJK, HENDRIK FOLMER, HENRY W. HERZOG, JR. AND ALAN M. SCHLOTTMANN

15.1 Introduction

An important aspect of labour market behaviour is migration. Several studies have shown that labour force migration and the probability of finding a job are positively related. Unemployment has also been found to stimulate migration. For instance, Van Dijk et al. (1989) found that personal unemployment strongly increased labour force migration within the Netherlands and within the US, ceteris paribus. However, such unemployment within the Netherlands promoted internal migration to another labour market solely for individuals who, in most instances, had 'contracted' for re-employment there. Conversely, estimates obtained for the U.S. provide indirect evidence of the existence of 'speculative' internal migration (i.e. migration without a job at hand). Among unemployed individuals, migration was also found to significantly augment re-employment prospects in the Netherlands while this was not the case in the US. This latter result lends further credence to the existence of speculative migration in the US., as well as to the risks assumed by migrants who undertake this form of job search. For a survey of related empirical findings, see Herzog et al. (1993).

In this study we consider and examine the impact of internal migration on earnings attainment in the Netherlands and the United States. We focus on migration between labour markets *within* each country and this implies that international migration is not taken into account. The main hypothesis is that migration has positive earnings effects, ceteris paribus. Closely related to migration are differential information and search costs of individuals. Although unobservable, such information and costs should vary (like earnings) across workers by human capital endowments, across regions by labour market conditions, and across and between occupations. With respect to the latter, it has been argued that white collar and blue collar workers employ quite different job search strategies, and that search outcomes (jobs and earnings) are likely to vary by quantity and quality of labour market information utilized in the process.

In addition to differential information and search costs, differentials in the wage setting situation have to be taken into account. Relevant aspects of the wage setting situation are information systems, unionization, collective bargaining and social security. A brief overview of differential labour market institutions is given in the following section. Next, a formal model of job search is developed in Section 15.3, where differential job search information and costs, as well as collective bargaining, are shown to impact reservation (minimally required) wages and, in turn, potential earnings attainment. The method by which such attainment levels are obtained from earnings 'frontiers' is also discussed. Separate econometric estimates of these frontiers for the Netherlands and the United States, in both the aggregate and for major occupational groups, are presented and compared in Section 15.4. Conclusions are presented in a final section.

15.2   Labour Market Institutions

In the United States, the role of family, friends and relatives in providing labour market information has often been emphasized. Such information networks have been cited as particularly important for blue collar and service worker migration. (Lansing and Mueller 1967).

A nationwide public employment service was established in the United States in the 1930s. Early case studies such as Wilcock and Franke (1963) attribute only modest success to this organization in disseminating employment information. More recent studies also indicate that neither potential employees nor employers appear to rely upon the Service as their primary source of labour market information (see US Department of Labour, 1983). The reliance of blue collar job seekers on information provided by friends and relatives on the one hand, and upon employer-directed information (often at the plant gate) on the other, is indicative of a more limited search network than that utilized by white collar workers (Swigart 1984). For the latter, the utilization of local and national newspaper and magazine advertisements, professional organizations, and private employment agencies both broadens the search process and limits the importance of the public employment service.

The functioning of the US Employment Service stands in marked contrast to its counterpart in the Netherlands, and particularly for blue collar workers. Within the Netherlands, computers facilitate job matching across space. Local databases are interconnected with one another, thus making it possible to obtain information in each regional office of the Public Employment Service concerning vacancies and unemployed individuals elsewhere. Several studies document the importance of the Public Employment Service in job search (Heijke 1986; Bouman and Van der Zwan 1996 and EC 1994). These studies are mainly based on interviews among unemployed job searchers. Employed job seekers may use different job search strategies from the unemployed.

It should be noted that laws concerning benefit entitlement in the Netherlands require the unemployed to register at the Public Employment Service, and to accept job offers which match individual qualifications. However, there is no requirement that an individual accept a job offer which does not match his or her job qualifications, or jobs that require relocation.

The opposite is true for information concerning vacancies since employers are not required to notify the Public Employment Service of their employment needs. There is evidence that employers prefer to fill vacancies for higher skilled workers through information channels maintained outside the Public Employment Service, such as informal networks to include friends and relatives as well as formal channels utilizing both local and national newspaper and magazine advertisements. Based on data obtained from a survey among firms, Russo et al. (1995) report that informal networks and advertisements are by far the most important recruitment channels for firms. The Public Employment Service is for many firms of minor importance.

The conclusions of various studies with regard to the role of the Public Employment Service in the job matching process are not unambiguous. This is partly caused by the fact that employers, employees and the Public Employment Service often disagree on the way job matches are settled, because this is often a process influenced by many actors in a complicated way (Bouman and Van der Zwan 1996). It should be observed that the Public Employment Service in the Netherlands is not only directly instrumental with respect to job matching in the sense that it provides job searchers with information on job openings and employers with information on potential workers, but also indirectly in the sense that it provides labour market information in general. Moreover, it is often instrumental with respect to training, application techniques, etc. (Bouman and Van der Zwan, 1996)

The results of a survey of employers by Gaspersz and Van Voorden (1987) indicate that personnel with lower qualifications are primarily recruited through the Public Employment Service (80 percent), in the internal labour market (75 percent) and by employment agencies (66 percent). Personnel with middle level qualifications are recruited mainly via advertisements in national newspapers and magazines (83 percent) or internally (75 percent), while professional and technical workers are almost always recruited through national newspapers and magazines (90 percent). Furthermore, Gaspersz and Van Voorden (1987) report that employers utilize on average 2.8 recruitment channels.

In summary, for lower skilled workers and job vacancies, the Public Employment Service is an important source of nationwide information, even in cases where migration and reemployment is ultimately finalized on the basis of other information. For higher skilled jobs, both job

361

seekers and employers rely on information provided in national newspapers and magazines, a situation not unlike that in the US.

Turning now to unemployment insurance (UI), both the duration of UI benefits and their relative magnitude in terms of the average replacement rate (benefits/past earnings) are significantly higher in the Netherlands than in the United States. (OECD 1991). Such UI benefits reduce the opportunity cost of unemployment and job search, and thus augment the effects of better labour market information by raising observed wages relative to potential (maximum attainable) wages.

A final institutional difference expected to impact relative earnings attainment in the two countries is the method or process by which wage setting occurs. Trade union density and collective bargaining coverage are considerably higher in the Netherlands than in the United States. Trade union density in the Netherlands is 26 percent versus 16 percent for the US. The collective bargaining percentage in the Netherlands is 71 percent, in the US 18 percent. Moreover, bargaining within the Netherlands is predominantly at the sectoral level, while in the U.S. it occurs at company, and often plant, level. Such bargaining coverage in the Netherlands, and particularly its position at the sectoral level, reduces the variance of effective wage offers, and in turn increases observed wages relative to potential wages (compared with the situation in the US).[1]

Based upon the above, each component of institutional difference between the countries (labour market information, search cost, and collective bargaining) works to the advantage of Dutch migrants. In this regard, observed wages among Dutch migrants (undifferentiated by occupation) are expected to be higher *relative* to their potential earnings than is the case for US migrants. However, the *degree* by which such relative earnings (hereafter 'earnings attainment') are recorded within wage regimes should vary by occupation. Among blue collar workers, earnings attainment will be significantly greater in the Netherlands than in the US because of the excellence of the Dutch job matching program. On the other hand, earnings attainment among white collar migrants will vary less between countries to the extent that such workers utilize similar job search information channels maintained *external* to the public employment service. Within country differences in earnings attainment between migrants and non-migrants should also vary in a predictable fashion. In this regard, migrant wage regimes (and measured earnings attainment) are responsive to job search information and costs, while non-migrant regimes (comprised primarily of continuous job holders) are not. Since collective bargaining diminishes the wage variance of both new and continuous employees (migrants and non - migrants), intercountry comparisons of migrants and non-migrants provide knowledge, albeit indirect, of the *combined* effects of job search information and cost differentials on relative earnings attainment. These arguments are investigated below within a formal model of migrant job search, and by an econometric technique explicitly designed to measure potential earnings, and in turn earnings attainment.

362

15.3 Job Search and Earnings Attainment

15.3.1 The Job Search Model

Workers (migrants and non-migrants) are assumed to obtain observed wages, W, through optimal search activity.[2] Based upon the job search model, observed wages are dependent upon: (1) a group of personal attributes (inputs) traditionally assumed to augment human capital stock, H; (2) job characteristics, J; (3) regional labour market conditions, R; and (4) labour market institutions, L. Inputs in H include education and work experience, while job characteristics, J, relate to duties performed (often proxied by industry of employment). Considered above, labour market institutions include activities of the Public Employment Service, level and duration of unemployment benefits and other social security payments, and the wage setting environment, represented here by job search information, I, marginal search costs, C, and parameters of the wage offer distribution, F(.), respectively. Notice that $I'(H) \geq 0$, $C'(H) \leq 0$ and $C'(I) \leq 0$. In addition, F(.) likely varies with H, J and R. However, since L is not observed, but rather inferred from alternative estimates of W(H,J,R) in Section (15.4), derived earnings attainment levels are ceteris paribus with regard to these effects. Thus, L = L(I, C, F (.)), and

$$W = W [H, J, R, L (I, C, F(.))]. \qquad (15.1)$$

Migrants (non-migrants) are assumed to obtain W through optimal search in destination (local) labour markets. For an individual characterized by H, J, R, and I in equation (1), the amount of search will depend upon the cost of generating job offers, C, and the wage offer distribution, F (.). Under the job search model, search will terminate when a wage offer, W_o, either equals or exceeds W_r, the latter 'reservation wage' determined to equate the marginal cost of obtaining one more job offer with the expected marginal return from further search.

Given optimal search activity, one expects $W'[I] > 0$ in Equation (15.1) based upon the fact that better labour market information most likely:

a   decreases the marginal cost of search,
b   increases the likelihood of receiving a job offer during any time period, and
c   decreases the variance of (effective) wage offers.

Since (a), (b) and (c) each increase W_r, W will be augmented accordingly (ceteris paribus).[3] In addition, since marginal search costs and UI benefits are inversely related, and $W'[C] < 0$ in Equation (15.1), then W is an increasing function of unemployment benefits. Finally, collective bargaining agreements, and particularly those negotiated at the sector level (vs. company or plant), decrease the variance within the wage offer distribution F(.). Thus, like $W'[I]>0$ above, W in Equation (15.1) is likely augmented by such bargaining practice. As described in Section 15.2, I, C and F(.) vary, in a predictable fashion, by country, occupation and mobility status, a fact exploited below in Section 15.4.

Another assumption required for the job search model is that a potential or maximum attainable ('frontier') wage offer, W^*, exists for each worker, and is commensurate with H, J and R in Equation (15.1). However, with $C > 0$, then $W_r \leq W^*$. Thus, virtually all individuals will demonstrate less than 100 percent earnings attainment ($W \leq W^*$) once they find a job, and the magnitude of such underpayment is related to I, C and F(.) in equation (15.1). In this regard, better labour market information, lower search costs, and/or reduced variance in the wage offer distribution improve the job-matching process, and thereby augment earnings attainment. In addition, although we observe the job search process ex post through variation in *observed* wages (rather than wage offers W_o), $E(W) > W_r$ due to the optimal stopping rule considered above. Finally, even though 'like' individuals will have equivalent W_r and W^*, their actual (observed) wages obtained through search ($W_r < W \leq W^*$) will likely differ due to the stochastic nature of the search process.[4]

In what follows, it is convenient to base comparisons of job matching and earnings attainment upon the ratio W/W^* rather than upon the difference $W^* - W$. In this regard, better labour market information, more generous UI benefits and/or reduced wage offer variance should increase W/W^* in the Netherlands relative to the equivalent measure for the United States. Such a comparison, of course, requires estimates of W^* for each individual, and it is to this issue that we now turn.

15.3.2 Measuring Earnings Attainment

Starting point for the derivation of the wage equation are the basic earnings function (Mincer, 1974) and the segmented earnings function (see, among others, Holmlund 1984). The basic idea underlying these earnings functions is that, given job characteristics and personal characteristics such as age, education, earnings depend on the amount of and the returns to human capital accumulated within and outside the current job as well as previous search activities. Based upon the discussion in Section 15.3.1 we arrive at Equation (15.2), which will be estimated separately for each country as

$$W = W (H, J, R), \qquad (15.2)$$

with major occupational groups represented initially by a binary independent variable, and subsequently by individual equations for the two occupational groups. Also, the potential or maximum attainable wage for each worker, W^*, is solely a function of the wage offer distribution, F(.), and thus of its determinants H, J and R above.

Consequently, for each individual characterized by H, J and R, $W^* = \max [W (H, J, R)] \geq W$.

Earnings attainment (efficiency of job matching) varies directly with W/W^*, and for any group of workers, with $E (W/W^*)$.[5] Thus, measuring earnings attainment requires that a potential wage, W^*, be determined and compared with the observed wage, W, for each individual within our research sample (described below). In addition, such a determination must be 'ceteris paribus' in terms of the inclusion of independent variables for the estimation of Equation (15.2), as well as the disaggregation of the analysis to accommodate unmeasurable institutional attributes of job search (L in Equation (15.1)) that vary by country, occupation, and mobility status. Finally, based upon the job search model outlined above, our estimating equation must explicitly reflect a stochastic wage with a two-sided distribution as well as a separate earnings attainment term $(W^* - W)$ which is non-negative.

Such a model (wage equation) can be stated as

$$W = f(\mathbf{z}) + v - u, \qquad (15.3)$$

where W is again the observed wage, $\mathbf{z}$ is a vector of all wage determining variables representing human capital stock, job characteristics and regional labour market conditions, v is a symmetric error, and u is a non-negative error. The symmetric error term relates to the usual randomness of the frontier wage (i.e. omitted variables, measurement errors and randomness in human behaviour). The non-negative error term represents the stochastic variation in the earnings attainment term $W^* - W$. Hence,

$$W^* = f(\mathbf{z}) + v. \qquad (15.4)$$

This model has the same general form as the stochastic frontier production function of Aigner, Lovell and Schmidt (1977), and is similar to the earnings frontiers developed by Herzog, Hofler and Schlottmann (1985) and Hofler and Murphy (1992). Based upon Equations (15.3) and (15.4), notice that $W/W^* = 1 - (u/W^*)$. In addition, note that: (1) $u = 0$ when $W = W^*$, (2) $u > 0$ when $W < W^*$, and (3) u varies across individuals as W/W^* varies. Finally, because the non-negative error term satisfies these three characteristics, it is asserted that u in Equation (15.3) captures the effect of underattainment. Thus, this wage frontier, Equation (15.3), is the explicit equivalent of Equation (15.2).

For any N individuals (migrants or non-migrants) within a given country and major occupational group,

$$E(W/W)^* = (1/N) \sum_{i=1}^{N} [1 - (U_i/W_i^*)] . \qquad (15.5)$$

365

When Equation (15.3) is defined in semi-logarithmic form and -u is exponentially distributed, Equation (15.5) can be expressed as

$$E(W/W^*) = E[\exp(-u)] = 1/(1 + \mu_u), \qquad (15.6)$$

where μ_u is the mean of u. Comparisons of mean earnings attainment between countries, by mobility status and occupation, can then be made on the basis of Equation (15.6) because u is estimated for each individual and μ_u can be calculated for various subgroups in the sample at hand.

15.4 Econometric Results

15.4.1 Data

A comparative empirical examination of the job search process (described above) is made possible by the availability, and consistency, of survey data in the two nations. The Dutch OSA-survey (Vissers et al. 1986) provides labour force data for a national sample obtained in April, 1985, and is the most complete file of its type in the Netherlands containing wage information. Individual records of the Dutch survey provide information on such characteristics as weekly wages, age, education, occupation, industry and mobility status.

Although alternative micro-data sources were available for the United States, this study utilizes individual records obtained from the Survey of Income and Program Participation (Nelson et al. 1985). This Survey (SIPP) is the only major US data source which permits wage comparisons with Dutch individuals as of April, 1985 for a large number of observations, and for personal characteristics defined consistently between the two countries.[6]

The common universe for our comparative analysis was designed to maximize labour force participation as well as sample consistency. Both samples include white male members of the civilian labour force aged 16–60, and exclude individuals attending college, members of the armed forces, and inmates of institutions. The self-employed, as well as part time workers, were also excluded from the research population in order to better represent within our analysis the job search process described in Section 15.3.1. Based upon these restrictions, the resulting samples consist of 1,142 and 8,117 observations for the Netherlands and United States, respectively.

Of particular interest to this study are variations in individual attainment of potential earnings between the two countries, by major occupational groups. In this respect, the blue collar/white collar distribution is essentially the same within the Netherlands and the United States. The distribution of employment by industry is also quite similar between the countries, although a higher proportion of workers in the

United States are employed in wholesale and retail trade compared to the Netherlands. The opposite is true for employment in the commercial services and public administration.

15.4.2 Earnings Estimates

Based upon the discussion above, the natural logarithm of 1985 weekly earnings (wage and salary income) was regressed against sets of variables representing both personal and region characteristics, as well as industry affiliation. Personal characteristics (H in Equation (15.2)) include age (and age squared), years of education, family size and marital status, the latter represented by a binary variable set equal to unity for single individuals (and zero otherwise). In addition, a variable denoting number of weeks an individual reported looking for work or on layoff was included as a measure of work interruption (and reduced experience).[7]

Regional characteristics (R in Equation (15.2)) were included within the analysis to adjust for intra-country differences in local labour market conditions. For the Netherlands, a single variable was set to unity (vs. zero) to reflect higher (versus lower) relative unemployment in peripheral (non-metropolitan) areas. Two binary variables were employed within the US regressions, and were designed to obtain consistency with the Dutch data. These latter variables were set to unity (and zero otherwise) for individuals residing in non-metropolitan areas and/or in states with above average unemployment rates. Finally, job characteristics (J in Equation (15.2)) relate to duties performed while at work, and are represented within the earnings analysis by a regime of dummy variables reflecting industry of employment.

For both the Netherlands and the United States three separate male earnings frontiers were estimated by maximum likelihood techniques using the statistical package LIMDEP version 7.[8] For each country one model is estimated for the entire sample and in addition one model for blue collar and one model for white collar workers. This procedure provides consistent estimates of all parameters, after which the two-component error term, v-u in Equation (15.3), can be decomposed into separate estimates of v and u for each individual.[9] In this regard it was assumed that v and u in Equation (15.3) are independent, that v is normally distributed with a zero mean and finite variance, and that u is derived from an exponential distribution with mean μ_u and variance μ_u^2.

Earnings frontier coefficient estimates are provided in Tables 15.1 and 15.2 for the Netherlands and United States, respectively. In both tables, estimates shown in the first column were obtained for the entire sample, major occupation groups being distinguished by a dummy variable (white collar workers comprising the omitted category). The latter two columns of each table provide earnings estimates by major occupation, and will subsequently be utilized to investigate how earnings attainment likely varies within each country by job search methods.

Notice in Tables 15.1 and 15.2 that estimates on personal characteristics are robust across models (columns), and are consistent with other studies of earnings determination. In addition, the similarity of estimates between the Netherlands and United States is notable. In this regard, weekly earnings are augmented by additional years of education and age (albeit at a declining rate for the latter). On the other hand, such earnings are depressed among single individuals, as well as those with recent interruptions to their work experience. In addition, weekly earnings in the US demonstrate a negative association with family size. Turning to regional characteristics, peripheral (non-metropolitan) locations and high local unemployment diminish earnings in both countries, and especially in the United States. Also, for the United States, earnings within agriculture, forestry and fisheries, wholesale and retail trade, and commercial services and public administration are consistently below those in the reference group manufacturing, ceteris paribus. Conversely, Dutch workers employed in commercial services and public administration consistently outperform their counterparts in the manufacturing sector. Finally, estimates in the first column of each table indicate, for equivalent H, J and R in Equation (15.2), the earnings disadvantage of blue collar employment.

15.4.3 Earnings Attainment

Given the earnings estimates in Tables 15.1 and 15.2, non-negative errors (u) for individuals within each country and model can be determined by Equation (15.3). Equation (15.6) can then be employed to calculate $E(W/W^*)$, the mean ratio of actual to potential earnings for members of the Dutch and US labour force. Because u is available for each individual in the sample on which the model is estimated, mean μ_u can also be calculated for subgroups within the sample at hand. This permits for each country a comparison of W/W^* between migrants and non-migrants within the entire sample or within the subsamples of blue and white collar workers when separate frontiers are estimated by occupation. As discussed above, better labour market information, more generous unemployment benefits, and/or reduced variance within the wage offer distribution increase this ratio and, by inference, earnings attainment. Thus, for any model (or partition of observations by mobility status), differences in the mean level of earnings attainment between countries can be imputed based upon statistically significant differences in $E(W/W^*)$.

Observations employed in the estimation of the aggregate and occupation specific models in Tables 15.1 and 15.2 were partitioned by mobility status to provide estimates of mean W/W^* for migrants and non-migrants.[10] These are listed, along with the ratio of US to Dutch estimates, in Table 15.3. In each instance, equality of W/W^* between the two countries is rejected at the 1 percent level. Confining our attention initially to the upper panel of Table 15.3, and specifically to the results listed on the first line, notice that Dutch migrants apparently garner 92.4 percent of their potential earnings while U.S. migrants garner only 73.5 percent. Thus, earnings attainment among U.S. migrants is roughly 80 percent of that achieved by their Dutch counterparts (last column), a finding consistent with the discussion in Section 15.2.

However, the *degree* by which earnings attainment is registered within wage regimes should vary by occupation in the first instance, and by mobility status (migrants, non-migrants) in the second.

Notice first in this regard that intercountry differences in W/W* are maintained when migrant earnings regimes are disaggregated (estimated separately) by blue and white collar occupations. Since UI benefit schemes in each country are invariant across occupations, *within* country (row) variation in migrant W/W* derives, for the most part, from differential labour market information and wage bargaining.

In each country, the public employment agency can affect labour market information through the level of services provided, and in two distinct ways. First, these institutions can endow individuals with a general understanding of the *process*, or methods, by which one secures employment, either at home or in a distant region. Second, and more directly, such agencies provide searchers (migrants) information relevant to *specific* labour market conditions and/or opportunities. Both approaches are employed within the Netherlands, with programs particularly targeted at blue collar and service workers. On the other hand, the discussion in Section 15.2 indicated that blue collar migrants in the United States rely quite heavily upon employer-directed information (vs. that provided by the US Employment Service), as well as upon information provided through networks of family and friends.

On the other hand, earnings attainment among white collar migrants should vary less between countries due to their joint utilization of job search information channels maintained *external* to their respective public employment services. However, note in Table 15.3 that although white collar migrants in each country demonstrate higher earnings attainment than their blue collar counterparts, such *within* country differences are quite small (94.8 vs. 92.5 percent in the Netherlands and 75.0 vs. 72.5 in the US). When combined with the near constancy of blue and white collar W/W* relatives listed in the third column, little evidence is provided in support of information differentials between the two countries, at least to the extent that such knowledge is reflected in migrant earnings attainment. We tentatively conclude such differences likely stem from the more generous UI benefits, the high relative union density and collective bargaining incidence in the Netherlands. Regarding the latter, bargaining within the Netherlands is predominantly at the sectoral level, whereas in the US it occurs at company, and often plant level.

**Table 15.1   1985 earnings estimates for males: The Netherlands[a]
(dependent variable is LN weekly earnings)**

	By Occupation:		
Variables	Total Sample	Blue Collar	White Collar
Constant	5.061***	5.392***	4.433***
Personal Characteristics:			
Age	.044***	.029***	.065***
Age Squared (10^{-3})	-.453***	-.312***	-.669***
Education	.027***	.017***	.034***
Single	-.104***	-.116***	-.115***
Family Size	.003	.001	.004
Weeks Looking for Work/Layoff	-.001*	-.001*	-.002**
Regional Characteristic:			
Peripheral Area (Non-metro, High Unemployment)	-.034***	-.028**	-.031**
Industry:			
Agriculture, Forestry, and Fisheries	-.121**	-.060	-.090
Construction	.029	.016	.119***
Transportation, Communication and Public Utilities	.013	.039	.019
Wholesale and Retail Trade	-.013	-.010	-.001
Commercial Services and Public Administration	.060***	.074***	.066***
Occupation:			
Blue Collar	-.114***		
N	1,142	565	577
R^{2b}	.46	.26	.46
log-likelihood	313	211	151

* t-test significant at the .10 level.
** t-test significant at the .05 level.
*** t-test significant at the .01 level.

[a]   Figures shown are maximum likelihood estimates. All variables as well as the estimation technique are defined in the text.

[b]   Defined as the squared correlation between Y and $\bar{Y}$.

**Table 15.2   1985 earnings estimates for males: The United States[a]
(dependent variable is LN weekly earnings)**

Variables	Total Sample	Blue Collar	White Collar
		By Occupation:	
Constant	3.718***	4.007***	2.943***
Personal Characteristics:			
Age	.126***	.113***	.151***
Age Squared (10^{-3})	-1.382***	-1.277***	-1.620***
Education	.022***	.010***	.030***
Single	-.217***	-.203***	-.202**
Family Size	-.030***	-.037***	-.031***
Weeks Looking for Work/Layoff	-.010***	-.008***	-.018***
Regional Characteristics:			
Non-metro	-.073***	-.048***	-.132***
High Local Unemployment Rate	-.018	-.004	-.028
Industry:			
Agriculture, Forestry, and Fisheries	-.306***	-.295**	-.130***
Construction	-.005*	-.002	-.093*
Transportation, Communication and Public Utilities	.038	.121***	-.042
Wholesale and Retail Trade	-.276***	-.354***	-.149***
Commercial Services and Public Administration	-.242***	-.319***	-.175***
Occupation:			
Blue Collar	-.196***		
N	8,117	4,216	3,901
R^{2b}	.411	.40	.42
log-likelihood	7666	3579	3838

* t-test significant at the .10 level.

** t-test significant at the .05 level.

*** t-test significant at the .01 level.

a   Figures shown are maximum likelihood estimates. All variables as well as the estimation technique are defined in the text.

b   Defined as the squared correlation between Y and Ȳ.

Table 15.3 Mean 1985 W/W* by country, mobility status and occupation[a]

W/W* (%)

Mobility Status/ Occupation:	Netherlands (1)	United States (2)	2/1 (%)
Migrants[b]	92.4	73.5	79.5
Blue Collar[c]	92.5	72.5	78.4
White Collar[d]	94.8	75.0	79.1
Non-migrants[b]	91.8	67.7	73.7

[a] See Equation (15.6) in Section 15.3.2. For each mobility status/occupation, t-tests indicate significant differences at the 0.01 level in W/W* by country. Within countries only for the US significant differences (at the 0.1 level) are found in W/W* between migrants and non-migrants for the entire sample. The difference for white collar workers is larger than for blue collar workers.

[b] Determined from estimates in column 1 of Tables 15.1 and 15.2.

[c] Determined from estimates in column 2 of Tables 15.1 and 15.2.

[d] Determined from estimates in column 3 of Tables 15.1 and 15.2.

Turning now to comparisons between (total) migrants and non-migrants in the upper and lower panels of Table 15.3, notice in the US that W/W* among migrants is significantly higher than the comparable figure for non-migrants (73.5 or 67.7 percent), whereas in the Netherlands such estimates are quite similar. Hence in the US migration pays off.

15.5 Conclusions

In this study we have examined internal migration and potential earnings within the Netherlands and the United States against the backdrop of labour market institutions and the services they provide in matching jobs and workers across space. Variations among workers in the attainment of potential (maximum attainable) earnings – the downside of which results in job 'mismatches' and underemployment – is often attributed to differential information utilization and search costs within the relevant labour markets. Such information and costs, and in turn earnings attainment, likely vary among countries, and reflect important differences in the role, and level of effort, of national governments in matching workers with job opportunities in a spatial setting. Also considered is the wage setting environment in each country, and specifically how earnings attainment is likely impacted by differential levels of unionization and collective bargaining.

Predictions from a formal job search model indicate that differential institutions in the two countries work to the advantage of the Dutch labour market, and likely result in higher measurable levels of earnings attainment among Dutch workers (migrants and non-migrants) in comparison to their American counterparts. Such an advantage was revealed in the frontier earnings estimates for the two countries, where US migrants reached no better than 80 percent of the earnings attainment levels achieved by Dutch migrants.

This comparative advantage in earnings attainment, and perhaps job matching efficiency as well, was attributed to activities of the Dutch Public Employment Service, greater Dutch UI benefits in size and duration, and the wage setting environment there. However, inter- and intra-country comparisons of earnings attainment estimates by occupation and mobility status provide, at best, only limited support for the notion of differential job search information between the two countries. Based upon these results, one must appeal to other labour market institutions to explain the high relative earnings attainment among Dutch migrants. Such attainment likely stems from the higher relative union density and collective bargaining incidence in the Netherlands. Moreover, bargaining within the Netherlands is predominantly at the sectoral level, a situation which reduces the variance among wage offers there, and in turn increases observed earnings relative to potential earnings.

Regarding the more generous UI benefits (higher replacement ratios) in the Netherlands, a number of studies have documented the unintended results of such insurance on unemployment and search duration. In this regard, both higher UI replacement rates and an extended period of eligibility likely reduce the opportunity costs of job search, and thereby extend search duration and measured unemployment rates. In addition, our earnings estimates indicate a negative relationship between search duration and individual earnings. Thus, although higher relative UI benefits (lower search costs) likely augment reservation wages, the commensurate increase in search duration apparently diminishes observed wages, the latter a potential result of stigmatization by potential employers or a downward adjustment of the reservation wage. However, our findings are supportive of the view that the benefits of higher UI payments (increased earnings attainment) more than offset such costs of extended job search and measured unemployment.

Although in the present paper the frontier method is applied to the analysis of internal migration, the method can also be used to study the effects of international migration or cross-border migration. An example of such a study is Daneshvary et al. (1992) in which the earnings attainment of immigrants to the United States are analysed by means of the frontier approach.

373

As mentioned in the introduction, in a previous study among unemployed individuals in both countries, internal migration was found to significantly augment re-employment prospects in the Netherlands while this was not the case in the US (Van Dijk et al. 1989). The present study shows that employed migrants within the US obtain higher wages than non-migrants within the US, where in the Netherlands there is hardly any difference between migrant and non-migrant earnings.

References

Aigner, D., Knox Lovell, C.A. and Schmidt, P. (1977), 'Formulation and Estimation of Stochastic Frontier Production Models', *Journal of Econometrics*, vol. 6, June, pp. 21–38.

Bouman, A., and Van der Zwan, A.L. (1996), *Hoe Zoeken Werkzoekenden? - Rapportage '95*. (How do the unemployed search? – Report '95), The Hague: Arbeidsvoorziening Nederland, O&A-rapport 96–04.

Daneshvary, N., Hofler, R. Herzog, H. and Schlottmann, A. (1992), 'Job-Search and Immigrant Assimilation: An Earnings Frontier Approach', *The Review of Economics and Statistics*, vol. 74, no. 3, August, pp. 482–92.

Ehrenberg, R.G., and Smith, R.S. (1991), *Modern Labor Economics: Theory and Public Policy*, Harper Collins Publishers Inc., New York.

EC (European Commission) (1994), *Employment in Europe 1994*, European Commission, Luxembourg.

Gaspersz, J.B.R. and Van Voorden, W. (1987), 'Aspecten van Wervingsbeleid van Ondernemingen', (Aspects of Recruitment Behavior of Firms) *Sociaal Maandblad Arbeid*, March, pp.144–51.

Greene, W.H. (1995), *LIMDEP version 7.0 User's manual*. Bellport, Econometric Software, New York.

Heijke, J.A.M. (1986), *Migratie van Mediterranen: Economie en Arbeidsmarkt* (Migration of Mediterraneans: Economics and Labor Markets), Stenfert Kroese, Leiden.

Herzog, H.W., Jr., Hofler, R.A. and Schlottmann, A.M. (1985), 'Life on the Frontier: Migrant Information, Earnings and Past Mobility', *Review of Economics and Statistics*, vol. 67, August, pp. 373–82.

Herzog, H.W., Schlottmann, A.M. and Boehm, T.P. (1993), 'Migration as Spatial Job-Search: A Survey of Empirical Findings', *Regional Studies*, vol. 27, no. 4, pp. 327–40.

Holmlund, B. (1984), *Labor Mobility*, The Industrial Institute for Economic and Social Research, Stockholm.

Hofler, R.A. and Murphy, K.J. (1992), 'Underpaid and Overworked: Measuring the Effect of Imperfect Information on Wages', *Economic Inquiry*, vol. 30, July, pp. 511–29.

Jondrow, J.C., Knox Lovell, A., Materov, I.S. and Schmidt, P. (1982), 'On the Estimation of Technical Inefficiency in the Stochastic Frontier Production Function Model', *Journal of Econometrics*, vol. 19, August, pp. 233–38.

Lansing, J.B. and Mueller, E. (1967), *The Geographic Mobility of Labor*, Michigan Survey Research Center, Ann Arbor.

Lippman, S.A. and McCall, J.J. (1976), 'The Economics of Job Search: A Survey', *Economic Inquiry*, vol. 14, June, pp. 155–89.

Mincer, J. (1974), *Schooling, Experience and Earnings*, Columbia University Press, New York.

Mortensen, D.T. (1986), 'Job Search and Labor Market Analysis', in Ashenfelter, O. and R. Layard (eds), *Handbook of Labor Economics*, North-Holland: Amsterdam, pp. 849–919.

Nelson, D., McMillen, D.B. and Kasprzyk, D. (1985), 'An Overview of the Survey of Income and Program Participation: Update 1', Working Paper Series, Bureau of the Census, No. 8401, U.S. Department of Commerce: Washington.

OECD (Organization for Economic Co-Operation and Development) (1991). *Employment Outlook 1991*, OECD, Paris.

Polachek, S. and Bong Joon Yoon (1987), 'A Two-Tiered Earnings Frontier Estimation of Employer and Employee Information in the Labor Market', *The Review of Economics and Statistics*, vol. 69, May, pp. 296–302.

Russo, G., Rietveld, P., Nijkamp, P. and Gorter, C. (1995). 'Labour market conditions and recruitment behaviour of Dutch firms', Discussion paper TI 5-95-247, Tinbergen Institute, Amsterdam.

Schmidt, P. and Knox Lovell, C.A. (1979), 'Estimating Technical and Allocative Inefficiency Relative to Stochastic Production and Cost Frontiers', *Journal of Econometrics*, vol. 9, February, pp. 343–66.

Swigart, Richard P. (ed.), (1984), *Managing Plant Closings and Occupational Readjustment: An Employer's Guidebook*, National Center on Occupational Readjustment, Inc.

U.S. Department of Labor, Bureau of Labor Statistics (1983), *Handbook of Labor Statistics*, Bulletin 2175, U.S. Government Printing Office: Washington.

Van Dijk, J., Folmer, H., Herzog, H.W. Jr. and Schlottmann, A.M. (1989), 'Labor Market Institutions and the Efficiency of Interregional Migration: A Cross-Nation Comparison' in Van Dijk et al. (eds), *Migration and Labor Market Adjustment*, Kluwer Academic Publishers, Dordrecht, pp. 61–83.

Vissers, A.M.C., de Vries, A.M. and Schepens, T.H. (1986), *Arbeidsmarktgedrag ten tijde van Massale Werkloosheid* (Labor market behaviour during a period of mass unemployment), OSA No. 12, The Hague.

Wilcock, R.C., and Franke, W.H. (1963), *Unwanted Workers*, Collier-MacMillan, London.

Notes

1. See Section 15.3.

2. For an excellent survey of the job search literature see Mortensen (1986).

3. See Lippman and McCall (1976).

4. See Ehrenberg and Smith (1991), pp. 607–14.

5. Hofler and Murphy (1992) interpret W/W^* as an inverse index of 'underpayment', and demonstrate how such underpayment varies with labour market information.

6. The United States data is comprised of individuals within the sample as of April, 1985 (Wave 6), and allows linked records back to September, 1983 (Wave 1). The Dutch OSA Survey asked individuals for retrospective information back to January, 1980.

7. Intervals utilized for this determination extend back to 1980 in the Dutch data and to 1983 in the U.S. data. See note 6.

8. For details about frontier estimation with LIMDEP version 7, see Greene (1995, Chapter 29, pp. 679–92.).

9. See Schmidt and Lovell (1979) and Jondrow, Lovell, Materov, and Schmidt (1982) and Greene (1995) for a discussion of the frontier estimation technique. Polachek and Yoon (1987) and Herzog, Hofler, and Schlottmann (1985) have also obtained consistent and asymptotically efficient estimates of earnings frontiers by maximum likelihood techniques.

10. A similar procedure was employed by Herzog, Hofler and Schlottmann (1985) on a US earnings equation for all repeat migrants in order to discern differential W/W^* estimates between non-return and return migration. Here, migrants include all sample individuals with a 1980-1985 move between provinces in the Netherlands, or a 1983–1985 interstate move in the U.S. See note 6.